BEYOND EMPATHY

BEYOND EMPATHY

A Therapy
of Contact-in-Relationship

Richard G. Erskine
Janet P. Moursund
Rebecca L. Trautmann

Routledge
Taylor & Francis Group
New York   London

Routledge
Taylor & Francis Group
711 Third Avenue
New York, NY 10017

Routledge
Taylor & Francis Group
2 Park Square
Milton Park
Abingdon Oxfordshire OX14 4RN

First issued in paperback 2014

Routledge is an imprint of the Taylor and Francis Group, an informa business

© 1999 by Taylor & Francis Group, LLC

International Standard Book Number-13: 978-0-87630-963-6 (Hardcover)
International Standard Book Number-13: 978-1-138-00514-3 (pbk)

Library of Congress Cataloging-in-Publication Data

Erskine, Richard G.
    Beyond empathy: a therapy of contact-in-relationship / Richard G. Erskine, Janet P. Moursund, Rebecca L. Trautmann.
        p. cm.
    Includes bibliographical references and index.
    ISBN 0-87630-963-5 (alk. paper)
    1. Eclectic psychotherapy. 2. Object relations (Psychoanalysis). 3. Self Psychology. 4. Therapeutic alliance. 5. Psychotherapist and patient. I. Moursund, Janet. II. Trautmann, Rebeccca. III. Title.
RC489.E24 E768   1999
616.89'14—dc21   99-20272

Visit the Taylor & Francis Web site at
http://www.taylorandfrancis.com

and the Routledge Web site at
http://www.routledge.com

*This book is dedicated to our thirteen children and grandchildren,
who conduct an ongoing Human Development Seminar
that never fails to educate, amaze, and delight us.*

CONTENTS

Preface   ix

1   Basic Concepts   1

2   Inquiry   19

3   Attunement   46

4   Involvement   83

5   Relational Needs   121

6   Through the Keyhole   156

7   Greta: "Mother, Come Home"   176

8   Sarah: Therapy With a Regressed Client   205

9   Edward: Exploring the Function of Defenses   237

10 Loraine: Therapy With an Introjected Other (Part I)   262

11 Loraine: Therapy With an Introjected Other (Part II)   290

12 Integrative Psychotherapy With Couples   314

13 The Keyhole Revisited   336

References   369

Index   375

PREFACE

Why would anyone bother to read the Preface in a book like this? Most likely, to get an idea of whether the book itself is worth reading. So let us begin by talking about what this book is about and what we have tried to accomplish in writing it.

We set two major goals for ourselves in writing *Beyond Empathy: A Therapy of Contact-in-Relationship*. One was to describe our theory of therapy in a clear and readable way, and the other was to provide similarly clear and readable suggestions about how therapists can actually implement that theory in clinical practice. We recognize, of course, that no book can take the place of working with clients, of supervision, or of watching a master therapist conduct a therapeutic interview. Because of the importance of examples that bring the theory "into the trenches," the real-life interchange between therapist and client, we have provided numerous examples taken from transcripts of actual therapy sessions that we have conducted with our clients.

Integrative psychotherapy, the method of therapy upon which this book is based, focuses on relationship. We believe that to be psychologically healthy—in fact, to be fully human—is to be in relationship with others. We need relationship: we need to spend time with people who respect and value us, who support our efforts to express ourselves as unique individuals, and who will nurture us when we need nurturing and yet will applaud and celebrate our ability to take care of ourselves. Psychological health and growth result when people with whom we are in contact acknowledge these kinds of relational needs, and when those people respond to our relational needs appropriately. Psychological dis-ease, in contrast, arises from relational failure: the cumulative experience of relational needs not met.

In order to participate in health-enhancing relationships, one must be able to make and maintain contact with oneself and with other people. Contact is the touchstone of relationship; it is what makes relationship possible. A psychotherapist's first and most fundamental job is to build his or her client's ability to maintain contact: internal contact (contact with oneself) and external contact (contact with others). Internal contact involves full awareness of one's internal experiencing, including thoughts, emotions, desires, attitudes, and sensations. External contact, similarly, involves awareness of all that is available in the external environment, and especially that part of the environment made up of other people. In a psychologically healthy individual, internal and external contact interact; each depends upon the other, and neither can exist in isolation.

As people weather the inevitable traumas of life, large and small, they develop ways of protecting themselves from pain. These self-protective patterns, helpful (sometimes even necessary) at their inception, may become destructive as one moves into new life phases. Unfortunately, what has been learned as a response to a specific traumatic situation tends to generalize, to become a habitual and more or less out-of-awareness way of responding to the world. To the degree that one's responses are governed by such patterns, one's ability to make full contact is impaired. An automatic script has replaced spontaneous, creative, contactful interaction with self and others. The therapist's task, we believe, is to help clients break out of such script patterns and to rediscover their ability to relate contactfully by reintegrating the parts of themselves that were lost to awareness and, as a whole person, to engage the world once again.

In this book, you will learn how to assist clients in the process of replacing script patterns with genuine, contactful relationships. You will learn about the three therapeutic elements that we believe can further this process: inquiry, attunement, and involvement. Through skillful inquiry into what the client is experiencing, careful attunement to that ongoing experience, and appropriate involvement in the therapeutic process, the integrative psychotherapist can lead clients to acknowledge and transcend the self-protective patterns that, although once necessary for survival, are now disruptive.

"Integrative" psychotherapy is becoming a very popular description, and with popularity comes a plethora of definitions. In both this book and our earlier volume, *Integrative Psychotherapy in Action*, "integrative" has two meanings, two implications for what is happening in therapy. First, as described above, we help the client to integrate his or her self: to bring back to awareness the sensations, the responses, the abilities, the hopes and dreams and fears and fantasies that were split off and driven underground as a result of acute or cumulative trauma. In short, integration means becoming whole again, with full access to all that one is and may become.

Second, "integrative" refers to our theory of therapeutic method, which integrates concepts and techniques from a wide range of approaches. We gratefully acknowledge and utilize the insights of client-centered therapy, transactional analysis, Gestalt therapy, and of contemporary psychoanalytic perspectives, particularly the intersubjective approaches and British object relations theory. Unlike an "eclectic" approach, we have attempted to build a therapy that is logically consistent, one in which each element or technique grows out of a basic and clearly defined set of concepts about the nature of human relationships. And we have reserved the right to pick and choose: to incorporate only those aspects of other theories and approaches that fit within a consistent and comprehensive theoretical framework and that have proven to be clinically useful.

If you have read this far, we hope you are thinking something like, "Hmm, sounds good. But there are lots of books out there, and many of them make similar claims. Why is this one any different?" That's a fair question, and we will try to answer it.

Somewhat to our surprise, one of the claims to uniqueness of *Beyond Empathy* emerged more or less by accident. Experienced therapists reported that they found this book useful and stimulating; they told us that our writing was somehow "stratified" and that with each reading they discovered new layers of meaning that they had not noticed before.

But beginning therapists, too, found value in the book and could understand it and apply it to their work with clients. We now realize that our efforts to create a readable, jargon-free explanation of how we view therapy have resulted in a book that can be read and used by people with a wide range of therapeutic skills and backgrounds.

Perhaps part of the reason for this wide range of usefulness is that *Beyond Empathy* tends to deal primarily with the "middle ground" of therapeutic competence. It is not a book about basic listening skills, about those foundation techniques with which nearly every therapist begins his or her training. But neither is it a narrowly focussed, technique-oriented approach, wedded exclusively to a single way of viewing human interactions. Rather, it has grown into a kind of bridge that connects the basic, everyone-has-to-learn-them-but-where-are-they-going skills to a comprehensive and coherent view of the therapeutic process. Because the therapeutic theory on which our work is based is "integrative," in our second sense of the word, it brings together parts of many different theories. Practitioners of all of these theories will, we hope, find our ideas useful.

The methods of therapy described in this book are broadly applicable. They provide a set of guidelines for "traditional" individual psychotherapy, as can be seen from most of the transcripts we have included. They are useful in both short- and long-term work; we and our students have utilized the approach with clients who have been in therapy for months and even years, and we have also used it in settings where the contract is for only a single session of therapeutic work. As can be seen in chapter 12, our focus on relationship makes integrative psychotherapy particularly relevant to work with couples. And, as we have discovered in both regular ongoing therapy groups and in training seminars and workshops, it provides a highly effective framework for group therapy.

A word about the structure of *Beyond Empathy* may be appropriate at this point. We have divided the book into two major sections. The first section lays out our theory of therapy and describes the methods we employ as we utilize that theory. We have provided many examples taken from actual therapy sessions. Some are quite short, with only a few transactions, and others are up to a page or so in length. By the time you finish these first six chapters, you should be reasonably clear about what we attempt to do therapeutically and why we attempt to do it.

In the second section of the book, we move to long transcripts, so that you can see how integrative psychotherapy actually unfolds in our work with clients. These transcripts include most or all of a given therapy session. No matter how clear a theory may be, real-life clients can be depended upon to do something unique, to take the work along paths that cannot be predicted. We want to show you the details of that process, to show you pieces of work from beginning to end, with no gaps or shortcuts. The transcripts are liberally annotated with our comments about the work and discussions of the therapist's choice of intervention and the effects of these choices on the progress of the work.

As is most often the case in books about therapy, our final chapter provides a wrap-up, a retrospective. We attempt to put all of the bits and pieces back together again, within a framework that will help you to see how each relates to all the others.

Well, the task is almost complete. (Funny, how we authors always write the first bit of a book last, isn't it?) What remains is to acknowledge the people whose ideas, creativity, and support have made our task possible. In a very real sense, this is not just our book. It is built upon the work of so many others: our predecessors, many of whom appear in the references and upon whose shoulders we stand; our contemporaries, whose ideas and arguments have stimulated our thinking and from whom we have absorbed more than we can possibly know; and our clients, who continue to teach us as we work with them.

There is no way that we can acknowledge all of the specific people who have shaped our thinking. There are too many of them! Moreover, we are acutely aware that we have absorbed ideas from others and made them our own to such a degree that we can no longer tell what is theirs and what is ours. Often, we suspect, it is both; not surprisingly, several intelligent people viewing the same phenomena may reach similar conclusions. Such is the path of science, and such is the nature of the integration of ideas . . . and while it can make for a well-rounded and broad-based approach, it certainly complicates the task of giving credit where credit is due. We have attempted, in the first section of the book, to provide fairly extensive referencing; this will allow the interested reader to trace ideas back to others whose work has prefigured, influenced, or confirmed our own thinking. In the transcript chapters and in our summary chapters, we have omitted this extensive referencing; to do otherwise, we decided, would be redundant.

There are two groups of folks whose contributions must be acknowledged specifically: First are the members of the ongoing professional development seminars and training programs of the Institute for Integrative Psychotherapy. A number of discussions in these programs were devoted to a careful and critical analysis of therapy transcripts (many of which can be found in *Integrative Psychotherapy in Action*), and this analysis led to the development of the concepts of inquiry, attunement, and involvement as fundamental to our approach to therapy. Our colleagues in the Institute for Integrative Psychotherapy programs have helped us hammer out ideas, have argued passionately with us, and have forced us to clarify, edit, and amend our work. Their influence pervades *Beyond Empathy*, and without them this book would be quite different, and much less. As we are proud of our work, so should they be as well.

Second, we want to acknowledge the help we have received from the folks at Brunner/Mazel. From the encouragement we received on submission of our first, partial manuscript, through the long process of bringing a book into being, they have been extraordinarily helpful. The response of the three anonymous reviewers was gratifying, and the editors and production managers, Lansing Hayes, Toby Wahl, and Catherine Van Sciver could not have been more supportive.

To all, many thanks! And thanks to you, dear reader, as well, for staying with us through this long Preface. And now, let us move on—on *Beyond Empathy*—to a therapy of inquiry, attunement, and involvement.

1

Basic Concepts

For generations, psychotherapists began their training by learning the skills of active listening. They studied Rogers' (1951) three "necessary and sufficient" growth conditions: genuineness, unconditional positive regard, and accurate empathy. Most—perhaps all—carry these foundation skills into whatever additional approaches they use. Empathic understanding, offered in the context of honesty and respect, is the basic principle that holds the therapeutic relationship together.

When Rogers first wrote about his new "client-centered" approach, the fields of counseling and psychotherapy were quite different from today's therapeutic landscape. There were, essentially, two kinds of therapy available: psychoanalytic and behavioral. Psychoanalysis was expensive, demanding, and somewhat esoteric. Behavioral approaches tended to be brusque, cut-and-dried, no-nonsense procedures. Rogers offered a much-needed alternative, a way of providing an arena where people could sort out their pain and their problems and be in charge of the kinds of changes they wanted to make.

But one innovator—one pioneer—can only go so far. There is a kind of synergy about the development of psychotherapy, in which each of us builds upon the work of those who came before. The Carl Rogers who wrote *Client Centered Therapy* could not have known about the theoretical and practical contributions of the psychotherapists and psychiatrists of the last 40 years. He could not incorporate into his thinking the work of the Gestalt therapists, the neo-Freudians, the psychoanalytic self-psychologists, the transactional analysts, the British object-relations theorists. Brick by brick, each of these schools—and others as well—has contributed its

1

ideas to the structure of what psychotherapists are doing as we move into the twenty-first century (Wheeler, 1991; Kohan, 1986; Greenberg & Mitchell, 1983). Many of these modern psychologies are referred to as "integrative" in that they attempt to integrate the best and most useful aspects of several different approaches (Norcross & Goldfried, 1992; Erskine & Moursund, 1997).

The authors of this book have been practicing and teaching an integrative psychotherapy for many years. It is an integrative therapy with a particular focus on relationship. We believe that psychic dis-ease arises from relational failure: the repeated failure of one's significant relationships to meet basic relational needs. Similarly, we believe that healing occurs in the context of a relationship that actively responds to or meets those needs.

This book is intended to describe our therapeutic methods. In it, we talk about how to create, maintain, and enhance a healing psychotherapeutic relationship, a relationship that utilizes many different understandings and approaches to people and their problems. These understandings have grown not only from our own ideas, but also out of the research and clinical experience of a host of other therapists. All of these therapists, no matter how widely their theories may differ, share a common debt to Carl Rogers, who made the word "empathy" almost synonymous with the notion of therapeutic relationship. And all of them, each in his or her own way, have gone beyond empathy, making their own unique contributions to the field. We, too, acknowledge that debt as we embark on our own journey beyond empathy.

In order to understand a method, it is necessary to know something of the theory on which it is based. That is what this first chapter is about: our perspective about how people come to be all that they are, how problems arise in that process of becoming, and how a healing therapeutic relationship can help one to deal with those problems. Once we are all on the same theoretical page, we can move on to the real purpose for which the book has been written: describing a method of effective psychotherapy.

☐ Contact and Healthy Development

One of the most consistent of all the activities of the developing human is our striving for contact with others. This movement toward contact is as natural as the movement of a flower toward the sun; it is the first observable manifestation of the need for relationship that characterizes all human organisms throughout the course of life. This striving of infants to achieve contact in relationship is a two-way street: the newborn responds to appropriate contact by engaging in behaviors that indicate pleasure and comfort, and adult caretakers (and noncaretakers as well) are re-warded by the baby's response. The satisfaction of feeling a tiny hand curl around one's finger, or seeing a pudgy face light up with a smile, is nearly universal. And although the infant cannot tell us in words about its cor-responding satisfaction, we can certainly infer from its searching and seek-ing behaviors, and its cuddling or smiling or relaxation when interper-sonal contact is achieved, that satisfaction is indeed there (Bowlby, 1969, 1973, 1980). Contact with others is a primary motivating experience in human behavior; humans strive for it from birth and, when it is appropri-ately provided, are universally rewarded by it (Guntrip, 1971; Fairbairn, 1952).

Not only is such interpersonal contact rewarding, it is necessary. With-out relationship—without reciprocal interaction with other humans—babies do not grow up to be people. Indeed, there is convincing evidence that they may not grow up at all (Spitz, 1954); the old term "marasmus" and the more modern "failure to thrive" both refer to the physiological effects that lack of contact in relationship can have on an infant. The psychological consequences of lack of contact in relationship are also dev-astating. Even if a child manages to survive physically, in the absence of adequate human contact, it will be unable to function normally in a hu-man environment. When children do not experience interpersonal con-tact—when they are deprived of reciprocal relationships with other people—they are unable to behave and interact in ways that we would consider "human." The damage to the person's sense of self and to his or her ability to relate to others is probably irreparable. Self—the human self—is a product of relationship, relationship that is a part of the infant's environment from birth (Fraiberg, 1987; Stern, 1985, 1995). The child who grows up with inadequate responsive relationships, with insufficient contact, cannot develop an adequate sense of self (Winnicott, 1965). Chil-dren need human caretakers to provide the necessities of life, and simple contact with those caretakers is as much a necessity as food or shelter.

In the course of normal development, the hours and minutes of wak-ing life are punctuated by many different sorts of interactions with the world around us. One of the first tasks for the growing infant is to sort out this new and complicated world: parts of self from parts of the environ-ment; living things from nonliving things; people from not-people. Con-sidering the complexity of the variables involved, babies are remarkably good at figuring out these differences; by the end of the first year of life most of us have our environment pretty well categorized and have made a sizeable start on the social and interactional nuances with which we contend for the rest of our lives (Bowlby, 1969, 1973, 1980).

What is it about contact with others that is so important for human development? Or, from the other side of the question, what is it about the lack of such contact that is so traumatizing? Why, if a child's physical needs are met (ignoring the possibility that there may be some actual physiological necessity for active skin stimulation through same-species contact), should that child not be able to grow and develop in a reasonably normal fashion, whether or not it is in relationship with other people? The answer lies in the nature of the psychological makeup of human beings. Humans are unequivocally social animals. The essence of our humanness is inextricably tied up in the ways we relate to others. We are conceived and born within a matrix of relationships, and we live all our lives in a world that is inevitably and constantly populated by other humans—both externally (most of the time) and internally (all of the time) in fantasies, expectations, and memories. *To be human is to be in relationship with others.* Developing these relationships is a fundamental aspect of our growth (Bergman, 1991; Jordan, 1989; Miller, 1986; Surry, 1985). We cannot live as humans without them, and our environment must provide us opportunities to develop and use them as we move through life. Relationships in which a child is neglected, physically abused, or emotionally attacked are traumatizing to a child, but no relationship at all is far worse.

☐ Internal Contact

Thus far, we have been referring to contact in terms of relationship with others. There is another aspect of contact, though, that is equally important: contact with oneself. Just as fully functioning humans are aware of and able to relate to the external world and the people in it, so they must also be aware of and able to relate to their internal world. This internal world is the world of sensations, emotions, ideas, fantasies, wants, and needs. It is all that goes on inside of our skins, as transmitted to and organized by the central nervous system. The nervous system and brain of the newborn infant is, of course, not yet fully developed; its organization of all this internal material must be somewhat primitive. Curiously, though, in some ways the young child may be more aware of internal reality and may be more in contact with it than many adults. Young children have not yet learned that it is unacceptable, or nonuseful, to know about and respond to all internal events. The stomach contracts: cry. Waste moves in the bowel: expel it. Want of mother occurs: seek mother. Healthy children, children who have not been damaged by their environment, do not know how to censor themselves in the way that adults have learned to do. They do not push annoying or unwanted internal events out of awareness; as needs arise the baby attends to them immediately. When this occurs, children are in full contact with their ongoing internal experience.

Of course, there is no way that anyone—infant or adult—can attend to everything all at once. There is just too much, internally and externally, to take into account! Our attention moves from one thing to another, from internal to external, and from this need to that perception and back again. Contact is really a verb, not a noun; it is dynamic rather than static. It is similar to a flashlight beam playing over the contents of a darkened room, lighting up first this object and then that one. It is not a random movement, though; in full and healthy contact there is a shuttling between internal and external events, with neither overbalancing the other. We move from awareness of self to awareness of our environment and especially of other people in that environment. From self to other to self and back to other again (Perls, 1973; Perls, Hefferline, & Goodman, 1951).

There is much more that could be said about the development of external and internal contact and how both change over the course of one's life. But this is a book about psychotherapy and only incidentally about general human development. Psychotherapy, as we view it, is a relationship that can be utilized to heal the cumulative trauma of previous ruptures in relationships (Erskine, 1993/1997, 1997; Lourie, 1996; Khan, 1974). We turn now to the role of relationship in human development, and specifically to how our contact with other people affects the way we understand and experience the world.

☐ Relationship and Becoming Human

It is through relationships that a child learns to make interpersonal contact in increasingly sensitive and inclusive ways. It is through relationships that this same child learns to set and maintain boundaries: he or she learns that *I* and *me* are separate and distinct from *you*. It is through relationships that the child learns to accept and use appropriately all the aspects of internal contact: to recognize needs, to daydream, to be angry or sad or joyful or scared. To join internal with external contact: to ask for help or to enjoy the interpersonal transactions that make us fully human. And, finally, it is through relationships that the child develops social interest, the sense of relatedness and empathy and compassion that allows us to survive as a species on this planet.

When healthy relationships are not available, children must take care of themselves. They, like all humans, must learn to cope with both painful external events and with the discomfort of internal needs that are not met. When children have been deprived of contactful and need-responsive relationships, they are likely to develop the expectation that nobody will be there to help them—really help them, with the kind of help they need—now or in the future. Bowlby and his students have identified this expectation as "avoidant attachment" (Bowlby, 1988; Ainsworth, 1969; Ainsworth, Blehar, Waters, & Wall, 1978), and that phrase gives us a flavor of the ambivalence and the tension that such a person must live with. Wanting with no hope of getting, or needing with no possibility that the need will be met, is terribly painful. The result can be that one learns not to experience one's emotions fully (because experiencing them alone only makes it hurt more), not to recognize one's need for relationship (for the same reasons), and eventually to split off unruly thoughts and feelings and wants and needs into a separate and barred-from-awareness part of the psyche (Tustin, 1986; Guntrip, 1968; Bettelheim, 1967).

Relationship is nurturing, stimulating, and restorative. Responding to another, and being responded to in turn, allows us to discover who we are, what we want, how we feel, and what we think. When this process of discovery is impeded by unresponsive or absent relationships, the coping skills that we develop will tend to interrupt both internal and external contact and to split, fragment, and deny important aspects of the self.

Much has been written about trauma and how traumatic events can leave psychic scars that influence a person's ability to function throughout life. Usually, however, it is not the traumatic event itself that creates such scars: it is the event unmitigated by healing through relationship (Erskine, 1993/1997, 1997). A single abusive experience is just that—an experience. For a child who can work through that experience in relationship with a caring and sensitive adult, the experience will become just one memory among many others. What is truly damaging is the absence of a healthy relationship following such an experience. When we have been traumatized by the actions of others or by some circumstance of life, we need a reliable other who will listen and respond to our pain. The overwhelming, helpless-making nature of a traumatic experience threatens our cognitive and emotional stability as well as our physical security: it is natural and instinctive to reach out for help when such experiences occur. Following an undeserved punishment, a beating, or any other abusive experience, there is an intense need for someone who will to talk with us about what happened and how we reacted, offer a realistic way of understanding the situation, keep us safe while we recover, and protect us from future trauma (Lourie, 1996).

Even when there is no active abuse, the absence of relationship is in itself abusive and damaging. Neglect and isolation produce a kind of cumulative trauma, a growing set of expectations that others will never be available and that life is difficult and painful. Many psychotherapists work with people who have suffered from cumulative trauma (Kahn, 1963). These people cannot identify any single or repeated experience that they can use to account for their sense of dis-ease, and they often feel guilty and ashamed about their need for help. They may even imagine that people who have been raped or starved or beaten are better off—at least those people have something to point to that will help them understand their pain. The cumulative trauma of contact deprivation, in contrast, leaves one with feelings of longing, of emptiness, and of "something's wrong," but with no way to make sense of those feelings.

When a reliable other is not available, a person's need for relationship is met only sporadically and unpredictably, if at all. If there has been abuse, the pain is compounded: now the need for relationship is intensified, and still nobody is there to help. What to do? Don't feel it, push it down, and split it off. Tell yourself that it isn't/wasn't really that bad, that you ought to be tougher/stronger/more grown up, that others are much worse off. Try to forget about it. Thus begins the process of isolating and excluding experiences and, in more extreme situations, isolating even aspects of one's self from awareness. The "bad stuff," the part of self that felt so lonely or frightened or angry or devastated, is tucked away where it is immune to the kinds of normal integration and updating that occur as a part of growing up. It resides, an undigested lump, with the affect and understandings of the developmental stage(s) the person was in at the times the traumas occurred (Federn, 1953; Weiss, 1950; Berne, 1961). Beliefs and expectations that are split off in this way cannot be questioned or challenged because they are out of conscious awareness; needs and feelings remain unrecognized and unresolved. The split cannot be healed until full contact, with self and with others, is restored.

Many names have been given to this process of splitting off and hiding away (Guntrip, 1961, 1971; Fairbairn, 1952). It is, of course, a defense: a protection against the pain of unmet needs and unexpressed emotions, including both the reaction to the original trauma and the reaction to the absent or inappropriate relationship (Fraiberg, 1982, 1987). It is a kind of dissociation, a making into "not me," a something that is too uncomfortable to own or recognize. It may be accomplished through denial, repression, or any of the more complex defensive maneuvers: disavowal, dissociation, desensitization, or depersonalization (Basch, 1988; Freud, 1937). Whatever form they take, these defenses serve to maintain stability, reduce awareness of discomfort, and allow the person to disengage from the pain of their needs not met and get on with the business of living. As a way of coping, such defense mechanisms are useful and perhaps even necessary processes. But they have a cost, and the cost can be very great.

☐ Needs

When a need arises, is met, and fades away, the person can move on to the next experience. When the need is not met, it persists, demanding attention and energy—a sort of psychic glue that refuses to let go and go away. The needs engendered by the absence of healthy relationships, past and present, are no different: they keep reemerging, intruding, and getting in the way of making ongoing contact with self and others. When the absence of relationship has been coupled with some form of abuse, the reemergence may take the form of flashbacks, fantasies, nightmares, or obsessive rumination; when there has been no clearly identifiable abusive experience, the person is more likely to feel sadness or anger or a nagging sense of emptiness and may be unable to figure out why he or she is in such distress. It is no wonder people try to split themselves off and to push all that pain out of awareness! Yet the attempt is never completely successful: just when they think they are "over it," the environment provides a reminder. Out pop the old feelings, as green and fresh as when they were first experienced, and sometimes just as painful.

Clearly, the wish to keep unpleasant experiences out of awareness is in direct conflict with the need for contact with self and others. One cannot have full contact with internal sensations, feelings, needs, thoughts, and memories while at the same time pushing some of those internal events out of awareness. And contact with the external world, with other people, is also impaired: meeting another person authentically requires a full acknowledgment of one's own self. Since relationships between people are based on contact, a major effect of trauma (both acute and cumulative) is damage to one's ability to form and maintain relationships. The result is an ever-increasing fragmentation, a growing inability to integrate new experiences. Awareness of anything that might remind one of the old pain must be blocked off: needs, feelings, perceptions. And people.

Gestalt therapy has given us a useful way of understanding how needs shift and change in normal life. It uses the concept of figure-ground relationships: a vast complex of potential needs and wants lie in the background of our experiencing. At any given moment, one of these needs is figural: it comes to the foreground; it enters our awareness. When that need is dealt with appropriately, it recedes into the background and another need becomes the figure (Perls et al., 1951; Perls, 1944/1947). We move ahead, not so much propelled by instinctive drives (as Freud believed) but by acting purposefully to satisfy the shifting patterns of our needs. Those needs include what will allow us to survive physically; they also include the psychological needs for stimulation, for contact with self and with others, for structure and predictability, and for relationship (Berne, 1966). Indeed, the dynamic pattern of experiencing and meeting a need is the essence of contact. What happens, then, to a child who has learned that no one will be there to meet those needs and that allowing a need into awareness just creates more pain? The need cannot be dealt with and allowed to recede naturally. Yet it does not just go away (there's that psychic glue again), so the child must find some other, artificial way to take care of it (Lewin, 1938)—more splitting, more pushing into the background. As such children continue to grow, they develop collections of strategies, generally out of awareness, to extricate themselves from the stuckness of needs-not-met. They deny; they deflect; they disavow their experience; they feel something else instead. They do whatever is necessary to keep the forbidden thought or feeling out of awareness. Gradually, the artificial strategy becomes habit, a life script, a well-learned schema of internal or external behavior or both (Stolorow & Atwood, 1989; Andrews, 1988, 1989; Stern, 1985; Perls & Baumgardner, 1975; Berne, 1972; Arlow, 1969a, 1969b).

☐ The Fixed Gestalt

As we learn to function in the world, we combine individual actions into blocks, sequences of behavior, that are performed with little or no thought. Do you want to go from one room to another? You do not think about lifting your arm, curling your fingers around the door knob, twisting your wrist, holding the tension, pulling toward yourself, partially relaxing your fingers, pushing sideways just hard enough to make the door swing further open. You simply open the door and walk through. The sequence has become a schema, a single, smoothly integrated action. It is only when that single action does not work, when the knob turns in the opposite direction or the door must be pushed rather than pulled, that we take the schema apart and modify it appropriately. Similarly, patterns of perceptions and experiences that occur together, over and over again, tend to blend and blur until we no longer differentiate among their separate parts. "Mother" is everything about mother: how she looks, how she sounds, and how we feel and what we expect when we are with her. The German word "gestalt" best describes these sets of parts-become-one-unit. A gestalt is a whole, indivisible pattern. We lose track of the fact that the gestalt was once lots of individual parts and that we have constructed the whole out of those parts. And the whole is qualitatively different from the sum of its parts, just as the notion of a "square" is qualitatively different from the notion of "four equal-length lines set at right angles to each other." Gestalten (more than one gestalt) are difficult to define, simply because defining them in terms of their component parts destroys that qualitative difference. Yet we all live in a world filled with gestalten: "my room," "partner," "running," "birthday" (Kohler, 1938).

Gestalten are important to us as psychotherapists because they are the patterns that one uses to organize one's behavioral schemas. People build up habits, response clusters, on the basis of their experiences and expectations. The more seamless and grown-together the gestalten on which such a cluster of responses are based, the more difficult it is to modify or adapt components of the cluster so as to deal with changes within and outside of ourselves.

Habitual responses, based on experiential gestalten, are not good or bad; they are simply a part of how all organisms negotiate their environment. It would be almost impossible to function without such clusters: imagine trying to figure out each small muscular component of taking a step every time you need to walk from here to there or thinking through exactly what you want to say and how to say it as you converse with a friend. When development is proceeding in a healthy way, the gestalten and the larger patterns that we build from them are useful and appropriate. They allow the child (and the adult!) to recognize an emerging need, find the resources to deal with it, and move on. But when acute or cumulative trauma occur—when a child is abused, neglected, deprived of reliable and nurturing relationships—gestalten and related behavior patterns can serve a different purpose. Rather than helping the individual meet his or her needs, they serve to deny or distort needs that cannot be met.

Think of a child who is experiencing a need to make physical contact with a nurturing adult. The need that emerges is, "I need touch." For the child who has no one with whom to meet that need, the next immediate awareness is, "No one is here." Those two adjacent awarenesses soon fuse: "When I need touch, no one is here." This is a typical *script belief*, a conclusion drawn from experience or learned from a significant other that becomes an unquestioned, out-of-awareness part of one's way of experiencing the world (Erskine & Moursund, 1988/1997; Erskine & Zalcman, 1979; Berne, 1972). The script belief, "When I need touch, no one is here," implies that the need for physical contact cannot be satisfied—there is no way to meet it. But needs, once experienced, have a demand quality: they must be dealt with somehow. If they cannot be taken care of naturally, by meeting the need, people find a way to close them off artificially: "I don't really need touch; I'll entertain myself instead." So the "need-touch" experience fuses with an artificial closure, a way to push that nagging, demanding need into the background. In the short run, this artificial closure is reinforcing: the need does seem to go away, but the demand abates. And so the pattern repeats itself the next time that need emerges. Repeat, reinforce, repeat, reinforce. Gradually, the whole thing becomes fixated, seamless, and indivisible. What was once an experience of "need touch" is now experienced as a need to entertain oneself; thus the "fixed gestalt" is born. Because the original need has been distorted and the whole pattern fused together, there is no way to undo or adjust it to fit changing circumstances. The need for touch will not be satisfied, because it is no longer allowed into awareness; unsatisfied, it will never fully subside (Perls et al., 1951).

Fixed gestalten are strongly resistant to change for several reasons. First, they are out of awareness—how can you change something that you do not even know you are doing? Moreover, they are based on a distorted view of the world (remember, both internal and external experiences are constantly being censored, so as to keep at bay the original need that cannot be satisfied), and so the current response feels like the only possible reaction or choice available. If you do not know that your discomfort is caused by an itch, scratching it will not occur to you, much less staying out of the poison ivy! And, finally, the fixed gestalt is reinforced: it works; it does help to split off or push away the experience of needs-not-met.

When we have developed a pattern of script-driven responses, responses that protect us from the pain of awareness, those patterns are used—*must* be used—whenever awareness threatens to emerge. They are used even when some other behavior would seem, to an observer, much more logical, helpful, or appropriate. They are used because, to us, they are simply the only thing to do. We do not even think about it; indeed, not thinking about it is one of the basic characteristics of the fixed gestalt. "Why did you go outside, walk around the house, and come in at the back door in order to get to the kitchen?"—"Because I wanted to go to the kitchen." "You look sad; what are you sad about?"—"I'm not sad, I'm angry." "What are you experiencing right now?"—"Nothing."

A fixed gestalt may be relatively harmless, if it only circumscribes a small portion of one's behavior. The fixed gestalten that are developed to deal with the absence of relationship are generally broader. Many sensations can trigger the memory of a painful experience, suffered alone: do not feel them! Many needs remind us of the old needs not met: do not experience them! Aspects of current relationships can call up threatening wants and recollections: stay away! The result is a life script that forms the basis for ever-broadening interruption in both internal and external contact, a growing inability to be fully aware of one's experience and to form full and authentic relationships (Yontef, 1993).

☐ Trauma and Symptoms

The earlier in life an individual experiences that the need for a relationship is not being met, and the more consistent that experience is, the greater and more disruptive its effects. Small children do not have the variety of resources that are available to adults; internal defensive mechanisms may be their only option for self-protection. If there has been abuse in addition to relationship deprivation, the likelihood of an internal defensive response is even higher. There is no one to help; survival feels threatened; the child learns to freeze, to withdraw (Fraiberg, 1982, 1987), to deny, and to transmute the painful affect into something more bearable (Tustin, 1986; Bettelheim, 1967). Part or all of the experience of abuse and neglect must be split off and pushed away. Unintegrated, it becomes the basis of an ever-expanding pattern that ultimately distorts perceptions, inhibits spontaneity, and limits flexibility and relationships with other people (Erskine, 1980/1997). And thus are born "pathology," "symptoms," and eventually the whole panoply of disorders found in the pages of the psychiatric *Diagnostic and Statistical Manual* (*DSM*).

Symptoms, as presented by our clients, begin as coping strategies. They are the external manifestations of fixed gestalten, distortions of reality and internal interruptions to contact, that protect the client from painful awareness. The external and internal aspects of such fixed gestalten are mutually reinforcing. It is necessary to block out aspects of current relationships in order to support internal keeping-from-awareness; internal splitting and defensiveness are necessary in order to maintain the distortion of interpersonal contact and to limit relationship to the outside world.

You can easily see, by now, where this discussion is leading. If symptoms are the result of patterns of fixed gestalten, then the remedy is to dissolve those fixed gestalten. If psychological disruption and emotional pain arise from lack of full external and internal contact, then restoring contact should cure the disruption and ease the pain. All that the therapist needs to do is to help the client work through and integrate the old trauma, bring the split-off aspects of self back into awareness, and regain full internal and external contact. "All," indeed! Accomplishing such a task is hard work. The client cannot do it alone, for it is based on the unfolding of awareness through *relationship*. The therapist nurtures the relationship with his or her client, enters into it fully, and that relationship becomes the vehicle for growth and healing.

☐ The Function of the Therapeutic Relationship

The first phase of psychotherapy involves exploring what is known. In the context of the therapeutic relationship, the client is encouraged to discover his or her feelings, needs, memories, thoughts, and perceptions. As these experiences are described, the client is offered the therapist's interest and involvement; the therapist is interpersonally contactful, available, and committed to understanding the client's world as the client understands and experiences it. As the client's ability to experience this relationship grows, the boundaries of awareness expand, and old memories and needs and aspects of self begin to emerge.

Contact, then, is the key. Contact, contact, and more contact. Contact facilitates dissolving the defenses, allowing more and more of those split-off, threatening bits of experience to come to awareness. As they come to awareness and are described or acted out, the therapist attends to them with interest, sensitivity, and encouragement. Within this contactful relationship, each newly discovered piece can be integrated into the self, and the split-off parts reclaimed and reowned. The therapeutic relationship is not like those relationships (and nonrelationships) of the past; the old defenses are not needed here. The goal of a contact-oriented, relationship therapy is to dissolve the client's fixed gestalten—those fused-together patterns of thinking and feeling and behaving—so that their original components can be brought to awareness: with awareness comes the possibility of reestablishing contact with self and others (including the therapist), of replacing the old, automatic beliefs and behaviors and disavowals and distortions and of dealing with current experiences spontaneously and flexibly.

The process is ever expanding. Just as establishing a fixed belief or attitude tends to set up a cycle of self-protection in which more and more of one's experience must be kept from awareness, so dissolving that fixed gestalt reverses the cycle. Disowned, denied, unresolved experiences, born of neglect and trauma and thrust into the limbo of unawareness, are brought to light and made part of a cohesive self. Simultaneously, hitherto unexperienced aspects of current relationships can now be taken in and attended to. Each new awareness makes the next step possible, in a continuing and ongoing integration of new and remembered material discovered and shared in the therapeutic relationship.

Does it sound simple? Perhaps too simple; perhaps an oversimplification There is a host of things that happen in therapy, as in any relationship. Different therapists, espousing different theories, focus on different aspects of the client's internal and external behavior. Remember when we described contact as being like a beam of light, illuminating first one part of a dark room and then another? In just such a way, the therapeutic dialogue moves in different directions and in different patterns, depending upon the therapist's interests and beliefs, and, equally, upon the client's view of the world, understanding of the problem, willingness to risk, and intensity of affect. All of these shape the course of therapy.

It is our contention, though, that whatever combination of problems and distress the client may be experiencing, and whatever theoretical perspective guides the therapist's treatment plan, the underlying and essential element of successful therapy is contact in relationship. Contact in psychotherapy is like the substructure of a building. It is seldom seen, but it undergirds and supports all that is above ground. It is this therapeutic contact that provides the safety to drop defenses, to feel, to remember, to try out new behaviors, to experience and integrate all that one truly is and can become.

The person who is damaged by the continuing experience of needs not met develops a pattern of fixed gestalten that resembles a kind of psychic log jam, blocking the possibility of new learning and growth. Like a log jam, it is ungainly and clumsy; the logs stay afloat but at the cost of freedom and movement. Log jams are difficult to break up, and the breaking-up process can be dangerous and scary. Unjamming one part may reveal further tangles and blockages underneath; when a bit gives way it can do so with great crashing unpredictability that may threaten to overwhelm the logger who is working to solve the problem. The therapist, similar to a logger, will work with whatever part of the jam appears to be most available to change. It may be a cognition or a barely suppressed memory; it may be a bit of behavior; it may be an emotional experience lying just below the surface. Changing any one of these may shift the logs and begin to break up the jam. But if progress is to continue, and if the jam is not to re-form even more intractably, then every change must be fully supported by caring, supportive, need-responsive therapeutic contact.

☐ Retraumatization

The image of a re-forming log jam brings up the concept of retraumatization. One of the biggest problems in working with people who have experienced neglect or trauma is that the therapist may tend to try to work too fast or do too much and in so doing stimulate the pain, the fear, the memories, and the defenses of the original trauma. Sometimes we become impatient, we press ahead too quickly, or we insist on behavioral changes without sufficient inquiry into the important protective function of the old patterns. The net result may be a therapeutic relationship that is psychologically similar to those that were present when the client experienced earlier neglect or abuse. Noncontactful relationships do not allow or encourage a child to fully explore his or her feelings and thoughts and responses to painful events and can initiate a cycle of defensive reactions. Internal experiences that are not explored or supported must be thrust out of awareness; what has happened to one somehow becomes one's own fault, shameful, a signal of some not-rightness at the core of one's being (Erskine, 1994/1997b, 1995). Later, if the therapist appears to be unwilling to help with exploration, or is impatient, or is unable to support all of one's feelings and beliefs and fears and fantasies, the shame is rearoused, and the old defenses spring into action. It becomes even more important to restrict contact (this time, contact with the therapist as well with oneself) and to maintain the internal splitting and denial. "If even my therapist can't/won't tolerate all of my 'stuff,' then it *really* must be dangerous or awful, and because my 'stuff' is a part of me, that makes me crazy or dangerous or awful too." This is the essence of therapeutic retraumatization.

People who have experienced neglect may be retraumatized in the context of many ongoing relationships, following essentially the same pattern as described above, and the closer and more important the ongoing relationship the more serious the effects of retraumatization. It is perhaps more serious in the therapeutic relationship than in any other. In therapy, clients are encouraged to become increasingly vulnerable as they bring to awareness more and more of their long-buried and split-off material; it can be devastating to sense that the therapist rejects, disapproves of, or fears what is so hesitantly exposed.

Notice, again, how retraumatization can quickly become a self-perpetuating process. Once danger has been sensed (and how sensitive the client will be to any hint of a negative reaction!) the door is opened to ever-greater distortion and misinterpretation of the therapist's response. Out of the large array of therapist behaviors, the client will selectively attend to those that most resemble the disapproval, withdrawal, or threat experienced (and fantasized) from others. Whatever the therapist says and does will be filtered through this mesh of expectations; things that fit what has happened or have been imagined in the past are taken as yet another reason to maintain the protective pattern, whereas things that do not fit are often unnoticed, distorted, or not remembered. The therapist's responses, in turn, may be shaped by the client's selective reactions. The whole interaction begins to replicate more and more closely the client's past relationships. Whatever the therapist says or does can be perceived and construed according to the client's protective frame of reference, and these perceptions and constructions create a strong yet subtle push for the therapist to provide even more misconstruable responses to the client. There is a juggernaut quality here: the pattern seems to take on a life of its own, sucking both therapist and client into its repetition and moving inexorably toward reactivating, yet again, the old fixed gestalten. It is the therapist's responsibility to attend to these inevitable patterns of relationship failure and to make the necessary corrections (Safran, McMain, Crocker, & Murray, 1990).

Therapeutic corrections are possible when there is contact in relationship. Only the therapist's ability to maintain full contact with both self and client can counteract the movement toward retraumatization. Some incident will occur, some verbal transaction, which will be major and clear enough that the therapist notices: "Here it is; the client just did *this* and I responded *so*. That's how it happens." At this point the therapist can draw back, unravel the pattern, and interrupt it. The client may be invited to share in the unraveling, or the therapist may choose to deal with it nonverbally. What is important is that something different must happen; the old, all-too-familiar routine of relationship disruption must be interrupted.

The earlier in the development of a therapeutic relationship such an interruption occurs, of course, the better. With every reinforcement, the re-creation of old traumatic patterns of relationship failure becomes stronger and more resistant to correction. To notice and respond therapeutically, it is essential that the therapist attune himself or herself to the pace, the affect, and the whole presentation of the client. Only by being attuned to the client's experience can the therapist provide the protection and permission and acceptance that clients need in order to penetrate the filter, to experience a different kind of relationship that is protective and permission-giving. Within such a relationship, clients can maintain a process of exploration that feels contradictory to all of the ways in which they have learned, over the years, to keep themselves safe. When they experience the inevitable setbacks, the return to old patterns of perceiving and responding to their experiences, they can learn to notice what has happened and to experience the contrast between long-buried protective mechanisms and new ways of being in the world. Sensitivity to the internal conflict between old and new, with appropriate and well-timed responses of support and understanding and encouragement, may well be the single most important ingredient in successful therapy.

☐ Inquiry, Attunement, Involvement

Inquiry is the process by means of which the therapist invites the client to explore his or her experiencing. The process is about asking, but not just with questions; a statement, a tone of voice, a gesture, or a lift of an eyebrow can all be part of therapeutic inquiry. The therapist inquires about every aspect of the client's growing awareness. By doing so, he or she conveys to the client that it is good to talk, good to explore, that no part of one's experience is forbidden, or unacceptable, or too threatening to be tolerated. Yet in the process of this inquiry, the therapist must be attuned to the client's here-and-now experience (actually, the past and the present flow together and are often indistinguishable in the moment of experiencing) in order to monitor and regulate the progress of exploration. Attunement involves sensitivity to, and reverberation with, whatever is going on for the client; we shall have much more to say about this in chapter 3. Attunement, in turn, can be maintained only if the therapist is fully present, aware of his or her own internal process as well as that of the client, involved in the relationship, and open to being moved and affected by it.

These three aspects of the therapist's behavior—inquiry, attunement, and involvement—compose the essence of a successful therapeutic relationship. With careful inquiry, sensitive attunement, and authentic involvement, the therapist will be experienced as dependable, consistent, and trustworthy. Experiencing such a relationship, clients can begin to reintegrate the parts of self that were split off in response to trauma and neglect; and with reintegration comes the possibility of full contact with self and with others, of true relationship, of being in the world as a whole person again (Hycner & Jacobs, 1995; Yontef, 1993).

It is important to keep in mind that full contact, "being in the world as a whole person," involves being fully aware of both internal and external events. Being in relationship requires that I be aware of myself as well as of the other person. These two aspects of contact, self and other, will not be equally balanced throughout the course of therapy. At the beginning, the focus is likely to be much more on the client's phenomenological experience: his or her life history, relationships, feelings, and beliefs—all of the internal experiences that are available to awareness. Focusing here leads to expanding the client's awareness in a gradual bringing to the surface that which has been hidden. Later, as the therapeutic relationship begins to hit the bumps and snags that signal reactivation of old patterns, the focus may sometimes shift to the relationship itself, to "what is happening between us." The therapist may share his or her own personal experiences and reactions, and the client's ability to make full contact-with-other begins to be challenged and to grow in the relative safety of the therapeutic session. The final movement is a free shuttling of awareness and contact, from self to other and back to self again. When client and therapist are both fully engaged in this shuttling process, it becomes an intricate dance in which each partner is responsive to the other as well as to himself or herself: the dance of authentic relationship. And, once experienced in the relative safety of the therapist's office, the dance may be taught to or danced with others in the client's life.

In the following chapters we will explore the therapist activities that invite the client into contact, authenticity, and relationship. We will examine in detail the concepts of inquiry, attunement, and involvement, and the ways in which the components of these three basic therapist attributes work together to enhance and support client growth. Throughout our discussions, we will illustrate the ideas and concepts with short excerpts from therapy transcripts. In the second part of the book, we will emphasize actual therapy interactions even more: each chapter will be based on a transcript of a full therapy session, with extensive discussion of the therapist's interventions and the clients' responses.

It has been our observation that good therapists, regardless of theoretical orientation, engage in inquiry, value attunement, and are concerned that their involvement be genuine and appropriate. Even when neither therapist nor client is specifically aware of these processes, their presence or absence has a profound effect upon the course of treatment. By deliberately cultivating one's skills in inquiring and attuning oneself to the client, and by constantly maintaining a stance of authentic involvement, the therapist of any stripe or persuasion can enhance his or her effectiveness in working with clients.

CHAPTER

Inquiry

Inquiry is the foundation of every variety of psychotherapy. Psychodynamic, behavioral, or existential—all use explicit or implicit questions to help their clients begin the journey toward self-discovery and healing. Even the most conservative of person-centered therapists are, in their selective responses, constantly inviting their clients to consider questions: What am I experiencing? How do I feel? What do I want and need?

Similarly, the process of inquiry cuts across all diagnostic categories and all sorts and types of clients. Depressed, anxious, angry, withdrawn, old or young, male or female, if clients are appropriate candidates for a talking therapy, that therapy will include inquiry. If the therapist is skilled, the inquiry will lead the client back into the memories, decisions, defenses, and vulnerabilities that were (and are) so painful, helping him or her to establish full contact with self and with others, and thus to discover a new way of being in the world. Therapeutic inquiry keeps the client focused on this process of exploration, while still respecting the client's own wisdom about what things will be important and helpful to talk about. And the whole process is carried out in such a way that it will not retraumatize, will not needlessly reopen old wounds, will not frighten the client into retreat or escalation. The competence and sensitivity with which interventions are made (and, more importantly, with which the client's responses are further explored) is critical to the outcome of the therapy (Safran et al., 1990).

In integrative psychotherapy, our inquiry begins with the assumption that the therapist knows nothing about the client's subjective experience. As therapists, we ask clients to teach us about that experience, and we

explore it together. The ultimate purpose of inquiry is to help clients discover the ways in which they have learned to interrupt internal and external contact. As they recognize their patterns of contact interruption,
they can develop new and more authentic ways of relating to themselves
and to others. And with this new authenticity come spontaneity, flexibility, and satisfaction. It sounds pretty straightforward, right? Straightforward, but not obvious. Simple, but not easy.

Part of what makes good inquiry difficult for beginning therapists is
that it follows a different set of rules from the question-asking we have
been doing all of our lives. From the time we began to use words, we
have been taught to use questions in order to get information. "Where is
baby's nose?" The child who points to its nose is rewarded with hugs and
praise. "Did you remember to put the dog out?" "What did you do in
school today?" "Will you marry me?" "Have you seen my cane?" Questions are universally used in order to get answers, and the answer is the
end of the questioning.

Therapeutic inquiry, however, is much less concerned with the answer
itself than with the process of getting to an answer. In therapy, the question that can be answered clearly and unequivocally is not always useful.
The therapeutically potent question is one that invites the client to search
for answers, to think in new ways, to explore new avenues of awareness.
Discovering a previously out-of-awareness response to the therapist's inquiry is much more important than the actual content of the answer.
Asking questions and making comments that encourage and support this
kind of self-searching, while still respecting the skill and courage with
which the client has maintained his or her defenses, is the essence of
therapeutic inquiry.

Searching for answers is necessary, of course, because the mechanisms
that we use to protect ourselves psychologically are outside of conscious
awareness (Guntrip, 1971). Otherwise, we would not need the help of a
therapist to figure ourselves out: we could observe what we are doing,
feeling, and thinking, and make changes on our own. The essence of a
psychological defense, though, is that it *is* unaware (Freud, 1937). We
protect ourselves by blocking out, shutting off, and hiding away. And,
just like that elusive name that you cannot remember, the one that is
right on the tip of your tongue, the harder we try to use brute force to
find the answers, the further they retreat. Skillful inquiry helps people
get to their own unique answers by inviting them to look in places and in
ways that they would never have thought of (or dared try) on their own.

Another difference between therapeutic inquiry and other question–
answer processes has to do with whom the answer is intended for. Ordinarily, if I ask you a question, it is because *I* want an answer. But in
therapeutic inquiry, the therapist asks questions primarily so that the *client* will find an answer. Or, more productively, the client will not find one

or will find one that just leads to another question, and then will be able to explore what is happening in that ongoing process. The point is that the response to any question is for the client much more than for the therapist. That is not to say that therapists do not learn from inquiry—of course we do! Our learning, though, is secondary. The primary benefit is to the client, as he or she begins to rediscover a sense of his or her long-lost self through the awareness-enhancing questions with which the client is grappling.

As the inquiry proceeds, the therapist becomes increasingly attuned to the client's process. Therapeutic understanding grows, and with it comes a clearer sense of where to point next and how to draw the client's awareness to just the right next tiny step forward. The therapist is interested in "figuring out" the client only insofar as that figuring out will eventually help to guide the client. It is sometimes easy to lose track of this aspect of inquiry, to become so fascinated with the client's dynamics that our own understanding becomes the focus. When that happens, it is time to pull back, regroup, let go of our need to be wise or clever. This is the client's show, the client's drama. The client is the central character, the protagonist; the therapist is merely a member of the supporting cast.

We hope that it is becoming apparent in this discussion that the inquiry process, when done properly, is healing in and of itself (Mendelson, 1972). It does not just get us somewhere; it *is* the somewhere. One of the reasons why therapeutic inquiry is such a powerful tool for healing is that it is carried out in the context of an authentic relationship between client and therapist. We shall have much more to say about the nature of this relationship in later chapters; for now, it is enough to say that the client–therapist relationship is a context in which the client can safely experience himself or herself in new ways, and can experience being with another person in new ways as well.

The relationship of the client with the therapist is also the subject of inquiry. In fact, this relationship may be the most important subject of all, because the newness of the experience invites the client into new levels of awareness. Instead of hashing over old, well-worn ideas and beliefs and interactions, we can talk about what it is like now, how the client is responding to a person who does not do the expected and does not repeat the old patterns. The client is repeatedly encouraged to notice how the therapy relationship is different from, and similar to, other relationships; and the therapist can then inquire about those comparisons and what happens when they are experienced (Stolorow, Brandschaft, & Atwood, 1987).

As trust in the relationship grows, the therapist may invite the client to attend to specific aspects of his or her phenomenology—his or her subjective experience (Yontef, 1993). Often the therapist will start with what is going on physiologically for the client, the flow of kinesthetic stimuli that is so seldom the focus of one's attention (Kepner, 1987). There is no hidden agenda here, no expectation that the client will come to some particular predetermined bit of insight: it is simply the therapist's genuine investment in the process, coupled with the knowledge that the greatest learning usually comes from looking more and more closely at what we are experiencing and what we do with that experience. Listen to this bit of work with Cheryl, who started by talking about feeling frightened and sad and how she often blocks herself from fully owning or understanding those feelings. As she talks, her face does not reflect sadness or fear, but her body seems tense and strained. The therapist asks her to pay attention to what she is doing with her body:

Therapist: *Stay with your body now, Cheryl.*

Cheryl: *I am, partly.*

Therapist: *Can you teach me about that? What do you mean, partly?*

Cheryl: *Well, I'm in here* (indicating her left side).

Therapist: *That side of your body.*

Cheryl: *Yeah.*

Therapist: *And the other side of your body?*

Cheryl: *Oh, it's there.*

Therapist: *"It's there."*

Cheryl: *I can feel it. From outside.*

Therapist: *Not like you're in it . . . and you've shifted all to the right side.*

Cheryl: *Yeah, to my arm, just to this portion.*

Therapist: *And there's a real important reason that you're living only right in there. And this side can only be felt from the outside.*

Cheryl: *Yeah.*

Therapist: *Is there anything that you're prepared for, when you're in this position?*

Cheryl: *Yes . . . if . . . if someone touches from here, or from the parts that I'm not in, um, then I don't react.*

Therapist: *You don't—how wonderful!*

Cheryl: *Yes, I can just keep it numb.*

☐ Characteristcs of Inquiry

The excerpt above, from Cheryl's work, illustrates a number of important aspects of the inquiry process. We continue to refer back to it as we begin to lay out the major characteristics of therapeutic inquiry.

Respect

Respect for the client is the foundation of therapeutic inquiry. The therapist who does not respect his or her client or who does not clearly show respect in the inquiry process will be unable to provide the kind of contact that the client needs in order to feel safe. Without respect, inquiry can be artificial, technique-bound, or mechanical. Or it can be bullying and brutal, an inquisition or an interrogation rather than a genuine inquiry. Respect and skill are the two fundamental ingredients of consistent therapeutic success. The skill can be acquired over time and can vary from one therapist to another. Respect, though, is a constant requirement, and it must be constantly present.

Respect, of course, does not mean that the therapist must always agree with clients, always approve of or support what they do. The respect is for the essence of the person, the person who was born a valuable and loveable human being and who has been surviving as best he or she can. It is respect for the struggle, the courage, and the commitment to survival. Respect is expressed in the therapist's consistent invitation to interpersonal contact, in the support given as the client moves into increasing awareness, and in the therapist's recognition of and involvement in the client's growth.

Notice how this respect is played out in the excerpt from Cheryl's work. All of the therapist's comments direct Cheryl's attention to herself, to her internal process. Cheryl is respected for who she is and what she is doing. The respect becomes explicit in the therapist's comment, "There's a real important reason that you're living only right in there" —an antidote to any sense of shame or embarrassment that Cheryl might have been feeling. And it is even more openly expressed at the end of the segment, when the therapist's exclamation, "How wonderful!" is a spontaneous appreciation of the skill Cheryl has developed in protecting herself from pain.

Genuine Interest

It is difficult to point to any single part of a therapeutic inquiry that exemplifies interest on the part of the therapist. Genuine interest is conveyed not so much by words as by the tone of voice, the facial expression, all the nonverbal aspects of the exchange. And it is evidenced in its consistency: interest in everything, not just in occasional parts that happen to capture the therapist's attention. In the work with Cheryl, the therapist's questions are motivated as much by the therapist's interest as by any therapeutic technique. How has Cheryl managed to narrow her awareness down to one small part of her body? How is it useful to her to do so?

What is she preparing herself for? To a skilled therapist, an individual's patterns of contact and noncontact, and the purposes served by these patterns, are never-ending sources of wonder.

In one way, this characteristic hardly needs specific mention: it is usually a natural outgrowth of respect. How can you truly respect another person and not be genuinely interested in his or her experience? But interest has some important consequences of its own, and thus deserves a place on our list. One of these consequences is that it makes the therapist's job much easier: it tends to relieve the therapist of the burden of figuring out what to do. The genuinely interested therapist follows up that interest by asking for more of the client's ideas, experiences, and understandings. From "What's it like to be responsible for so many important decisions at work?" to "How did you handle it when your dad used to come home drunk?" conversations motivated by genuine interest take on a life of their own. Each question is generated by the previous answer; sometimes the questions come so fast that they almost have to wait in line.

Good teachers know all about how genuine interest propels the dialogue between student and teacher. Imagine that you are asking me questions designed to lead me to an understanding of, say, how to do calculus, and that I am truly invested in learning. We certainly will not run out of things to talk about. Each of your questions will invite me to extend my knowledge just a bit further; our mutual interest and pleasure in my learning will keep us involved until I have mastered the task.

Fortunately, genuine interest on the client's part is seldom a problem. There is nothing so fascinating for me to talk about as myself; clients can generally be counted on to be interested in their therapy. It is the therapist's interest that can sometimes wander. And when that happens, it will interfere with the process of inquiry—guaranteed. One of the first consequences of losing interest is not knowing what to ask about next. The client has answered your question and is sitting there, waiting. What in the world should the next question be? Where should the inquiry go now? Without genuine interest on the therapist's part, he or she has to fall back on technique, and that is often not enough.

A more serious consequence of therapist disinterest is its effect on contact. If we are uninterested, our attention inevitably turns elsewhere, and contact is lost. Even if we realize what is happening and try to repair it, there is still contact disruption. If we find that we have lost interest, our internal response is likely to be one of guilt or shame: cover it up, don't let the client know that we do not really care about all this! So we pretend an interest that we do not have. Pretending always distorts the quality of contact and the authenticity of the encounter. By being less than genuine, we destroy the essence of what makes therapy work.

Genuine interest, in and of itself, is both intrinsic to and an important characteristic of therapeutic inquiry. At the risk of sliding from a description of the process into a description of how to accomplish it (which is the next section of this chapter) let us anticipate a question that you may be asking: "What do I do if I wander off mentally, if I truly am not (in this moment, at least) interested in this client?" First, use whatever information your loss of interest may provide. Your mental wandering off did not happen in a vacuum; it happened in the context of what is going on, right now, between you and your client. Perhaps the client is talking about something that is hard for you to hear, that may be stirring up some of your own unresolved issues. Perhaps you are providing for the client the same kind of disinterest that the client received from other important people in his or her life, past or present. Or your lack of interest (or your avoidance) may reflect some lack of interest (or avoidance) on the part of the client. The point of all these suppositions is that, undesirable though it may be, losing interest in what a client is saying can still be useful—if we are aware of what is happening and are alert to the information it carries (Bollas, 1987; Racker, 1968).

Once you are consciously aware of your internal process, you may choose to set it to one side, to come back to later, or you may deal with it in interaction with the client. If it is your own personal "stuff" that has been stirred up by what the client is talking about, it might be wise to find a third party to help you sort it through. If it has more to do with the interaction between you and the client, you may choose to talk with the client about it, watch to see if it happens again, or tuck it away for later use. Simply noticing and making the decision should allow you to interest yourself once more in what is going on in the therapy session. If that does not happen, if you find yourself increasingly plagued by wandering attention and flagging interest, then it is time seek consultation. Something is going wrong, and you need to find out what it is. Remember, genuine interest is a natural outgrowth of respect; if you are not feeling either of them, there is something in the way.

Open-Endedness

There is not a single therapist comment in the Cheryl excerpt that can be answered adequately with a simple "yes" or "no," or for that matter with a simple statement of fact. Even those clarifying reflections to which Cheryl agrees with a single "yeah" are movement-oriented, are preparatory for a next step. "Teach me about that" is the sort of inquiry that both focuses the client on a particular phenomenon and also allows her to talk about it in any way that makes sense to her. Even the focus is, in essence, chosen by the client. By using the word "partly," Cheryl pointed to an important aspect of her experience that the therapist inquired about immediately. The comment, "not like you're in it" picked up on Cheryl's "from outside." Wherever the client goes, the therapist follows, but always inviting the client to open her awareness just a bit more, to look just a bit beyond what she has just said.

Theory Does Not Bias the Inquiry Process

There is, of course, no way that a therapist can—or should—be theory-free. Theories about how people grow and change and what sorts of relationship qualities will facilitate growth will always govern the way we conduct ourselves with clients. And yet in the inquiry process our theories must not limit the client's exploration (Sullivan, 1953). We must make sure that we do not, deliberately or accidentally, conduct our inquiry in such a way as to nudge the client to meet our own theoretical expectations (Naranjo, 1993).

The therapist's question, "can you teach me about that," to Cheryl does not presuppose any particular meaning about her rather cryptic "partly." Whatever she says as she attempts to "teach" the therapist will be accepted as valid for her at that moment. As she goes on to discover that she has shifted her sense of self to her right arm, excluding the rest of her body, the therapist invites her to consider the implications of that shift: "There's a real important reason. . . . " In one sense, that is an obvious comment: it is highly unlikely that such a shift would be made for no reason, or for an unimportant one. Yet making the comment, and getting Cheryl's agreement, allows the therapist to ask the next question: "Is there anything you're prepared for?" Without confirmation that there was an important reason, that next question would have imposed, presupposed, the therapist's ideas. It would have gone beyond inquiry into interpretation.

The question about being prepared for something warrants another word of explanation. Without knowing Cheryl's body language, one might wonder where the question came from and whether it did, in fact, impose some theoretical bias. A video of the interaction would show something quite different: Cheryl has twisted herself up, curled around that right arm where all her feeling has gone. Her whole body is saying, "protection!" Given the force of that nonverbal statement, asking "Is there anything you're prepared for?" is again rather obvious. People do not protect themselves like that unless they are preparing for something (Epstein, 1972)! And now it is Cheryl's choice whether to acknowledge the something and whether to talk about what it might be.

When we do not impose our theory on our clients, we are free to follow them wherever they need to go. Not infrequently, clients find this somewhat confusing. After all, isn't the therapist the authority? Therapists are trained to understand people. A good client should listen carefully to the therapist and do what that therapist says, right? It is truly paradoxical: implicit in the inquiry process is the instruction to *not* do what I say, but to follow your own way. But if the client does that, he or she is following instructions.

The constant thread that leads both client and therapist through the confusion is contact. Even if the therapist misunderstands, goes off in the wrong direction with a question, or misses something important, the contactfulness of the therapeutic relationship provides an opportunity for therapist or client to make the needed correction and get things back on track. The therapist simply stays in the moment, stays with what is happening, and reminds the client of this when necessary. Look at this short excerpt from a piece of work that the therapist does with another client, Nell. Nell is a professional woman in her early fifties, who experienced a great deal of childhood neglect, insults, and family discord. In order to deal with the pain and inconsistency of that environment, she learned to depend upon guessing and imagining rather than on her perception of reality; now, as an adult, she experiences a great deal of emotional confusion around close relationships. It is not surprising that this confusion emerges in her work. She is frustrated with her inability to move forward; and she frightens herself with the fantasy that the therapist will abandon her. The therapist responds:

Therapist: *Let's sort out all the things you imagine, all that stuff you call "crazy." Like imagining that I went away.*

Nell: *I know you haven't. . . . I don't know what to do.*

Therapist: *Go back inside. Just let yourself know what's happening for you.*

Nell: (pause) *I'm trying to stay with you. I don't know what to do with the silence.*

Therapist: *You don't need to stay with me. My job is to stay with you.*

There could hardly be a clearer statement of the principle of not imposing our ideas on the client: "You don't need to stay with me. My job is to stay with you."

Constant Attention to Contact

The contact between client and therapist is the context within which the client can begin to explore his or her own internal experience. In a sense, contact *between* is the bridge to contact *within* (Orange, Atwood, & Stolorow,

1997; Bollas, 1979). The therapist is constantly attuned to the quality of the client's internal contact, constantly asking questions that will increase the client's awareness of feelings, needs, memories, perceptions. Moreover, the questions are asked and answers received in a way that enhances the relational contact as well. The two aspects of contact, internal and external, intertwine: each provides fuel for the growth of the other.

With Cheryl, the therapist's questions and comments consistently invite her to open her awareness and to notice what she is doing/thinking/feeling/expecting. Again, what does not come across in this printed transcript is the warmth of the therapist's nonverbal communications: tone of voice, facial expression, gestures, posture, all convey involvement with Cheryl's exploration. The therapist is fully herself, fully open to her own reactions and feelings; and she is open to as much contact with Cheryl as Cheryl is willing to tolerate. It is this contactful quality of the therapist's questions, undergirded with interest and respect, that allows Cheryl to move ever more deeply into her own experience.

Expanding Awareness

No matter what a client says, there is a multitude of things to be interested in and to ask about. It is not particularly helpful to jump all over the map, skipping from this thing to that. So, how can the inquiry process be purposeful and productive and yet avoid leading the client where the therapist, rather than the client, wants to go? The answer is fairly straightforward: inquiry concerns itself with whatever will invite the client to become more aware—aware of self and aware of his or her relationships with the external world (Kepner, 1987; Zinker, 1977).

An important implication of this principle is that the inquiry process often does not follow the rules of etiquette and of ordinary social discourse. The explicit and implied questions asked of Cheryl would seem odd and even inappropriate in most other social situations. We do not ordinarily ask someone to stay with their body (and, implicitly, to tell us about that experience) over a cup of coffee, or suggest that they tell us what they are preparing for in the way they are curling themselves into a ball. But therapeutic inquiry is not about social chatting or even ordinary problem-solving. It is about becoming increasingly aware of oneself and of one's interactions with others.

Not only does therapeutic inquiry deviate significantly from the ordinary social rules of conversation, but it also refuses to be distracted by the social exterior presented by the client. Cheryl began her piece of work by relating an incident that had occurred earlier that morning as she walked to the therapy session: she had stopped to pet a cat and found herself talking to it in French. By focusing on the internal meanings of that story, rather than on its external details, Cheryl was led gently to the point at which our excerpt begins. Therapeutic inquiry consistently asks about what lies below and beyond the social exterior. Stories of the "I did this, then he did that, so I did thus-and-such" are not dealt with just at face value, but are rather taken as disguised comments (disguised, perhaps, from the client's own conscious awareness) about deep feelings, needs, hopes, and fears.

One of the most difficult things for beginning psychotherapists to do is to put to one side the conversational conventions that they have used all their lives. We have already alluded to one of these conventions, the expectation that questions are asked in order to get clear, unambiguous answers. Another convention that does not fit is the one about making the other person comfortable. Good conversationalists are experts at this: they know how to keep the flow of talk going so that the other person enjoys it and wants to continue. But the goal of inquiry is not to help clients feel comfortable, or shore up their defenses, or provide them with an enjoyable 50-minute interlude in their day. It is to help them discover things they have been unable to discover on their own, to explore aspects of self that they may be uneasy with, and to experience ways of feeling and thinking and being that can be frightening and sometimes quite painful. In this process, social rules are much less important than furthering the therapeutic process.

As we have said, interest, respect, and willingness to learn from the client undergird the inquiry process. They allow us to suspend the usual social conventions and to have the client nevertheless experience our comments and questions as helpful and safe. The client is in charge; the client decides how far he or she is willing to go in the process of exploration. Each new awareness enhances contact and invites the client to take another step, to reclaim one more bit of self. Inquiry lies at the core of therapy; it guides the process yet leaves the client free to choose his or her own direction.

☐ The Techniques of Inquiry

Thus far, we have simply been describing inquiry, its purpose and its characteristics. Now it is time to talk about how to make it happen.

Contracting

The basic principle of respect for the client requires that nothing be done without the client's consent and cooperation. This means that the client must agree with the therapist's intent and must essentially contract with the therapist that they will do the work together. Every moment of therapy, every transaction between client and therapist, occurs in the context of a therapeutic contract (Steiner, 1974). Moreover, the contract can be renegotiated at any moment; there should be a clear understanding that either client or therapist can back off, question what is happening, or clarify and fine tune the process. Working *with* the client, rather than working *on* the client, makes the client a partner in the therapeutic enterprise. Resistances and dead ends become problems to be solved jointly (Safran et al., 1990). The client's sense of efficacy and control are enhanced, and with efficacy and control comes a greater sense of safety and willingness to risk (Basch, 1988).

An important aspect of inquiry, then, is inquiry about the unfolding process of the therapy itself (Mendelson, 1972). Implicitly, we ask the client, "Is this working? Is it okay to explore here? What do you think would work best for you?" In the following excerpt, the client, Dan, is describing his relationship with his father. Dan is becoming increasingly aware of how old behavior patterns that developed in that relationship are now affecting his ability to be contactful in present-day interactions. The therapist believes that it would be helpful for him to reexperience the old relationship in order to bring it to full awareness. Asking Dan what he would prefer, and respecting his wishes, leads in a different direction:

Therapist: *Is it important that you tell this story to me, Dan, or would it be more beneficial to tell it directly to him? Or would you prefer that I talk to him?*

Dan: *I don't know. I need, I just need you to know, I think.*

Therapist: *I understand. And I was looking to see what else you need. Would you like to know what I know?* (Dan nods) *That is, that you need all three. And I was just looking to see if you had a preferential order. So since you're not real clear, let's continue with your telling me about it.*

Later in the session, Dan himself moves comfortably into an imagined dialogue with his father. He does so when *he* is ready, not when the therapist decides. By renegotiating the contract, the therapist has suggested/signaled that she is open to this sort of fantasy work but that Dan is in charge of whether and when it will occur.

No Presuppositions

Inquiry begins with the assumption that the therapist knows nothing about the client's internal experiences. Easier said than done! We all tend to suppose that others will react to situations more or less the way we our-selves would. "Oh, that's too bad" or "You must have been furious!" are common responses to our friends' stories about themselves. Such responses represent empathy; they are usually based on putting ourselves in the friend's place and knowing how *we* would feel. Most therapists are trained to do this sort of thing as a part of "active listening." It is a part of our training that we would do well to deemphasize as we learn to inquire in a way that goes beyond empathy.

Presuppositions can seriously derail the inquiry process in at least two ways. First, what if the therapist's "empathic" response is quite different from the client's experience? To say, "that made you angry" or "you were sad about that" when the client felt neither, leaves the client with a vague sense that his or her response was somehow odd, wrong, or abnormal. What to do next? Correct the therapist? That's pretty uncomfortable. Go along with the therapist's interpretation? That doesn't feel right either. Maybe just change the subject or talk about something else; this therapist obviously doesn't understand me too well.

Even if correct, though, therapist presuppositions still detract from the primary purpose of inquiry (Sullivan, 1953). By acting on a presupposi-tion, we imply to the client that we have "got it." The client does not need to explain any more; the therapist understands. But the therapist really does not understand—not fully, not completely. Nor, for that matter, does the client. Exploring meanings and feelings is like peeling an onion: there is always another layer. Inquiry is intended to peel down those layers, each response leading into a new level of awareness. Neither thera-pist nor client knows what the next level will bring—that is what inquiry is all about (Naranjo, 1993).

This is not to suggest that we tune out our own affective responses to the client or that we ignore the nonverbal signals the client sends us. Those responses and those signals are a fundamental aspect of therapist–client communication and contact (Cashdan, 1988; Bollas, 1979, 1987; Berne, 1961). We use them, though, to formulate questions rather than answers. Not, "You must have been furious," but rather, "You look angry right now. What *are* you feeling?" or "It looks like that incident was deeply meaningful to you," with a voice tone and a pause that encourage the client to talk about his or her meanings. If the client's responses to such explicit or implicit questions continue to confirm our sense of having the same reaction, we may share that sense. (As we shall see in a later chap-ter, knowing that one's therapist has had similar experiences can some-times be very helpful and meaningful to a client.) But we are always careful to do so in a way that will invite further exploration, rather than closing it down.

Here is another short excerpt from Dan's work. Early in the therapy session, Dan and the therapist had been talking about a paper that Dan had written for a conference. The therapist talked about her own interest in the paper, and then noted an expression of discomfort on Dan's face. Notice how both of the therapist's questions follow Dan's own exploration, inviting him to take the next step without in any way suggesting what that next step should be:

Therapist: *I remember being fascinated by it . . .* (as Dan frowns) *What's going on inside, Dan?*

Dan: *All sorts of put-downs. About, well, it didn't work very well, and I'm not sure it's applicable, and all those sorts of things.*

Therapist: *And do those put-downs, "it didn't work very well," and "it's not completely applicable," and all of that, does that motivate you or does that stop you?*

Dan: *It decreases my satisfaction. In something that's actually okay. Just takes the edge. Always takes the edge off.*

As the inquiry continues, Dan explores the meaning for him of "taking the edge off." This leads him to memories of interactions with his father in which his father's reaction "takes the edge" off his pleasure and satisfaction, and paves the way for him to eventually work through his by-now-automatic damping of enthusiasm for his own accomplishments.

Everything Is Important

Just as nothing is presupposed in therapeutic inquiry, so also is nothing unimportant. Every word, every gesture, every shift in voice tone or posture is connected to some aspect of the client's experience and is thus worthy of exploration (Smith, 1985; Langs, 1981). There is always something to ask about! The challenge to the therapist is not so much what to explore as it is what to postpone until later.

Think of the client's phenomenological or subjective experience as a vast sea of memories, feelings, dreams, and expectations. Some of this material is immediately available to awareness; much of it is not. A task of therapy, as we have said, is to reestablish internal contact so that the client has access to all of his or her experiencing, to every part of self. Whatever the client says or holds back from saying, each bit of communication, rises out of that sea of selfhood. Inquiring about it leads the client back in toward the source.

While inquiry most often deals with phrases, sentences, even entire stories, there are times when inquiring about a single gesture or an individual word can open whole avenues of awareness. As a rule, ambiguous words and vague pronouns are fertile ground for inquiry. In many families there is an unspoken pact not to call some things—usually disturbing or uncomfortable things—by their right names. Unquestioned acceptance of this sort of verbal avoidance not only fails to follow up a promising lead; it also reinforces the old pattern. It encourages the client to continue to use vague generalizations as a way of splitting himself or herself away from awareness of what and how things really are. In the following excerpt, the therapist has arranged a two-chair encounter (Erskine & Moursund, 1988/1997; Perls, 1967) in which the client, Janelle, imagines her mother sitting in a chair across from her. Janelle "talks to" her mother about her mother's failure to deal with Janelle's abuse at the hands of her grandfather. The family pattern is to avoid, ignore, and deny what is happening, and Janelle's language reflects that pattern even as she experiences her anger and frustration:

Janelle: (to mother) *No! I won't forgive it!*

Therapist: *Tell her about the secret word.*

Janelle: *What secret word?*

Therapist: *The one you've used five times here in this room.*

Janelle: (to mother) *Oh, you crazy woman! You are so crazy!* (breaking off, and looking at the therapist) *One word? I don't know what you. . . .*

Therapist: *Yeah, you were saying "it." "Until you admit it." "I won't forgive it."*

Here Janelle's use of "it" serves to further her avoidance of full awareness of her grandfather's sexual abuse. "It" maintains both the secret and Janelle's response to it. As a child, that splitting of awareness made sense, because Janelle's mother would deny and quite possibly punish her if she talked openly about the sexual abuse; hiding it in a neutral pronoun and then pushing it out of awareness allowed Janelle to continue to be a part of the family. The cost to her was loss of internal awareness, and with that loss came an inability to make full contact in relationships, to be spontaneous and flexible, and to be fully herself. Focusing on the "it" and inquiring about its real meaning is an important step in reversing that pattern.

Another thing to notice and come back to is the word that is used frequently, or the word that is relatively unusual in its context. Inquiry about such words need not always be in the form of a question; simply reusing them calls attention to them and invites the client to explore their significance. Here Allen is talking about his father:

Allen: *My father gave quite heroically from a place of neediness in his own background. And yet there's always that something that I've been terrified of in him.*

Therapist: *He gave when he felt needy himself?*

Allen: *Yeah . . . giving, and general resentment, rage. . . . Um, yeah, or seeing my mother give it, feeling those same things. I imagine he wanted a lot; I'm sure he wanted a lot for himself. From my mother or what he didn't receive from his mother.*

Therapist: (pause) *I'm trying to link that with what you said before, about being able to accept being cared for and given to when you were sick.*

Allen: *Yeah. Given to generally, I think. Not specific to being sick. Yeah, receiving nurturing. And myself being vulnerable as well, like, for me to cry is almost impossible. Still, even after . . . in real desperation, real pain I'll cry, now; but I still almost never cry.*

Therapist: *So what were the kinds of things he gave to you that were so heroic? How would he do that?*

At first reading, the therapist's last question seems to be an abrupt shift. Looking more closely, though, we can see that it neatly links Allen's own heroics (never crying) to those of his father. Allen is being invited to look at the relationship between how he handles difficulties and how his father handles them. Attending to that single, rather unusual word sensitized the therapist to the parallel pattern and offered a way to sensitize Allen to it as well.

Respect the Client's Perspective

There are inevitably points in the therapeutic inquiry at which the client chooses not to answer or not to answer fully. The client may deny the significance of something that the therapist is interested in, or he or she may choose not to follow the therapist's suggestion for how to move past some stuck place. The therapist may be certain that a particular technique or strategy will be helpful to the client, but the client may resist using that strategy. Such resistance is significant and deserving of respect; it is serving an important function in the client's whole self-protective system. Rather than trying to batter down or crash through a client's resistance, integrative psychotherapists welcome the resistive behavior as a signal that the client may be at the edge of some new awareness or some previously unaware area of experiencing (Brisser, 1971).

Trying to persuade clients to explore in a way that they are not ready for is not only a waste of important information, but it is also an abrogation of the therapeutic contract. It erodes, rather than strengthens, the client's sense of efficacy. And it generally does not work: the client either continues to resist openly or is compliant in a grudging and half-hearted way. In either case, the contactfulness of the therapeutic relationship is ruptured. Anxiety and resentment on the client's part, and frustration or exasperation on the therapist's part, begin to block progress. Little will be accomplished until the relationship can be mended. Coerced work is similar to bad carpentry; it has to be torn out before something solid can be built in its place. It is much better not to have built the shoddy stuff at all!

So what do you do when the client resists, ignores your suggestion, or does what you think will not be helpful? Follow the client's lead. Continue to inquire. Save your suggestion for later, when the client is ready. You may find that "later" comes sooner than you expect! As in this interchange with Paul, who is talking about his inability to relate to women as he would like to and is discovering that this inability connects somehow to his early experiences with his father. The therapist suggests that Paul dialogue in fantasy with his father in order to begin to experience a different kind of contact with him. Paul makes a rather half-hearted attempt to do so, but he almost immediately directs his remarks to the therapist again. In order to move Paul into a more emotionally powerful encounter with his father, the therapist suggests that he close his eyes.

Paul: *That's the bewildering part, Dad . . .*

Therapist: *Close your eyes, now, and keep going.*

Paul: (still looking at the therapist) *This is the bewildering part to me . . .*

Therapist: *If you need to talk to me, open your eyes. If you want to talk to him, you close your eyes. And you can have it either way.*

Paul: *I, I need to talk with you a little bit. He doesn't know shit about this, how to do it. That's one of the problems I have with him.*

The therapist has put Paul in charge, letting him decide whether and when to move into an emotional experience with his father. And Paul chooses to stay, for the moment, with an emotionally safer focus on the therapist. However, just a few transactions later he slides easily and naturally into a fantasy interaction, but with his wife! He notices what he has done and puzzles over it; the therapist again puts him in charge:

Paul: *She's, she's so there . . .* (looking again at the therapist) *Don't know whether to do this with her, or do it . . .*

Therapist: *Do it any way you want to do it.*

Paul: (as if to his wife) *You're so there, all your wants, all your feelings . . . and I think at the moment I really want to take care of you; I don't know how; all I know how to do is act like I'm taking care of you. Something happens to me, and I end up getting angry at you, and annoyed with you. And you're very disappointed with me. . . . And I feel like I want my father to have shown me what to do right now. I know how to get up every day and go out and work—provide food and money. . . . And I know how to be gentle, and I know how to be warm, and I know* *some other things. But when you as a woman somehow blend into my mother as a woman, then all I know to do is to not ask* (sigh, pause). *Then I think I'm supposed to know.*

Therapist: (pause; then softly) *Now see what happens if you close your eyes and look at Dad. . . . Just start, "She's your wife."*

Reading Paul's body language, the therapist realized that he was now ready to deal with his father. The last statement was much more an invitation than a command, and Paul heard it as such. He readily moved into the interaction with father.

☐ An Inquiry Menu

As we have said, the focus of inquiry is the internal experience of the client. But that is so broad! The client's "internal experience" is everything he could possibly know about. Is there a way to narrow it down a bit, to provide some more specific guidelines about the sorts of things it can be therapeutically useful to inquire about? Indeed there is. Here is a list with examples:

1. *Physical sensations.* Ask about what the client is experiencing in his or her body. This is particularly useful with clients who have difficulty recognizing and expressing emotions (Smith, 1985). Physical feelings are often the pathway to emotional feelings. We recognize our emotions by the physiological sensations that accompany them, and people who have learned not to recognize feelings have done so by closing off awareness of sensation. Nell is one of those people:

Nell: (continuing with a long, rather monotone narrative) . . . *so I was a good girl. Real good. But it wasn't enough—*

Therapist: (interrupting) *Feel your body while you say that.*

Nell: *Huh?*

Therapist: *Feel your body while you say that.*

Nell: *Oh, yeah, it's tight through here* (indicating her chest). *Real tight.*

Nell and the therapist can now decide, together, whether to explore the tightness or to continue the story. Exploring the tightness may help Nell to feel the emotions that she has walled off, and she may or may not be ready to do that. The therapist has offered the invitation; Nell is free to accept it or turn it down.

2. *Physical reactions.* Different from sensations, in that these questions have to do with how the client's body is behaving, quite possibly outside his or

her immediate awareness (Kepner, 1987). If such a reaction has to do with an emotional response that has not yet emerged into awareness, inquiring about it often helps clients to recognize, consciously, what they are feeling.

Physical behaviors—clenched jaws (or fists), tilted heads, or swinging feet—may also be part of an old pattern that has been learned and then pushed out of awareness. Pushing the whole thing out of awareness allows people to avoid the uncomfortable or painful feelings that were present at the time the patterns were formed or reinforced or both. Awareness, along with the original complete set of behaviors, is gone; but small fragments of the pattern remain, like crumbs left on the table after the meal has been cleared away. Calling attention to those bits of behavior invites the client to recover the rest of the pattern and the memories that go with it. The physical reaction becomes a sensory bridge back to what has been kept out of awareness for so many years.

Therapist: . . . *and you keep trying to figure out what you did wrong.*

Monica: *Yes. And I can't. Everything I did is wrong! (*she is crying with the remembered pain)

Therapist: *But mom and dad keep telling you to do more.*

Monica: *Do more, get going, figure it out! I can't figure it out! If she's drunk, for God's sake, how can you figure it out?* (her legs begin to move back and forth with a kicking motion)

Therapist: *Those legs sure want to figure it out—legs are figuring it out. Do you want to just give her a kick when she's drunk?*

Notice, also, the therapist's use of the present tense. Monica mixes present and past: "I *can't* . . . everything I *did*." Such mixing of tenses is typical of a client who is shuttling rapidly between present and past experiences, who is involved with the therapist and also involved with the past traumatic memory. By consistently referring to the past events as if they are happening now, in the present, the therapist encourages Monica to immerse herself in the experience so as to reclaim full contact with the split-off memory.

3. *Emotions.* This hardly needs mentioning; it is probably the most common topic of therapeutic inquiry. Emotions seep into awareness from old repressed memories; emotions connect here-and-now experiences (of which we are fully aware) with then-and-there experiences (that have been split off from awareness; [Jones, 1995]). But skilled inquiry goes beyond simply asking about the surface quality of a feeling. Therapists inquire not only about the feelings that are being expressed, but also about those that do not seem to be present: either or both can be significant.

Inquiry always points to the next layer, encouraging the client to make the emotional connections from here to there and back again to here, from now to then and back again to now, and to become more and more fully aware of all the feelings that undergird their experience of themselves (Nathanson, 1992). To tap into that experience, we inquire particularly about the client's affective responses to the therapy situation itself, and to the person of the therapist. In this excerpt, the therapist is talking with Billie about an earlier interaction, when Billie was upset and wanted the therapist to notice and to help her to work with her feelings.

Therapist: *What was it like for you, Billie, when I didn't ask about your feelings?*

Billie: *I felt really lost.*

Therapist: *Also like it wasn't coming from the other side. I had lost you.*

Billie: *Um-hmm. Like I didn't matter.* (she is weeping)

Therapist: (pause) *You don't matter. People miss you. You know a lot about that. And you don't dare get angry about that—is that right?*

Billie: *That's right.*

4. *Memories.* These, too, are a stock in trade of therapy. Recent memories and early memories, memories of childhood and adolescence, of pleasant and unpleasant experiences. In a very real sense, anything from the out-of-therapy world that is discussed in therapy is a memory, even though it may be a memory of what happened only a few hours earlier. Memories, though, involve much more than the story of what happened. They are shot through with feelings, meanings, script beliefs, all of the texture that makes life three-dimensional. Memories can be inquired into in terms of every other item on this therapeutic menu that we are constructing. Here is an example of a request that opens this kind of inquiry: "So tell me what you remember about what you experienced, what you thought at the time, and then the different things that happened after that."

The therapist may go on to ask about the emotions that this client experienced and about her sense of what it all meant (both back then and now) and will be alert for hints of decisions and expectations that may be related. There is really no end to it; everything is interconnected, and a single memory could form the basis for hours of useful and highly therapeutic inquiry.

A memory need not be fully formed in order to be inquired about. Memories can flash across our awareness in a second or less; if they are not captured by inquiry they quickly dissolve into the background again. Here, the therapist has been talking with Martha about her tendency to be self-critical. Martha breaks in to report such a quick but vivid memory:

Martha: (sigh) *Yeah. What I heard then was a very, very strong—I heard my mother's voice, a much—it's actually difficult to reconcile, 'cause I heard a much stronger voice than she's got now, 'cause she's now an old lady and she looks like a sweet old lady, but there's pure venom underneath. And what I heard was her saying, "You can't expect anything else but to get slapped around when you've behaved like you do."*

Therapist: *Now is that an actual memory or is that an elaboration?*

Martha: *No, I was raped when I was in my twenties. And I worked through it in therapy, but before I did I actually told my mother. I don't know why I told her, but I was living a long way away from her, and I was going there for the weekend, and I told her what had happened, and she just said, "What do you expect when you behave like you did?" She was totally, totally unmoved. And I actually told her friend first, 'cause I thought my mom would be upset. So I went with her friend to tell my mother. She was expecting to support my mom. She didn't need any of that. That was just a flash that I had, when you said that.*

"Just a flash," but an important one. By inquiring about it, the therapist helps Martha move back into one of many experiences that led her to learn how to criticize herself first, before mother (or anyone else) had a chance to do so. Working through that painful pattern may allow her to develop a different way to take care of herself, one that will serve her better in her current life situation.

5. *Thoughts.* Although the client's emotions tend to capture our interest and attention, we must not lose sight of the cognitions that accompany those emotions. Nor must we assume (so easy to do and so potentially damaging!) that we know what the client is thinking. Guesses about the client's thought process are just that—guesses. It is important to ask about thoughts; it is equally important to make it clear that we are *asking* and not telling the client what they are or should be thinking. Again, thoughts about what is happening here in the therapy session, in relationship with the therapist, are particularly useful.

Dan's work provides a good example of this sort of inquiry. You may remember an excerpt earlier in this chapter in which the therapist asks Dan whether it would be useful for him to have a fantasy conversation with his father. In this next short segment, the therapist has again invited Dan to tell his father directly about his feelings, rather than simply talking about them.

Dan: (sigh) *Now I'm stuck again.*

Therapist: *Is there by any chance something you want to disagree with me about?*

Dan: *Hmm. . . . Yeah, there is. I think the idea of telling my father anything just strikes me as such a waste of time. I just don't want to do it.*

Asking Dan what he is thinking about his interaction with the therapist yields important information about his here-and-now experiencing as well as about his relationship with his father. Either can be pursued with questions about how he handles his disagreement with the therapist, or about his decision that telling his father anything would be a waste of time, or about the experience of expressing his want ("I just don't want to do it") clearly and directly.

6. *Conclusions and decisions.* Disruption of contact with self and with others usually involves some sort of decision, conclusion, or survival reaction. Rarely a part of our conscious awareness, these decisions and reactions trace back to early experiences that have taught us some survival strategy (Greenwald, 1971, 1973; Goulding & Goulding, 1979; Berne, 1972). The problem is that such strategies then tend to be applied—and misapplied—to current situations. Because the conclusion or decision is often either out of awareness, or is experienced as a natural and inevitable response, it cannot be challenged or updated; when it leads to problems, we are often bewildered, hurt, or confused. Dan's belief that telling his father (and, by extension, anyone else) anything would be a waste of time is an example of such a conclusion; it has led him to keep his opinions to himself and to refrain from openly expressing his wants and needs. Asking a client about decisions and conclusions helps to bring these responses back into awareness, where they can be reexamined from the perspective of an adult's knowledge and experience.

In the following excerpt, Alice has been talking about a pair of roller skates that her brother bought for her when she was a child. The gift stands out in her memory, not only because she loved roller-skating, but also because she had never had such a gift before; her neglectful parents never gave her presents. Notice how the therapist supports her exploration of the decision that grew out of her early deprivation by bringing out details that have important implications for how she lives her life:

Therapist: *So those skates were very important to you, Alice.... What else was important?*

Alice: *Deciding I would never be like them.*

Therapist: *Tell me what you mean.*

Alice: *I decided when I was little that I would never, ever, ever be like them, wouldn't raise my children like that, wouldn't be like that, wouldn't marry a man like my father. I wouldn't be like my mother. I wouldn't be drunk. I wouldn't fight. I wouldn't have violence.*

Therapist: *Wouldn't marry a man like your father, and you wouldn't have violence; you would never fight. . . .*

Alice: *That's right.*

Therapist: *There would be no anger, or anything like that—*

Alice: *That's right. We would never raise our voices.*

Therapist: *Hmm. What an important decision!*

7. *Meanings.* Notice, in the above excerpt, that when Alice first stated her decision, the therapist immediately asked her what that decision meant. People assign meaning to experiences and decisions and words in such varied ways that it is always risky to assume that we know what a statement really means (Efran, Lokens, & Lokens, 1990). Before we make such an assumption, we need to inquire, to ask about it. "Inquiring about" meanings opens up a vast array of possible questions: nearly everything can have a meaning, and even when it does not, the very absence of a meaning can be meaningful. (Hmm, what a complicated sentence. . . . I wonder what it means!) Inquiry can concern itself with the meaning of what a client says, what a client feels, and what a client is doing. Wherever it points, the purpose is the same: enhance awareness and bring the client back into contact with what has been lost.

The following segment is taken from work that was done in a therapy group that had been meeting for several sessions. Janelle has been sitting somewhat back from the group while other participants work. She has started to cry, huddled up on a couch, and her body is shaking. There is a curious, contradictory quality to her behavior, as if she does not want to interrupt, but yet she wants to be noticed. Finally, after finishing a piece of work with another group member, the therapist asks her to talk about what is happening. She begins to describe a set of painful memories, and the therapist invites her to look at the meaning of her focusing on those memories at this moment.

Therapist: *And do you experience a sense of urgency about all this?*

Janelle: *No, I can put it away. I let it, I let it develop, 'cause I thought there would be time for me to work in group this morning. I think I can put it back in, but. . . .*

Therapist: *Do you* experience *a sense of urgency about this?* (Janelle does not answer; her tears continue) *How do you make sense of your weeping?*

Rather than assume that she understands what looks so obvious, that the expression of strong feelings is a natural part of Janelle's process, the therapist has asked Janelle about the meaning that *she* assigns to what she is doing. By asking about it, the therapist opens up the possibility of exploring not just the memory, but also the way Janelle is dealing with it and her hopes/fears about how the therapist may react—which, in turn, may lead to other decisions, meanings, and awarenesses.

8. *Expectations.* Many of the activities we engage in are shaped by our expectations about what will happen next (Epstein, 1972). We avoid one sort of behavior because we expect it to lead to negative consequences; we do something else because we expect it will result in something good. As with so many other things, though, these expectations are often out of conscious awareness: it feels as if we are doing this or that almost randomly or because there is no other course of action available. Our expectations (both in and out of awareness) generally come from past experiences. What we hope for, fantasize about, or fear is based on what has happened to us in the past. Nowhere is this truer than in our relationships with others. We build our expectations about future relationships—how people will treat us, whether they can be trusted, whether they will understand us or like us or even notice us—on our understandings and recollections about previous experiences with people.

Inquiring about expectations— about themselves, about others, about life in general—helps clients to become aware of how they make choices as well as to recover the context in which their expectations were developed. It moves into conscious awareness the fact that their fears are of things that have already occurred and that their hopes are often for what was needed and not provided in the past. Again, this inquiry is often most profitable when it concerns expectations about the therapy itself or about the therapeutic relationship (Orange et al., 1997; Stern, 1994). These expectations are right here; they can be discovered from the client's own phenomenology and checked against the reality gauge of what the therapist will actually do. And, of course, expectations about therapy do not exist in isolation; they are, more often than not, a distillation of other expectations that shape the client's way of being in the world outside of therapy.

In the excerpt below, the therapist is inquiring about Jolene's expectations of her. Even in these few transactions, it is apparent that the inquiry is uncovering something that governs the way Jolene views the world, and that significantly affects how she interacts with people.

Therapist: *What are you feeling right now with me?*

Jolene: (pause) *Uh, a bit threatened.*

Therapist: *Are you? Can you tell me about that?*

Jolene: *Uh, . . . 'cause it's like . . . I want to sort it out . . . but I feel you, you're missing me, and I don't know what's missing.*

Therapist: *What's going to happen if I see you differently than you see you?*

Jolene: *I might get attacked.*

Therapist: *Attacked. You're afraid that I'm going to attack you?*

Jolene: *You might do it to me.*

Therapist: *Like other people have done . . . and if I were going to do that, can you give me some sense of what your anticipation is? What will I do; what will I say?*

Jolene: (pause) *You'd humiliate me.*

9. *Hopes.* Expectations, at least those of greatest therapeutic interest, most often have to do with negative outcomes. We expect, and we dread what we expect, so we construct defensive strategies to ward off that dreaded outcome. But people can and do conceive of positive futures as well, even though they are usually framed within a context of not having had such experiences in the past. These hopes of things to come are not so often mentioned spontaneously by clients; somehow, clients do not seem to think that therapy is "supposed to" focus on a positive future. But they are important, not only because they can serve as goals to work toward, but also because they can help both client and therapist understand the deep wants and needs that thread through that client's life (Mitchell, 1993).

We have seen, over and again, how inquiring about an aspect of a client's experience opens whole vistas for further inquiry. Inquiring about a hope is no different: any question may open a whole storehouse of information. It is rather like walking around a sculpture, with each step showing a slightly different side, revealing a bit that could not be seen before. Sometimes there is a surprise—a kitten hides at the hem of the sculptured figure's gown or the hand on the far side holds a dagger. Or sometimes there is simply more richness, more detail, and more material for reflection.

In this example, the therapist continues the dialogue with Jolene. Jolene has been talking about how she turns herself "to stone" in order to protect herself from being humiliated by the reactions of others. Rather than pursuing the details of the negative expectation, the therapist asks Jolene about her hopes:

Therapist: *What would feel most gratifying to you—instead of being told they're not your feelings, instead of having to turn to stone—what would you want to have someone else do in response to you?*

Jolene: *Acknowledge the depth of my hurt. And not tell me it's silly. Take it seriously.*

Therapist: *Take it seriously? And to feel it with you?*

Jolene: *I wouldn't want them to feel it.*

Therapist: *Based on the way you seem to respond to other people's feelings, I wondered if it would feel most intimate, most loving, most sharing, if someone were able to do the same with you?*

Jolene: *As long as they didn't have to feel all of it.*

Therapist: *Why not feel all of it?*

Jolene: *'Cause I wouldn't want anybody to feel that much hurt.*

10. *Fantasies.* And beyond hopes are fantasies: imaginings unlikely to come true, imaginings we do not expect to experience in reality. Imaginings of horror and fear or of love and delight. Metaphoric symbols of things that cannot be contained in ordinary language (Klein, 1964; Fairbairn, 1952). Fantasies are important because they tap into the worst and the best that the client can conjure up. Their symbolism is often a thinly disguised clue to the world of banished-from-awareness, the world that has been for so long out of contact with the conscious self, the world of experiences that one cannot and must not consciously recall (Bettelheim, 1967; Sandler & Nagera, 1963). By inquiring about a client's fantasies, we can gain useful information about those symbols and what they may represent. More importantly, by taking time to deal with and ask about fantasies, we demonstrate in a very concrete way that we do take the client seriously and that everything about the client's experience is important and significant. Watch what unfolds as the therapist talks with Martha about her fantasies:

Therapist: *It seems like there's no place in your life for you to have these praises, to feel grand and glorious, lest you be like your mother, your mother-in-law, that teacher, women you don't like. When do you get to have your own grandness?*

Martha: *I get it from my supervisor about my work. I don't, no, I don't get to.*

Therapist: *My sense is that you also underplay it in yourself.*

Martha: *Yeah, I think you're right. (pause) Yeah, I think you're right, I do. It's. . . .*

Therapist: (pause) *Then does it show up in fantasy?*

Martha: *I don't know what I do in fantasy. My kind of fantasies are things like having days off to just wander in my garden, and unplug the phone, and, and just. . . . I think my real fantasies are about time out.*

Therapist: *Going back to your quiet place.*

Martha: *I don't do that enough, and it's real important for me, my quiet place.*

Therapist: *It's your alone place.*

Martha: *Yeah. Yeah, I don't take people with me in that fantasy.*

Therapist: *I'm sure if anyone else were there you couldn't really be yourself.*

Martha: *No. No, cause I think that I would criticize myself for being self-indulgent.*

This excerpt, like the whole menu, could go on much further. There is never a really good stopping place for inquiry; there is never a point at which we have learned all we need or all that might be useful. But books, like readers' patience, are finite in length; we must move on. We leave it to your own fantasy to imagine what may happen next with Martha and with all the other clients whose work we have visited.

3

CHAPTER

Attunement

"He-she-you-they just don't understand!" Is there anyone in the world who has not said these words? The desire to be understood—truly and deeply understood—is a universal yearning. It is part of our human hunger for contact and for relationship. When we do not feel connected in this way, we tend to pull back, protect ourselves, and shut down. When we do feel it, we open up and seek more contact.

Feeling understood and in contact involves more than someone knowing the logical, rational meaning of our words. It involves having them know how we feel about those words and sensing that they share or reverberate with how we feel. It involves their being *attuned* to us, to where we are coming from and why the words are important to us, and what we want from them as we say those words. Attunement begins with empathy; it is the relational quality within which interpersonal contact thrives. And it goes beyond empathy, because it involves the deeply personal response of the hearer as well as the intent of the speaker (Stern, 1985). It is about the "in between," the space where two people meet in a kind of joined awareness (Tustin, 1986; Bettelheim, 1967).

In this chapter we look carefully at attunement: at what it is, how it is achieved and communicated, and what its effects are in a therapeutic setting. As we do so, we will find ourselves looking back at the inquiry process and forward to the quality of involvement. These three—inquiry, attunement, involvement—are inextricably intertwined in the therapeutic relationship. To the extent that any one of the three aspects of attunement can be primary, however, that one must be attunement. It is attunement that guides the therapeutic inquiry, and it is attunement that shapes the nature of therapeutic involvement.

Attunement is a two-part process. The therapist who is attuned to the client must first be aware of that client's sensations, needs, feelings, desires, or meanings. Maintaining such awareness, the therapist must also communicate to the client that he or she *is* aware, *does* understand, and is willing to shape his or her responses accordingly. Nicholas Evans, in his novel *The Horse Whisperer*, describes the ideal relationship between horse and rider: "It's about trust and consent. You've gotten hold of one another. The man's leading but he's not dragging her, he's offering a feel and she feels it and goes with him. You're in harmony and moving to each other's rhythm, just following the feel" (1995, p. 122). So it is when the therapist is attuned to the client. In the dance of attunement, the therapist most often follows, may sometimes lead, but never drags; the client feels the attunement and moves into the next layer of awareness.

☐ Functions of Attunement

Attunement fosters a sense of rapport between client and therapist. But that is really a cliché: *whatever* the therapist does right is likely to further rapport. Let us look, more specifically, at what happens as clients sense that their therapist is attuned to them.

Respect

To the degree that the therapist is attuned to the client and conveys that attunement, the client feels respected. "This therapist is attending to *me* and is in synchrony with *my* process. It must be okay for me to be doing/ saying/feeling this way, because my therapist understands and validates my reasons for doing so." The therapist, sensing the client's pattern of focusing here rather than there, of dealing sometimes with cognition and sometimes with affect, of talking or of remaining silent, responds with understanding and presence. And the client recognizes that these patterns will be taken seriously. The therapist's respect for the client becomes a seed that will grow into the client's trusting and respecting his or her own wisdom.

Attuned to the client's process, the therapist can respond so as to further that process. Clients experience a variety of needs as they move more and more deeply into self-discovery: needs for support, protection, and information. When these needs are recognized, the client's sense of being respected is enhanced; when they are met with a response attuned to the client's total experience-in-the-moment, that sense of being respected is even more fully enhanced. For example, in the following exchange with Cheryl, the therapist complies with a request for information. More importantly, she does so with language and voice tone that convey total respect for Cheryl's question and for her need for an answer. Cheryl, for whom English is a second language, is talking about a cat in her garden; this excerpt precedes the one from chapter 2:

Cheryl: . . . *and another thing I realized concerning that was, um, I was out in the garden and the cat came. Jumped on my chair, and I talked French to the cat. And I haven't even been thinking French all these days now. And now I was wondering if this is, is regression, or resistance. Whatever, is there an explanation for that?*

Therapist: *Well, Freud thought that regression was resistance. And I don't completely agree with that perspective. I have certainly seen regressions that are resistance. But I've also seen regressions that aren't resistance, and I've seen regressions that are in the service of what Freud called the development of the ego. What do you think it was?*

A less-attuned therapist might well have responded to Cheryl's question with another question, inquiring as to her feelings, thoughts, expectations, or reasons for initially asking the question. Instead, attuned to all of what Cheryl is bringing to the moment—her hesitation and nervousness, her impulse to self-criticize, as well as her honest curiosity about the meaning of her language shift—this therapist becomes, momentarily, a teacher. By doing so, she responds directly to Cheryl's expressed request. She tells Cheryl, implicitly, that her question is worth answering, that she is behaving appropriately, that she, the therapist, values and respects Cheryl's interest in this topic. And, after sharing her own ideas, she asks Cheryl to share hers. Cheryl is invited to experience herself, not as someone being "worked on" by an expert but rather as a valued partner in the therapeutic process.

Many clients bring to therapy the fear that they will somehow do it wrong, say the wrong thing and cause the therapist to be displeased. They worry that they will embarrass themselves or be shamed as they expose things that they themselves are embarrassed about or ashamed of. Staying attuned to this underlying fear, as well as to the intricate and ever-changing blend of needs and wants that the client experiences from moment to moment, allows the therapist to work with full respect for all parts and facets of the client and to convey that respect clearly and unambiguously.

Safety

The importance of providing the client with a sense of safety can hardly be overemphasized. Fritz Perls talked about the "safe emergency" in which the client can take the risk of trying something new and still know that he or she will survive (Perls, 1967, 1973). The prospect of working with a therapist is inherently frightening for many (most?) people. Carl Rogers speaks tellingly about the client's perception of the therapist·

> I'm afraid of him. I want help, but I don't know whether to trust him. He might see things which I don't know in myself—frightening and bad ele-ments. He seems not to be judging me, but I'm sure he is. I cannot tell him what really concerns me, but I can tell him about some past experiences which are related to my concerns. He seems to understand those, so I can reveal a bit more of myself. (1961, p. 67)

Only a sense of safety and stability in the therapeutic relationship can allow the client to move into frightening places, to dissolve his or her denial, and, if necessary, to fully regress into old traumatic experiences in order to reclaim the lost parts of the self (Guntrip, 1971). Only a sense of safety can enable him or her to bear the pain of comparing the failed relationships and unmet needs of the past with the richness of the thera-peutic experience. Sensing the therapist's attunement, the client feels pro-tected: "This therapist won't attack, won't go too fast (or too slow), won't insist on doing things that I don't want to do, won't make fun of me or be disgusted by me. I feel safe because this therapist is with me and tuned in to me, every step of the way."

Reclaiming Old Experiences

One of the basic assertions that characterize a relationship-based therapy is that present discomfort and dysfunction arise out of the ways in which people have learned to cope with relationship failures in the past (Spotnitz, 1969). In such past experiences, the person's needs and feelings may not have been acknowledged or attended to. Over time, as such experiences are repeated, one learns to disavow the feelings and needs, to split off the needy parts of the self, and to seek out relationships that repeat the famil-iar patterns while avoiding relationships that might reawaken old pain. An important task of therapy, then, must be to reclaim the denied expe-riences so that the hurt can be repaired and the client can lay a new foundation for relating to self as well as to others.

Through attunement to the client's reexperienced emotional memo-ries, the therapist validates the significance of those memories while at the same time providing a contrasting relational experience (Brandchaft, 1989). The client discovers what it is like to be with someone who attends to needs and feelings and who is interested in and sensitive to the things that were so consistently ignored or devalued before: "Somehow, contrary to all expectations, this person really cares about and values what is going on inside me!" The fully attuned therapist will often be aware of aspects of the client's experience even before the client notices them and can help the client notice and find language for what is happening (Kohut, 1971), as occurs in the following segment. The client is Billie, whom you met in chapter 2:

Therapist: *"You don't matter." That's what you figured out? You know a lot about that. And you don't dare get angry about that, huh?*

Billie: *No.* (cries; her legs make small kicking movements)

Therapist: *Even though those legs are kicking up a fuss, you don't dare get angry.*

Billie: *Uh-uh. No. Don't make a fuss.*

Therapist: *Who said that?*

Billie: *Umm. . . .*

Therapist: *"Don't make a fuss."*

Billie: *That would be my mother. And you* knew *not to with my father.*

Therapist: *There's a fuss all the time in you, isn't there? Quite a fuss in those legs.*

Through this kind of exploration, Billie can begin to reclaim her anger—the anger that at first she is only able to hint at by making slight kicking motions with her legs. Observing the slight leg movement, the therapist responds to both Billie's anger and her attempt to disavow it. With this kind of support, Billie can begin to move her legs more freely and, in that movement, reverse the disavowal. The more she allows her body to express her feelings, the more her awareness grows. Reclaiming the disavowed emotion is like lancing a festering but scabbed-over wound: the infected fluids pour out in an angry gush, and the wound can then be cleansed and begin to heal.

Dealing with Therapeutic Misses

Staying attuned not only helps the client to access and heal memories of relationship failures from the past, but also to deal with those inevitable instances of therapeutic failure in the present (Ferenczi, 1988). No matter how sensitive and skillful they are, therapists do make mistakes.

Attunement can never be perfect; clients get missed sometimes. And they notice, and the therapist's failure is added to the long list of "proofs" that reinforce their script beliefs: "My needs won't be met," "People can't be trusted," "Life is hard." The therapist who is committed to maintaining attunement with the client, in spite of occasional misses, will be aware of the shift that occurs in the ongoing relationship when such a miss occurs. And the shift itself can be used therapeutically to gain another entry into the client's out-of-awareness coping strategies as well as to communicate the therapist's intent to stay attuned (Safran et al., 1990). Dan's work provides us with an example of how to use a therapeutic miss. In the excerpt in chapter 2, Dan was talking about his father. Later in the session, the therapist drew an analogy which did not fit Dan's experience; Dan did not question it, but his responses became less animated.

Therapist: *Dan, are you shutting down?* (Dan nods) *Then I'm going to assume that I've done something. . . . That I have not connected with you.*

Dan: *I think it was your analogy. I think I'm okay with; I think where we missed, where you missed me. . . .* (he looks frightened) *I think it was when you said the only thing I need to do was tell you if you were wrong. And I think, when I know that you're off I get quiet.*

Therapist: *When I miss you?*

Dan: *'Cause sometimes I don't know it. Sometimes I just, sometimes it's really difficult for me to. . . .*

Therapist: *Twice here I think you cooperated with that miss by saying, "I get quiet." What if you were to drop that vocabulary and say, "My shutting down indicates that you've missed me"?*

Not only does the therapist pick up on the shift, when Dan begins to shut down, but she also suggests a meaning for the shutting down. When Dan confirms the hypothesis, the therapist moves quickly to offer a solution. In doing so, she both takes responsibility for causing the "miss" and suggests that Dan may also, out of awareness, be contributing to it. This, in turn, paves the way to invite Dan to help the therapist stay more fully attuned as they continue to work together. Even more important, Dan now has a new strategy for dealing with disruptions in relationship.

One of the characteristics of attunement is this move to take responsibility. The therapist fully owns his or her contribution to therapeutic failures (Orange et al., 1997). Such ownership again conveys respect and fends off the client's tendency to blame himself or herself (or to believe that the therapist blames him or her) for whatever goes wrong. It also provides a powerful contrast to previous experiences of relationship failure in which the client *was* blamed and the other person did *not* take responsibility. The longer segment below takes place a week after the client, Jolene, had done the piece of work excerpted in chapter 2. You may recall that, in the chapter 2 excerpt, Jolene was talking about the therapist "missing" her. At the end of that piece, Jolene seemed to feel unfinished and somehow disappointed. Notice how, in this later work, the therapist refers to her failure to connect with the client, initiating a discussion of what happened and returning, again and again, to its effect on their relationship:

Therapist: *Jolene, I wanted to ask you about something. I had the sense last week after we finished working that had I lost you. And I wondered if you had that experience, and if so if we could talk about what happened.*

Jolene: *I, I don't know whether you really lost me, but I think what happened, and I've only realized that today, was that I was ramming my hand in my mouth, and I think you needed to persuade me to take it away. Because what was happening was, I was holding my mouth (a) to stop things going in, but (b) it meant I wasn't letting out what I needed to let out. And I think that might have been what you sensed—that I hadn't been able to process or identify. Would that make sense?*

Therapist: *Yeah, it does. What was the effect of my not noticing that and not facilitating you letting out? What happened to you inside?*

Jolene: *Um, I guess it stopped me really letting out a scream. And I can see that I would, I mean, I've noticed a lot, since long processing, that I do cover my mouth, as a protection. And obviously. . . .*

Therapist: *And as a way of holding. . . .*

Jolene: *. . . It's a way of holding in, and stopping things going . . . maybe positive things. It stops positive things coming in. And stops bad things coming out.*

Therapist: *Bad things?*

Jolene: *Well. . . .*

Therapist: *Or things that people have responded to badly?*

Jolene: *Things that people have fed me with. I mean, what I felt I was spitting out was semen, but . . . um, you know from all the food difficulties that I have, and I suspect part of that is 'cause I was force-fed with a lot of stuff that really would have been better for me not to consume. Food, beliefs, semen. . . . So I think that might have been what was missing.*

Therapist: *What effect has it had on our relationship?*

Jolene: *Um, I don't think it's. . . . I don't think it's been negative. Um. . . . I suppose it, if I try and analyze it, it just concerns that message that maybe I have given away a few times here, that I cannot necessarily expect people to get it right for me.*

Therapist: *Which implies some disappointment.*

Jolene: *I guess so, yeah. . . .*

Therapist: *I think I sensed that. I used the words "I lost you" or "You slipped through my fingers"—I didn't know what happened. But I experienced it as some kind of break.*

Jolene: *Yeah. And I couldn't have told you at the time. Um, I can usually work it out afterward, but by that time it's gone. . . . But I think it was because I was feeling so young, that I very much relied on . . . whoever.*

Therapist: *Someone else has to figure it out.*

Jolene: *Figuring out for me. Yeah.*

Therapist: *Sure. Sure.*

Jolene: *Um, and often when I find that I haven't got words, in all sorts of situations, or I seem to be dumb when I know I'm not dumb. Because at that level, somehow, people didn't—haven't—figured it out right for me. So that's where I think I need some repair work. That somebody can actually pick up what I need and give it to me, to help change that belief.*

Therapist: *Um-hmm.*

Jolene: *'Cause it's not unrealistic, for people to read what I need. . . . But I know I had to teach my former therapist how to work with me. 'Cause she was screwing up.*

Therapist: *And is that working now? Are you getting what you need from me?*

Jolene: *Yes, very much so. And. . . . But, I suppose my main reason for coming to you was because I felt, that . . . you could work with me at that level. It, it often gets me missed.*

Therapist: *Um-hmm. And I'm sorry I missed the importance of that gesture.*

Admitting our mistakes and owning our responsibility for therapeutic failures is a difficult thing to do. After all, the client expects us to be the professional and to get it right! We fear that if we admit that we were wrong, the client will never trust us again. The reality is quite the opposite: most clients tend to be more, rather than less, trusting of a therapist who acknowledges his or her errors. Attuning ourselves to the client's response to us allows us to notice when we get off track, own up to the miss, and explore its consequences. And *that* process will be a therapeutic hit, not a miss.

☐ Kinds of Attunement

Attunement means being aware of and responsive to a wide variety of client behaviors and experiences. There are so many things to be attuned

(margin note: # categories ↓)

to! It may be helpful to break down these various aspects of client experience into some major categories, so as to talk about how attunement is maintained and expressed for each. Remember, though, that we break them apart just to make it easier to talk about them; in the actual ongoing therapeutic relationship, the categories blend together and the therapist must attend to them all simultaneously.

Cognitive Attunement

Understanding the client's cognition—what the client is thinking about and the content of his or her remarks—would seem, on the surface, to be relatively easy. It is what we generally do best. In fact, sometimes it is what we have to let go of in order to tune in to the emotions that may be bubbling underneath the words. Before we dismiss it as trivial, though, let's take a closer look.

Cognitive attunement is more than simply attending to content. It is not the same as "understanding the client's cognition," because it goes beyond simple understanding. It involves attending to the client's logic, to the process of stringing ideas together, to the kinds of reasoning that the client uses in order to create meaning out of raw experience. It is about *what* the client is thinking, but, more importantly, it is about *how* the client is thinking it. As we attune to the client's cognition, we enter the client's cognitive space, moving into a kind of resonance with the client and using our own thoughts and responses as a sounding board to amplify the tiny cues that the client is giving. We bring the client's words and nonverbal expressions into ourselves; take on their meanings, implications, and connections; and experience this way of thinking ourselves in a kind of internal "as if."

Our internal "as if," though, is not infallible. It must always be treated as hypothesis rather than fact. One of the surest ways for us to be out of attunement, to miss the client, is to assume that we understand or that the client's way of thinking about things is the same as our own (Efran et al., 1990). It is certainly safe to assume that anecdotes, stories about things that happened yesterday or last week or many years ago, have some important meaning. *(margin note: the intention behind account)* Cognitive attunement depends upon listening for, and asking about, that underlying meaning, rather than simply attending to the content, assuming that we understand, and moving on. The inquiry may request clarification of a detail of the story, or it may go directly to the story's underlying significance—the message that the client is unconsciously trying to communicate to us. Either way, the important part is that the attunement be enhanced and deepened, so that we can follow the client at both surface and underlying levels of meaning. Here, for instance, Dan is talking about his relationship with his father. Notice how the therapist's questions invite Dan to discover how he makes meaning from his experience:

Dan: *He would not own who he was. He had an office of 200 people and he described himself as a clerk. I never knew what he did. I went to his office when I was about 30, and it was like a palace. I thought he worked at a desk in a room with 50 people.*

Therapist: *And in what you describe, what did you discover?*

Dan: *I discovered that he had an office, and that he was responsible for almost 200 people. And he had a photograph of me on his desk. I didn't know. . . .*

Therapist: *A photograph of you on his desk. . . .*

Dan: *I didn't know he cared. I was completely astonished.*

Therapist: *An adult photograph, or a child photograph?*

Dan: *Graduation photograph. But I was, I was so furious. Because he never gave me—I was 30—he never gave me any indication that it mattered.* (sigh) *And I still can't disagree with him; if I argue with him, he'll argue black is white; when I point out that they're different he'll agree with me as though that's what he said all the time.*

Therapist: *Which leaves you feeling—*

Dan: *Negated. Just . . . as if I don't matter.*

Attunement to Dan's cognitive process allows the therapist to search out the meaning underlying Dan's story. Resonating to that process, putting himself into a similar frame of reference, the therapist constructs questions that lead Dan to discover how his ways of understanding and thinking about the world have structured his beliefs, his choices, and his sense of self.

That the therapist take on the client's frame of reference, experience his or her cognitive attunement to the client, is only one side of the cognitive attunement phenomenon. The client, too must experience the resonance. The deepest, most sensitive therapeutic attunement would be useless if the client felt consistently misunderstood. Being attuned, though, the therapist knows when the client believes himself or herself to have been missed and takes steps to heal the rift. In the following example, therapist and client have been talking about a tiny doll that the client left with the therapist some months earlier. The client, Melinda, is quite obese, and the therapist remarked that she had considered putting stuffing in the doll's clothes to make it look more like Melinda. Melinda was offended and hurt. Rather than simply apologizing to her for what might, on the surface, have appeared to be a therapeutic error, the therapist explored with Melinda the meaning those remarks had for her.

Therapist: *How do you see the baby in you?*

Melinda: *Like a baby.*

Therapist: *Thin baby? Chubby baby?*

Melinda: *No, I wasn't a chubby baby. I mean, I wasn't a chubby little kid. As a little kid, I was skinny. Well, not skinny, but I was tall and thin.*

Therapist: *So this* (holding up doll) *is more about how you were as a baby. This is the way you* want *to be thought of.*

Melinda: *Yes. That's right.*

Therapist: *Makes good sense. So if I tell you about a thought I had one day, about making her [the doll] round, then I'm not, in a way, in tune with your thoughts of how you want to be seen.*

Melinda: (very softly) *Yeah.*

The therapist demonstrated first that she *wanted* to understand Melinda's meanings, and then that she *did* understand them. The softening in Melinda's voice may indicate that cognitive attunement has been reestablished; further inquiry into the softness of the "Yeah" will take us more deeply into her phenomenological experience.

Of course, cognitive attunement alone is not enough. Thoughts are always intertwined with feelings. The therapist who simply follows thoughts and meanings with no sensitivity to the feelings that go with them will not further the therapeutic relationship. As clients tell their stories and sort out the meanings of those stories, they are delving deeper and deeper into awareness of their experiencing, and this emerging awareness is often painful and frightening. An attuned therapist talks about meanings as they relate to affect, helping clients to become aware of that affect and the defensive behaviors they use to protect themselves from it. In the work with Melinda, the therapist demonstrated that she was attuned to Melinda's thoughts and intentions about the doll. They next begin to explore the way she defends against the pain of dealing with her weight. The weight issue has, of course, been talked about before; in fact, part of the initial therapy contract involved working on it. Melinda talks about her response when the therapist mentions her weight:

Melinda: *You never keep quiet about that very long, and . . . and that's important that you don't.*

Therapist: *Based on your request.*

Melinda: *Right. I know. But I still feel bad when you do it.*

Therapist: *Um-hmm. Like I'm putting my finger on a sore spot.*

Melinda: *Right.*

Therapist: *Even though you know I need to do it, your first reaction is, "Get away from here!"*

In this excerpt, we see again how inextricably meanings and feelings are bound together. It is time to turn our attention to those feelings and to the nature of affective attunement.

Affective Attunement

Affective attunement refers to the therapist's sense of the client's affect and responding with a reciprocal affect. This is different from empathy: in an empathetic response, the therapist feels what the client is feeling. He or she metaphorically crawls inside the client's skin and shares the client's affective experience. The affectively attuned therapist goes beyond empathy, meeting the client's affect with his or her own personal and genuine affective response. We have much more to say about this reciprocal response in chapter 4 when we discuss involvement; for now, we will focus on the receiving part of affective attunement rather than the therapist's resonating response.

Characteristics of Affective Attunement

Affect involves both type and intensity; it is both qualitative and quantitative (Stern, 1985). The affectively attuned therapist takes both into account. As affective intensity increases, the client may become frightened of that intensity: another layer of affect is created. This is particularly true for clients who have been victims of trauma, either acute or cumulative. If they are getting very close to old emotional memories, the richness of the therapeutic involvement heightens the intensity of their affect even more. In the following short exchange, for example, Dan (who has been talking about his growing professional success) is beginning to make a connection between feeling abandoned by his father and feeling alienated from others in his adult life. The therapist is attuned to Dan's self-reaction—that is, his emotional response to his own internal process—and attending to that self-reaction allows Dan to continue to expand his awareness of the connection between then and now:

Dan: *Something's happening. It's to do with, um, feeling abandoned . . . and it's to do with not being seen. And I can be contrary, and I can be adversarial, in role. So in my work, especially in the last 2 years, I've really become powerful. I can really be solid and clear, and I can really make an impact. But not...the more important it is to me, the more personal it is, the more essential it is for me not to be left, abandoned, in the relationship.* (his voice breaks) *It just gets too risky.*

Therapist: *Yeah. Now you are so scared, it implies you already know this. About being left.*

Dan: (sigh, pause) *If I ever disagreed with my father, he'd just wipe me out. He'd just—it was not acceptable to disagree.*

The therapist's comment acknowledges and affirms the emotion that has not yet been named (Basch, 1988); it also affirms Dan's ability to recognize his own responses. It acts like a kind of cement, holding together the first tentative bits of understanding and recognition that Dan is uncovering, and creating a firm platform from which he can explore even further.

Affect is more than just emotional fizzing and erupting. It is a form of communication, a way for a client to tell the therapist about things that cannot be formulated in words. Maybe saying it in words would be too scary or too vulnerable-making. Or perhaps the words are not there. The absence of words may reflect an emotional regression to a preverbal experience (Tustin, 1986; Janov, 1971; Bettelheim, 1967). In order to be affectively attuned, the therapist must hear what the client's emotion is communicating. All of the facets of affect are important: the feelings themselves, the meanings they have for the client, and the message (request, need, or even rebuke) they have for the therapist. Here is Dan again. He has now brought into awareness a clear connection between his old experiences with his father, and an earlier incident in which the therapist had to leave a session in order to attend to a personal emergency. The therapist attends to Dan's ongoing and emerging feelings as well as to the underlying request:

Therapist: *If you were to put aside the part of you that understands my leaving, I wonder if you're also angry with me for leaving.*

Dan: *Well, it's funny you say that. I think I made it okay for you to leave.*

Therapist: *You did. But the other side might be . . . .*

Dan: *That's what I always did with my mother. And, I dunno, I hadn't thought of it before, but you just said it. But, uh, yeah, I suppose you abandoned me and I feel a little—*(long pause)

Therapist: *Did you get scared?*

Dan: *—Ohh!* (pause) *Yeah, I wanted you there. I'd forgotten that you said earlier that you might have to leave. And I did what I always do, which was make it okay.*

Therapist: *Tell me what you're feeling, Dan.*

Dan: *I'm feeling sick. I don't want to do this any more.* (pause) *Will you say something?*

Therapist: *I'm thinking about how to respond to that. Um, what I'm thinking is I'll make sure that I don't put you in a situation where that becomes an issue. I'll make sure that your session doesn't end with you feeling abandoned.*

Affect comes in layers. There is often more, often a next level ready to push its way into awareness. Clients may welcome that next level, experiencing the release and relief that comes with reclaiming and reintegrating a lost part of themselves. Or they may react defensively in order not to experience some intense emotional memory. Failure in attunement to this latter possibility—the need to defend against overwhelming emotions and memories—can lead to retraumatization, in which the therapy situation itself recreates the same kind of pain and invites the same defenses that the client experienced in the past. Affective attunement, then, not only helps us move the client forward; it also signals us when it is better to move slowly and to pause and give the client time to regroup and attend to his or her current emotional needs.

Although affective attunement has to do with all categories of affect, it is especially critical to be attentive to the affect of shame. Attunement to shame reactions is important because shame is both complex and commonplace (Nathanson, 1992; Goldberg, 1991; Kaufman, 1989). It is commonplace in that many—perhaps most—clients experience it in the course of their work. And it is complex because it involves several layers of affect: hurt, at not being accepted as one is; the fear of rejection and isolation; anger, which is being disavowed and turned against the self; and compliance with the image or criticism of some disapproving other (Erskine, 1994/1997; Erskine, 1995). A sense of shame invites the client to distort or disrupt contact with the therapist and to retreat back into the psychological closet where he or she can hide and hurt alone (Lewis, 1971, 1987). By being attuned to each layer of affect, the therapist can help him or her to deal with it as it begins to emerge, before it has time to swell into a monstrous and unbearable flood of shame.

Rhythmic Attunement

Rhythm forms a ubiquitous background for all human activities. An infant's earliest awareness is accompanied by the constant rhythm of the mother's heartbeat. Throughout life, our physiological processes mark the rhythms of passing time: brain activity, digestive cycles, internal patterns that mirror the movements of sun and moon. And each of us, as we grow into a unique individual, expands and elaborates these rhythms in different ways. We develop cognitive, affective, behavioral, and physiological rhythmic patterns that are so fundamental and feel so inevitable that it is difficult to recognize that anyone could function any other way. Yet people do:

each of us has our individual rhythmic patterns, unnoticed and taken for granted until they are disrupted in some way.

It is the therapist's job to notice and respond to the client's rhythms. Rhythmic attunement means that we tune ourselves to the client, rather than expecting the client to match us. Our inquiry and our involvement must be paced so that they best facilitate the client's processing of information and affect. And because people use different rhythms for different kinds of activities, this means changing tempo as the client moves from cognitive to affective processing, from exploring here-and-now to remembering then-and-there, from imagining and fantasizing to planning and making decisions.

Although each person's rhythms are unique, there is one rhythmic "rule" that holds for all of us: we tend to process affect slower than cognition. This may be a function of mental translation. Cognition is generally done in words, or at least in thoughts that are relatively easy to express in words. The affective processes are not word oriented, and, in fact, seem to be related to brain activity that occurs literally in a different location than the activities associated with cognition (Jones, 1995). So, while the *experience* of affect can be lightning fast, talking and thinking about it occurs much more slowly. When the therapeutic process focuses on affect, then, on exploring feelings and bringing them to awareness, the pace will generally need to be slower than when the client is working at a more cognitive level (Janov, 1971).

Psychotherapy is about integration—integration of awareness of internal and external sensations, integration of thinking and feeling, integration of taking the world into oneself and of putting oneself out into the world. Rhythmic attunement is about finding a rhythm for therapy that allows this kind of integration. Problem solving is unlikely to lead to lasting changes if it does not take into account the affect that is stimulated by the problem; deep affective work will be no more than temporary catharsis unless there is time to process that work cognitively. Most often, becoming rhythmically attuned to the client's needs means slowing down, giving the client time to find and sort through and integrate all the pieces that he or she is uncovering.

Finding examples to demonstrate this kind of slowing down is difficult, again, because the printed word does not convey well the pacing of transactions between client and therapist. Try reading this next excerpt into a tape recorder, counting to 10 slowly and silently every time you come to a (*pause*), and reading the words of both therapist and client rather slowly as well. Then listen to the tape you have made and feel the importance of those silent spaces and that slow pace:

Dan: *I just had a flashback to when my mother used to go out dancing. I used to cry until I was sick.*

Therapist: (pause) *Because you were so scared about being left?*

Dan: (pause) *The house was dark, and they never left any lights on. . . .* (crying)

Therapist: (pause) *You were left alone. . . .*

Dan: *My grandmother was downstairs. It was a great big house.* (pause) *I was always too scared to try and get to her* (pause). . . .

False Rhythms

Sometimes a client will try to override the natural rhythm of the work, speeding up in order to meet some imagined therapist expectation. The therapist may be misled by this false rhythm, only later noticing that the work has taken on a shallow, brittle, no-time-to-do-more-than-talk-about-and-move-on quality. Or the therapist may move into his or her own natural rhythm, forgetting for a moment to adjust to the client's pace. When this happens, it can be helpful to stop and ask the client about it and inquire if the pace is right or if it needs to be adjusted.

Loraine: *I want to say, "No." I want to say, "I don't want it."* (pause) *I want to say what I don't want. And I don't really care about those examples I told you about; they're just examples. That's how it came to me.*

Therapist: *The things you don't want.*

Loraine: *That's right. And* my *space.*

Therapist: *And how is this connected to your Mom and those interactions with her?* (pause) *I wonder if I went too fast, if you need to stay with your discomfort here. What do you think, Loraine?*

False rhythms can be learned and become habitual through life experiences. They often begin in school when children are pressed to keep up with classmates or teachers, are pressured to come up with an answer *now*, and are punished or shamed when they fail to do so. Or they can begin even earlier, as a young child tries to meet the demands of adults and of older siblings. Conversely, a child who has a naturally fast cognitive tempo may learn to slow himself or herself down in order to maintain relationship with a slower-processing parent or peers. Over time, the false rhythm of the pushing forward or the holding back comes to seem natural. Like other adaptations, it is grafted on so thoroughly that the person is no longer aware that it does not really fit. The discomfort is accepted as simply a part of who he or she is.

These false rhythms interfere with contact and integration. Have you ever experienced the clumsiness that results from trying to do a familiar task too quickly? Or have you become frustrated (and sometimes equally clumsy) by having to slow yourself down to match someone else's tempo? Imagine the psychic effect of *always* having to be off pace and out of synch with oneself. Part of the therapist's job is to help clients move out of a false, adaptive tempo and rediscover their natural rhythm and pace. This is accomplished partly by modeling a different rhythm than that presented by the client; the therapist can also point out the problem and invite the client to deal with it, bringing the whole notion of rhythm and pacing into awareness.

Nell: *I wasn't a good enough daughter, which is my old stuff; couldn't do it right—and didn't want to do it right—I'm not locking in so much to "I can't do it right"* (talking faster and faster)—*I didn't want to—I was angry—and part of me wanted—no—I wanted—*

Therapist: (speaking slowly) *You're starting, I think, to go faster than your own natural rhythm.*

Nell: (surprised) *Hmmm?*

Therapist: *Are you going faster than your own natural rhythm? How about you taking half a minute and focusing on that. "I—didn't—want—to—do—it—right."*

Nell: (quickly shakes her head "no")

Therapist: *You said it.*

Nell: *No—I'm saying, "no"—I didn't want to do it right—I'm agreeing with you. . . .*

Therapist: *Just take some time to appreciate that. It's a very wonderful statement.*

With her last comment, the therapist suggests that there is much more to this "wonderful statement" than appears just on the surface. By taking time to focus on all those possible meanings, Nell is also encouraged to appreciate her own patterns and rhythms—her affects and cognitions—that would be a natural part of her experiencing if she did not escalate in her frantic attempts to "do it right."

Developmental Attunement

As people begin to reclaim lost aspects of themselves, in the nourishing environment of the therapeutic relationship, they inevitably recover thoughts, feelings, behaviors, and memories that are associated with previous developmental stages. These patterns of experience—what Eric Berne (1961) referred to as the "archaeopsychic" or "Child" state of the ego—manifest themselves as client *regression*: the client is able to experience both self and others in the same way as he or she did at that earlier time (Federn, 1977; Weiss, 1950). Through therapeutic regression, a client can reexamine relationships, access and change old decisions, and heal the cumulative trauma of childhood through enacting and experiencing in fantasy what was not available in reality.

In order to facilitate these processes, it is essential that the therapist be developmentally attuned: to recognize and respond to the client at the age to which he or she has regressed. A client who is (for the moment) experiencing the world like a 5-year-old may not feel understood or supported by a therapist who uses adult language and concepts. Indeed, to treat regressed clients as if they were fully adult is likely to pull them out of the regression, missing the opportunity for increased contact and integration and quite possibly reinforcing their old self-protective patterns. On the other hand, talking down to a person who is only partially regressed may be disrespectful. Finding words that are appropriate for both the adult client and the client at a previous developmental age requires not only sensitivity, but also a thorough knowledge of the developmental process.

Regression often takes the client back to some critical point in life, a time when a particular trauma occurred or an important life decision was made or reinforced. Because splitting off, disavowal, desensitization, dissociation, and the whole array of self-denying defenses tend to be centered around these life incidents, the regression points at and opens the way into the psychic space in which the therapeutic work needs to take place (Ferenczi, 1988; Erskine & Moursund, 1988/1997; Balint, 1959). The survival decision of the past becomes the therapeutic arena of the present, in which the client strives to break free from once-needed but now inhibiting strategies. Developmental attunement is critical, then, not only because it enhances and deepens the relationship between client and therapist, but also because it sensitizes the therapist to the fact that the client is moving into a crucial aspect of the therapeutic process. The client is beginning to deal with the issues that most need to be resolved, beginning to access memories and experiences that have been kept out of awareness until now.

Responding to regressed clients requires a kind of therapeutic "double vision," the ability to maintain contact with both the regressed-to-childhood person and the self-observing adult (Federn, 1977; Berne, 1961). Both are psychically present in the therapeutic situation. The therapist will decide which one to address, depending upon the kind of focus most likely to facilitate the recovery of lost emotional memories or responses or both. The adult is given suggestions as to how to expand and deepen the experience, while the child is offered protection and support. In the following excerpt, Margaret is talking about her caretaking role in her family. As she allows herself to remember more and more vividly what it was like for her to be that caretaker, she begins to regress. Notice the subtle shift as the therapist begins by inviting Margaret into her feelings and gradually moves to language (and voice tone, although this is left for the reader to imagine) appropriate for a small child:

Margaret: *I had to take care of the house; I took care of the house. . . . I took care of Tommy, my brother, when he came, 'cause my Mom had to work. I took care of everybody. . . .*

Therapist: *Feel that, Margaret.*

Margaret: *Very good at taking care of everybody. . . .*

Therapist: *I bet you were.*

Margaret: (beginning to cry) *Yes, especially the laundry; I did all the laundry; I did all the cooking; I cleaned house. . . .*

Therapist: *Yeah. I hear you, Margaret. And it's too much for a little girl, especially when she sees her daddy just sitting around. She needs help.*

The above segment is an example of regression to a relatively young age, and the therapist's last response is to that young child. But regression can be to any previous developmental stage. Often, decisions and beliefs and rhythms developed in adolescence and young adulthood serve to strengthen and crystallize earlier coping strategies; it may be necessary to work through several layers, going backward through time, in order to finally tap into the core emotional experience that lies at the root of the client's contact disruptions. In the excerpt to follow, Dan and the therapist are discussing an interchange that Dan observed between the therapist and another member of a therapy group that Dan attends. The group member had offered the therapist a suggestion that the therapist found helpful. Dan contrasts the therapist's reaction with Dan's father's way of handling opposition or criticism. This contrast recalls the pain of his father's absence and Dan's experiences of being angry with his father yet still wanting to love and respect him. Dan appears to be accessing a part of himself characteristic of the late teens, when he was well practiced at making excuses for his father and creating an armor for himself against his own pain. Attuned to Dan's developmental stage, the therapist, for the moment, provides good parenting—an experience that Dan needed and did not get as a young man.

Dan: *When he said that, you said, "Okay, let's try it a different way."* (sighs)

Therapist: *It would be stupid to do otherwise.*

Dan: *That never stopped my Dad.*

Therapist: (chuckles) *From being stupid.* (pause) *Sorry; didn't mean to label him like that.*

Dan: *No. He's not stupid; that's the sad part about it.*

Therapist: *But that is a stupid thing to do, Dan, not to learn from somebody's unique and different approach. Not to take the advice of his wife, if his wife were to say "You missed our son." That doesn't seem like it's very good emotional intelligence or relational intelligence. You're smart enough to know that in these days, folks who really make it are the folks who understand emotions and relationships.*

Dan is an intelligent man, a highly competent businessman in his own right. Surely, at an adult level, these last remarks are not telling him anything he does not already know; saying them to a nonregressed Dan would have been inappropriate or even condescending. Similarly, they would have been inappropriate had Dan been regressed to an earlier age, since that type of language does not connect well with a small child. Only by correctly assessing the developmental level of Dan's regression and by being developmentally attuned was the therapist able to meet him exactly where he was and to provide the therapeutic experience that he needed.

With a developmental focus, the therapist can help the client access the age level at which contact in relationship was absent, the age level at which the child learned to provide artificial need-meeting structures to take the place of the interpersonal contact not provided by his or her environment (Fromm & Smith, 1989). Sorting through these structures can be difficult: small children have their own logic and their own way of using (or not using) language. The therapist must be patient and sensitive, must attend to small details of language and gesture, and must be willing to ask about rather than assume understanding. In the example to follow, Cheryl is regressing to a very early age. The therapist first guides her into the regression and then helps her explore the experience. Staying with her emotionally is complicated by the fact that she uses her observing adult ego to report what she finds; thus her language is sometimes more adult than her physical and emotional experience. The therapist respects this dual presentation, using language that a child can understand, while framing the inquiry in a way that is respectful of the adult.

Therapist: *Let yourself go back inside. See if you can just relax that busy mind. If you can't, will you just tell me about it? Just remember, my first comment was to let your body be the boss.*

Cheryl: *(pause) I feel sick, like throwing up and just tearing everything out.*

Therapist: *Okay. I'll clean it up. . . . Notice how each expression, each thought, you try to stop. Like right now, you stopped yourself from being sick.*

Cheryl: *Well, because when you said, "I'll clean it up," I know where it goes now; I, I thought, "Well, you'll clean it up, but you'll still be mad." Well that was—*

Therapist: Still *be mad?*

Cheryl: *Yes. Maybe that's it. Whenever I get into this thinking business, at the end it's, "Will you still be mad?"* (cries hard)

Therapist: Still *be mad . . . Who is mad?*

Cheryl: (cries hard) *Oh, so I can be good and I can be not good and it's all the same, and . . .*

Therapist: (long pause; Cheryl continues to cry) *Is that, "You'll still be mad" like, "You'll still not want me?"*

Cheryl's tears and body language as she cries out, "Will you still be mad?" are indications that she has moved into a regression. Attuned to the regression, the therapist moves with her: "Who is mad" refers now to a relationship from childhood, rather than to the person who might have to "Clean it up." Cheryl follows the shift easily. Her next sentence clearly relates to old pain rather than to present relationships and allows the therapist to construct an inquiry that captures the desperation of a child whose caretaker is forever and unchangeably rejecting.

Assessing the Developmental Level of the Regression

The ability to assess and respond appropriately to the current developmental stage of the client is based on four kinds of information. The first is the client's own phenomenology: sometimes the client will report directly what his or her phenomenological age is. Clients may say, "I feel little," or "I feel just like I did when I was in first grade." Another set of useful cues is the information the client may previously have given about his or her personal history. Knowing that this client lost a special teddy bear at age 5, or that mother was hospitalized when the client was 8, or that the client was raped during her senior year in high school, allows the therapist to place emotional memories within the appropriate developmental framework. Third, the therapist's general understanding of developmental psychology, of the patterns of behavior typical of different stages of development, will help in recognizing nonverbal (as well as verbal) cues and formulating hypotheses about the level to which the client may have regressed. The therapist draws on his or her knowledge of normal child development, gleaned from the professional literature (Greenspan & Pollock, 1989; Kagan, 1984; Stern, 1985; Dinkmeyer, 1965; Fraiberg, 1959; Piaget, 1952; Erikson, 1950) as well as from personal experience with children, to make sense of age-level patterns embedded in the client's ongoing behavior. Finally, the therapist's internal response to the client provides an important guidepost. Does the client *feel* young to me—do I experience an impulse to respond to this client as I would to a small child or to an adolescent? Is there a countertransferential pull to respond to this client as if he or she were a younger person? Our affective response to a client is not just a random occurrence; it contains information that is no less valuable simply because we find it hard to translate into words (Bollas, 1987).

These same four areas of knowledge—phenomenological, historical, developmental, and social/transferential—help the therapist to formulate responses that will resonate with a developmentally regressed client (Berne, 1961). We respond out of our knowledge of general developmental patterns and developmental needs and out of our knowledge of this particular client's unique history; we are sensitive to our internal affective impulse toward the client and to what that client may be telling us about his or her awareness of regression. Our attunement is conveyed in our choice of words and even more in our voice tone, our expression, and our gestures. In the excerpt below, as work with Cheryl continues, notice how the therapist puts into words the fears and longings of a small child:

Therapist: *I keep thinking about this little girl who wanders around from place to place. "Who'll have me now? Who wants me now?"* (Cheryl cries) *"Who can I be okay with now?"* (Cheryl cries harder) *"It won't last long, because they're going to get tired of me and send me somewhere else. So where can I be now?"*

Cheryl: (sobbing) *Yes. . . . It's that, when they get tired of me, or—I don't understand what they—but somehow I have to go away. . . .*

Gradually, bit by bit, Cheryl's old decision and its consequences are being unravelled: "people may want me around for a while, but they'll 'get tired of me.' Sooner or later I'll be sent away. So how can I protect myself from the pain of rejection and banishment?"

The fact of having regressed to an earlier developmental pattern is sometimes in the client's awareness and sometimes not. We can all remember instances in which we behaved "childishly" but were not aware at the time that we were doing so, and most of us have experienced engaging in similar patterns with full or partial knowledge of what we were doing. Therapeutic regression is the same: a client may regress deliberately and purposefully, or the regression may be spontaneous, done without conscious intent. The client may be unaware of moving into regression; this is often the case when the client is talking about a current event but the affect or beliefs connected with the experience are from an earlier time in his or her life. Or (as in the above example with Cheryl), an observing adult ego may be present, an adult ego that can be called on at any time to assist the process. Whether or not the client is aware that he or she has moved into regression, the developmentally attuned therapist will recognize the shift. The attunement may, in fact, be more powerful in its impact when the client does not know that a regression has occurred; all he or she is aware of is that the therapist is somehow there, somehow saying the right things, somehow making a kind of bone-deep, emotional sense even though the words may fly in the face of adult logic.

Developmental attunement helps to melt the self-protective resistance of the client, not rip through it with the attendant risk of retraumatization but move gently and supportively past it and into the pain of the archaic experience. It sidesteps the client's homeostatic tendency, the tendency to keep things as they are in order to avoid the dangers and terrors of the unknown. Because the therapist is on the client's side and is present in a way that did not happen historically, the client can experience now the kind of safety, relational support, and respect that enhances growth and change. Developmental attunement allows for a kind of psychic parenting, an acknowledgment of and response to early needs that were so painfully unmet in reality.

☐ Conveying Attunement

Throughout this discussion, we've made references to the need to convey one's attunement to the client: what the therapist knows and understands will be of little use unless that knowledge and understanding allows the client to experience the therapist's fully attuned presence. Although conveying attunement is in many ways an art form, a way of being-with that defies analysis, there are nevertheless some specific guidelines that can help us to stay on track. In the concepts and examples to follow, no attempt will be made to differentiate among different kinds of attunement. The principles hold across all the varieties of attunement that we have discussed: cognitive, affective, rhythmic, and developmental. They all tend to merge into a single stream of relationship between client and therapist.

Attend to the Client's Nonverbal Communication

The voice tone and body language of the client help us to determine which part of the verbal content we need to attend to most closely (Kepner, 1987). Sometimes we should take the content at face value; this tends to be the case when the verbal and nonverbal parts of the message are consistent with each other. When there is inconsistency—when the words say one thing but the tone or the face or the gestures say something else— this is usually a signal that there is something more important than the content that we need to be attuned to (Smith, 1985). Sometimes there are no words at all; the client who is regressed or deeply involved in an emotional memory often cannot find words to express what is going on inside. By being attuned to the nonverbal signals, the therapist can find the words to move the client more deeply into his or her process.

In the following short segment, Margaret has been telling the therapist about what it was like to live, as a child, with a father who would neither work to earn money nor help around the home. The father insisted that he was disabled, sat day after day in a darkened room, and lived off the efforts of the rest of the family. Yet he was the adult that Margaret had the most contact with, and it was important to her to keep alive the belief that he could somehow be a good daddy.

Therapist: *Put your dad here—talk directly to him, instead of telling me about him.* "You *moocher! You lived off my mother!"* (Margaret breaks eye contact with the therapist, stares into space, says nothing) *Just close your eyes. . . .* (As Margaret's eyes close, her face begins to crumple into tears) *Yeah . . . your compassion for him comes out. . . .*

Margaret: *Yes. . . . yes, it does.*

Therapist: *Such a struggle. . . .*

Margaret: *Yes—oh, yes. . . .*

Sensitivity to nonverbal messages may mean simply noticing them and acknowledging them in some way through the therapist's own nonverbal response. It may, as in the example above, involve actually commenting about them. Or the therapist may invite the client to notice or even exaggerate some bit of body language.

Dan: *. . . because I have no respect for him. If I was to tell him anything, it would be that.* (sobs deeply)

Therapist: *Feel that hand across your mouth, holding that comment in.* (Dan cries harder, hand held hard against mouth) *Just say that comment that you've been holding in. . . .*

Decenter

Although attuned therapists are aware of their own experience and use that experience as a kind of amplifier for what the client is presenting, it is nevertheless the client's process that must be at the center of the therapist's awareness (Stolorow et al., 1987). Whatever the client presents is, by definition, an important communication; the therapist's awareness of self is used in the service of client awareness and contact. This is particularly important when the client is expressing feelings about the therapist. No matter what the client directs toward the therapist, from anger to adulation, the therapist attends to and experiences his or her own response and then decenters from that response, putting the client's experience, meanings, and needs into the foreground. Nell, in the piece of work excerpted below, began by relating a fantasy in which she was exploring a gray, featureless place; the experience was very significant and also very frightening to her. She both wants and does not want to go there again; to protect herself from her fear she resorts to old, out-of-awareness avoidance techniques. One of these techniques is to split herself into parts, become helpless and confused, ask the therapist to rescue her, and then fight about it.

Nell: (in a frightened voice) *Let me hold your hand? I need. . . .*

Therapist: *I could do that very easily. I have no difficulty, for my sake, holding your hand. But I think that would be a way of you stopping yourself from going where you need to go. Now if you tell me I'm wrong, I'll hold your hand.* (pause) *Now watch your reaction to what I just said.*

Nell: (dramatically) *I stood up to people for years and didn't ask for that. I dared to ask you for it, and I didn't get what I asked for!*

Therapist: *And when I implied, "No," what was your response inside?*

Nell: (agitated, talking very fast) *Back away; I don't want to be close; I don't trust you.*

Therapist: *And what did it mean to you, when I implied, "No"?*

Nell: (agitation continues to increase) *Rejection. Again. I finally dared to ask, and I still didn't get it. So why the hell bother. . . .*

Therapist: (calmly) *So I imagine you didn't hear the reason why I implied, "No."*

Nell: *My head heard it; the rest of me didn't. Yeah, I can tell you—*

Therapist: *Wait, let's get something straight. It's only with your brain that you listen and understand.*

Nell: (screaming, furious) *I KNOW THAT! I'M NOT STUPID!*

Therapist: (calmly) *You said, "My head knows this; the rest of me doesn't get it." But you are desperately working to avoid going into that gray place. And inventing a rejection is a wonderful distraction.*

Being misunderstood and screamed at by a client is not a pleasant experience; a self-focussed response might well have been for the therapist to defend against Nell's rage. Decentering from her own needs, however, the therapist is able to deal calmly and appropriately with Nell's avoidance, which leads us to the next guideline.

Be Sensitive to, and Respectful of, Defensive Maneuvers

Even when confronting Nell's defensive strategy, in the example above, the therapist is respectful and supportive. Nell herself is respected; she is treated as an intelligent woman who has partially and temporarily regressed into a confused and angry child. The therapist's calm and firm intervention invites her to move out of her nonproductive attempt to escape her confusion through anger and come back to the business at hand. And even the defense itself is respected: it is a "wonderful distraction," a skilled way of protecting herself, which has served her well in the past.

Noticing these sorts of defenses, being attuned to their underlying meaning, affect, rhythm and developmental age, and dealing with them directly, is often affirming. The client is made a partner, almost a cotherapist (Baker, 1982; Greenson, 1967). It is as if the therapist is saying, "You need to help make this process work. Here is what I think has been happening; what do you, my colleague, think we should do about it?" Not only is this kind of approach respectful and supportive, but it also seeks information from the best possible source: the internal experience of the client. Margaret, in her compassion for her father and her need to protect him (and her image of him) from criticism, has trouble describing what really went on in her family. In the short exchange to follow, the therapist is closely attuned to her affective and cognitive process; she senses Margaret's avoidance and invites her to pay attention to what she is doing:

Therapist: *Margaret, do you experience yourself now saying these things in the vaguest possible way?*

Margaret: *No, I'm trying to get the words out.*

Therapist: *My experience of you is that you're working to keep this as mild and as vague as possible. Probably so you won't have to feel it. . . .*

Here is another example. This time the client, Janelle, is engaging in a dialogue with her mother, who she imagines sitting across from her. She hints that mother is being phony and is not willing to deal directly with the fact that Janelle's grandfather was sexually abusing Janelle; yet she herself is talking in hints and euphemisms. The therapist chooses to frame the confrontation as a series of suggestions about what Janelle might tell her mother. Again, it is the therapist's attunement to Janelle's process—to her cognitive, affective, and developmental level—that allows her to construct suggestions that Janelle will use and that will lead to increasing awareness:

Janelle: (to mother, breathlessly) *And you told me, you told me, you told me, you told me, you said. . . . I asked you, I asked you, what happened to me when I was little.*

Therapist: *"What I won't ask you, Mom, is. . . . "*

Janelle: (pause, then crying) *Ohhhh—what happened? Did you know? Did you know? I think you knew; I think that's why you have to have me be okay all* *the time. I think you knew, and I think if I have anything ever wrong with me you get scared!*

Therapist: *Because. . . .*

Janelle: (angrily) *Because you wouldn't tell me it affected me! So you have to pretend everything's fine with me always! Always, always, always, always, always. . . .*

Therapist: *"And I pretend too, Mom, by. . . ."*

Janelle: *Ohh. . . . I act like I'm okay all the time; I just look for that little look on your face, that little tiny look, and I back right up and I won't say any more, just shut up, 'cause I don't want you to have that look on your face 'cause I want you to think I'm. . . . .*

Therapist: *"Because I won't ask you. . . ."*

Janelle: (pause) *I won't ask you . . . ohh . . .* (cries again, hard) *Did he screw you, too? Did you know? Did you know?*

Timing

It is fairly obvious that timing is a critical element in rhythmic attunement. Being sensitive to the pace and rhythms of the client and adjusting your timing to them is, essentially, what rhythmic attunement is all about. But timing is important for other kinds of attunement as well. The therapist's timing and pace let the client know whether that therapist is indeed in tune with affect, with cognition, and with developmental age.

In general, as we mentioned earlier, the therapeutic pace may need to be slower for affective work than for cognitive work. There are likely to be more silent spaces in affective work, spaces in which the client's lost sense of self can emerge along with the emotional memories. Allowing, and even encouraging, these spaces is a subtle invitation for the client to move from a cognitive to an affective focus. In this context, silence is itself an intervention (Pine, 1985). The therapist who leaps to fill silent moments with words, or who permits the client to do so, has lost a powerful tool.

Developmental attunement is also partly a function of timing. Usually, the younger the developmental level, the slower the pace. Small children need small words, often with large spaces between them; older people can deal with large words and smaller spaces between them. A regressed client also may need explicit permission to create quiet spaces or to accept them when they are offered by the therapist: "Go inside to that quiet place," or "It's okay to take time to think," or "Sometimes it feels good to not say anything at all for a moment" can be helpful reassurances.

The need for space and for matching the client's tempo is especially critical when the client is *both* regressed and dealing with affect. Trying to hurry a sad, scared, or angry child is a prescription for therapeutic disaster: the best thing that can come of it is adaptation, moving out of the therapeutic regression and back to old, fixated, self-protective patterns. It is much better to pause, to listen, and to use all of one's senses to understand and value the fragmented communication of that child.

Attunement Through Scheduling

Timing involves more than just the flow of words and the spaces between them. It also has to do with the length of time a client can use for a given session. Some clients, for instance, have retreated deep inside themselves and have shut their most tender and vulnerable selves off from the world. They spend their lives in a desperate oscillation between retreating from a terrifying outside world and fleeing the emptiness and loneliness of their internal hiding place. Working with these people requires that the therapist slow down, wait quietly and say little or nothing, and allow plenty of space for the client to discover that here it is, indeed, safe to engage in relationship. Such clients may not be able to finish a piece of work in the traditional 50-minute hour. They need more time—time to reach out to test the therapeutic waters and then retreat back into their safe loneliness before emerging again.

Other clients, particularly young children or adults who have a limited attention span, may not be able to tolerate even a full hour of therapeutic intensity. For them, shorter sessions work better; if a session is too long, they may begin to fidget, evade, and retreat into familiar defenses. Similarly, clients who are in acute crisis may benefit more from short, frequent sessions than from longer, more widely spaced ones (Efran et al., 1990).

What all this means is that the therapist must adjust his or her scheduling of sessions, as well as the rhythm within the session, to the client's pace. And, when it is not possible to provide an ideal appointment pattern, the therapist should acknowledge both the problem and the difficulty of solving it, demonstrating understanding of, respect for, and attunement to the client's needs even when they cannot be fulfilled.

Language

This chapter has been filled with examples of how language can be used to demonstrate attunement. Words have been the therapist's stock in trade since Freud and his colleagues began using the "talking cure" with their patients. Here are some of the principles that frequently guide our use of language in the therapy session:

Attuned therapists use language to reflect and describe the feelings, cognitions, and beliefs that underlie the stories that clients tell them. The words demonstrate not only that the therapist is attending to the content of the story, but that he or she is also sensing why the story is important. "That really hurt" or "You needed someone to be there with you" supports and respects the client's experience and invites movement to a deeper level of awareness.

The choice of verb tense is particularly important for developmental attunement. For an adult describing an incident of childhood, a past tense response is appropriate: "You *were* scared" or "You *didn't* want to." When that client is regressed and experiencing the incident as if it were current, use of the past tense is likely to jar him or her out of the regression. No longer regressed, he or she is back to talking-about, disavowal of affect, and disruption of contact, and doesn't know quite what happened. The guideline, then, is that the therapist uses present tense verbs to express attunement to a regression experience: "You're scared . . . " or "You don't want to . . . " (Perls, 1967, 1973).

Use of the client's own language enhances attunement. We saw this with Allen, in chapter 2, when the therapist repeated Allen's word "heroic." Similarly, after Cheryl (who was dealing with the pain of criticism and rejection throughout her childhood) has described her internal experience as, "It's as if a thought comes up, it goes to here, and then this is like iron, and even with claws to it, and it makes the thought go away, and then I can't think anymore, and it just hurts in my head, and. . . . " The therapist, much later in the work, says, "It's real important that those iron claws keep that thought from coming into your head."

Words, of course, are only a part of our language repertoire. Words do little to communicate attunement unless accompanied and supported by appropriate nonverbal expression. Indeed, verbal and nonverbal aspects of communication are like the two sides of a coin: we can look at them separately, but in reality dividing them would be to destroy the coin itself. Voice tone, gesture, and facial expression deepen and flavor the message of the therapist's words. Most importantly, then, the nonverbal messages that we send to the client need to fit what we are saying in words. The verbal and nonverbal messages sent by the therapist are similar to the instrumental voices of a symphony. When one or more of those voices is out of key or off tempo, the whole piece sounds wrong. Moreover, just as we respond to one piece of music or another depending on the state or mood in which we find ourselves, the client will respond differently to different therapist "symphonies" depending on his or her own state—dealing with affect or cognition, regressed or not, energized or fatigued, and so on.

The musical metaphor makes sense, and it is no accident that we use it to understand the notion of "at*tune*ment." Hearing all of the nuances of the client's melody and rhythm and responding from and with the harmony of our whole therapeutic orchestra, verbally and nonverbally, is what attunement is all about.

☐ Attunement and Other Therapist Tasks

If the only thing required of a therapist were to be attuned to the client, to hear all of the client's voices, and to convey to the client that he or she has been heard and understood and responded to, that would be no small thing. Adding more tasks seems almost too much. How can one possibly attend to anything more when attunement itself is so demanding? Yet the therapist can and does do more—much more. The "more" is done in the context of attunement, and therapeutic attunement helps the therapist to decide just what sort of "more" will be most helpful at any given moment. In this section we will take a look at three of the most common of those "more" tasks and how they can be carried out to enhance rather than detract from the therapist's attunement.

Giving Information

Sometimes a bit of client behavior, in or out of the therapeutic session, is a clear statement of lack of information. The client does *this* because he or she is unaware of other options, says *that* because he or she has been misinformed, or asks the therapist to provide needed information. Whether or not to provide an interpretation, answer a question, or correct a misunderstanding, is always a therapeutic judgment call. Being attuned to the client's internal experience helps therapists to decide whether it will be more helpful to give information or to help the client discover it for himself or herself, to determine whether a request is straightforward or a disguised way of saying something else, or to know whether a bit of behavior is to be taken at face value or understood as a plea that someone pay attention to what's going on at a deeper level.

If we decide that it would be helpful and appropriate to provide information, the next challenge is to do so while still remaining attuned. Switching focus back and forth, from self (what I have decided to tell this client) to other (how the client is responding to my message), the therapist moves with the flow of the interaction. Like a canoeist paddling down a stream, carried along by the current, the therapist uses the client's reactions as a guide to what to do and say next or how to get from here to there. In the excerpt below, Dan is criticizing himself for how he acted in a previous session with the therapist. Although a sophisticated businessman, sensitive in understanding other people's behavior, Dan uses a different standard for himself: he takes full responsibility for the relationship and does not see it as a joint product of two separate people. This overresponsibility, in turn, limits his ability to relax and enjoy relationships when they are good or to solve problems effectively when they are not. The therapist decides to suggest a different way of looking at things:

Dan: *It's really hard for me sometimes, with you.*

Therapist: *Based on what behavior of mine?*

Dan: *I don't think it has anything to do with your behavior.*

Therapist: *Oh, I bet it has a lot to do with me, Dan. And in other situations, with other men, that also has a lot to do with how they behave.*

Dan: *I'm prepared to believe you, but I just don't know that myself.*

Therapist: *It's not just a one-way street. What I'm saying to you is that my appropriate behavior is important.*

Dan: *Yeah. Yeah, that's true.*

Therapist: *The appropriateness of my behavior is critical to your response.*

Dan: *That's true.*

Therapist: *That's the simple point I want to make. It's not just what goes on inside your head.*

Here, as in a previous excerpt, Dan was emotionally regressed to adolescence, and it is a bright adolescent that the therapist is talking to. Developmental attunement helps the therapist choose words and tone that are most likely to be assimilated by a regressed client. Contrast the tone of this example with another segment from this piece of work, after Dan has emerged from the regression. He has gone through an intensely emotional dialogue with an internal image of his father, and, as the session ends, he is trying to develop a cognitive perspective for what he experienced. The therapist, aware of his need for this sort of structure, offers an explanation. Notice the different quality of the therapist's words and phrasing: here the client is a man, not a young boy, a man coming to grips with the sadness of what he missed in his relationship with his parents:

Therapist: *I think I may have understood something just now. In the back of my mind, I kept thinking, "Why would a man like your father, whom you describe as so authoritarian, present himself as being not very professionally successful?" It seems very contradictory. And what I just realized was, by not being successful, you can't ask anything of him. He's just sort of a poor humble clerk. So what can you expect? Do you think that fits?*

Dan: *Yes. Yes. I was just thinking that they used to, they never used to ask anything of me very much. Exams and things like that, they'd say, "Well, do the best you can...."*

Therapist: *They didn't ask much of you, and you weren't to ask much of him. And mother wasn't to ask much of him either.*

Confrontation

Confrontation involves a statement or question used by the therapist to bring a discrepancy into the client's awareness (Berne, 1966). The discrepancy may be between words and behaviors, between what the client actually does and how he or she describes it, between thoughts and affect, or between expectations and actual events. Discrepancies like this, when unnoticed, support the splitting off and disavowal of parts of oneself. As long as one does not have to be aware of one's contradictory feelings and behaviors, as long as one does not notice that one's behavior does not really match one's understanding or that one's perception of events is different from what actually happened, it is relatively easy to maintain self-protective defenses.

Confrontation of discrepancy, done without sensitive attunement, is likely to produce a reaction of shame and drive the client even further into defensive maneuvering (Goldberg, 1991; Wurmser, 1981). If the therapist leaps in, caught up in the excitement of having noticed something important and paying no attention to the damage his or her "big boots" may cause, it makes perfect sense for the client to get out of the way, retreat, and defend. In order for a confrontation to be effective, it must be framed within the context of attunement. In such a context, a confrontation is also a confirmation—a confirmation of the therapist's respect for and commitment to the client, a confirmation that the client and therapist are working together in the service of the client's growth, and a confirmation of the genuineness of the therapeutic relationship.

Nowhere is the need for attunement in confrontation more critical than in the case of "acting-out" behavior. "Acting out" is too often misunderstood as somehow bad or negative, and confronting it can be turned into a kind of therapeutic "gotcha!" that only intensifies the client's defensiveness and pushes feelings and needs further out of awareness. In fact, acting out is an attempt to communicate; it is the client's way of expressing in action that which cannot be expressed in language. It often tells the story of some important problem or issue or relationship from the client's past. Appropriate, attuned confrontation simply calls the behavior into awareness, with no sense of criticism. In the segment below, for instance, the therapist has invited Janelle to talk directly to her (imagined) mother, rather than talking to the therapist about her mother's behavior. Janelle resists:

Therapist: *Will you talk to your mother?*

Janelle: *This feels real—a big part of this is, until someone takes care of my sisters, I can't . . . can't . . . deal with her. . . . Just something, I had to stay, I stayed, I had to stay okay with her to make them okay.*

Therapist: *Now just tell that to her.*

Janelle: *I'm so scared of her myself. I couldn't, I think I couldn't ever let myself know that, because I was always taking care of them. So I stayed out of my own feelings about her.*

Therapist: *Tell her now, because I think as long as I let you just talk about her to me, I'm not protecting you.*

Janelle: *Why?*

Therapist: *Why? Because one of the best protections for you is to encourage you to take a risk.*

Janelle: *I'm very scared of her.*

Therapist: *Is she going to beat up your sisters because you tell her you don't like her?*

Janelle: *Or hit me.*

Therapist: *Well, that's a risk you'll have to take, isn't it?* (pause) *Has she ever hit you?*

Janelle: *Um-hmm.*

Therapist: *And when you've told her other things you don't like, does she go and hit your sisters?*

Janelle: *I only told her once. Once I said, "If this is the way marriage is, I don't want to get married." And she whacked me across the face. I was a teenager. And my sisters remember. My mom is real unpredictable, but. . . .*

Therapist: *So you're using a one-time occurrence to hold yourself back from talking to her now.*

In one sense this confrontation might seem harsh: it cuts through the fuzz of feelings and explanations and evasions and goes directly to the underlying purpose of Janelle's behavior. Yet, in the context of a respectful and attuned relationship, it is supportive. It acknowledges the meaning and purpose of her defensiveness. There is no value judgment, no "you're bad or wrong for doing this." It is simply a statement of what the therapist sees happening, a putting into words what has only been acted out before, so that Janelle can now use all of her resources to deal with the problem.

Confrontation is only useful if the client can acknowledge it, remember it, and use it to enhance awareness (Adler & Myerson, 1973). This kind of client response will seldom occur if the confrontation is humiliating or if it expresses a therapist one-up position. In contrast, the confirmation that acknowledges the behavior as a coping strategy, a solution that was worked out for some very good reason but that is no longer useful, is much more likely to be experienced as supportive because it emphasizes the function of the behavior.

Discrepancies and archaically expressive ("acting-out") behaviors are not random events: they have a purpose and a function. They are (or have been) protective for the client; they continue to be a part of the behavior repertoire because their function is important. A supportive confrontation invites the client to shift that function to the therapeutic relationship itself. The confrontation says, in essence, "I understand that this is important for you, that you feel as though you need it. But if you experiment with letting go of it right now, here with me, I'll help you deal with whatever happens."

When they feel valued and respected, clients can listen rather than deny, can expand awareness rather than retreat behind familiar defenses, can allow the therapist to support their changes. Like a child learning to ride a bicycle, they gain confidence from the dependable presence of that other person keeping things steady, catching the child when she wobbles and being there to reassure and comfort her if she falls.

Supporting Regressive Work

Purposeful therapeutic regression is hard for many people to accomplish. They have spent most of their lives being told things like, "Grow up," "Don't be such a baby," "Don't feel that way." Regression, when they do experience it, feels like being out of control—like going crazy, or being unacceptably dependent—and is very uncomfortable. In contrast, other people regress easily and often, but their regressions are not generally helpful. Their regressions tend to be out of awareness and often represent an old, no-longer-appropriate solution for a here-and-now problem (Guntrip, 1962; Balint, 1959; Federn, 1953/1977). For both kinds of clients, it is attunement, more than anything else, that allows them to regress in a way that is therapeutically useful. Attunement helps them feel safe and supported, so that they can allow themselves access to emotional memories without all of the defenses and resistances that have been keeping them stuck and frustrated.

The therapist needs to be attuned to clients who regress easily and spontaneously and often self-destructively, and to those who find it hard to regress at all. When a client begins to move into regression, the therapist should be alert to the possibility that some aspect of self, previously denied and defended against, may now begin to emerge. He or she helps to give that part voice and helps the client to experience and express and reclaim what was lost. Notice, in the following segment of Dan's work, how the therapist actually speaks for Dan, so attuned that she can begin a thought that Dan then finishes. Dan has moved deeply and intensely into an emotional memory of being with his father and is now able to experience telling his father what he could never say in reality:

Dan: (to father) *I wanted you to set an example for me. Just . . . just to . . . if you just claimed you were good at something . . . if you'd been proud of what you'd done . . . if you'd showed me how to be proud, instead of hiding yourself in some hole in a corner. . . .* (sobs)

Therapist: *'Cause I need . . .*

Dan: (to father) *I need you to show me the way to be in the world as an intelligent, sensitive person, who is clever at things—not some self-effacing creep.* (crying softly)

Therapist: *And I need . . .*

Dan: (to father) *I need you to stand up for me. I need you to stand up for me and not shrug things off. If you excelled at just one single thing, and would say so, just . . . just admit your success . . .*

Therapist: *That would mean . . .*

Dan: (to father) *I could admit mine. I could be proud instead of ashamed.* (He sighs, then turns to the therapist) *I didn't know that. I never knew that.*

There are many important things going on in this excerpt, and this chapter has already grown quite long. So we will only ask you to notice how the therapist is able to follow Dan's process and how each of her statements primes the pump, allowing Dan's self-interrupted experience to flow again, leading but not directing, and helping Dan to explore needs and meanings previously lost to awareness.

☐ Conclusions

We have spent a great deal of time discussing the need for attunement in therapy, the various kinds of therapeutic attunement, and some guidelines for achieving and maintaining attunement. Before moving on, let us sum up the effects of attunement on the client and on the client's progress through therapy.

Therapeutic growth is anchored in relationship (Jordan, 1989; Miller, 1986). It is through relationship that contact with self and with others is enhanced, memories are recovered, and the self is reintegrated. Without a contactful relationship between therapist and client, therapy is at best a mechanical, symptom-bound process: figure out what behaviors are not working, change them, and get out. A relationship-oriented therapy, in contrast, concerns itself with the whole person and with recovering fragmented aspects of oneself and bringing them together—the basis of change (Hycner & Jacobs, 1995).

The first and most obvious consequence of therapist attunement is that it enhances this therapeutic relationship. It allows the client to experience that the therapist is contactfully present, and acknowledges, validates, and normalizes his or her experience. The therapeutic environment is safe: the client will not be attacked or misunderstood and will be asked to do only what is in his or her best interest. As the therapist demonstrates attunement to cognition, to affect, to rhythm and to developmental age, the client can begin to trust; with the growth of trust comes willingness to risk both internal and external contact; with increased contact comes growth and healing.

Another consequence of attunement is the challenge to the self-protective belief system that the client has been maintaining (Erskine & Moursund, 1988/1997; Erskine & Zalcman, 1979). Old beliefs and expectations, once useful but now self-defeating, are continually contradicted as the attuned therapist recognizes them, acknowledges their historical significance, and validates their current psychological function. As the client, too, begins to recognize those old coping strategies and to both value them (as serving an important purpose) and question them (as perhaps no longer the best way to serve that purpose), he or she becomes more and more able to risk trying out new ways of being, not only with the therapist, but with himself or herself, and even with others outside the therapeutic setting. Remember that log jam we talked about in chapter 1? As soon as one log shifts or one script belief is given up, the whole structure may become unstable. New ideas and possibilities begin to multiply, contact breeds more contact, and the pattern of ever-increasing rigidity and restriction is changed into one of exploration and learning.

The attuned therapist not only understands the client's experience, but also supports and validates its connection to script beliefs, memories, and defenses. This stance directly contradicts the self-negating responses that originally led to fragmenting and denial: the client's belief that he or she "shouldn't be this way," "shouldn't feel these feelings," or "shouldn't think these thoughts." Emotions and memories and wants and needs that were split off and denied because they were painful, shameful, or dangerous are now respected and valued. In such a climate, lost memories can be reclaimed and reintegrated. With the memories come fragments of self that have been walled off and denied. And the self-perpetuating therapeutic process continues: awareness begins to expand, and relationships deepen.

For people who have been neglected, whose needs have been ignored or misunderstood or who have experienced acute trauma with no supportive relationship to help them through it, having someone be attentive and caring and understanding flies in the face of all expectations: The world is not like this! People do not treat each other this way! It is simply too good to be true. Their first reaction may be suspicion, anger, withdrawal, or even further denial or dissociation. Juxtaposition of their old relationship experiences, on the one hand, and their experience with the therapist, on the other hand, first creates disbelief; later, they may experience anger and grief as they allow themselves to feel—perhaps for the first time—how painful those old situations really were. We shall have much more to say about this juxtaposition response later, when we examine in detail the whole notion of relational needs.

We have reached the end of this chapter, but it is not really an end at all. It is, rather, a beginning—or at least a bridge—to the last of the three basic components of the therapeutic relationship. We have talked about inquiry and attunement, and in the next chapter we will explore the concept of *involvement*. The reason that the present chapter cannot really be concluded or cannot be brought to a neat ending is that attunement cannot be fully discussed or understood without also talking about involvement. They are two parts of the same thing, similar to the inhaling and exhaling that make up breathing. Neither can be present without the other. Because a book is a linear thing, with one idea following another, it has been necessary to consider them in sequence; in reality they interpenetrate and interact with each other through every moment of the therapeutic interaction.

CHAPTER

Involvement

Psychotherapy draws upon both art and skill. To get an idea of the balance between them, imagine a continuum with skill and technique and all those teachable behaviors on one end, and art and attitude and emotion and all the other intangibles on the other (Figure 4.1). On such a continuum, inquiry, which was discussed in chapter 2, would fall toward the skill side. Although there is certainly a kind of artistry in good therapeutic inquiry, it depends more upon skills and techniques than do many other aspects of therapy. Attunement, the subject of chapter 3, involves more of the intangibles: attitude, emotion, the sort of "withness" that defies scientific definition or measurement. Yet attunement, too, utilizes teachable skills. It is in the middle of the continuum. And therapeutic involvement would certainly go toward the art/attitude/emotion end. Appropriate involvement requires skill, of course, but it is more importantly a matter of attitude, of emotion, and of art. Inquiry is about what a therapist *does*; involvement is not about *doing* so much as about *being*. Being therapeutically involved means being fully present, fully contactful, an ordinary person with needs and blemishes and all the other baggage that comes with being real, while still being a therapist who is with and for the client (Buber, 1958).

For many therapists, involvement is difficult. It would be easier to stay uninvolved, remote, and untouched by the clients' struggles. Therapists see so much pain! Why in the world should we choose to be affected by it? The answer is simple: therapy occurs in the context of relationship;

FIGURE 4.1. A continuum of therapeutic activities.

relationship requires contact; contact requires involvement. Relationship is a two-way street.

Having said that, let us back up and qualify it a bit: at the beginning of a therapeutic relationship, many clients are not ready for full contact. They are not fully aware of either themselves or others; parts of them are split off, denied, labeled "unacceptable," and locked out of awareness. To the extent that this has occurred, the early therapeutic relationship *is* a one-way street. It is part of the therapist's job to coax the traffic to move in both directions. A therapy of contact-in-relationship uses the involvement of the therapist to invite the client into becoming more and more authentic, aware of himself or herself, and open to relationship. That process, that invitation, is what this chapter is about.

☐ The Nature of Involvement

Willingness to Be Affected

Involvement means, first, that the therapist is willing to be affected by what happens in the relationship with the client. Involvement cannot happen without taking risks (Ferenczi, 1988). When I allow myself to truly care about you, to be touched by you, I risk being made uncomfortable. What if you do not like me? What if you are in pain? What if things go badly in your life? If I am involved, I cannot just sail past those kinds of things. I must feel them, too; I must respond. As you grow and change, so do I as well.

The notion of therapist involvement is not a new one. In 1961, Carl Rogers said, "If I am to facilitate the personal growth of others in relation to me, then I must grow, and while this is often painful it is also enriching." (p. 51) Enriching? To be sure. Disturbing? Often. Exhilarating? Occasionally. And always—real, authentic, fully in contact with one's own responses as well as attuned to those of the client.

Resonance

Attunement to the client's responses, in this context, implies more than just noticing—however closely—what the client is thinking and feeling and doing. The involved therapist not only notices, but also resonates with the client's response. The client's affect is not merely something to attend to and understand; it evokes a reciprocal affective response from the therapist. The client's thoughts and his or her struggles to understand and change and grow set off trains of thought (and perhaps struggles as well) in the therapist. A fine crystal has no "choice" but to vibrate to the sound of a pure tone; that response is an intrinsic part of what a fine crystal is. Just so, the involved therapist has no choice about resonating to the client. As the client moves into the work, experiencing feelings and thoughts and memories, the therapist is not "just listening"—the therapist, too, feels and thinks and experiences. Resonance is a part of what relationship is all about; it is intrinsic to contact and authenticity. In a therapeutic relationship, this resonance is a kind of unconscious communication between client and therapist; blended with attunement, it serves to guide the inquiry process (Bollas, 1987).

Developmental Appropriateness

A part of the therapist's responsibility is to be sensitive to the developmental level of the client: the level of functioning at which the client finds himself or herself at any given moment. The quality of therapeutic involvement must take these developmental levels into consideration. One does not respond in the same way to a toddler as to a 10-year-old; one is not impacted by an adolescent's affect in the same way that one is impacted by that same affect in an adult. The appropriately involved therapist not only notices and evaluates the client's developmental level, but also responds internally to the client as if the client truly were at that age (Winnicott, 1965; Fairbairn, 1952). Indeed, this internal response is, as we discussed in chapter 3, one of the ways in which an attuned therapist can assess the developmental level at which a client is operating. Developmental appropriateness is genuine, not contrived. With a regressed client, the therapist is no more "pretending" to respond to a younger person than is the client "pretending" to be phenomenologically young. Regression, if it is to be therapeutically useful, is a two-person phenomenon: the client experiences it, and the therapist responds to it.

Commitment

Involvement begins with the therapist's commitment to the client's welfare. Here lies the fundamental difference between the therapeutic relationship and a friendship. The therapeutic relationship is *for* the client; the therapist is there for the client's benefit. The therapist may (and often does) reap some additional benefit from the relationship, but this is a side effect; the primary focus is on the client. Commitment to the client's welfare, an unswerving and unquestioned awareness that the client comes first, is the bedrock that makes therapist involvement possible. Without this commitment, the therapist could be tempted to shift the focus when his or her emotions were aroused: to become defensive, to attack or criticize, to leave the relationship, or use it to meet his or her own needs. When commitment to the client is solid, the therapist's involvement enriches and vitalizes the therapy. It allows relationship between two real human beings, each challenging and enhancing the authenticity of the other.

Professionalism

If commitment to the client's welfare marks the fundamental difference between appropriate therapeutic involvement and the involvement of other close relationships, then professionalism is what makes that commitment therapeutically effective. Professionalism provides direction and structure for our commitment. It includes knowledge, skills, and values, and it implies constant self-monitoring to be certain that one relates to the client appropriately, authentically, and fully aware of one's own psychic baggage. It means recognizing when we are in over our heads, when we need to ask for help or to refer a client to a colleague more skilled in some area than we are. It means setting clear limits, for both ourselves and the client, so that feelings can be experienced and expressed safely. Professionalism and commitment, together, form the skeleton that gives shape and strength and dependability to the blood and tissue of the therapeutic relationship.

☐ The Expression of Involvement

Acknowledgment, validation, normalization, and presence are both the manifestation and the goals of involvement. They are the outward signals by means of which the client senses the therapist's involvement. And they are goals in that as they are enacted, the relationship is enriched, and the client can grow. Let's consider each in turn.

Acknowledgment

Acknowledgment of the client begins with attunement to the client's affect, needs, rhythm, and developmental level. It says to the client, "Yes, you are who you are; you really are experiencing this; I'm aware of your thoughts and feelings and needs and they matter to me." In acknowledging the client's presence, the therapist too becomes present. It is the overture to the symphony: we are both here, with all our voices and complexities; now we begin.

Often the therapist will sense needs or responses or affect in the client that the client himself or herself has not yet brought to full awareness. Acknowledging these—tentatively, always respecting the client's right to deny or postpone or disagree—can help the client to become more fully aware. It can help the client to make connections between emotions or physical sensations or both that relate to long-buried memories and thus reclaim those memories and the parts of self that were buried with them (Kepner, 1987). In many cases, clients have experienced relationships in which needs and feelings were not acknowledged. If this happened early enough or consistently enough, the client may not have developed or may have lost the vocabulary to express such needs and feelings; again, acknowledgment by the therapist opens the door to awareness and expression.

In order to acknowledge the client's phenomenological experience, the therapist first demonstrates that he or she is aware of what the client is feeling. Straightforward reflection can accomplish this, and it also puts into words what the client may not have known how to say. At other times, reflection is not necessary: a simple comment such as, "That's sad/ scary/infuriating," a sympathetic, "Ouch!", or a nonverbal expression or gesture, conveys a world of acknowledgment. Indeed, it is because the nonverbal component of acknowledgment is so important, and is often unaccompanied by words, that it is difficult to present examples of how such acknowledgment is demonstrated. Here is one exchange, for instance, in which the therapist's words (although clearly acknowledging the client's feelings) carry much less impact than the gentle, respectful, caring tone in which they are delivered. Jolene, who had little difficulty expressing herself when she began to work, has gradually become quiet and almost withdrawn.

Therapist: *You look really scared right now. Are you scared?* (Jolene nods) *Can you tell me what's scary to you right now?*

Jolene: (pause) *Well . . .* (pause) *People in the past kept telling me I wasn't really feeling things.*

Therapist: *That's pretty confusing, isn't it? You're feeling something, and someone tells you you're not feeling it. . . . What would seem most gratifying to you? . . . Instead of being told they're not your feelings, instead of having to withdraw, what would you want to have someone else do in response to you?*

Note that in this example the therapist has actually gone beyond simply acknowledging that Jolene's scared and confused and needy feelings exist. She has invited Jolene to follow those feelings, to let them inform her of what is needed, and to share the information. And all is done with a quality of caring and commitment to Jolene's welfare.

In another example, Billie, the client, has been talking about her ambivalence about being close to the therapist. She desperately wants the therapist's comfort and support, but she is afraid of the feelings and memories that the comfort and support may trigger. As she struggles to express herself, the intensity of her feelings becomes so great that she protects herself by closing down. The therapist comments that Billie has cut off her feelings, an acknowledgment of what is *not*, rather than what is. She (the therapist) goes on to take responsibility for distracting Billie and gently invites her back into her stream of experiencing. Acknowledgment of all that is going on—the shift of attention and its importance, as well as the feelings that were being avoided—allows Billie to take another step toward recovering an emotional memory:

Therapist: *What happened to what you were feeling just a minute ago?*

Billie: *I don't know; it just went . . . I start thinking . . .*

Therapist: *And what did you start thinking?*

Billie: *About what you said.*

Therapist: *And that was my responsibility. I'm sorry.* (pause) *But my guess is, it was also maybe . . . convenient? Because you were starting to feel something very important. You said something about . . . something about wanting something . . . and too much . . . What did my words stimulate?*

Billie: *I feel like I'm just gonna explode.*

Therapist: *Would you have wanted me to hold you together somehow while you explode?*

Billie: *I would have to be able to get away, though.*

Therapist: *So you imagined me holding you together, and taking care of you, but you don't want to be trapped.*

You may have noticed that there is a confrontation as well as an acknowledgment in this excerpt. The therapist suggests that although she did distract Billie from her process, it was also "convenient" for Billie to be distracted. Confrontation, calling the client's attention to discrepancies between different parts of what he or she is presenting, is inevitably a part of acknowledgment. Clients do present discrepancies, and the sensitive therapist cannot help noticing them (that is a good thing, because such discrepancies are usually pointers to the work that the client needs to do). After noticing, and believing that what is noticed is significant, we see that acknowledgment is the natural next step. Here, for instance, Nell has begun to become emotionally confused again. Her self-description is a child's frantic attempt to protect herself from that confusion and to avoid the pain of being close and hence vulnerable to criticism. To leave this description unchallenged would be to collude with the avoidance and to tacitly support Nell's defensive self-criticism. Instead, the therapist acknowledges the discrepancy (between what Nell is saying and what she is actually capable of) with a confrontation:

Nell: (almost frantically) *I don't know anything at all; I don't have much information; I don't know what's going on. . . .*

Therapist: (reasonably) *Now, Nell, you don't expect me to believe that, do you?*

Nell: (pause) *I don't. . . .*

Therapist: *I mean, if that were actually true, then you wouldn't belong in this kind of setting. You'd belong in a residential treatment facility.*

Nell: (offended) *Well, thanks a lot!*

Therapist: *You're absolutely welcome.* (pause; then very gently) *If you were as bad off as you just claimed to be, then you'd belong in a very different place.*

Nell: (pause) *I really don't think I'm that bad.*

Therapist: *I don't think so either. So it's important that you not get so frantic. Just stay here, with me, and I'll take you seriously.*

In her agitation, Nell was behaving in a way that narrowed internal and external awareness and contact rather than enhanced them. To continue with the inquiry at that point would most likely have increased the agitation, and the therapeutic relationship would be weakened rather than strengthened. Instead, the therapist chose to focus on Nell's agitation and escalation. The confrontation acknowledged what was going on (before Nell was consciously aware of it) and broke through the pattern. The agitation diminished, therapeutic contact was reestablished, and inquiry could continue.

Often, in addition to acknowledging a particular experience or behavior, confrontations acknowledge the underlying function of some experience or perception (Adler & Myerson, 1973). One of the effects of this kind of acknowledgment is to reduce the "sting" of the confrontation. The therapist is saying, "I see what you are doing, and it doesn't make sense on the surface, so let's look at the underlying way in which it does make sense." The client may feel criticized, which is one of the dangers of confrontation, but the sense of respect potentially outweighs the criticism. Let us listen in on Nell again. In an excerpt used in chapter 3, Nell had asked the therapist if she would hold her hand and was upset when the therapist did not respond in the way she wanted. Nell has now come back to that incident, using it to "prove" that she "always" gets rejected when she asks for something.

Therapist: *It seems interesting to me, Nell, that you focus on that one moment when you reached out and I didn't respond. . . .*

Nell: (agitatedly) *I wanted, I wanted. . . .*

Therapist: *Just a second—*

Nell: (refusing to listen) *This is not, this is not, I wanted. . . .*

Therapist: *May I finish, please? And about five minutes later, you reached out again and I did respond. And I held your hand. Do you remember that?* (pause) *So I think there's some importance for you in your hanging on to the experience of my not responding, which outweighs everything else. Is that possible?*

One of the most important guidelines for effective confrontation is that clients must experience them as being for their benefit. That is, the confrontation must not be experienced as a put-down or a "Gotcha!" Rather, even though it may be something they would prefer not to hear, clients still sense that the confrontation is an acknowledgment, that it is intended to help, and that the therapist still cares and respects and believes in them. When this rule is followed, a confrontation can be useful in two ways: it can break through a set of behaviors, perceptions, or beliefs that are interfering with the client's ability to use the therapeutic relationship; and it can call attention to an underlying dynamic, a need not met, that prompts such behaviors or perceptions or beliefs. It follows, then, that the confrontation will be successful to the degree that it accomplishes one or both of these purposes. If the confrontation fails to change a dysfunctional pattern and leads to no new awareness, then it has not worked; the therapist needs to repair the therapeutic disruption (Safran et al., 1990). He or she may need to question whether the basic guideline has been followed: did the client experience the intervention as intended to enhance his or her welfare? If, on the other hand, the client's behavior (including self-report of internal events) does change, if awareness does expand, or if the client indicates by affect or words that new understandings are now present, then the confrontation was successful. Nell's work is a case in point. She has had a difficult time; the therapist's comments were painful for her to hear. Yet, at the end of the session—after one last distortion and confrontation/acknowledgment—she finds herself in a new place:

Therapist: *You are quite willing to do bizarre, crazy-looking things in order not to go into that confused, scary place inside yourself.*

Nell: *Yeah, but not too bizarre.*

Therapist: *Everybody's got their limits, of course.*

Nell: (pause) *Yeah, I've done some pretty bizarre things. To me.*

Therapist: *Like those fantasies of me going away, not staying with you, and then getting real scared. And making whatever I do fit those fantasies—that kind of bizarre stuff?*

Nell: (talking faster) *You didn't—you don't believe me. You're like all the rest of them. You don't believe me. You're not taking me seriously. I must be crazy, because you're not taking me seriously. Makes it real scary. . . .*

Therapist: (calmly) *And as long as you choose to sit there and imagine my not taking you seriously, you get caught up with that and you don't have to look at what you're really scared of.*

Nell: (pause) *Yes . . . . yes. . . .* (begins to cry)

During her childhood and adolescence, Nell experienced the cumulative trauma of neglect and emotional abandonment. Her way of coping with this trauma was to become extremely competent intellectually, while staying confused about and often unaware of her emotional experience. Now, in adulthood, she recognizes that this solution has cost her the ability to enter into full and rich relationships. Like a child with a scraped knee, she cries out for help even as she frantically tries to protect herself from being touched. Her words and her tears at the end of the above intervention are evidence that the therapist's caring confrontation has broken through and quieted the frantic child trapped inside. Acknowledging the discrepancies between what she is doing and what she needs to be doing (and is capable of doing) has served as a preparation, readying her for the next step of her work.

Validation

In a sense, we have already begun to talk about the process of validation. Validation is a special case of acknowledgment; it is the acknowledgment of the significance of the client's experience (Wolf, 1988; Kohut, 1977). We can all remember times when our feelings or wants or behaviors were acknowledged but not validated. The other person certainly recognized what we were doing, and maybe even how we were feeling about it, but they missed the underlying purpose, the reason behind the behavior or the belief that supported the feelings. Or, if they did understand the "why" of what we were doing, they discounted its significance: "Oh, you're just upset" or "You just think you want that; you'll change your mind." Even though our experience may be acknowledged, without validation that acknowledgment is hollow and unsupportive.

Validation is particularly important in the therapeutic setting, because clients themselves may not be sure of the significance of what they are experiencing (Bach, 1985). They may be afraid that their experience is wrong, or crazy, or that the therapist will judge it that way. They cannot see the forest but only the trees: caught up in the immediacy of the experience, they cannot step back and examine what is going on for them. They cannot conceive of an alternative way of understanding or responding to their situation. Therapists, in contrast, although involved in and committed to the therapeutic relationship, are not so enmeshed in the client's perspective. Their job is to provide a different perspective, underscoring the significance of what is going on for the client and validating it.

Validation conveys to the client that the therapist takes him or her seriously. Nell, in our previous excerpts, got hold of an important concept, but she got it backward. If the therapist *had* believed that Nell was crazy, she would have taken it very seriously indeed. It was because Nell was clearly *not* crazy that the therapist could focus beyond the bizarre content, validating the behavior by underscoring its significance in protecting Nell from the terror of her "scary place." In simultaneously acknowledging and validating what she is doing, the therapist helps Nell to appreciate, rather than being ashamed of, her phenomenological experience. The therapist invites her to attend to the underlying purpose of her behavior.

Therapist: *That bizarre stuff is actually well-rehearsed material. "I'm incompetent; I can't think; I'm crazy; I'm this and that. . . ." That's well rehearsed.*

Nell: *Yeah, it is. Real well rehearsed.*

Therapist: *It must be getting boring, Nell. Don't you feel bored with it?*

Nell: *Sure, I do.*

Therapist: *That's what I thought. It's getting boring.* (pause) *What are you thinking?*

Nell: *What am I thinking? You just put into words what's been in a secret part of my mind. It's boring. I'm sick of it.*

Therapist: *And yet you continue to do all the fantasizing and presenting yourself as a very troubled woman, for a very important reason.*

It is particularly important to validate behavior and experiences growing out of relationship issues between client and therapist. Clients often have strong feelings toward a therapist. They want to do well, look good, gain the therapist's approval. Or they are angry, or disappointed, or fearful that the therapist will see too much and understand them too well. Or maybe all of the above! The involved therapist resonates to these feelings, but he or she also knows that they go well beyond the client's response to the current situation. They are part of a whole pattern of being-with-others and of perceptions, expectations, hopes, and fears that grow out of old relationships and affect current and future ones. Validation of their significance can be straightforward or subtle; it can point out similarities directly or promise opportunities for the client to discover them for himself or herself. Martha, for example, is therapeutically sophisticated, understands the concept of transference, and recognizes that her feelings toward the therapist have to do with much more than simply the therapist herself. The therapist, attuned to Martha's level of understanding, promises to participate fully in her exploration of the feelings and the enactment of their significance; the promise is a powerful validation.

Martha: *I think I'm scared about telling you that I've got a negative reaction to you. I actually like you on a personal level, but at the same time I'm really scared of you, because I remember having a really bad time with another therapist, and she didn't like me, and she wouldn't admit it. . . . She had really bad feelings about me.*

Therapist: *Bad feelings about you?*

Martha: *Oh, yes. And when I told her, she just said to me, "Well, I'm not your screwed-up mother." So, I know you're not my screwed-up mother, but I still find your eyes very scary.*

Therapist: *Well, maybe you need me to be?*

Martha: *Yeah, maybe. . . .*

Therapist: *So perhaps I've got to learn how to become your screwed-up mother, at least part of the time.*

Martha's "screwed-up mother," according to her description, was unreasonably and invariably critical. Martha described growing up under a constant barrage of put-downs and discounts, thinly disguised as suggestions for her own good. Introjecting this critical attitude, she found herself as an adult living with an equally persistent internal critic, constantly second-guessing herself and finding herself "not good enough." The self-criticism did serve an important function for her, however: she used it to drown out her memories of being belittled and degraded. As long as she was distracted by her self-criticism, she didn't have to acknowledge the pain and terror of that old relationship; she could deny it and lock it away, as if it had never happened. The problem with this strategy, however, was that it resulted in her splitting off and locking away a part of herself. In the piece of work that began with the excerpt above, Martha was able to trace through the connection between her self-criticism and the early abuse and begin to reclaim her lost emotional memories. At the end of the session, the therapist suggests that Martha continue to validate the significance of her self-criticism. Instead of trying to get rid of it, as a useless holdover from childhood, she is invited to recognize its function and use it to continue her therapeutic work:

Therapist: *Now, what if you were to spend the next day or so noticing every internal criticism and thinking about every one as a defense against the memory of the abuse?*

Martha: *Yeah. . . .* (sigh) *Yeah.*

Therapist: *Whatever critical thing you just said to yourself . . . just now . . . if you just said, "This criticism is a defense. What would I be remembering if I weren't criticizing myself?" All those criticisms you've been talking about. "What would I be remembering if I weren't telling myself I should replace the mug I broke?"* [Just before the session she had broken a coffee mug.] *"What would I be remembering right now, as I put on my new shirt, if I didn't tell myself I'm so fat?" Or whatever the nature of the criticisms might be.*

Martha: *Yeah. . . .*

Therapist: (pause) *What are you experiencing?*

Martha: *Much better. Yeah, much better. Better with you, too.*

Therapist: *Were you expecting that I would be critical of you, too?*

Martha: *Yes. Yeah, I was.*

Therapist: *So either one, whether it's what you hear from yourself or what you expect to hear from someone else, might serve the same function.*

Martha: *I'm going to stay with that and think about it.*

We have been talking so far about the effect of validation on the client: how validation helps the client to understand and use his or her experience, rather than feeling confused or shamed by it. But validation is also important in helping the therapist maintain genuine involvement. Looking at our clients' resistant behaviors as a way of communicating what they do not yet fully understand, and as attempts to protect themselves in an uncertain and often-threatening world, allows us also to appreciate what they are trying to do (Tustin, 1986). It inoculates us from impatience, irritation, and frustration. It allows us to truly value the client— and without that genuine sense of valuing, our involvement would be shallow at best and phony at worst. Validation, then, works in both directions: as we help our clients to appreciate their process—the function of their responses, if not the responses themselves—we help ourselves to do the same thing.

Normalization

Many—perhaps most—clients come to therapy with a deep sense of shame about who they are and what they do. They have been told, implicitly and often explicitly, that there is something wrong with them (Lewis, 1987; Morrison, 1986). Their need for therapy is often taken as a proof that they are sick, or flawed, or are doing something wrong. The purpose of normalization is to counter these self-denigrating beliefs and to help clients to realize that their behaviors and their internal experiences are normal and predictable responses to their life situation, their environment, and their genetic makeup. They are not "responsible" for all of the barriers they have had to overcome, either those that they were born with or those imposed upon them externally. Anyone (if they were clever enough) might have been expected to respond to those barriers in a similar way. Our clients, no matter how odd or bizarre their behavior may seem to an outsider, are essentially normal people who have had to cope with abnormal problems.

Shame is a powerful reason to hide, split off, and deny parts of self. If there's a part of ourselves that we believe to be bad, selfish, ugly, pathetic, or unlovable, then we are not about to show it to anybody else, and we will try not to look at it ourselves. Better to shove it underground and pretend it's not there (Goldberg, 1991; Wurmser, 1981). Learning that we are not much different from anyone else, that we are not some sort of grotesque object, makes it much less difficult for us to reown those denied and disavowed parts.

Normalization often takes the form of simply giving information. Clients need to be told—sometimes again and again—that what they are doing and feeling is a normal human response. They need to be told about other people who respond in the same way that they do. Melinda, for example (the woman who was offended by the therapist's comments about "stuffing" her little doll), experiences a great deal of shame over both her obesity and her internal experiencing. Her shame gets in the way of using the therapeutic relationship optimally. Early in therapy she would not allow herself to be fully in contact with the therapist and to experience the acceptance and caring that she yearns for; rather, she alternately argued or held herself back so as not to show her neediness. Now, after many sessions, she is discouraged because she still feels needy and still wants nurturing from the therapist. The therapist comments on how she has changed and how her needs are both important and normal:

Therapist: *What I hear is that you're making a lot of changes. And you still need me. You're getting there, but you're not there yet. It's working. So keep at it. Keep doing what you need to do, Melinda, and trust that. It's not enough yet.*

Sometime it will be enough from me, but for the rest of your life it won't be enough from everyone.

Melinda: *Say that again?*

Therapist: *At some point you will have gotten enough from me, but that doesn't mean you've gotten enough, period, and you'll never need to be taken care of again in your whole life. People always need that. Everybody needs a sense of being cared for by others.*

Some clients carry an enormous invisible load of guilt and shame about past behaviors. We have all done things we are not proud of, things we would prefer others did not know about. But for these clients, the past behaviors (or thoughts or feelings) are more than just something that happened, something we are sorry about, something we wish had been otherwise. They are monstrous and unforgivable. They loom over the psychic landscape, casting a grim shadow over anything good the client does. In the client's mind, those past experiences can never be made up for; he or she is spoiled beyond the possibility of repair. Not only does such a belief make it useless to try to change ("Why bother, if I'm never going to be any good anyhow?"), but it also, paradoxically, provides a means of avoiding pain. By concentrating on the shame of the past—so well known, so familiar, the discomfort almost comfortably consistent and predictable, like a decrepit old armchair—they can avoid dealing with the present. Like the soldier with an intentional self-inflicted wound, the pain of what is known is preferable to the terror of the unknown. Normalizing what such clients have done or felt can be a struggle; nobody gives up a defense easily! However, when the normalization succeeds, it allows them to let go of that unchangeable past and focus their energies on the changeable present.

Here again is Nell. Earlier in this chapter, we saw how desperately she defended herself from exploring her inner experience. Even though she knows, intellectually, that she needs to revisit that inner space, she is still terrified of it. In this segment, she continues to wrestle with her fear. Here, though, the tactics have changed: instead of becoming frantic and acting "crazy," she uses her guilt about how she treated her mother, when her mother was dying, as a way to avoid awareness. Notice how she maintains the defense and how the normalization invites her to let it go:

Nell: *In my mother's last months of life, I ended up being like a mother to her, and I didn't want to, and I guess my perception of it was I wasn't a good mother. . . .*

Therapist: *Well, that's. . . .*

Nell: (speaking faster) *And I began to get angry, because I wasn't getting taken care of by her, and I was very—*

Therapist: (trying to be heard) *Nell, wait. Listen—*

Nell: (even faster) *—I was very hesitant to get back to her, I didn't want to visit...*

Therapist: *—Nell, lest you go and make this a big deal for yourself, probably almost everyone your age has had a parent die—and it wasn't exactly the same story—but at the dying of their parents, they've had to parent their own parents. And most people never could do it good enough, because there's nothing you can do to take away their aches, their pains, their depression, and the fact that they're going die.*

Nell is neither unique nor monstrous in her reaction to her mother. She is just like many other people dealing with dying parents. If she is willing to accept this normalization, she can move out of the defense of self-castigation and on to something more therapeutically productive.

We have seen that normalization can be a straightforward giving of information so that the client can put his or her own behavior in perspective. In less straightforward situations, it allows the therapist to enter into the client's conflict between the desire to grow and change and the fear of giving up old defenses. It is this conflict that keeps so many clients stuck: unwilling to move back and yet terrified of moving forward. In such situations, normalization underscores the discrepancy between the client's exaggerated view of himself or herself as unusual and different from most others, and the reality of ordinary human responses. In our final example of normalization, Allen is trying to let go of his learned ability to dissociate and to turn off his feelings. He now recognizes that dissociation has become an automatic response and that it is no longer helping him.

Allen: *And I have . . . when I get moved towards crying and let myself be vulnerable in other ways, fear and sadness maybe and those kinds of emotions, then I can, I can do that.* (snaps fingers) *I can just stop myself from getting into . . .*

Therapist: *From getting into?*

Allen: *From getting into my vulnerability, sadness, and fear, neediness. I can. . . . When I was first in therapy it was traditional Gestalt therapy. The therapist would tell me to breathe more into it. So I'd breathe more into it, and it would go away. "You stop breathing; you're stopping your sadness; breathe more." So I'd breathe more and dissipate it. It's like I can do anything to dissipate. So, I'm well practiced at it.*

Therapist: *Including this conversation?*

Allen: *I can use anything, yeah. . . . Which, um, well, I'm undoubtedly proud of in some ways, I think. . . . There's an element of me that. . .*

Therapist: *. . . That would be culturally consistent for you, given how you were schooled.*

Allen is the product of a boarding school education. At the age of 8, he was shipped off to live subject to the whims and cruelties of his schoolmates and with little or no kindness or protection from adults. Dissociation was a practical solution back then: if one could not escape the unbearable, it made sense to lose the ability to feel it. The therapist's last statement provides a normalization to forestall the self-criticism that Allen is about to move into: if one is behaving in a culturally consistent way, then it is harder to criticize or blame oneself for that behavior.

Presence

You may be wondering how normalization, which would appear to be a more or less standard therapeutic technique, fits into the notion of therapist involvement. In part, it is because normalization has the same effect on the therapist as validation: it helps the therapist to keep perspective and to avoid getting lost in the client's struggle. In a larger sense, though, all three of the factors we have been discussing—acknowledgment, validation, and normalization—emerge naturally from the aspect of involvement that is most important of all: presence.

Of all therapist behaviors, presence is both the most intuitively obvious and the most difficult to define. It is, in the vernacular, "just being there." But it is more than simply contactfulness (although there is very little about contactfulness that is "simple"). It is contactfulness combined with therapeutic intent and therapeutic competence (Yontef, 1993). It is "being there" for and with the client, committed to that client's welfare, able to put one's own feelings and needs into the background, yet emotionally responsive to all that occurs. It uses all the information gained through inquiry, and all the sensitivity of attunement, to maintain a genuine, caring, and responsible relationship within which the client can find the support he or she needs in order to grow and change.

How does one learn to be therapeutically present with a client? How can we cultivate this most important of all therapist qualities? Irving Yalom (1980) has suggested that, just as a master chef goes beyond a written recipe by adding "throw ins" that cannot be completely specified, that which characterizes excellent therapy also defies specification. The difference between true presence and mere technique may be a "throw in," born of an I–thou relationship (Buber, 1958) and incapable of being reduced to words.

Having acknowledged that possibility, however, it is still possible to talk about some of the ingredients of presence. The chef's gourmet creation does have ingredients, all of them necessary, and without which the "throw ins" would be useless. Let's look, then, at the basic ingredients of presence, keeping in mind that each therapist must put them together with his or her own unique "throw ins" in order to create a full therapeutic relationship.

Contact

We have already talked at some length about the nature and importance of contact, but it is so central to the notion of presence that it bears reviewing once more. Contact, you will remember, involves awareness of both internal and external events. It requires a kind of shuttling process, moving from what is going on inside myself to what is going on with this client (Perls et al., 1951).

External contact is the basis of attunement. The therapist decenters from his or her own feelings and needs, putting the client squarely in the foreground of awareness (Stolorow et al., 1987). But external contact alone would remove the therapist as a person from the relationship. Our history, our needs and sensitivities, our values, and our training and experience, are all part of who we are as therapists and are essential to our therapeutic presence (Bollas, 1987). Attending to them allows us to respond as a genuine, unique human being rather than as an empty "professional" shell.

It's a balancing act, this business of contact. It is more than back and forth, more than just the shuttle. Each aspect feeds, informs, and enhances the other. My awareness of the client evokes a response in me that is flavored and deepened by my awareness of my own internal process. Each potentiates the other, and together they create a climate that invites relationship.

Interest and Curiosity

Presence includes a genuine interest in the client's intrapsychic and interpersonal world and a genuine curiosity about what will reveal itself next. People are fascinating; they present the most complex phenomena that science has ever attempted to understand. We become therapists in part because we feel that fascination. Without it, our therapeutic presence would be a façade, a "have to be here" rather than a "want to be here." When we are (temporarily, for whatever reasons) uninterested, the client senses it; safety and support and respect are dissolved by the hypocrisy of pretending an interest that does not exist; and the relationship begins to crumble.

Not only does the client sense the absence of genuine interest, but the therapist needs that interest and curiosity in order to motivate all of the other therapeutic activities. Interest creates the therapist's immediate reinforcer: whatever the client does and says is rewarding in that it both satisfies and whets the therapist's genuine interest. Interest enlivens us; curiosity makes our inquiry more than just a therapeutic technique. Even though the primary goal of inquiry is the client's growing awareness, we too benefit from the client's answers. We experience satisfaction as we understand more and more of what the client's inner world is all about. Everything the client does or says gives us new things about which to be curious and interested.

In this example, the therapist has just told Melinda that she still has the little doll Melinda gave her a year earlier. Notice how the therapist's interest and curiosity serve both to move the inquiry along and to convey respect and caring to the client.

Therapist: *What's it like for you, Melinda, to know that I still have it?*

Melinda: *It's real nice. But I was so, just scared to even ask if you did. I don't know what—oh, I get frustrated with myself for being so scared to ask that, you know?*

Therapist: *And when I said it for you, so you didn't have to ask, how was that?*

Melinda: *It was so, a relieved feeling. Such a . . .*

Therapist: *Relief from what?* (pause) *See, that's one of the things that I've never really appreciated about you. I understand the dynamics. But I don't have a sense of really appreciating your scare.*

In another example, Allen is invited to talk about his father. He does so, at some length. Rather than being bored or impatient, the therapist is genuinely curious about Allen's history. Staying with the details, allowing herself to resonate with them, allows the therapist to make an inference about Allen's internal process—an inference that moves the work to a new level:

Therapist: *So what was it like, growing up with him?*

Allen: *Well, his background was that he was born out of the country, because his father was in the army. And then when the war broke out, my father was nearly 5 years old.*

Therapist: *1940?*

Allen: *No, 1939. And my father couldn't speak English, because he'd been brought up by a local nanny, which, I mean, this is my supposition, since my mother tells me more than my father does about it; but presumably he didn't have much contact with his mother. And also, me knowing his mother, who's now dead, but recently; she couldn't cope with anyone who was ill; she hated it. And I imagine that was, that relates to his own feelings about being sick, or incapacitated.*

Therapist: *Hmm.*

Allen: *I'm piecing lots of stuff together. And my mother agrees with my, my sense, as well, that he was must have had a deprived first few years, around his mother. Um, then they came back to England for the war, and I think maybe stayed at home for a bit, and then he was straight off to prep school and off to boarding school and military boarding school, which is, I think, harsher than most boarding schools.*

Therapist: *They're not very compassionate?*

Allen: *That would be the last thing.*

Therapist: *Then you grew up in a military environment?*

Allen: *No, not really. Except for him. I mean, the harsh atmosphere around him, he created his own . . .*

Therapist: (pause) *I've never heard you speak of him before.* (pause) *No wonder, in that kind of atmosphere—not environment, atmosphere—you would want to retreat to a safe place inside. That harshness was there not just at school, but at home too.*

Allen: (softly) *Yeah.*

Openness

Interest, genuine and spontaneous, helps the therapist to maintain presence. Its usefulness to the client, however, will depend upon whether the client can actually sense it and feel it in the therapist's responses. And in order for this to happen, the therapist must be willing to have his or her internal responses known. He or she must be open, expressing feelings and wishes, satisfactions and disappointments. Openness involves spontaneity and genuineness; it is the opposite of hiding behind a veneer of detachment and "professionalism."

But wait—we said earlier that professionalism is an important factor in involvement. How can we have it both ways? The answer lies in the therapist's commitment to and genuine interest in the client's welfare. When we are truly focused upon the client, our professionalism is not a veneer; it is a part of who we are at that moment. It provides the necessary limits and boundaries, so that our openness—like everything else we contribute to the therapeutic relationship—is in the service of that client's growth. We can be open and spontaneous precisely because we are professional, because we know that our inner experience will be appropriately centered on the client.

Remember Melinda and the little doll? She was startled and offended when the therapist said that she had thought about stuffing it with cotton so it would look more like Melinda. That comment was a part of the therapist's openness and willingness to share her thoughts and feelings with Melinda. When Melinda expressed her hurt, the therapist did not offer a pro forma apology or become defensive; instead, she shared even more of herself and her feelings:

Therapist: *When I told you that, I was trying to communicate to you the inadequacy of this little doll—when I was cleaning out my desk, I saw it right there, and I was looking at it, and my memory of you was of you being much rounder than the little doll. And I thought, huh, I ought to fatten it up. I felt that as a connection, between me and you.*

Melinda: *Hmm. Well, maybe that's nice. I mean, I hear what you're saying. . . .*

Therapist: *And if I'm going to have something that would remind me of you, I'd like it to be more reminding.*

Openness serves to dissolve the client's fantasies of being rejected or of disappointing or boring or shocking the therapist. Virtually all clients have these fantasies, born of their memories or their own internal self-criticism. They are painfully aware of what they dislike in themselves and find it difficult to imagine that anyone else could fail to dislike it, too. The response they imagine in the therapist is so strong and seems so inevitable that it often outweighs what the therapist actually says. Melinda is no stranger to this sort of fantasy. We have seen her struggle with the therapist's response to her little doll, early in her work. Later in that work, she reaches a point at which she is ready to describe an experience that was difficult and painful for her. She asks, very hesitantly, if the therapist will hold her hand as she talks; she needs the support of physical contact, but she is ashamed of needing it and afraid of the therapist's rejection:

Melinda: (looking at the floor) *I think I'd like you to hold my hand. . . .*

Therapist: *I would be glad to do that. And, wait just a second. . . .*

Melinda: *What?*

Therapist: *I was going to suggest that you say that again, looking at me this time.*

Melinda: *Oh.*

Therapist: *You didn't want me to notice that?*

Melinda: *It's just so hard to do. . . .*

Therapist: *Um-hmm. And it's so important to do. So that you can see my response.*

In spite of all of her issues around shame, Melinda managed to find the courage to ask the therapist for the kind of support she needed. She feared, though, that the therapist would be reluctant to give it to her, would give it grudgingly, and would think less of her for asking. For the therapist to simply tell Melinda how she felt about Melinda's request would probably have had little effect on that fear; Melinda knows that words can be used to conceal as well as reveal. But a nonverbal response bridges the communication gap; it is much more likely to be genuine, and thus it is more emotionally impactful. As she sees the caring and respect in the therapist's face, Melinda is more likely to accept her support without distorting or discounting it. In that moment, she makes contact with the real person rather than with her own projected, disapproving fantasy.

Vulnerability

One cannot be truly open without being vulnerable. In choosing openness, the therapist inevitably risks being touched, impacted, and changed by the client. Like everything else in a relational therapy, vulnerability is a two-way street: the client is invited to become vulnerable—that is, to allow himself or herself to be both defenseless and impacted—with the therapist, but in order to make that invitation credible the therapist too must risk.

Letting oneself be vulnerable *is* a risky business. It is risky for the therapist, who cannot remain defended and untouched behind a shield of professional detachment. It is doubly risky for the client: not only is the client encouraged to become vulnerable to the therapist, but also to a therapist who, because of his or her own imperfections, will not always be objective, clear, or correct. In short, a vulnerable therapist is a human therapist, with all the possibilities for error that such humanness entails. The therapeutic relationship captures in microcosm the paradox of all human relationships: one must have contact with others in order to become fully oneself, but that self is inevitably changed through the very contact that allows it to survive.

Let us come back to a more practical consideration of therapist vulnerability: how is it expressed, and how can it be contained and directed to best serve our clients? As to the first question, our vulnerability is expressed through our openness. A therapist who is truly open to his or her inner experience will, naturally and inevitably, reveal the ways in which he or she is impacted by the client. When sadness, amusement, or impatience, for example, arise in the therapist, they are welcomed into awareness. In the example to follow, Nell has been evading and defending for some time. In spite of the therapist's understanding the function of these behaviors, she is beginning to feel frustrated. She cares about Nell, and because she cares she is vulnerable to this sense of frustration: she wants to help; she wants to see Nell break through the old patterns, and Nell is not doing so. Rather than pretend an acceptance that she does not (at this moment) experience, the therapist challenges Nell:

Therapist: *Why, Nell, I don't believe what you just said. And if you want to change your life, then you're going to have to take some risks with me.*

Nell: *I thought I just did.*

Therapist: *I don't experience you taking risks with me. I experience you wanting to do with me the same pattern you do with everybody else. You just got done quoting yourself: "I'm going to do with you what I do with my mother." Now, if you want to change your inner life, you're going to have to take some risks with me and treat me differently than Mama. Are you willing to be different with me?*

This example is particularly interesting in that it leaves open the question of whether the therapist's challenge was motivated more by her own level of frustration or by what she thought would be most helpful for the client. However, by posing that question we set up an artificial dichotomy. The therapist's expression of her own feelings, her own vulnerability, *is* most helpful for the client. Technical expertise without caring and vulnerability would be sterile and unproductive; caring and vulnerability without therapeutic competence would be self-indulgent and unethical. Together, each informs and guides the other; the combination is the essence of the therapeutic relationship.

Appropriate therapist vulnerability walks a fine line between not caring enough (too little vulnerability, so that the client feels personally unimportant and the relationship becomes a sham), and overinvolvement or overcaring (so that the client feels intruded upon or unsafe). At some level, and at some times, clients need their therapists to be larger-than-life magical creatures who, untouched by human fallibility, are completely focused on and invested in the client's experience. At other levels, and at other times, clients would like their therapists to stop being therapists, to be friends, to lean on the client and need help themselves for a change. The fine line of appropriate vulnerability marks the tension between these opposites (Kohut, 1971). As is so often the case, much of this blending of opposites is conveyed nonverbally, by voice tone and body language. Dan, for example, began a piece of work by talking about his feelings of abandonment when the therapist, for personal reasons, had to leave a previous session early. He went on to talk about other instances of feeling abandoned and how painful they were for him. In this short exchange at the end of the work, the therapist expresses genuine caring and real vulnerability to Dan's pain and real regret for her own share in creating it. But at the same time she sends a clear nonverbal message that she is still in charge of herself, very much aware of Dan's therapeutic needs, and fully intent on responding to them professionally.

Therapist: (very long pause) *Is there anything more you want to say?*

Dan: *I don't think so.*

Therapist: *I'm sorry I left you. And I was glad that you said, "Don't do it again."*

Patience and Consistency

A few paragraphs ago, we saw an example in Nell's work of the therapist's expression of frustration and impatience. Such expressions, indeed, such internal responses, must be the exception rather than the rule if the therapist's presence is to be therapeutic. Momentary digressions to the contrary, therapeutic presence is characterized by patience, consistency, and reliability (Khan, 1974). Engendered by genuine respect for the client's efforts to deal with his or her unique situation, the therapist's patience provides an arena in which the client can work through his or her own personal drama, reenacting the old patterns in a new and different context. It puts old wine into a new wineskin (just the opposite of the Biblical parable!). And in this new context, this new container, the old pattern looks and feels and works differently.

Nell provides us with a poignant example of an old pattern that is no longer effective. We have seen her trying, in many different ways, to protect herself from her inner emotional confusion. She is caught in a trap that seems to be closing down on her: the very part of herself that she needs to reclaim is the thing she most fears. In the example to follow, she has summoned all her courage to peek hesitantly into one corner of her hidden self and then flees back into the painful familiarity of her dramatic defenses. She sits with her eyes closed, crying for help:

Nell: (in a tiny voice) *I'm alone. . . . I can't go back, and I can't go in.* (cries, then calls loudly) *Where are you?*

Therapist: *Right here, same place you left me when you closed your eyes.*

Nell: *I didn't leave you; you left me. I'm all alone!*

Therapist: *That's nonsense.*

Nell: (speaking quickly) *If that's nonsense, then I'm nonsense! And my ideas are nonsense, my mind is nonsense, my ability to try and sort this out is nonsense! Don't tell me I'm nonsense!*

Therapist: (calmly) *Will you be quiet and listen to me?*

Nell: *What?*

Therapist: *Be quiet, and listen to me.*

Nell: (angrily) *Don't tell me to be quiet!*

Therapist: (reasonably) *I can tell you to be quiet.*

Nell: *That's not respectful! I want respect from you.*

Therapist: *I thought that was the most respectful thing I could say. Be quiet and listen, so you can hear me. You couldn't hear me when you were talking over me.*

Nell: *Don't tell me to be quiet; I can't listen to you like that.*

Therapist: *Yes, you can. . . . You were busy chattering, so you didn't get to hear what I had to say . . . that I'm right here, and won't leave you as you go inside.*

There is no rejection here, no abandonment. The therapist offers consistency, interest, commitment, and contact. She refuses to be distracted by Nell's anger or her other self-protective maneuvers. She continues to do her job: to remain present, fully herself, open and aware of both Nell's behaviors and what those behaviors evoke in her.

Professional Intent and Ability

We asserted, at the beginning of this chapter, that professionalism provides direction and boundaries to the therapist's sense of commitment to the client. Now we would like to look at a slightly different facet of professionalism: the intent and ability that contribute to the quality of therapeutic presence.

Professional intent has to do with why the therapist is here, in relationship with this person at this time in this place. The person might be someone who, in another situation, could have been a friend or a colleague, with the bonds of friendship or collegiality cementing the relationship. Conversely, it might be someone whom the therapist would not be at all likely to choose for a friend. But here, in this therapeutic setting, such matters are irrelevant. The therapist's sole purpose for being here, now, is to provide therapy for this client; that is the basic bedrock of the relationship. And it is the bedrock of therapeutic presence: *therapeutic* presence, presence in the service of therapy.

Professional ability, too, colors the nature of therapeutic presence. We therapists can no more divorce ourselves from our abilities than shed our skins. We know what we know, see what we see, and believe what we believe; and our knowledge and perceptions and beliefs inevitably shape our interactions with others. But more than that, given professional intent, our knowledge and perceptions and beliefs will affect our conscious and deliberate choices of which course to follow, which of many responses to share, and what suggestion to make or withhold.

There is another essential aspect of professional intent and ability, an ineffable something that we might call "groundedness." Groundedness allows the therapist to be impacted by the clients' emotions, to be moved by their experiences, but yet to maintain his or her own psychic balance. Clients need us to respond to their fear but not be frightened by it; they need us to respect their anger but not become defensive; they need us to feel compassion for their pain but not be overwhelmed by it.

Grounded, focused, and clear as to professional intent and ability, the therapist's contactful presence calms and contains an agitated client; it encourages and energizes a passive one. In both cases, presence serves to relax fixated defenses so that needs and feelings and memories can be reclaimed and reintegrated. Of course, the client seldom is aware of these details. When we do our work well, the client's experience is of our warmth, respect, and confidence and of our willingness and ability to help untangle the knots and put together the pieces that the client has been unable to deal with alone. As in this short exchange with Monica, we do not do our work with great fanfare or lengthy explanation; we just do it. It is who we are and why we are there.

Monica: *I've got to tell you about what's going on for me. It's really scary; this is just going to come out the way it is and I don't know if it's going to make any sense, okay?*

Therapist: *Well, that's my job.*

Monica: *It's all so crazy; it doesn't make sense.*

Therapist: *My job is to make sense out of it. It's your job just to spit it out.*

Or, again with Nell, who has finally recognized her self-defeating pattern but does not know how to break out of it:

Nell: *How do I stop doing this?*

Therapist: *By listening to me, making what I see at least as important as what you imagine. . . . Let me be important to you. Let what I say matter—matter enough that while I'm talking, you stop thinking about your scary thoughts for a minute. And think about what I'm saying. Then you can think about you. And I'll listen. . . . We can take turns; then you don't have to do it all alone.*

Presence, then, communicates intent and ability. It is an expression of the therapist's full internal and external contact, carefully framed so as to facilitate the client's discovery of self in relationship. It allows the client to experience the therapist's responsibility, dependability, and reliability. It says to the client, "I'm here, I care, and I'm big enough and strong enough and knowledgeable enough to deal with what needs to be dealt with." Presence emerges from contact, contact that shuttles from internal to external awareness and back again, and that invites the client to learn to do the same. It is more than just what the therapist says or does and more than simple communication: it is a kind of communion, the essence of the "in between" of relationship that both separates people and binds them together.

☐ Affect

We have referred many times to the nonverbal aspects of client–therapist interactions, those aspects of the therapeutic exchange that cannot be captured on the printed page. Nowhere are these nonverbal aspects more important than in the expression of affect. Affect is transactional and relational in its nature; it is a communication that demands a corresponding, reciprocal affect—an involvement—from the other person. When appropriate reciprocal involvement is present, therapeutic movement can occur: relational needs are responded to, awareness is enhanced, and there is an invitation to full contact (Erskine, 1994/1997b).

For the client, affect is often a bridge to awareness (Jones, 1995). Clients who have learned to shut off or to distort emotional expression in order to avoid the discomfort of experiencing the intensity of their feelings have—by definition—split off a part of themselves (Guntrip, 1968; Federn, 1953/1977). They can no longer be all of who they are. It is a costly solution: they have had to give up significant parts of their spontaneity, their flexibility, and their capacity for intimacy, and they must also use increasing amounts of psychic energy in order to maintain the split. Their inability to feel emotions is a defense against emotional overstimulation. It protects them from having to deal with the denied parts of themselves, but it does so at the expense of contact, wholeness, and relationship.

A significant function of therapeutic involvement is that it sensitizes us to client affect and allows us to provide our own emotional resonance for the expression of that affect. Through involvement, we help the client to access, experience, and integrate emotions. This does not mean that we teach our clients to spew out their feelings regardless of the situation. It means, rather, that they learn to experience the totality of their emotional response and find a workable balance between expression and containment of that response. One way in which this is accomplished is by helping clients understand the function of their emotions. Encouraging the client to go ahead and escalate and to fully express and even exaggerate whatever emotion is on the surface helps him or her not only to go beyond that surface into a deeper level of awareness, but also helps the client appreciate the way in which the surface experience may have been used to maintain emotional disavowal.

Here is Paul, who was ignored by his father during most of his childhood. Throughout his adult life, he has kept the grief and despair of that abandonment locked away and out of awareness. Whenever those feelings threaten to break through, he becomes angry instead. The effort needed to control the anger then blots out and overrides his pain.

Paul: *I've been thinking a lot about my Dad—how he left me to fend for myself, which I did, because I had to.*

Therapist: *Would you like to make yourself angry right now?*

Paul: *Make myself angry? I'm already angry.*

Therapist: *I know that. Would you like to make it more, in order not to feel the loss?* (pause) *That's a question, not a statement.*

Paul: *If that, if that will let me get through all this, then I'll do it, I'll trust your . . . .*

Therapist: *I wasn't giving you a prescription. I don't have a prescription. What I was watching was, with each sentence you were tightening your jaw more.*

Paul: *Yeah.*

Therapist: *And I was wondering if you were making yourself angry to have more sense of power or control over a rather helpless loss.*

As his work continued, Paul did allow himself to become angrier. With the therapist's support, he expressed the fullness of that anger. Eventually, as the result of expressing, rather than controlling, his feelings, he was able to access what was hidden below the anger. Paul ended his work softly and sadly:

It's about what you could have been, Dad. Just between you and me. You didn't do anything about it. Oh, God! I want more, more, more. You could have been enough. I never got enough of you. I never. I never. Ever. (begins to cry)

Paul's work is not completed with this discovery of deep sadness, of course. He has much to explore and many more emotional memories to own and integrate. But the door is open now; he is much more aware of his relational needs, of the loss of relationship with his father, and of the way in which he escalates his anger in order to control that awareness.

An adult who ignores a child, or uses put-downs and sarcasm, is likely also to shrug off the importance of such transactions: "It wasn't anything; s/he is just too sensitive/demanding/fussy. . . . " So the incidents pile up and are never fully acknowledged or dealt with. In therapy, awareness of this accumulation of discounts can be overwhelming: frightening, painful, infuriating, more than one can bear. Involvement allows the therapist to resonate to the client's fear and pain and frustration and to respond by providing an environment of safety and security. With such encouragement—literally, providing courage—the client can access experiences that have been blocked from awareness. Like the physical therapist who encourages a patient to stretch cramped and constricted tissue in spite of the pain, the psychotherapist helps the client to move through pain into growth and healing. Here is Cheryl, the woman whom we met in chapter 2, protecting herself by numbing one side of her body and curling up into a ball. She is so terrified of her emotional memories that she feels physically sick. Yet the compassion and support of the therapist help her to move into her fear, and to gradually recover her awareness of her childhood experience.

Therapist: *You're tightening yourself up for some very important reason. There's an experience that that position was meant to cope with.* (pause) *And it's real important that those iron claws* (pointing to her fingernails digging into the sofa) *keep that thought from coming to your head and that you keep your body tense and that a small portion of you wants me to come close, but mostly you want the control. That's all important, what you're doing. So just close your eyes for a minute, and just go back to that. . . .*

Cheryl: *To "I don't know"?*

Therapist: *. . . to any of those things, because I'd like to take your scare seriously.*

Cheryl: (pause) *That's, that's weird. When you say, "I'd like to take your scare seriously" it's as if I can't believe it.*

Therapist: *I'd also like to take your care seriously.*

Cheryl: (crying) *I heard that one.*

Therapist: *May I take both of them seriously?*

Cheryl: *Yeah. But . . .*

Therapist: (pause) *Your scare, so I can provide the care?*

Cheryl: *Yes, and still there is—there is so much in the way, to believe, or to . . . to trust . . .* (crying) *as if I always have to think of both sides. Like for you, and for me, it's not as if something is sad, and I can just take it in. It's always that I have to find out the person that is meaning that, and it goes on and on and on and I will always find something to, to, to maybe criticize or to say, oh, this cannot be because . . .*

Therapist: *Such a busy mind.*

Cheryl: *Yes . . . it's afraid.*

Therapist: *Let yourself go back inside. See if you can just relax that busy mind. If you can't, will you just tell me about it . . . just remember, my first comment was to let your body be the boss.*

Cheryl: (pause) *I feel sick, like throwing up, and just tearing everything out.*

Therapist: *Okay. I'll clean it up. . . .*

Different kinds of affect demand different kinds of response from the therapist, and the wrong response will be taken (often accurately) as evidence that the therapist is not appropriately attuned to and involved in the relationship. Attunement, combined with therapeutic intent and competence, almost guarantees that one's first impulse of affect will be the right one and will resonate with the client. Let us look at the major categories of affect and the corresponding reciprocal therapeutic response: attunement and involvement, in harmony.

Anger

An angry person needs to be taken seriously. Anger is a serious business. An angry client demands a therapist who is attentive to that anger and does not discount it or retreat from it, but meets it with respect. Alice, for example, has been trying to stifle her anger for years. She had a miserable childhood, filled with poverty and isolation. She has given her children all the things she never got for herself—and they hardly notice. She is furious with them and, at a deeper level, even more furious with her own parents for their neglect; yet, as a strongly religious woman, she is ashamed of her anger.

Therapist: *Would it be okay with you, Alice, if I respect how angry you are? Even if you try to pray it away? Even if you try to push it into the past? . . . If I recognize that each Easter egg for your children is, just for a fraction of a second, an angry reminder? And each toy at Christmas, each bowl of oatmeal, each clean-smelling sheet on the bed is a moment of anger that has to be shut off? Is that close to your experience, Alice?*

Alice: *I'm ashamed of that.*

Therapist: *Oh, please don't be. Just tell me about it. There's no need to be ashamed, because I'm not going to put you down for being angry, and you don't have to be ashamed in my presence. Now I understand that you made a promise to yourself to forgive them. But I wonder if that promise was there because you are so angry at them.*

Sometimes a client's anger is directed not toward someone else but toward the therapist. The therapist may be a stand-in for the target of the anger or may in fact have done or said something that the client is angry about. If the latter is the case, the therapist's response to anger must include some act of correction, perhaps an acknowledgment, an apology, or a reparation. Without such correction, the client may not feel that he or she has been taken seriously; whatever affective response the therapist may have, it will feel contrived and insincere to the client.

No matter whom the anger targets, the first and most important response of the therapist is a sense of his or her own solidness, groundedness, and capacity for holding (Fromm & Smith, 1989; Winnicott, 1965). It is the response of "I take you seriously" combined with "I'm not frightened or hurt by your anger" that allows the client to continue. If the anger is at someone other than the therapist, the therapist may need to share the anger/outrage—to experience his or her own anger at what has happened to the client (Erskine, 1997, 1993/1997). But the therapist's anger must not exceed the client's anger. If it does, the client may switch to defending the target person from the therapist or fear that the therapist is too angry to hold and contain the client's own emotion.

In the following example, the client, Althea, has been talking about her aging mother and how the mother has become neglectful of her personal appearance. She compares this with her grown daughter's behavior. Althea is a very proper woman, for whom doing "the right thing" has been an enormously important way of coping with the alcoholism in her family of origin. "What will people think?" is her greatest means of control. She was angry when her daughter violated her rules of "proper conduct," yet she is hesitant to voice that anger.

Althea: *They had school uniforms with knee-length skirts. And she'd roll hers over so that it was a mini skirt.*

Therapist: *That's the way the kids then liked to wear their clothes. . . .*

Althea: *But she'd cut the sleeves off things, and just wear it!*

Therapist: *I understand. And what concerns me is the effect of that on you. For you, it's like seeing your mother wear her cardigans inside out when she was drunk.*

Althea: *Yeah. . . . Yeah!*

Therapist: *It's like your daughter marrying someone whose family drinks. It's the shame that you're always fighting against—trying to be a proper, dignified woman, with a family that looks good, that you can be proud of, and hold your head up high about. And she throws the whole thing into the garbage bin for you!*

By expressing her own indignation, resonating to Althea's feelings, but careful to calibrate that expression to Althea's level of intensity, the therapist demonstrates that she does indeed take this client's anger seriously— and is still focussed on the client's needs. It is the combination of feelings and focus that is important here: the therapist's genuine affect, channeled and expressed in the service of the client's well-being.

Fear

The client who is afraid requires the therapist to respond with affect and action that communicate security. A part of this response involves simply acknowledging the fear without being distracted, dismayed, or frightened oneself. To recognize, understand, and appreciate the fearfulness of a situation, without being afraid of it yourself, is perhaps the most supportive and calming response that can be made to a frightened client. Here, for instance, Dan is talking about a group therapy session some months earlier, in which Rebecca disagreed with Richard:

Dan: *My first memory of that was that time in group when Rebecca told you that you had made a mistake with me.*

Therapist: *You mean, that she corrected me in some way?*

Dan: *Yes. And I thought the sky would fall in.*

Therapist: *You must have been awfully scared.*

Dan: (his face crumples) *Oh, yes!*

Therapist: *Are you remembering something right now?*

Dan: *Uh-huh . . . Like, my Dad. . . .* [He begins to relate an incident from childhood.]

There is no single word that fully captures the essence of this kind of security-making responsiveness. Even calling it "security-making" is misleading, because that terminology suggests that the therapist intends to do something for the client. But the security-making response is not about how the therapist is going to fix things for her client—it is about the therapist's internal experience and her feelings. It's similar to saying, "I'm sorry" when told about something bad that happened to someone. It is not an apology, nor is it taking responsibility for what happened, but rather it is an expression of one's feelings about the other person's pain. The therapist's "security-making" response is her feeling about his fear, rather than her intention to fix it or her suspicion that he cannot handle it. It says that she understands, she is impacted, she feels protective, and she cares.

Sadness

The reciprocal response to sadness is compassion, not pity, which implies a one-up, one-down relationship between client and therapist, but compassion, feeling with. In compassion, the therapist moves from experiencing the client's sadness empathically to experiencing his or her own caring about what is happening with the client.

Compassion is perhaps the most difficult response to illustrate in print, because it is never fully and almost never even partially expressed in words. It is a tone of voice, a gesture, a sigh, or a touch of the hand. In the following excerpt with Martha, the therapist only says nine words. In those words, and all that goes with them, there is a world of compassion:

Martha: *. . . and the teacher said "move backwards," and we were six little girls, and I was at the back of the line. So instead of turning around and walking for-*

wards, we all shuffled backwards. And I fell over something, and hurt my arm. And I went home and told them what had happened, and she said, "You stupid child for walking backwards." And I said, "But my arm hurts." And she said, "Oh, stop making a fuss." And in the night I was crying and she told me to stop making a fuss and it would get sorted out tomorrow. And it was broken.

Therapist: (tenderly) *Oh, Martha. . . .*

Martha: *And I've always been scared of making a fuss, because I don't. It's like, I carry so much, and I don't talk about it much. And when I hear people talking about their dark, scary places, I thought, "My dark place inside isn't scary. It's. . . ."* (long pause)

Therapist: (very softly) *Is it where you go to be safe?*

Perhaps the reason why compassion is most easily expressed nonverbally is that words tend to dilute or dissolve this most tender of feelings. We have listened to, transcribed, and searched through literally hundreds of hours of therapy, and inevitably the most compassionate moments are the most quiet ones as well. Words can acknowledge the moment, they can provide some evidence that the therapist really does understand what is going on for the client—but beyond that, they just get in the way. Here is Martha again:

Martha: (quietly, pensively) *One of my favorite places is going to the zoo. And, I haven't taken a day off and done that for a long time. I can wander between the cages and go and talk to all the different animals.*

Therapist: *Much like when you talk to your cat in the morning.*

Martha: *Yeah. I really enjoy a few minutes in the morning, just bending down and talking to my little white cat. It's nice.*

Therapist: *She doesn't talk back.*

Martha: *She's lovely, I really like her. She comes to me and, and it's really nice.*

Therapist: *You're crying inside, aren't you?*

Martha: *I do enjoy some quiet times with people. I really appreciated Paul this morning, when he talked to me.* (tear rolls down her cheek)

Therapist: *Those little things are so special. You allow yourself so little.*

The compassion is not in the words. It is in what surrounds them.

Joy

All of therapy is not fear and sadness and anger; there are joyous moments as well. Laughter can be healing; joy gives us the courage to deal with the less pleasant business of life. Joy is multiplied through being shared, and it evaporates when the other person in the relationship refuses to share it. As the children's song says, "It's just like a magic penny, hold it tight and you ain't got any; lend it, spend it, pass it around, and you end up having more. . . . " Sharing joy, though, requires that the other person participate. The reciprocal response to a client's joy is the expression of one's own genuine pleasure and enjoyment.

Dan: *I make presentations [at] about seven or eight conferences a year, with large audiences. That's something I take pride in.*

Therapist: *Wow, Dan!*

Dan: *And when I speak, I always get five out of five evaluations that are good.*

Therapist: *Congratulations! That's worth being proud of.*

Dan: *And I enjoy it, because I like communicating. I like to teach. . . . It's really hard for me to say that. I shouldn't boast, and it feels like boasting.*

Therapist: *You allow me to feel proud of you, by letting me know.*

When we are not preoccupied with our own problems, enjoyment and pleasure are usually easy to express. After all, we like this client, and we are truly glad when he or she does well. It is only if we have some sort of mistaken notion that therapy should always be serious business, a belief that moments of pleasure distract us from our "real" purpose, that we are likely to deny clients our shared, reciprocal pleasure in their joy. As with anger, though, we must take care that our joy does not exceed theirs. Too much intensity, and we will be experienced as insincere or out of contact.

Reciprocal joy and pleasure can be expressed through laughter, through echoing the client's words, and even through gentle teasing. Most of all, of course, it is expressed through the therapist's smile. And when the reciprocal response is genuine, the smile comes naturally.

Therapist: *What do you like about you?*

Allen: *Um, well, I like that I'm sensitive, as well. Passionate. Um, I like my ability to think, understand things. And, I like now, I like being able to come alive much more now—enjoy life, for the first time. It's really different, because I felt depressed for many, many years.*

Therapist: *Motorcycling. . . .*

Allen: *Motorcycling* (chuckle), *yeah. . . .*

Therapist: *Are you alive when you motorcycle?*

Allen: *Um-hmm.*

Therapist: (grinning) *You should see yourself!. I saw you one day, dressed in leather from head to toe.*

Allen: *I remember.*

Therapist: *You looked so great!*

☐ Inquiry, Attunement, Involvement

You have seen that, in discussing the therapist's reciprocal responses to affect, we are talking not only about involvement but about attunement as well. Particularly in the realm of affect, the two are inseparable: when one is involved, one is also likely to be attuned; and attunement cannot really be achieved in the absence of involvement. Sensing the client's affect (attunement) and valuing and responding to it (involvement) are like the yin and yang of Chinese philosophy; each fits with the other, and together they form a whole. They are the harmony, the rich and ever-changing background to the tune sung by the client. And inquiry is the countertheme, the other tune that weaves in and out, sometimes echoing and sometimes evoking each passage and each melody.

Inquiry, attunement, and involvement give substance and dimension to the technical practice of psychotherapy. Without them, we are simply going through the motions. With them comes the possibility of a true relationship, of the contact that nourishes that relationship, and the integration that emerges from it.

When the therapist inquires skillfully, is attuned to the client's rhythm/affect/cognition/developmental level of functioning, is involved in the client's process, and brings appropriate skills and knowledge to the therapeutic relationship, there are a number of specific outcomes for the client. In this final section, we will look at examples of each.

Safety

When a client is supported within an appropriate therapeutic relationship, the client feels safe. With that sense of safety, he or she can begin to relax old defensive patterns and expand awareness. The sense of safety is essential, because, to the client, letting go of defenses means risking the loss of self. It is as if the therapist, who is attuned to the client's fear and is emotionally present in the relationship, says, "I'll hold on to your boundaries; I'll take good care of them; and I'll make sure you get them back when you've finished your work."

In this excerpt, Monica had begun to scream and then stopped herself:

Therapist: *I'm right here. So you just go ahead and scream out whatever you need to scream out.*

Monica: (screaming) *OOOOOHHHH!* (breathlessly) *Are you going to leave me?*

Therapist: (matter of factly) *No.*

Monica: *If I go crazy you're not going to leave me?*

Therapist: *No. You're not going to stay crazy, you're just going to go crazy, right?*

Monica: *Right.*

Therapist: *And after that, we'll talk about what happened.*

With this invitation, Monica regresses again and begins to scream for her father to come help with her drunken mother, a demand that she never dared make as a child. The safety provided by the presence of the therapist allowed her both to reexperience the walled-off memory and to respond to the situation in a new and healthier way.

New Awareness

If, as Fritz Perls asserted, awareness is contact and contact is health (Perls & Baumgardner, 1975; Perls, 1973), then enhanced awareness must be the hallmark of successful therapy. Awareness, in this context, means more than understanding. It is not so much a cognitive phenomenon as it is a reclaiming of self (Perls et al., 1951). There is a recognition quality to a new awareness; there is an intense clarity, a sense of "I've always known this; why did it take me so long to find it out?" The involved, attuned, and inquiring therapist helps the client to stay with his or her process until the "aha" occurs, refusing to settle for explanations that only go skin deep. Monica, with the safety and protection of the therapist, was able to "scream out" her distress and, later, her demands for father's help. Near the end of the session, she begins to try to frame her work in psychiatric and diagnostic terms. The therapist intervenes:

Therapist: *Now, Monica, you're about to analyze this thing to death.*

Monica: *Do you want to stop working with me?*

Therapist: *No. And my wants aren't what's important here. What I want just isn't real important. I think you spend so much of your life figuring things out, that maybe this would be one of those occasions where it would be good just to experience it.*

Insight

Understanding, analyzing, and figuring it out can all be important, as long as they enhance rather than interfere with awareness. Cognitive understanding provides a frame for affective experience and heightened awareness. It gives the client words to attach to the experience, words that allow him or her to put it into context and to recall it to memory later, when the old patterns threaten to reestablish themselves.

Therapist: *And I've noticed that every time someone in your therapy group has worked on something emotional, that has any similarity to your own situation, you heavily identify with it.*

Nell: *With them, instead of with me, because there's no me? Because there isn't a me?*

Therapist: *Or, in search of "who am I?"* (pause) *Did you ever see the children's book about the little duck who gets separated from his mother? And he goes around and says, "Who am I?" "Are you my mother?" "Are you my mother?"*

Nell: *Which I used to think I knew.*

Therapist: *Who you were?*

Nell: *Yeah.*

Therapist: *A conglomerate of roles?*

Nell: *That was how I defined me. But yet, if I think about it more, more to your comment, I do have a sense of me. It's emerging, but there is a sense there. I'm beginning to understand. I remember writing in my journal yesterday, "I know what I know." It may not be a whole heck of a lot, but it's coming. I'm learning about me.*

New Behaviors

There's a story about a teenager whose mother sent him to a psychotherapist because he insisted on putting his food on the floor and lapping it up like a dog. After months of treatment, the boy was still eating his food off the floor. When his mother, exasperated, asked why he had not gotten anything from treatment, he replied, "Oh, yes I have—I still eat off the floor, but now I know why I do it!" The moral, of course, is that significant internal shifts seldom take place without some external sign that something has happened. If there are no observable changes, it is unlikely that therapy has been effective. Although our focus in this book tends to be on affective and relational issues, we nevertheless believe that behavioral change, too, is an essential outcome of successful therapy. Sometimes our clients show us exactly what those behavioral changes are and how they grow out of the therapeutic milieu. Loraine, for instance, ends an intensely emotional piece of work:

Loraine: *I think I'm just sad. I feel caved in and sad.*

Therapist: *Sad about. . . . Can you say more about that?*

Loraine: *I'm sad I can't fix things for my Mom, because I love her.*

Therapist: *Tell me more about being sad that you can't fix it.*

Loraine: *I'm sad that she's sad. I'm sad that . . .*

Therapist: *And the job she assigned you? The impossible task she looked for you to do?*

Loraine: *Oh, yeah. Make Mom's life okay.*

Therapist: *Did you want to do that job?*

Loraine: *I think I wanted to, originally. Yeah. It was . . . gave me a way to be with her. I thought the only way I could be with her was to take care of her, to carry her shit*

Therapist: *Yeah, that's important.*

Loraine: *To carry her shit. I don't want to carry it. I can't do it any more.*

Therapist: *But how are you gonna show her how grateful you are?*

Loraine: *Well, I mean, I am grateful. But I'm not grateful for that. She can have it. I feel like I filled up her buckets all the time, and she just dumped them out. She said, "Here, this is empty again." And I filled it up again. And I can't do that anymore.*

Therapist: *So what you're gonna do is. . . .*

Loraine: *What I'm gonna do is . . . take care of myself. And I'm gonna tell her when, when she's coming in on me, when her expectations are not real, when I can't meet her expectations. I don't know if she's gonna get it. I don't care if she only did have an eighth-grade education; I think she's smart as hell.*

Therapist: (pause) *Anything more to say about that?*

Loraine: *I don't think I need to say anything else right now. I think I need to do it for real. In life. I need to sit at the kitchen table with her, and just be clear. And not cave in. And not go away.*

And she did. Some months later, Loraine reported having two conversations with her mother, in which Loraine was clear, expressed what she wanted, and asked her mother what *she* wanted in the relationship. By the end of the second conversation, Loraine sensed that her mother was also different. She was less demanding and more interested in Loraine.

When everything is working as it should, it all comes together—the therapist's inquiry and attunement and involvement and the client's sense of safety and enhanced awareness and understanding and new behaviors. That's when the magic happens, when contact in relationship seems to transcend the rules of ordinary human interaction. The experience is transforming and numinous (Bollas, 1979). It is healing in the true sense of the word: it is making whole.

Clayton: *I think my parents messed up. Really messed up.*

Therapist: *So what about taking your life back?*

Clayton: *Well . . . since both of them didn't do what they were supposed to do, uh, I better look for other people to help me do it. And I did find some people; I don't think they would have approved of them originally. . . . I never told my mother I was in therapy—all the years she was alive.*

Therapist: *She didn't need to know?*

Clayton: *No, she didn't. She wouldn't understand anyway. I mean, I'm sorry. . . . I think my mother was smarter than I give her credit for . . .*

Therapist: *So if something would cause her to be anxious, what would she do? Dig at you somehow?*

Clayton: *Yeah. "Why would you want to do that?" she would say. "Are you trying to tell me I didn't do a good job?" Yeah, Ma, you're right. You didn't.*

Therapist: *So what do you know now?*

Clayton: *She really didn't do a good job. She didn't even know who I am. She didn't know me. She knew the outside. . . . No, but you know, she would say in her cards to me, "I pray to God that He gives you anything your heart desires."*

Therapist: *What a wonderful prayer.*

Clayton: *I wish that she would have carried it out. That's the part that bothers me.*

Therapist: *You mean that* she *would give you your heart's desire?*

Clayton: *Yeah. . . . So I think she recognized she didn't do it, as she once thought. Maybe her prayers could* (he begins to cry). *. . . I've worked so hard to get my life back again. . . .*

Therapist: *And what have you achieved—what have you got, out of all that work?*

Clayton: *I have freedom that I never had before. I can think for myself, choose for myself. Somebody loves me. And I have accepted it. And she knows that now— she finally knows the inside of me. . . .*

Therapist: *And the prayers. . . .*

Clayton: *All those cards, birthday cards and Christmas cards, that she sent. . . . "Hope God gives you what you desire . . ." It's happening, Mom. And I think that makes her happy, that I'm beginning to learn something she didn't teach me. That it's okay to be alive!* (cries quietly)

CHAPTER 5

Relational Needs

Our discussion of therapist involvement has taken us inevitably into the "in between,"—the domain that belongs exclusively neither to therapist nor client. Involvement is a part of the *relationship* and thus belongs to both participants. Having said this, however, we return to the fundamental tenet of psychotherapy, the ethic that supersedes all others: everything about this relationship and what happens as it develops is in the service of the client. Even though our therapeutic involvement has to do with our own genuine feelings and responses, and even though it is a process of the in-between, it is nevertheless focused on the client's welfare.

There is an apparent paradox here. The involvement of the therapist must be genuine and spontaneous; it emerges much more from attitude and affect than from technique (Yontef, 1993). Nevertheless, as we have seen in chapter 4 and will see again in the following pages, we can hone and direct our involvement, and we can train ourselves to use it in increasingly therapeutic ways. But how is this possible? How can one "train" a response and have that response remain genuine? Doesn't "directing" our involvement make it something less than spontaneous?

The resolution of the paradox can be found, again, in that fundamental notion of therapeutic intent. When I am with a client, my intent, attention, and interest are focused on that client's growth and well-being. I have made the choice to be in the relationship in that way for that purpose. My therapeutic involvement always emerges from the client-focused context (Jordan, 1989). Water in a stream is free to cascade over a log, swirl around a boulder, or linger in an eddy, but it stays within the streambed, so my involvement can be free and spontaneous within the streambed of therapeutic intent.

Involvement is about the therapist: how he or she feels, thinks, and responds to the client. It is about the client: how he or she perceives that the therapist is invested in and impacted by what happens in the relationship. It is about the in-between, the interplay between two human beings, the dance of interpersonal contact (Sullivan, 1953). It is about relationship needs felt and relationship needs met. In fact, this latter notion—needs felt and needs met—is so important a concept, so central to a therapy of contact-in-relationship, that it has been given a whole chapter to itself.

The types of needs that can be met through relationship are, of course, special kinds of needs (Erskine, 1998). They differ from the needs for survival and for physical safety that Abraham Maslow (1970) placed at the base of his hierarchy of human needs. They are the needs that grow out of human interaction and, conversely, feed and nurture the interaction. They are what I need and want from you when I am in relationship with you.

All people experience these relational needs; they are present in every relationship. Indeed, they can be said to define a relationship. Certainly no relationship is possible in their absence: if I need or want nothing from you, nor you from me, then we will simply not form a relationship. Relationship needs are not only needs of childhood or needs experienced by adults who have been relationship starved as children. They are components of relationship that are present every day of one's life. Most often they are out of conscious awareness, but they emerge into awareness when they are not attended to: they become more intense, more pressing, and are experienced as a kind of emptiness, a longing, or a nagging loneliness. If the deprivation continues, the person may become frustrated, aggressive, or angry. Further disruption can result in a loss of energy or of hope and can reinforce script beliefs such as, "No one is there for me" or "What's the use?" These script beliefs form a cognitive defense against full awareness of the pain of needs not met (Erskine, 1980/1997).

Although relational needs are present for both participants in every relationship, the therapeutic relationship is unique in that the needs of the therapist must be secondary to those of the client. The client's relational needs are in the foreground; the therapist's needs are in the background. It is the "streambed" of therapeutic intent that keeps it so: the therapist's conscious choice, motivated by genuine interest, to decenter from self and attune to the client (Stolorow et al., 1987).

Attunement to client needs is essential, but it is not sufficient. Relational needs must be dealt with in the therapeutic relationship. The therapist must not only be aware of the client's relational needs, but also must meet them with his or her own appropriate affective response. This appropriate affective response—genuine, spontaneous, caring—is the essence of a contactful relationship. It is what brings the relationship to life and puts flesh on the bare bones of technique.

The concept of trauma, acute and cumulative, has come up several times in previous chapters. With the introduction of the concept of relational needs, we can now understand how trauma damages and how cumulative neglect can often be more damaging than the acute trauma of outright abuse. For it is not the trauma itself that causes lasting damage to the human psyche, but the absence of a healing relationship during or after the trauma that does so (Erskine, 1997, 1993/1997). And a healing relationship is one in which relational needs are recognized and responded to appropriately.

Every person, and especially every child, requires relationships in which the other person is reciprocally involved. That is, we require the contactful presence of another person who is sensitive and attuned to our relational needs and who can respond to them in such a way that the need is satisfied (Clark, 1991). As therapists, we most frequently find ourselves working with clients for whom such relationships have not been consistently or dependably available; thus our clients experience not only the needs of the here-and-now relationship, but the unmet relational needs of the past as well. And our attunement and response must extend beyond the needs of the present to those old unmet needs.

Often, in fact, the intensity of old unmet relational needs overshadows and distorts the relational needs of the here-and-now therapeutic relationship. The therapist who is unaware of human developmental patterns (Basch, 1988), or of this particular individual's relationship history, may be surprised or confused when such needs are expressed. A client may ask for some input from the therapist or (perhaps more commonly) accuse the therapist of not having provided something, and the request or the accusation may seem to come out of nowhere. It does not come from nowhere, though; it is the echo of a cry for relationship that has been ringing in the client's psyche for years of deep internal loneliness and need (Bach, 1985).

We must not assume, though, that all of the client's intense relational needs are holdovers from early relational deprivation: relational needs are present throughout the entire lifecycle from early infancy to old age. People do not outgrow the need for relationship. These needs are the basis of our humanness.

Through patient and gentle inquiry, the therapist can tease out the threads of relational need and trace them to their origins in the present and in the past. He or she is sensitively attuned to the client's experience, is able to respond with genuine and appropriate affect to that experience, and so reweaves the threads into a tapestry of new and healing relationship.

Understanding and recognizing the nature of relationship needs and the reciprocal affective responses that they call for is clearly an important facet of therapeutic skill (Basch, 1988; Wolf, 1988; Kohut, 1971, 1977). The fully attuned therapist needs to be aware of the relational needs that are foreground for the client at any given time and respond appropriately. In the remaining pages of this chapter, we shall discuss eight of the most commonly encountered relationship needs and how the reciprocal response can be demonstrated therapeutically.

☐ Eight Relational Needs

Security

As mentioned earlier, Maslow (1970) posited that the needs for survival and safety are basic, primary, and usually must be met before a person is able to experience and respond to any other type of need. We find an echo of this in the relational need for security. In a relationship, too, one needs to survive and be safe. It is important to know that the relationship is a place where we can be who we really are, where we can show all of ourselves without fear of losing the other person's respect and affection for us. Contact is a risky business. Allowing oneself to be open and aware of all one's feelings and thoughts and memories, and sharing that openness with another person, means dropping defenses and being vulnerable to whatever response the other person may offer. The first, tentative moves toward relationship usually involve testing out whether this vulnerability will be honored and whether the other person is truly safe to be with.

If the relational need for safety is present in ordinary social relationships, how much more important it must be in the therapeutic setting (Fromm & Smith, 1989)! In therapy, the client is specifically invited to become vulnerable, to open more and more to self and to the therapist, to become aware of and share thoughts and feelings and wants and memories that have been hidden away for years. With each emerging awareness and each recovery of a disavowed or repressed experience, the need for relational security is experienced with new intensity.

Security requires more than verbal reassurances from the therapist. It is the visceral experience of having one's vulnerabilities respected and protected. And that respect and protection comes primarily from sensing that the therapist understands, accepts, views as human and natural everything that we experience. It is the absence of rejection or ridicule. It grows out of repeated experiences of sharing a new bit of self and discovering that the relationship is still there, still solid, still safe.

Many—perhaps most—clients fear that their inner experience will be unacceptable to others. They fantasize that their therapist will respond to them with shock, disgust, or censure. They may fear that the therapist will be overwhelmed by the intensity of their feelings and will push them away because they are "too much," or will laugh at them because they are foolish or stupid. They are hypersensitive to any nonverbal reaction from the therapist that will lend support to these fantasies. Only the genuine presence of the therapist, and the spontaneous and consistent expression of his or her regard, understanding, and acceptance, can overcome such fantasies (Rogers, 1951). Listen to Melinda, who is afraid that her wants are unacceptable:

Melinda: *Okay, you don't think that's awful? You don't think I've asked you enough times now that ought to be enough? You don't think, "Gee, Melinda, I've listened to that story a lot, how come I have to listen again?"*

Therapist: *That's your fantasy. You're telling me what* you *think.*

Melinda: (pause) *Yeah. . . . I'll say, "Gee, I'm doing it again. . . ." And you don't ever say to me, "I've already heard that, Melinda." You'd never say that. . . .*

Therapist: *Then why this imagination right now? Right now, this imagination, when I agreed to what you asked me for, has an important function.*

Melinda: *Some kind of protection. Weird protection . . . maybe, in case you should embarrass me about wanting to tell my stories. Or not; maybe that's. . . . I'm just feeling very embarrassed about what you said is a natural need and want.*

In the last two statements, the relational focus has shifted to include *valuing*, the second of the relational needs we will be talking about. Let us put that aside for the moment and come back to security.

In order to be secure in the therapeutic relationship, clients need to know that the therapist will *continue* to be the therapist and that the commitment to the clients' welfare will not waver. The therapist will not abandon them, will not decide that they are beyond help, and will not use their disclosures to hurt them or punish them. No matter how stuck they get, no matter how awful and shaming their discoveries of self may be, somehow this therapist is still there, is still on their side, still respecting and caring about and believing in them.

Although much of the security-making behavior of the therapist is nonverbal, and thus difficult to convey in a therapy transcript, some excerpts do manage to convey part of the quality of security-making. Do you remember this short passage from Monica's work, which we quoted in chapter 4? It is taken from the first part of a session that began, early in the morning, with Monica sobbing deeply. She had been awake most of the previous night struggling with memories and fantasies that were both confusing and terrifying; part of her terror was that nobody—not even the therapist—would understand what she was dealing with.

Monica: *I've got to try to tell you a little about what's going on for me. It's really scary. This is just gonna come out the way it is and I don't know if it's gonna make any sense. . . .*

Therapist: *Well, that's* my *job.*

Monica: *But it's all so crazy, it doesn't make sense.*

Therapist: *It's my job to make sense out of it. It's your job just to spit it out.*

Monica's need for relational security demands more than therapeutic intent; it also demands therapeutic competence. The therapist is not saying that she will listen and try to understand. It is her job to "make sense out of it" and, by implication, she knows that she will—with Monica's cooperation—be able to do so. Monica does not have to figure it out or feel ashamed that she cannot understand it. Her responsibility is to "spit it out," and the therapist will know what to do next.

Often, when a client is dealing with an intense feeling or is deeply regressed or both, it is the physical presence of the therapist that, even more than words, provides security. The therapist's affective attunement allows him or her to sense when the client needs to feel the physical presence of a strong, calm, respectful other. Physical touch, offered but never forced, allows the client to experience security without the need for cognitive processing or full adult awareness of what is happening in the relationship (Smith, 1997; Kepner, 1987). Here is Monica again, a bit further into the session:

Monica: (frightened; her eyes are closed) *Where are you? I need to know where you are!*

Therapist: *Here's my hand, right here.* (touches Monica's hand; she clutches at it) *Can you feel me holding on? I'll hold onto your hand; then you don't have to use so much energy to hold onto me. I can put most of the energy in. That's my hand. . . .* (Monica begins to sob) *You don't have to work to hold on; I can hold on. I'll stay here, and you'll stay here, too.*

Monica: *I'm really not going to fly away.*

Therapist: *You could even try it. I'll keep you anchored.*

Monica: *You'll keep me anchored?*

Therapist: *Yeah! Go ahead! Try and fly away.*

Monica: *And I don't have to hold on to you, you're going to hold on to me?*

Therapist: *I'm going to hold on.*

Monica, the competent adult, is surely aware that she will not sprout wings or float up to the ceiling. But for a small child whose only defense against abuse was to dissociate and "fly away" from her body, being anchored by a safe and gentle therapist (who holds onto her, rather than requiring her to do the holding on) is not only a metaphor for security, it *is* security.

Valuing

The need to be valued, cared about, and thought worthy is an obvious part of any relationship. Why would I want to be in relationship with someone who did not value or care about or respect me? But "valuing," as a relational need, goes even beyond this general sort of caring about. It has to do with being understood and being valued for that which is understood (Basch, 1988).

The idea of being understood, though, invites more questions: Understood in what way? Certainly complete understanding is not required for relational needs to be satisfied; complete understanding is not even possible. No one ever understands everything about someone else; no one even understands themselves completely! Nevertheless, one's valuing of another must be based on some sort of understanding of that other. If you do not even know who I am, what I do, or how I feel, how much is your valuing of me worth?

In a therapeutic relationship, the relational need for valuing is met by the therapist's valuing of the function of the client's words, thoughts, feelings, and behaviors (Bach, 1985). That is an extremely important concept: the therapist knows and asserts that whatever the client does has an important function, a purpose, and that that purpose is of value. The function of the behavior or response is worthwhile and worthy of attention, even though the response itself may be pain-producing or confusing or quite incomprehensible. At best, the therapist understands the function of the behavior; at worst, the therapist does not yet understand it but knows that it exists and that it is important.

Valuing, then, is very closely akin to the "validation" that we encountered in our discussion of involvement in chapter 4. It is a validation of the legitimacy of the client's needs, the significance of the client's affect, the function of the client's intrapsychic processes (Kohut, 1971, 1977). "What you are doing and feeling has a purpose," says the therapist. "It connects up. It is not just random stuff. It's important, it's telling us something; we need to pay attention to it." Here the therapist talks to Cheryl, curled into a self-protective huddle:

Cheryl: (long pause) *I can stay alone, just go inside myself, forever. Just. . . .*

Therapist: *Just?*

Cheryl: (crying) *Waiting.*

Therapist: *Has "ever" been about 40 years already? Sit there forever and just wait.*

Cheryl: *Forever. Yes.*

Therapist: *Waiting for what, Cheryl?*

Cheryl: *. . . a release? Yes, a release. Something, someone telling me, "This is not it. You don't have to be in that position all the time."*

Therapist: *You don't have to be there. You went to that position for some very important reason. So most people's words wouldn't be nearly as important as the experience that that position was meant to cope with.* (pause) *And it's real important that those iron claws keep that thought from coming to your head, and that you keep your body tense, and that a small portion of you wants me to come close, but mostly you want the control. That's all important, what you're doing, including your comment, "I don't know who Cheryl is."*

Cheryl's body language mirrors her psychological position: tense, guarded, closed. She believes that she needs permission to be in a different space and a different position. In fact, she needs more than permission. She needs the therapist to value the position she has been in for so many years, because it has an important function (Khan, 1974; Guntrip, 1968). Only when she can feel that function appreciated and can begin to appreciate it herself will she be truly ready to change.

There's a legend in rural America that the snapping turtle, once having bitten into something, will not let go until it thunders. Old, well-worn responses are like that snapping turtle; they do not let go easily. The "thunder" is therapeutic valuing: communicating the therapist's belief that a behavior, an affect, a physical sensation—whatever the client says or does or experiences—is related to something significant in his or her experience. By valuing a response in this way, we enhance the client's self-esteem and reduce the likelihood of defensive denial. Because we value the response, the client can begin to value it as well.

This is not to say, of course, that everything a client does is valuable in its surface manifestation. Some client behaviors and experiences are hurtful to the client or to others or to both. Even hurtful responses must be valued for their function, for the important purpose they serve and the important message they communicate. Ostensibly appropriate and helpful responses may have their own unaware functions and messages as well. In the following excerpt, Cheryl has been allowing herself to become aware of how deeply frightened and hurt she has been, and how she has been blocking off this fear and hurt for many years. She cries out her pain and then chokes down her sobs and says in a flat voice:

Cheryl: *I don't like to do that.*

Therapist: *Would you like to tighten up a little more? Maybe you could even tell me a joke or recite a school lesson.*

Cheryl: *Oh, it's tough. . . .*

Therapist: *Yes. It is tough. Come on; let's take a break. Shall we talk about what's in the news?*

Cheryl: *Oh, please don't. . . .*

Therapist: *No, I'm serious. I'm going to have as much respect for your way of managing and coping with this world as I am going to have for your pain. Your protection is there for an important reason: doing well in school, having a sunny disposition, telling jokes, talking about the weather. That's all been very important in your life, hasn't it?*

At first, the therapist's responses sound teasing and almost flippant. It is not until Cheryl objects that we see the sincerity underlying those responses. Cheryl's tightening up and thinking of other things has served an important protective function. The therapist will not take that function lightly; she will respect and value it.

Valuing a response also tends to normalize it, to help the client understand it as a normal reaction to an abnormal situation. Traced back far enough and deeply enough, all behaviors are concerned with meeting needs. Normal people do what they have to do to get their needs met. But when a need-meeting behavior is plastered over with rationalizations, distorted by shame and guilt and buried out of awareness, we may lose track of its survival function and begin to think of it as abnormal, unacceptable, as evidence of our own laziness or craziness. The intent of normalization is to redefine the client's internal experience of his or her behavior so that the function of that behavior can be appreciated, without shame or distortion or defensiveness.

Among the client responses that demand valuing are the relational needs themselves (Erskine, 1998). Experiencing such needs can be shaming to a client: the need feels very intense, because it has to do not only with what is happening here and now, but also with old unmet needs of the past. Clients may not be aware yet of all that old, unfinished stuff; all they know is that they need something from the therapist, need it badly and do not understand why. It is confusing and it feels out of control; the client may be embarrassed to talk about it but still, like the snapping turtle, is unable to let go of it.

How does the therapist experience and convey the appropriate reciprocal response to the client's need for valuing? It is essentially a three-step process. First, we must de-center (Stolornow et al., 1987). The client response that most needs to be valued is often not the response that the therapist had hoped to be dealing with; it may derail the treatment plan. It may involve a criticism or an attack on the therapist. The therapist's internal response is important, of course, but it is background (Erskine & Trautmann, 1996/1997). The client is and must be foreground; the need to feel validated, affirmed, and significant within a relationship involves the need that one's own experiences be more important than those of the therapist, for that moment.

Having decentered, we normalize the response. We assert what we know to be true, that the response is not crazy, or evil, or stupid; that it has evolved out of a need for self-protection; that it is the best way that this client could figure out to deal with a difficult situation. We may not yet understand how it came about, but we know enough about people in general, and this client in particular, to be sure of the general theme: this is a normal, even commendable, response to an abnormal situation. Here, for example, the therapist talks with Margaret about her habit of defending her father rather than dealing honestly with his abuse and neglect of his family:

Therapist: *You want him to give you some wonderful reason why he steals from the family. If only he could tell you how the neurons at the back of the base of his brain got all hard-wired the wrong way, and he has a gambling addiction, and that's why. And he can't help it. Wouldn't that be wonderful?*

Margaret: (sigh) *That's not a good reason.*

Therapist: *No reason's a good reason to a child. But all children try to find good reasons, anyhow.*

All children try to find good reasons. What you are doing is normal. With this frame in place, we can allow ourselves to become interested, or respectfully curious, about how the response *did* evolve and what else it *is* connected to. This respectful curiosity is the best possible evidence for the client that we really do mean what we say, that we really do believe there is some important and valuable function underlying the problem response. After all, why would we be so interested in finding it if we did not believe it was there?

When the client truly discovers and understands, right down to his or her bones, the function of a behavior or affect or physiological response, it usually marks a key point in therapy. It does so partly because this kind of discovery allows one to reclaim a denied aspect of self, to re-own what had been disowned. And it also is key because it reaffirms the therapeutic relationship and the therapist's willingness to meet the client's need to have his or her responses valued. Often, it is all mixed together; the client is not fully aware of what has happened. He or she just senses that something has slid into place, some emptiness has been filled, something is different. In this example, the therapist talks with Loraine about how she has felt responsible for taking care of her mother.

Therapist: *So, perhaps what we need to talk about is how important it's been to your sense of self, having that responsibility.*

Loraine: *Yeah, I want to do that. That's what I want.*

Therapist: *And if you give up being the family caretaker . . .*

Loraine: *I will lose my Mom. I will lose whatever semblance of approval I have from her, which is totally based on my being the family caretaker, even now.* (cries)

Experiencing her oversolicitousness of mother, the caretaking (which did not make logical sense, but which she somehow has clung to) as a child's desperate need for a relationship with a caring parent, she can finally feel the pain of her need-not-met and can weep as she reclaims that lonely, lost part of herself. And she can allow that reclaimed part to be valued by herself as well as by the therapist.

Acceptance

In making this list of relational needs, we struggled to find single-word designations for each need category. The category of "acceptance" gave us the most trouble, and we are still not satisfied with that word, because it is not just acceptance alone that one needs in a therapeutic relationship. One could be accepted, including being loved, valued, respected, and needed, by lots of people that one simply would not care to be in relationship with, much less have as a therapist. The qualities of the person doing the accepting are critical: one needs acceptance from a strong, stable, and protective therapist (Bach, 1985; Basch, 1988; Kohut, 1971, 1977).

Although the need for acceptance from such a strong and stable person is present to some degree in many relationships, it is particularly important in therapy. With the therapist, the client can reexperience old relational issues and the cumulative trauma of needs not met and (provided that those needs *are* acknowledged in the therapeutic setting) can integrate and reestablish internal contact. Support and protection and acceptance from the therapist are essential to this task; also essential is the client's experience of his or her own emotional response to that support and protection.

Each of us as children had the need to look up to and rely on our parents, elders, teachers, and mentors. We needed to have significant others from whom we could gain protection, encouragement, and information. Sadly, for many people that need was not met; and, unmet, it continues to intrude and demand and get in the way of being and becoming. With the kind of acceptance we have been talking about, the therapeutic relationship can be a place where this need can finally be satisfied. It is not just ordinary, garden-variety stability and protection and support that is needed from one's therapist, then: it is the larger-than-life stability and protection and support that a child needs from its parents.

And how do we, as therapists, meet this need? Fortunately, it is not necessary that we actually become that larger-than-life fantasized parent. All that is demanded is that we conduct ourselves so that the client can emotionally experience us in that way. In other words, we must respond to the client in ways that will not interfere with his or her emotional imaginings about us. We must act so as to allow the client to relate to us as a consistently stable, dependable, and protective parent. If the client needs such a (fantasized) parent, our behavior allows and even encourages that fantasy; if the client does not need it, our behavior is still appropriate to our professional and therapeutic responsibilities.

"Stable" and "dependable" are characteristics that pretty well speak for themselves: we are available, we are consistently focused on the client, and our therapeutic intent does not waver. We keep appointments and respond to phone calls. We are able to listen to the client without being upset or overwhelmed. We can be trusted and we can be counted on. If we are forced to do something upsetting to the client, we warn him or her ahead of time. If we make a mistake, we admit it and apologize. We are here, and we are the same person today as we were yesterday and will be tomorrow.

Showing that we are "protective" toward the client is a bit more tricky, because it requires that the client feel protected both from the possibility that we may let him or her down and from his or her own self-criticism or defensive escalation. Essentially, the appropriately protective therapist is experienced as saying to the client, "I won't do anything hurtful to you, and I won't let you hurt yourself, and I won't let anyone else that you bring here in fantasy hurt you either."

Often, when a client experiences acceptance from this kind of therapist, he or she will go through a phase of idealization. The idealization is, in part, an out-of-awareness request for protection, a request to be taken care of by someone bigger, stronger, and wiser than oneself. It is also often an echo of the idealization of parents that children need to experience: all children need a mother and father who are kind and strong and loving and wise. The therapist, involved and attuned to the client's experience and committed to his or her well-being, may be the closest this client has ever come to that kind of parenting; idealization is a natural consequence.

Since idealizing the therapist helps the client to experience being accepted by a strong, dependable, protective person, it should not (under ordinary circumstances) be discouraged or reasoned away. Like a toddler's fuzzy bear or raggedy blanket, the idealized therapist can be a powerful ally in confronting one's pain and fear. Of course, if therapist idealization begins to impede rather than enhance the work, it must be dealt with like any other self-protective behavior. More often, though, it should be simply and matter-of-factly accepted as a part of the therapeutic relationship. Dan, who talked in chapter 4 about feeling abandoned, is about to begin a piece of work, but he prefaces it with an expression of his feelings about the therapist:

Dan: *I need to say some things to you first. I need to tell you how important you are to me.*

Therapist: *Well, you've really been showing that in lots of ways.*

Dan: *Yeah. I think I need to tell you, though. I need to tell you why. I think you are, I mean, I know there's a lot of transference going on, but leaving that aside, you're the first person in my life who's been big enough inside for me to want to be like. And, um, I want to grow in my relationship with you, so I can be in an adult place with you as well as a kid, because I think what's happened in my life is that grown-ups weren't respected. They've always been, they've either been bosses or teachers. And it's not that way with you.*

Therapist: *I'm glad it's not . . .*

One of the reasons we have titled this book *Beyond Empathy* has to do with the phenomenon of therapist idealization. Carl Rogers, who introduced the concept of empathy as one of the necessary conditions of successful therapy, did not believe that it was necessary or even helpful for a client to idealize a therapist (Meador & Rogers, 1984). In his view, the therapist simply provided the fertile soil in which the client's self-actualizing ability could grow and flourish. In a therapy of contact-in-relationship, the therapist generally takes a more active role, and the client's feelings about the therapist become more than just a background for the work. In this context, therapeutic progress can be roughly characterized as going through three stages. Early in therapy, the client's feelings, needs, and concerns are virtually all that the client thinks about; the person of the therapist is clearly in the background. Gradually the client begins to use the therapist to satisfy relational needs, and the therapist begins to take over the functions of the client's script-based responses so that the client is freed to experiment with new ones. During this second phase of therapy, the therapist may become extremely important to the client and may frequently be present in the client's thoughts and fantasies. As the work progresses, the client's need for this sort of dependency diminishes, and the pendulum swings back to the center: the client is important, the therapist is important, and together they create a contact-enhancing relationship between two whole human beings.

Mutuality

The need for mutuality is the need to be with someone who has walked in your shoes: who understands what you are experiencing because he or she has experienced something similar, in real life or in imagination. In the context of a therapeutic relationship, mutuality is the need to be with a therapist who knows what it is like, either firsthand or empathetically, to feel/say/do/bear the same kinds of things the client is feeling/saying/doing/bearing. It is the need for the therapist to do more than simply appreciate the client's perspective, but also to have an affective and cognitive sense of that experience—to know what it is like to really be there and feel that way and thus be able to respond with support and sensitivity (Kohut 1971, 1977).

Part of this need arises from the natural desire to not have to explain everything fully, to be understood without words. When you are with people who have shared your experience, you don't have to tell them everything about it—they already know. Before the words are out of your mouth, the expression on their faces tells you that they are with you, that they know clearly what you are talking about. Even more important, though, is the experience of acknowledgment and validation that comes with mutuality. My reactions, perceptions, understandings are confirmed when you say, "Yes, that's how it was for me, too." This is a special kind of normalizing: not just a vague "everybody" has had this experience; but a very concrete and immediate recognition. You've had it too.

Because the therapist has had the same, or a similar, experience, the client can allow himself or herself to believe that the therapist really does understand and really does appreciate his or her experiences. Sometimes a sense of mutuality is the only route to feeling truly understood: a person who has been the target of discrimination or the victim of abuse, for instance, finds it hard to imagine that anyone without the same experience could ever know how it feels to be treated that way.

Mutuality does not require that the therapist had an experience that parallels that of the client in every detail. Often one will have experienced something that, although different on the surface, had the same essential quality that the client is describing. Or the bridge to mutuality may be a similar emotional response to some situation in one's own life or in one's imagination. The thread of similarity is what is important: the communication of "I've felt the same way," or "I've done the same sort of thing," or "I've wrestled with the same kind of problem" is key. In this short interchange with Melinda, for example, Melinda is talking about her reluctance to deal with the issue of her obesity. Even though the therapist has never been overweight, she still conveys mutuality by finding an emotional response in her own experience that is similar to Melinda's feelings:

Melinda: *It's like going to the dentist or something. You know you need to have it done, but. . . . You know?*

Therapist: *Now that example really hits home for me!*

Melinda: *Why, you don't like the dentist?*

Therapist: *I've got to go this afternoon and have a filling put in. Yeah, that's a feeling I know about. I need to do it, but I sure don't want to. It hurts to think about it.*

Melinda: *Yeah, that's it.*

When the client's need for mutuality is high, it is not helpful for the therapist to insist on focusing exclusively on the client. If the client needs to know *your* experience, needs to know if you have ever been through anything that will help you to understand what he or she is saying, and you refuse to respond to that need, the client may see you as insensitive, evasive, or phony. The client will probably be able to step past it once or twice, but eventually it will begin to disrupt the contactfulness of the therapeutic relationship.

Do you see the built-in tension between the need for acceptance, which we talked about earlier, and the need for mutuality? If the need to be accepted by a strong, dependable person is foreground, the client wants the focus to be on himself or herself, so that he or she will feel accepted and respected and will be taken care of. The need is for the therapist to be wise and protective, not for the therapist to share his or her own personal experiences. In contrast, when the need for mutuality is foreground, the client may want to know that the therapist has had to solve problems or is not perfectly wise and unfailingly competent. That the therapist is a real person who has had to cope with real life issues, and perhaps even has wept and suffered just like the client has.

Here is another example of a therapeutic response to the need for mutuality. Alice has been beginning to recognize how angry she is at her children for being unappreciative and, at a deeper level, for simply having so many things that Alice was deprived of as a child. She feels ashamed of her feelings and is more than ready to believe that the therapist will never understand and will criticize or condemn her for those feelings. At moments like this, when feelings of shame and guilt are strong, many people also experience an intense sense of aloneness: no one else has ever felt this way, been so bad, or behaved so unacceptably. The need for mutuality and confirmation of shared experience may be high. Sensing that need, the therapist frames her intervention in terms of her own similar experience:

Therapist: *But there's something your daughter can never understand. Alice, can I tell you a little story about how you and I are alike?*

Alice: *Sure.*

Therapist: *One day, back when my daughter was in kindergarten, I had a lot of things to do. But she had, the week before, complained that I was away and hadn't taken her to the park. So I rushed home to take her to the park. She said, "I don't want to go. I want to watch television."*

Alice: *Yeah.*

Therapist: *And I said to a friend, who was visiting us, "Look how ungrateful she is! Doesn't she know what it means to have somebody come and take her to the park?" And my friend's comment was "Nope. She doesn't know what it's like not to have somebody take her," because I'd been taking her to the park several times a week for several years. Nobody ever took me to the park. And my daughter will never, ever understand that, Alice.*

Alice: *That's right.*

Therapist: *My daughter will never understand how sad I felt when she wasn't grateful that I wanted to take her to the park. So there are things that your daughter will never be able to understand and appreciate about you. And I bet you get irritated with her when she doesn't understand.*

Alice's need for mutuality was addressed when the therapist demonstrated that she had indeed "been there." She not only understood Alice's feelings, but she had also felt similarly toward her own daughter. Having confirmed Alice's experience by sharing her own, the therapist could then invite Alice to take the next step: to fully own her original anger and sadness, so that they would no longer need to be defended against.

Once a client's need for mutuality is noticed, meeting it is usually not difficult. There are few human experiences that we cannot find some echo of in our own lives, and the use of metaphor, fantasy, and dream experiences can expand our repertoire further. When we can find no parallel, we simply share the closest experience we know personally, acknowledge the differences, and ask the client to help us bridge the gap between our world and theirs. More challenging by far is recognizing when the mutuality need is foreground and distinguishing between the client's need for mutuality and our own desire to be seen as understanding or compassionate or empathetic. Just as it is unhelpful to withhold when the client needs mutuality, it is also unhelpful to share personal experiences when the client wants the focus to be on himself or herself. Knowledge of the client's history of relationships and of the therapeutic relationship in particular, and careful attunement to the client's responses to what is being said, provide the best guidelines for when to share one's own experiences and when to refrain from doing so.

Self-Definition

The need for self-definition in a relationship is the need to experience and to express one's own uniqueness and to have the other person acknowledge and respect that uniqueness. It is, in some ways, the mirror image of the need for mutuality: it is the need to be different as contrasted with the need to be similar.

Expressing one's self-definition can be a hazardous business. All too often, expressing one's differentness is greeted with disapproval or ridicule. This sort of reaction is particularly common in childhood, when adults may react negatively toward a child's efforts toward independence, and in adolescence, when agemates insist on rigid adherence to the unspoken rules of the group. Children who grow up in an environment that demands conformity, unquestioning obedience to rules and norms, may never learn how to be themselves. Or they may learn that the only way to be unique is to rebel and suffer disapproval or rejection from the people around them. For such people, the need to be truly oneself *and to have that self valued and celebrated* is met seldom, if at all.

In order to meet the client's need for self-definition, the therapist must consistently support any expression of identity. The therapist normalizes the need to define oneself and is present and contactful and respectful even when the client disagrees or refuses to cooperate with the therapist's perspective or plan of treatment. Although the experience of the need for self-definition can fluctuate even from moment to moment, as can all relational needs, the client's efforts at self-definition should always be supported and encouraged. To do otherwise would be to discourage both self-awareness and interpersonal contact, which is the antithesis of what a therapy of contact-in-relationship is all about.

Beyond a constant attention to and support of self-definition, however, some clients benefit from active and explicit requests for self-defining statements. These clients are often people who have not been encouraged to express themselves freely, who have been "under the thumb" of some domineering person or environment, people for whom blending in, not being noticed, and being just like everyone else were important survival skills. Such clients often find it extraordinarily difficult to talk with pride about their qualities, their accomplishments, or even their likes and dislikes. And this is exactly what they need to do in order to become aware of their need for self-definition and to begin to satisfy it.

Therapist: *What does your father like about you?*

Allen: *This is all guesses, cause he'd never say. . . .*

Therapist: *I bet you can figure out some of the things, though.*

Allen: *I bet I can, yeah. I think he likes that I'm sensitive, and not violent, and not abusive in most kind of ways that men have traditionally been.* (pause) *Um, I think he kind of, he didn't like me separating myself from my family for so many years, but I think he understood it.* (pause) *I think now I'm coming back to being close to them, and he likes that. Um, and he likes that I've got myself a career, and a house, and the kind of practical material things that he values.*

Therapist: *What do* you *like about you?*

Allen: *Um, well I like that I'm sensitive, as well. Passionate. Um, I like my ability to think and understand things. And, I like now. I like being able to come alive much more now, enjoy life, for the first time, increasingly, having felt depressed for many, many years.*

Therapist: *Motorcycling. . . .*

Allen: *Motorcycling* (chuckle), *yeah. . . .*

Inability to meet the relational need for self-definition is often associated with depression or aggression. People who have no permission (internal or external) to define themselves as unique and valuable may become competitive and adversarial (Wolf, 1988); when these strategies fail, the next step is often one of shutting down and further restricting contact. It is interesting, in this context, to note that as Allen has begun to define himself and to express his uniqueness, he also has begun to emerge from the deadness of his depression and to "come alive."

One of the most common ways in which people avoid the risk of self-defining statements is to translate the statement into a question. "I want to do this" becomes "Do you think I should do this?" or "What do you think I should do?" "I want it now" becomes "When would be a good time for it?" Notice that questions like these not only avoid self-definition, but they also shift the responsibility for taking a position onto the other person, discounting the speaker's own ability to know and to act. Probably the most common of such translations is the "why" question: "Why did you do that?" instead of "I didn't like what you did," or "Why do you think so?" instead of "I disagree." This sort of question is the antithesis of the questions of therapeutic inquiry. Therapeutic inquiry enhances the sense of self by inviting the client to explore his or her internal experience, whereas responsibility-shifting questions often result in the loss of internal contact and diminish the sense of self. This is especially true when the questions are unanswerable: "Why won't anybody notice?" "How could she have done that to me?" "Why are they so mean?" In the excerpt below, Clayton is talking to the fantasized figure of his father, with whom Clayton has many unresolved issues. Notice how his initial self-defining statement slides into a focus on father's experience and how the therapist brings him back:

Clayton: *I am angry. I'm very disappointed that you didn't interfere when Mom was so tough and so critical of me . . .*

Therapist: *"And I'm angry that you didn't . . ."*

Clayton: *That you didn't stop her. In fact, you even believed her. Me going to college . . .*

Therapist: *Keep going, Clayton. . . .*

Clayton: *I heard that you cried for almost a week . . .*

Therapist: *"And you didn't . . . "*

Clayton: *. . . you didn't tell me. Why didn't you tell me?*

Therapist: *Make that a statement. "I don't like . . . "*

Clayton: *I didn't like that you didn't tell me . . .* (sobs) *would have felt so good that you missed me.*

Children—and adults too, for that matter—try to make meaning out of their experiences. As the therapist told Margaret, in an earlier excerpt in this chapter, "All children try to find good reasons." They seek explanations and ways of connecting a complicated and often confusing environment with something sensible and predictable. In the face of abusive, neglectful, or unfair treatment from adults, the need to make meaning can become a quest for a magical solution or an explanation that will somehow make everything all right again. Thus Clayton's "Why?" serves not only to disguise and distort his self-definition (avoiding the danger of confrontation), but also to deny the need that prompted the statement in the first place: "I need to define myself" becomes "I need to understand." Since abuse and neglect and unfairness are generally not rational or understandable, the result of such a shift is that nothing is satisfied. The question echoes off into the void, unanswered and unanswerable, and the child is left to deal with his or her pain. This is exactly what Clayton's question threatens to do; the therapist's suggestion to "Make that a statement" invites Clayton to come back to his original purpose of defining his own wants and needs, and abandoning the futile quest for an explanation that will temporarily take away the hurt.

A significant aspect of self-definition involves disagreement. Saying "No" is the 2-year-old's favorite way of telling the world who he or she is. We define ourselves, in large part, by contrasting what we are with what we are not and what we like with what we do not like. Quite frequently we do so by saying, "No" or "I don't want to" or "I won't." Fritz and Laura Perls made this process a central part of their theory of personality development, asserting that the healthy person must not only take in from the environment, but must also chew up, spit out, and reject that which is not good for him (Perls, 1944/1947). In the process of growing up, however, most children are taught that it is not a good thing to say, "No" (unless you are saying it to bad people), because it is rude, uncooperative, and selfish. An important part of the therapist's task in helping clients express and satisfy their need for self-definition, then, is to support their "No"-saying. Disagreement and "resistance" are not negative or countertherapeutic: they are important ways in which clients define themselves and should be accepted as such by the therapist.

We can easily say that the need for self-definition must be satisfied in any healthy relationship and that the therapist should accept and encourage self-defining behavior, but how, specifically, can this be accomplished? Beyond our own internal response to such behaviors (which will nearly always be conveyed to the client, whether we like it or not, by our nonverbal reactions), we can fall back on a number of general guidelines. First, encourage clients to describe themselves: "This is who I am," "This is what I'm like." Also ask them to describe what they are not: "This is not like me," "That's not who I am." Similarly, encourage them to state their likes and their dislikes; these too are a part of self-definition. Support disagreement by respecting it and inquiring about it. And, finally, be sensitive to questions or statements that are self-protective translations of self-definition and invite a retranslation. "Why?" can often be replaced with "I don't like. . . ." and "it" and "you" are frequently substitutions for "I" or "me." Invite the client to make the appropriate changes: "It's confusing" becomes "I am confused"; "Why do you act that way?" translates to "I don't like it when you act that way" (Perls, 1967).

Gradually, when these kinds of interventions are a consistent part of therapy, clients can come to believe that it really is acceptable for them to be different from the rest of the world, even different from the therapist! Difference makes contact possible: with no contrasts, there can be no coming together, only a sludgy, boundaryless mass of similarity (Perls et al., 1951). As the need for self-definition is met and as his or her individuality is expressed and acknowledged, the client can participate in a true therapy of contact-in-relationship.

Making an Impact

An essential part of any meaningful relationship is having an impact on the other person. In this context, "impacting" another means having the ability to influence the other in some desired way, to change their thinking, to make them act differently, or to create an emotional response in them. Not only is it important to have these effects on someone, but it is also important to be able to see the effects and to know that something has happened to the other person in response to one's input.

Functional, healthy relationships, which are relationships in which contact is open and free, foster growth. This is probably the most fundamental reason why relationship is such a central need for all humans. The process of psychological growth, or of self-actualization, as Rogers (1951) phrased it, requires interaction with others. And growth, in turn, both creates and arises from a sense of agency and efficacy, a sense of being able to attract another person's attention and interest and to influence that other person by changing their emotion, their thinking, or their behavior. When this sense is absent, the relationship is experienced as stifling or demeaning. Children may respond to such experiences by doing whatever is necessary to attract a parent's or a teacher's attention, even when such behavior results in punishment. But adults, too, struggle to have an impact in their relationships: "He never listens to me" and "She just doesn't care" are probably the most common complaints heard in couple's counseling.

Therapy itself is not exempt from this relational requirement: in the therapeutic relationship there must be a sense that each person can impact the other. That the competent therapist will have an impact on the client goes without saying; the whole purpose of therapy, after all, is to help the client to change in some way. The reverse is also true: the therapist must be capable of being impacted by the client. If the therapist is attuned and appropriately involved, he or she will almost automatically be affected by what the client says and does and feels. As therapists, though, we need to deal with that impact professionally and to use our response to the client in the service of that client's growth and health. The means of accomplishing this lies in the notion of the *reciprocal response*, which was introduced in chapter 3. Our response to the client, or our way of being emotionally impacted and the behaviors produced by that impact, are genuine, yet they are framed within our commitment to the client's well-being. We are not merely empathetic, feeling what the client feels. Nor do we allow our own internal experience to become foreground and dominate the interaction. Rather, the genuine impact the client has on us becomes an integral component of our concern for and caring about that client. This is therapeutic intent in its essence: the therapist, in full contact with his or her own internal response to the client, integrates that response so as to maintain and further interpersonal contact in the therapist–client relationship.

Here, then, is the therapeutic paradox once more. An affect that is genuine and uncontrived can be professional; the therapist's spontaneous response must also be therapeutically appropriate. Training, experience, and a sense of one's therapeutic competence all contribute to the integration of spontaneity and client focus. The experience of compassion when the client is sad, of pleasure when the client is joyful, of serious-taking when he or she is angry, or of wishing to provide security when he or she is frightened, are all genuine, spontaneous, and immediate for the appropriately impacted therapist. Yet all are focused on the client and are calibrated to the client's needs and to the intensity of his or her affect. Here, for example, Allen is reflecting on the changes he has made in his life as a result of psychotherapy.

Allen: *I used to write poetry, which is a way of expressing the pain I was in, and you know, I've not felt much pain, not recently, really, but I've had such a powerful expression of pain in the past. And the poetry I'm writing now is so different. . . . Yeah. . . .*

Therapist: (pause, her eyes are moist) *I think your parents should be very glad for you.*

Allen: *You really mean that, don't you?*

Therapist: *If I were your parent, I would feel so proud and glad.*

The therapist's affective response will not always be the same, or even from the same "family," as that of the client. The client's words and behaviors can affect the therapist in ways that are quite different from what the client is feeling and different from what the client expects, and still be impactful. The following dialogue occurred just before the interchange quoted above:

Therapist: *Are you feeling about what you're saying now?*

Allen: *Yeah. . . .*

Therapist: *What are you feeling?*

Allen: *Um, . . . sad . . . really sad.*

Therapist: *Because I found myself wanting to feel very proud of you, thinking that you're living proof that therapy works. Just sort of hold you up for everybody to see. . . .*

Even though the therapist's affect was not that of sadness, matching what Allen was feeling, she was nonetheless impacted by what Allen was experiencing. And her response was visible; Allen had clear and unmistakable evidence that he did have an impact on his therapist.

Many clients, particularly in the earlier stages of therapy, will not expect to have an impact on the therapist. Indeed, they may be so familiar with not feeling impactful and so conditioned to adapting to the needs of others that they avoid doing or saying anything that might make an impact. The more isolated, fragmented, and out of contact with self a client is, the more likely he or she is to fear and avoid genuine, impact-making contact with the therapist. With such clients, the therapist may need to actively solicit disagreement and even criticism from the client. The therapist can then respond by making changes to move closer to the client's demands and thus demonstrating that the client has, indeed, made an impact. The danger with such a strategy is, of course, that it may become a "strategy" rather than a genuine shift in response to the client. When we invite a client to criticize or disagree, we must be honestly open to the possibility—the likelihood—the *certainty*, that he or she has a valid point of view different from our own and that we will welcome the opportunity to be corrected. Here, Dan has been talking about his sense of pain and disappointment with his parents, who tend to be formal and correct but seldom warm and loving. The therapist encourages Dan to express his own wants, thus meeting the relational needs for both self-definition and having an impact.

Therapist: *Do your parents do what you need them to do?*

Dan: *Doesn't feel like it.*

Therapist: *Then they aren't doing the right thing. They may be doing the ceremony. The ritual, the etiquette book. But it's not the right thing for you.*

Dan: *I don't know; I don't know what the right thing felt like.*

Therapist: *You seem to know it when I do it.*

Dan: (pause) *Yeah. . . . Yeah, maybe I would know. . . .* (pause) *I feel a bit lost.*

Therapist: (pause) *Did I just miss you now? Is that how you got lost?* (pause) *You've got to tell me out loud, Dan.* (pause) *Did I just miss you, with what I said?* (Pause) *Probably just like Mom or Dad. . . . Somehow I missed you. . . . But you've got to criticize it, Dan, so I can learn from it. So I don't do that same mistake again.*

Dan was not ready to follow the therapist's lead; in fact, the therapist's questions may have confused him or taken him away from his own experience. Yet (like his parents) he was polite; he simply said he felt "lost." The last intervention above accomplishes two things: it demonstrates the therapist's willingness to be impacted (to "learn from it"), and it also calls Dan's attention to how the therapeutic relationship may be recapitulating what happened with his parents. The therapeutic "error" evoked in Dan the same sort of response that he felt when his parents isolated and ignored him in order to get him to "be good." By accepting the invitation to criticize, Dan can experience with the therapist what was not possible to experience with his parents. A cut-off aspect of himself—the part that does know how to be critical and demanding and self-defining—can begin to be reintegrated.

Meeting the client's relational need to have an impact is simple: be impacted. Let the client stir you up; let him or her make a difference to you. Care. It is simple, but it is not easy. Allowing ourselves to be impacted by the client means that we must be willing to let go of our own agenda, to change our treatment plan, to admit that we were wrong. It means that we must be confident enough to doubt ourselves and competent enough to make mistakes and recover from them. Even more difficult, we must be willing to be genuinely affected and genuinely changed. We cannot protect ourselves behind a screen of professional invulnerability. The therapy of contact-in-relationship is a two-way street: both people are there, both are real, and both are affected. Being changed by another is probably the most difficult and frightening thing we can ask our clients to do. And in order to help them do it, we must be willing to do it ourselves, in resonance with them.

Having the Other Initiate

In our discussions of the need to define oneself and the need to make an impact on the other, we focused on aspects of relationship that had to do first with the behavior of the client in the therapeutic relationship. That is, in meeting each of these needs the client acts first and the therapist responds accordingly: by supporting the client's self-definition, in the first case, and by being impacted, in the second. The client is the initiator by means of a self-defining behavior or a behavior that has an impact on the therapist or both.

Another relational need, however, is to have the other person in the relationship initiate the exchange. Any relationship in which I must always make the initial approach, always initiate, always take the first step, will eventually become dissatisfying if not painful. Although it is important that the therapist be attuned and respond to whatever the client says and does, it can also be important that the therapist begin the exchange and take responsibility for making something happen. And how does the therapist know when his or her initiation will be helpful? By being attuned to the client's needs, to the possibility that the need for other-initiation has emerged into foreground at this moment.

Taking the initiative in a relationship-enhancing way involves more, though, than attunement: it also requires genuine involvement. It means reaching out in a way that acknowledges and validates the client's importance to us. We may invite criticism, for example, not only because it is therapeutically useful to do so but also because we genuinely want to hear the client's reaction. We may take responsibility for providing direction not only because the client needs direction at that moment, but also because we honestly care about helping him or her find it. As with all responses to relational needs, therapist initiation arises from the intersection of professional competence and personal involvement. We do it because we want to and because it will be useful; and we want to be useful both because we are involved and because being therapeutic is our professional business.

It stands to reason that therapist initiation, when appropriate, will help the client move ahead in the therapeutic process. But that is not the only reason for including it in this list of relational needs. Therapist initiation also underscores the reciprocal nature of the therapeutic relationship. It makes the therapist's involvement believable. It says, unmistakably, "I care enough to take responsibility, to be active, and to take the lead for a while." When the need for therapist initiation is not met, the client is likely to conclude the opposite: "You don't care"; "I'm not important to you."

In the following segment, Melinda is unusually clear and open in expressing her need for therapist initiation. She is talking again about the little doll that she left with the therapist:

Melinda: *I don't want to have to be the one to remind you that you have her, okay? You said if I didn't bring it up, you'd never bring it up. . . .*

Therapist: *Yeah.*

Melinda: *Well, I don't want you to do that! Okay?*

Therapist: *I don't know. . . .*

Melinda: *'Cause that's not good enough.*

Therapist: *What do you mean?*

Melinda: *I want you to think of it first!*

Therapist: *But I have to think about lots of things.*

Melinda: *Well I know, but . . . I want you to think about that, too.*

Therapist: *Well, okay. . . .*

Melinda: *No, I want a "yes." I don't even want to have to ask you.*

Therapist: *You want me to bring her up?*

Melinda: *Right.*

The need for the other to initiate is present in all relationships. If you and I are in a relationship, and you must always be the one who initiates, that relationship is lopsided and you will soon begin to doubt my investment in it. If the lopsidedness continues, you may decide to end the relationship (and seek others who are more reciprocal) or you may confront my behavior and demand a change. Or, if you are less confident and have less experience with contactful relationships, you may turn inward, blame yourself for the problem, decide that you will never get what you want (and that it is probably unreasonable to want it) and try not to feel the need at all. Such conclusions are not likely to originate in one's adult experience, of course; they are old script beliefs that can be reinforced and underscored by the behaviors of one's adult friend/lover/associate/ therapist when that person is insensitive to one's relational needs (Erskine & Moursund, 1988/1997).

This latter situation is one that often has occurred among people seeking therapy. Because their relational needs have not been met, their script belief is that such needs cannot and will not ever be met. Because of that belief, they behave in ways that do not promote relationship: they restrict and distort contact both internally and externally. And because of that restriction, their needs are even less fully met, and so the cycle continues. If therapy is to be successful with such people, the cycle must be interrupted and reversed. Therapist initiation is a powerful means of doing just that. When the client's foreground need is for other-initiation, the therapist must sense that need and respond to it. This can be done matter-of-factly, without additional comment, or it can be underscored by an explanation of what is happening. Here, for example, the therapist responds to Loraine's need by offering to talk to Loraine's (fantasized) mother.

Therapist: *Would you like me to talk to her about that anger?*

Loraine: *You couldn't; you don't know her. You could. . . .*

Therapist: *That's never stopped me before.*

Loraine: *Oh, yeah . . . well, I know I need practice talking to her. I don't know if I really want to talk to her about it. But I could pretend to talk to her.*

Therapist: *Loraine, I'm willing to talk to her. And it will be real.*

Loraine: *Okay. You can. I don't know where it will go. I'm glad you offered.*

Therapist: *Then maybe for the first time in a long time, you won't have to be forced to take charge.*

Take particular notice of the therapist's comment in this example that Loraine will not have to take charge "maybe for the first time in a long time." The need to have the other person initiate is often particularly intense among people who have had to function independently and take care of themselves, and this is nowhere more true than for survivors of physical abuse or cumulative neglect. Such survivors learn, often with a great deal of pain, that the only person one can depend on is oneself, and if you wait for someone else to offer, you are likely to wait forever. For such survivors, then, it is especially important to be sensitive and to respond to the need for other-initiation, even though it will seldom be openly expressed.

Therapists who have been trained in Gestalt therapy or transactional analysis, among others, may find it uncomfortable to initiate with clients. These schools of therapy place strong emphasis on teaching clients to ask for what they want, on self-support, and on the "50% rule": if the therapist is doing more than 50% of the work, then he or she is doing bad therapy (Steiner, 1974). To do more than half the work, or take more than half the responsibility for how the session is going, is a "rescue" or "invites confluence" and is believed to be nontherapeutic. For the therapist to initiate contact or suggest a course of action would seem to fly in the face of such rules. Remember, though, that the need for the other to initiate is only one of many relational needs, and it requires attending to only when it is foreground. When other needs are foreground, the therapist chooses not to initiate, but to deal with those other needs instead.

Effective therapeutic initiation, then, has two major ingredients: knowing when to initiate, and doing so appropriately. Not surprisingly, the sense of when initiation will be useful comes largely from experience. It requires sensitivity not only to what the client is saying and doing at the moment, but also to the overall pattern of the client's behavior. By definition, a client cannot openly ask that the therapist initiate; to do so would create the well-known "be spontaneous" double bind. (If I ask you to do something without my having asked for it, there's no way for you to meet my request. Something of this sort may have occurred with Melinda's request that the therapist remember to talk to her about her little doll.) Perhaps the best rule of thumb is to experiment and pay close attention to what happens next. If you feel manipulated by a client's "passive" behavior, try translating that behavior as an expression of the client's need for you to step in and help, without being asked. If the client grows confused or does not know what to say, try offering a suggestion. If the work is furthered by this kind of intervention, fine; if you have not learned that—at least for now— this is not what your client most needs from you.

The most powerful therapist initiations are often nonverbal. Moving closer to the client, holding out a hand, or facilitating eye contact can say, "I'm here, and I won't be ignored or go away." Nonverbal initiations such as these tend to communicate affectively, bypassing cognitive and rational understanding. The client may not even be consciously aware that the therapist has initiated, but at a deeper level he or she experiences that the need for other-initiation is being met.

There is certainly some danger that clients may take therapist initiation as evidence that the therapist sees them as helpless or incompetent, and one must be sensitive to this possibility. Acting so as to fulfill any perceived relational need always carries the danger that we have misjudged and that this is not what the client really needed. Yet it is a risk that must be taken. Error is always a possibility in therapy; indeed, as long as therapists are human and fallible, error is inevitable. The error of mistimed or too frequent initiation can be dealt with by acknowledging it and by changing one's behavior. Too little initiation, in contrast, may create a relational lack that will never be dealt with; the client cannot bring it up (for reasons we have already discussed), and we are unlikely to notice that it is a problem.

To Express Love

In any close positive relationship, the participants experience caring, affection, esteem, and appreciation for each other. Expressing these feelings is a relational need; not doing so requires that one push aside and deny the internal experience—just like denying or trying to ignore any other need—and avoids self-definition within the relationship. Part of who I am with you is how I feel about you, and if I am to be fully contactful I must be able to express those affectionate feelings.

A therapy of contact-in-relationship creates one of the closest and most intimate of all human connections, and it is almost inevitable that the client will experience strong feelings toward the therapist. Many of these feelings will be positive, and the client will need to express them. Although some of the emotions may be transferential in nature, having more to do with feelings toward important figures of the past than with the here-and-now relationship, others will be genuine feelings of regard and affection for the therapist. All too often, therapists discourage clients' expression of such feelings by labeling them all as transference or as a sign that the client is becoming too dependent or too infantilized or is trying to manipulate the relationship.

When we stop and think about it, though, what could be more natural than feeling love and affection for someone who knows us so deeply and who continues to respect and attend to and care about us? Indeed, for a client not to experience such feelings would be a strong signal that there is something fundamentally wrong, either in his or her ability to love another person or in the quality of the therapeutic relationship.

One of the reasons why many therapists have difficulty when clients express their positive feelings is that we do not know what to say in return. We do not know quite what to do with what the client is telling us, and we may feel embarrassed and clumsy. Our training has been to treat such expressions with suspicion, and we may fear that in believing and accepting them we are behaving unprofessionally, and quite possibly making fools of ourselves in the bargain.

Rather than assuming that an expression of gratitude, a loving gesture, or an affectionate word must be a sign of some hidden agenda on the part of a client, at least until proven otherwise, we believe it is better to assume the opposite. We should take that expression at face value unless and until we have reason to interpret it in some other way. Just as it is natural to care for one's partner in a relationship, it is natural to want the partner to care for us: it is entirely appropriate that the therapist feel pleased when a client expresses positive feelings toward him or her. The therapist's feelings of pleasure may not need to be stated directly (the client's feelings are the figure; the therapist's are the background), but being comfortable with them makes it much easier to stay with the client's experience. And staying with the client is what allows the therapist to guide that client to the next level of awareness.

As clients begin to re-own the denied and dissociated parts of themselves, they are likely to recover the ability to feel more intensely. Many children learn, through abuse or neglect, that it is not safe to feel. They believe that it is easier and less painful to wall off feelings and not even know that they exist. A client who is recovering the ability to feel emotions will have a strong need to express them. Children are powerful lovers, and a re-owned "child" aspect of self is likely to need to love and to love intensely. The expression of such feelings is not only transference. The feelings are genuinely and appropriately directed toward the therapist and are not leftovers from some earlier, unfinished relationship. But they must be understood in the context of the client's process of integration. Within the therapeutic relationship, at this point in its development, they are strong, and spontaneous; later, as reintegration becomes more complete, they will mature into a more adult-appropriate form of caring and affection.

Because the need for love is present (at least as background) in any relationship, children who are abused or neglected by caretakers find themselves in an emotionally-confusing situation. If they allow themselves to feel the pain of the abuse, they risk losing their love for the abuser. And, because the abuser is not behaving lovingly toward the child, maintaining the child's own love for the abuser is the only way to have any love at all in the relationship. It is the only way to keep open the possibility that things will get better and that the caretaker will somehow, miraculously, change and become a good parent. The love of a child for an abusive parent is often noted and wondered at by those who attempt to intervene in such situations: children will go to extreme lengths to protect the very person from whom they need to be protected.

This need to feel and to express love toward one's caretaker can be a major factor in working through abuse issues in therapy. Even as adults, clients who have been abused may experience a sense of protectiveness toward their abusers that is so strong that it interferes with their ability to re-own the aspects of self that have been kept out of awareness since the time the abuse occurred. Billie is such a person: her mother was critical and rejecting, and Billie's way of maintaining the pretense/possibility of a loving relationship was to see her mother as fragile and needy. In order to see mother in this way, Billie had to distort and deny her own internal experience and her knowledge of what mother was really doing and her feelings about her mother's behavior. Now, as an adult, that distortion and denial have severely restricted her ability to make contact with others as well as with herself. Recognizing that the unfinished issues with her mother lie at the roots of her emotional constriction and that she needs support and encouragement to deal with them, the therapist suggests that she, rather than Billie, will talk with Billie's (fantasized) mother. Notice how she must move to counter Billie's overprotection of and fear for her mother:

Therapist: *I think it would be helpful if I talked to your mother—if I talked to her about what to do with a little girl.*

Billie: (her face is frozen; she seems to shrink in on herself) *I don't know; she'd just crumble.*

Therapist: *I doubt it.* (pause) *Hang on a second, Billie. I know that's really scary for you. . . . But this is not a fragile woman we're talking about. She has her ways of getting what she wants. One of her ways was by manipulating you. So I'm not so concerned about her crumbling. I know you experienced her that way, and you can be sure that I'll take care of her. This is not about beating up your Mom.*

Billie: *I wanted to take care of her.*

Therapist: *That's the other side of it. About taking care of her. About loving her, and wanting her to love you.*

Billie: (cries) *I'm scared. I don't want to lose her.*

Therapist: *By really talking to her. . . .* (Billie continues to cry) *That way we can try to understand her better. . . .*

By framing the therapist's talking to the mother about how she should have cared for her daughter (which Billie is sure will be mostly criticism) as a way to "understand her better," the therapist has taken over the job of protecting the mother. Reassured that mother will not be "beaten up" and will not have to "crumble," Billie can allow herself the experience of hearing the therapist deal with Billie's mother, as well as the vicarious experience of self-expression.

And what does all this have to do with the relational need to express love? It is all of a piece: the need to express love is present in every healthy relationship, be it with parent, friend, or therapist. It may even be present in abusive relationships, which may explain why, all too often, clients continue with therapists who behave improperly or abusively toward them. Such therapists, who have allowed their own needs to take precedence over those of the clients, crave and demand the client's affection and regard and manipulate the client so as to get it. A competent and ethical therapist, in contrast, accepts expressions of love and gratitude and caring with equanimity, understanding them as both therapeutically necessary and as an intrinsic part of the relationship between two whole and contactful human beings.

People who have heard us talk about the major relational needs often ask about a need to *be* loved. "Surely," they say, "the need to be loved, appreciated, and cared about must be present in any meaningful relationship. Why isn't it on the list of relational needs?" The answer is simple: when the eight needs we have discussed are attended to, consistently and with sensitivity to which need is in the foreground at any given moment, the overall experience is one of being loved. There is no reason to list it separately, for it is the sum of the needs we have been discussing. To have one's relational needs met is to feel loved.

☐ Juxtaposition

You have done a good job with this client. You have been fully present and attuned to the client's relational needs; you have inquired with care and skill; you have experienced your involvement and demonstrated it appropriately. But the client is not responding as you expected. Instead of growing and blossoming and moving into ever-expanding internal and external contact, he or she seems to be pulling away from you. You see distance, anger, a frozen face; you hear denial or diversion or story telling or nothing at all. What is going on?

In order to understand these kinds of reactions, one must be aware of the phenomenon of *juxtaposition*. Juxtaposition occurs when there is, for the client, a marked contrast between what is provided in the therapeutic relationship and what was needed and longed for but not provided in previous relationships (Erskine, 1994, 1997). As the therapist attends to relational needs, acknowledging and responding to the client's phenomenological experience, what may be stimulated in the client is a surge of emotional memories of what it was like, back then, when those needs were not responded to. And those memories are often very painful.

George, another client, grew up in an emotionally arid environment and learned, very early, that his feelings were not important to others and would not receive positive attention. George learned to cover up his sadness, his fear, and his longing for contact. Over the years, the covering up became second nature to him; by the time he reached adulthood, he had become so skillful at it that he hardly even noticed when he had feelings. He did get migraine headaches, though, and he did not have the kinds of close relationships that other people seemed to have; his marriage was in trouble, and his career felt like a dead end. So George began therapy to figure out what was wrong. And, quite unexpectedly, he found himself in a whole new world of being with another person. For the first time in his life, someone seemed to be genuinely interested in and affected by the things that he was experiencing. When he went through his automatic cover-up routines, this therapist cut right through them and responded to the feelings he was covering—and his cover was blown away, gone. George could no longer deny his knowledge of what he needed. And he did not feel just the pain of today, but also the pain of all those old experiences, those memories of being young and vulnerable and desperately wanting something from someone who would not respond.

This is juxtaposition, and it can be more intense than the client is able to bear. It's just too much! So the alarms go off, the troops rush in to man the defenses. "Push the feelings away; don't let those awarenesses emerge; don't let this therapist be close anymore!" Although juxtaposition shows up primarily as a break in external contact—pushing the therapist away—both internal and external contact are interrupted. Contact with the self is broken so as not to feel what has been stimulated, and contact with the therapist is broken so as not to get more of what has proven to be so painful.

Therapists are often confused when faced with a client's juxtaposition reaction. That last session was so powerful, and the client made a real breakthrough—why did she cancel her next appointment? Or why did he come late and fill what little time was left with superficial "talking-about"? Or why did she blame the therapist for not understanding, for focusing on the wrong things, or for making everything worse instead of better? Juxtaposition reactions may be mistaken for negative transference or as signs that the therapist has missed the client and is not doing a good job. They can also be powerful invitations to the therapist to slide into countertransference: to respond to the client by pulling back, breaking contact, using one's own out-of-awareness defenses against what feels like rejection or even outright attack.

A juxtaposition reaction does not mean that the therapist is missing the client. Quite the contrary! It usually indicates that the therapist is right on target. If there has been a therapeutic error, it is that the therapist was *too* on target and has moved the client too quickly into contact with what has been buried and split off from awareness. The therapist has not taken the client to the wrong place; rather, they have gone exactly where they needed to go, but have gotten there before the client was ready to deal with it.

Responding to the Juxtaposition Reaction

There are several levels of response that can be useful when a client exhibits a juxtaposition reaction. The first level has more to do with what goes on inside the therapist than with what is actually said to the client (although, of course, internal process always affects external behavior). Before trying to figure out what to do, one must first recognize the client's reaction for what it is. "Oh, this isn't what I expected. Is it possible that I've created a juxtaposition and the client is responding to it?" Once this possibility has been recognized, the therapist can begin to put the client's behavior into therapeutic perspective; this allows us to avoid responding defensively or second-guessing our handling of the therapy.

Not only does recognizing a juxtaposition reaction allow the therapist to avoid self-blame and defensiveness, but it also clears the way for us to understand the function of the client's behavior. Remember that validation is an essential aspect of therapist involvement, and that validation has to do with the purpose and the goal of whatever the client may be doing. The behavior itself may not be helping the client—juxtaposition reactions usually do not seem helpful; they are likely to look like a step in exactly the wrong direction— but they have a valid purpose and are being carried out in order to serve some important function. In this context, a juxtaposition reaction may be quite helpful, illuminating both the out-of-awareness experience of contact deprivation as well as the behaviors the client has developed in order to cope with that experience.

Respecting the function of the client's reaction, the therapist will adjust the pace of the therapy and the focus of attunement. This is not only respectful of the client's unconscious communication, it is just common sense. When someone says, "Too much!" you do not immediately force him or her to take more. Of course the therapist should continue to be present and attuned to the client's process, but the intensity of the therapist's presence, and the rate at which new areas of internal and external contact are opened, can be reduced.

A juxtaposition reaction, whatever its external form, is essentially an interruption of contact. It is a way for the client to back off, get some breathing room, and get stable again. More often than not, the client does not realize this, and the first concrete step in dealing with the reaction may be to help him or her explore what is happening. What is this moment like for him or her? What are the thoughts, emotions, and physical sensations that he or she is experiencing? What is the body language, and how does it translate into words? In the presence of a juxtaposition reaction, careful inquiry into the phenomenological experience of the current interruption to contact may restore (or partially restore) contact, and may also help the client begin to explore the painful emotional memories that prompted the reaction in the first place.

It can also be helpful to return to the original therapeutic contract, and reclarify or renegotiate what the client wants from the therapy relationship. Such a return is useful in several ways. First, inviting clients to think about their expectations may lower the emotional intensity to a bearable level. Rather than being overwhelmed by feelings and emotional memories, the client can return to cognition and to familiar patterns of problem-solving and control. For clients who are more open to contact through thinking together than to contact through feeling emotion together, this is indeed a respite, a breathing space. Second, by returning to the original contract, both client and therapist can stand back and look at the way the work has gone. It provides a kind of formative evaluation in which both participants can decide which avenues have been fruitful and should be explored further and which are not likely (at least for now) to be helpful. Finally, and perhaps most important of all, renegotiating the contract allows clients to begin to explore their present behaviors (of which the juxtaposition reaction is primary) in the context of the wants and needs that originally brought them into treatment.

Such exploration, within a contactful therapeutic relationship, lies at the heart of the therapeutic process. The skill and sensitivity of the therapist is critical here, because the client is being invited to move into exactly the area that he or she had to defend against and the very experiences that prompted the original juxtaposition reaction. There is a fine line between exploring what must be explored, on the one hand, and re-injuring the client, on the other hand; the therapist's attunement and involvement, both internally experienced and externally communicated, makes it possible to find and respect that line.

With some clients, it may be helpful to provide information about the nature of juxtaposition and people's response to it. Information of this sort may help clients to understand and respect their own behavior. Normalizing a juxtaposition reaction (by describing it as a common and understandable response to being flooded by painful memories) decreases the likelihood that the client will experience shame over his or her response. For other clients, in contrast, the therapist may choose to attend first to phenomenology, staying with the client's ongoing experience, demonstrating that, whatever happens, this therapist will continue to be present, involved, and available. Ultimately, the client will probably benefit from both phenomenological exploration and cognitive understanding. Attunement to the client's rhythm and to his or her shifting relational needs will help the therapist know which to attend to first.

And so we have come full circle, back to the notion of relational needs. Cumulative trauma and psychological dis-ease occur when one's social environment does not respond to these needs; paradoxically, the juxtaposition reaction is most likely to occur when the therapist does respond to them. And yet, perhaps it is not such a paradox after all: if someone has spent his whole life learning how not to be aware of that which is painful, can we be surprised when he or she finds it difficult to feel that pain? Opening a festering wound is not fun; pulling off a scab hurts; and most folks shrink from such experiences. But when the scab is removed and when the wound is drained, it "hurts good"! Perhaps that is the single most descriptive (if ungrammatical) thing we can say about a therapy of contact-in-relationship: yes, it hurts. It hurts good.

6
CHAPTER

Through the Keyhole

A friend once told us a story about a little boy who was fascinated by bugs. Any small thing that walked, crawled, or flew was a source of endless interest for him. He hunted them and watched them and asked questions about them: "Where did they come from?" "Where were they going?" and, most often, "How did they work?" One day he captured a beetle, put it in a box, and watched as it explored its new world. He could not understand how such a tiny creature could actually move. And then came the inspiration: he would cut it apart and find out what was inside that made it go. So he did. And, of course, once he had cut it up it did not go anywhere; in fact, it was not even a beetle anymore, but just a collection of dead parts.

Our discussion of a therapy of contact-in-relationship has been something like that beetle. We have had to cut the whole thing up in order to explain its various aspects. But, cut apart, it really does not function. It is a collection of parts, rather than a living, breathing therapy. Now it is time to put it back together and to discuss how the parts relate to each other and work in harmony to create relationship and further the process of a therapy of contact-in-relationship.

Let us begin by backing off and looking once more at our beginning premises about the nature of healthy and unhealthy development and the role of relationship in that development. We have said, first, that relationship is a necessary part of growing up. People are not people unless they are in relationship with others; no true human can exist without real or fantasied relationships.

The notion of relationship brings us immediately to the notion of contact. Relationship is built on interpersonal contact. But true interpersonal contact is possible only if one is in contact with oneself. I cannot be open to you unless I am open to myself; I cannot share myself with you if I am unaware of me. Each kind of contact, internal and external, potentiates the other: my contact with you (especially if you are supportive and respectful) enhances my internal awareness, and as I become more internally contactful I am increasingly able to be aware of you and to share myself with you.

Relationship is especially critical when a person experiences stress or trauma. When we are in physical or emotional pain, or when we feel threatened by the prospect of pain, we instinctively try to defend ourselves. For a child without the support of healthy relationships, these defenses often involve closing down and shutting off: the child hides from the danger or pushes the pain out of awareness. Children may deny their fearful thoughts, disavow their uncomfortable feelings, desensitize themselves to physical distress. With these processes comes loss of self, for every thought or emotion or sensation pushed out of awareness is a loss of internal contact and a barrier to relationship.

Since some pain and some dangers are inevitable (the world being less than perfect), everyone must occasionally experience conflict between the need to protect, defend, and hide and the need to be in contact with self and others. When one feels threatened, the natural tendency to grow and to self-actualize collides head on with the equally natural tendency to close off and retreat. Out of such conflicts we develop patterns of compromise and ways of experiencing and understanding and interacting with the world that seem, in the short run, to resolve the conflicts but that in the long run perpetuate them by disrupting our ability to be in full contact with ourselves or with the world around us. These patterns of compromise form a life script—an unconscious plan, an interrelated set of fixed gestalten—composed of beliefs, fantasies, emotions, and memories that shape, predict, and give meaning to relationships.

To the degree that healthy relationships are maintained and internal and external contact is not disrupted, fixed gestalten do not form. The child who can go to a loving and understanding adult for protection and support will not experience long-term damage in the presence of trauma, because he or she will not need to close down, restrict awareness, cut off parts of the self. It is not so much the trauma itself that produces lasting damage; it is trauma in the absence of a protective, healing relationship. And the cumulative trauma of continuing, consistent relationship deprivation (which can be as damaging as an acute traumatic experience) is obviously the antithesis of contact-in-relationship.

The function of therapy is to reverse the pattern of fixed gestalten, self-protective contact disruption, and restricted awareness. The therapist's raison d'etre is to provide a relationship that will allow and invite the client to become increasingly contactful, internally and externally, to dissolve the fixed patterns or schema and to recover the parts of self that have been lost to awareness. This is what a therapy of contact-in-relationship is all about; this is the function of the inquiry, attunement, and involvement that we have been describing in such detail.

Psychotherapy is aimed at shifting the client's level of functioning from "distress" to "health," as shown in Figure 6.1. To do so, therapists create and maintain a therapeutic relationship. It is contact, within this relationship, that invites, encourages, and pulls the client into increased awareness, away from distress and toward health. Inquiry and involvement and attunement are the hallmarks of such a therapeutic relationship. These factors do not function independently; they are intertwined and commingled. Each depends upon the other two to build and sustain the relationship between client and therapist.

As the therapeutic relationship develops, it can be characterized as moving through a series of phases or foci. This characterization is, of course, a kind of distortion: no relationship ever builds smoothly from start to finish. In real life we go forward and back; we progress and we stumble; we open to the other person (and to ourselves as well) and we retreat. Nevertheless, the notion of phases will help us to understand how relationship develops and how a therapy of contact-in-relationship brings about growth. We are going to cut the beetle apart again, in a different way; nevertheless we are still cutting it apart. This time we will be cutting across the three factors of inquiry, attunement, and involvement, and cutting into "phases" instead of factors. But please remember that the cutting is artificial; it is a temporary learning device. The beetle is not really alive as long as we keep chopping it into pieces.

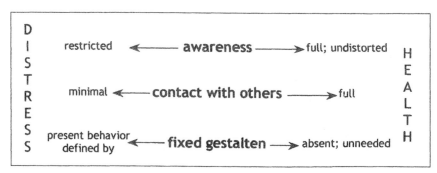

FIGURE 6.1. Awareness, contact, and fixed gestalten as they relate to health and distress.

☐ The Keyhole

How do you talk about everything at once? Where is the starting point of a circle? Just as the mythical worm Ouroboros, continually devouring and re-creating itself, has no beginning and no end, so the therapeutic relationship must be seen at once, whole over time, to be fully taken in. Words do not do that; they are linear. The therapeutic process requires a picture or a diagram. The "keyhole" is our attempt to show all the facets of a therapy of contact-in-relationship together, in dynamic relationship. Figure 6.2 shows the keyhole. We will be looking at it again, with different parts highlighted, as we work our way along.

First, notice that each of the major topics we have discussed is included in the keyhole: attunement is at the bottom and forms the foundation or

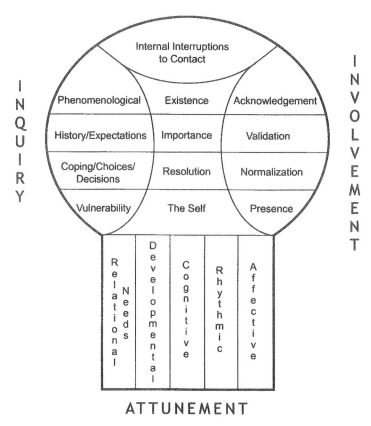

FIGURE 6.2. The basic contact-in-relationship Keyhole.

"stem" upon which everything rests; involvement is to the right, and inquiry (with some new terminology) to the left. Down the middle is a list of the levels or degrees of contact interruption.

We are going to work our way through the diagram, starting at the top of the keyhole and moving down, showing how the processes interact. We begin with a discussion of the internal contact disruptions.

☐ Interruptions to Contact

Contact interruption is both a response to and a cause of psychic pain. We have seen how the impulse to close down, move away, and hide inside is a natural reaction when one feels threatened or has been hurt. Just as a small animal hides itself away when it perceives danger, so humans hide away psychologically. And the more often we experience ourselves hurt, ignored, or humiliated by others, the more likely we are to close ourselves off from human contact.

Interruption of internal contact is perhaps less intuitively understandable. It makes sense to hide from a dangerous external world, but why hide from oneself? One answer has to do with avoiding whatever hurts. Do the things I am thinking about make me uncomfortable? Then stop thinking about them. Am I experiencing painful emotions? Learn not to feel emotion. Do the sensations in my body remind me of memories or needs or fears that I would rather not be reminded of? Make those sensations just go away.

Another facet of internal contact disruption has to do with the ways in which we make meaning out of our pain. People, especially very young people, are highly egocentric. They experience themselves at the center of their world; everything that happens is in relationship to them. One of the consequences of this egocentricity is overestimating their own importance. Things seem to be done *to* them, *about* them, and *for* them. They are somehow involved and responsible for all the important events of life. Children feel guilty when bad things happen: a sibling gets sick, parents divorce, or someone dies. It is easy to find the remnants of this kind of thinking in ourselves: imagine yourself talking with a friend when suddenly, with no explanation, the friend gets up and hurries out of the room. It is a rare person who would not experience at least a flash of "What did I do?"

Adding to the natural egocentric sense of responsibility that children feel are all the instances in which others in the child's life, intentionally or unintentionally, reinforce the child's negative perceptions of self. A parent's exasperated outburst ("You *never* clean up after yourself!"), being chosen last for a playground game, or doing badly on an exam, are all invitations to see oneself as bad or lacking in some way. In the absence of healthy, supportive, affirming external contact, such messages will be introjected and used as definitions of self: "I'm lazy," "I'm unlikable," "I'm stupid."

"I'm lazy," "I'm unlikable," and "I'm stupid" are not comfortable thoughts. Memories of believing them, or even just being told them, are not comfortable memories. Memories of being in pain, with nobody to help, are not comfortable either. To lessen the discomfort, people block out such memories. And then block out ideas and sensations and feelings that would tend to call them forth. And then block out other ideas and sensations and feelings that might remind them of the ones they've blocked away . . . and the spiral of disruption of internal contact has begun.

Internal contact disruption takes a number of forms, and we have already mentioned three of them briefly: denial, disavowal, and desensitization. Denial is disruption of our cognition. It involves an active choice: "I won't think/know about that." Repression of memories, inability to solve problems, not understanding or making connections—all of these can involve denial and disruption of contact with our cognitive abilities. Disavowal, in contrast, has to do with affect. If denial is "I won't think about it," disavowal is "I won't have any feelings about it." "Yes, I was abused, but that was a long time ago and it is no big deal." "It's true, my spouse cheated on me, but there's nothing to be gained by getting angry about it." Feelings, especially painful ones, are not tolerated; they are disavowed, covered over, blanked out.

The third form of this disruption triumvirate is desensitization: loss of contact with body sensations. People who have desensitized themselves may report feeling "numb" or "spacey." Or they may report nothing at all; they have been out of contact with their bodies for so long that they cannot imagine being any other way. For these folks, the body is a machine that is used to carry oneself from place to place; it only gets attention when it threatens to break down.

These three forms of internal contact disruption all involve cutting off a particular function and leaving the others intact. There are two other forms that cut across all of the functions—cognitive, affective, and sensory. These are depersonalization and dissociation, and they are the "big guns" of defensive self-protection and are generally not used unless the person is dealing with fairly serious trauma. Depersonalization involves a kind of psychic abandonment of the body, and even of the sense of self. "It's not really happening to me; I'm not really here." And dissociation is the classic splitting defense, dividing awareness into separate parts that may even function as independent personalities.

Clearly, if the goal of therapy is to enhance awareness, it is important to recognize and reverse these processes of contact disruption. In doing so, we often work through a number of defensive levels (Schiff, 1975). These levels can involve any or all of the forms we have just described. We will discuss them in order, as they are highlighted down the center of the keyhole in Figure 6.3.

The first and simplest level of contact disruption is to restrict one's awareness of the *existence* of a problem. If something is likely to make one uncomfortable, one just blocks that something out of awareness. This is the strategy characterized by Scarlett O'Hara's famous "I'll think about that tomorrow" in the novel *Gone With The Wind*: "I won't feel it; it isn't happening; I don't remember."

But a problem need not be blocked from awareness in order for contact to be disrupted or distorted. One can be aware of something and still deny

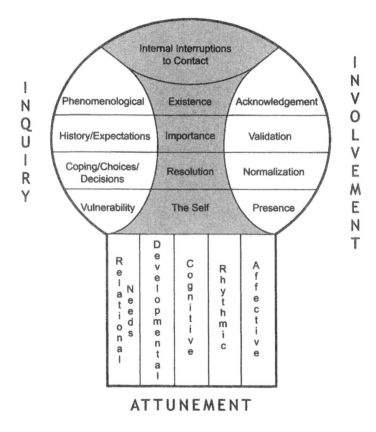

FIGURE 6.3. The Keyhole and interruptions to contact.

that it has any *importance* or significance. "Sure, I know it's going on, so what?" "Yeah, I was sad about that. Lots of sad things happen in life. Being sad is a waste of time." "I remember that I was beaten by my Dad, but it didn't affect me." At the second level of internal contact disruption, the event or memory or experience is there, but it has been emotionally and cognitively sanitized. It is a photograph in an album, rather than a living, breathing, three-dimensional part of oneself. And because it is not important, one does not have to deal with it or be bothered by it.

At the third level of contact interruption, the person is aware that a problem (feeling, memory, or situation) exists and that it is important, but he or she denies that any *resolution* is possible. "That's just the way it is; I'll have to live with it. Sure, it hurts; sure, the memory is keeping me awake at night; sure, I'm upset by what's happening between you and me, but nothing can be done about it. Better to just not talk about it, not keep dragging myself over the coals. What can't be cured must be endured. . . ." So the client pretends that he or she is okay (that is the right thing to do, isn't it, when one's problems are not solvable anyhow?) and tries not to bother anyone too much, and tries to keep himself or herself busy with other things. Not exactly a recipe for contact and relationship, is it?

If the first three levels of contact interruption have been worked through, and the person is able and willing to be aware of the existence, the importance, and the resolvability of a problem (cognition, affect, physical sensation), there may remain a denial of the value of *self*: one's own, personal, individual and unique ability to deal with the feelings and resolve the situation. The possibility of a resolution, out there somewhere, is no longer denied; it is just that this particular person cannot do it. "Somebody else could probably do something about it; lots of other people have dealt with worse things in the past. It's just me, just the kind of person I am; I can't handle it and never will be able to. It's better not to even let myself care, not to feel the needing or the wanting." Notice how neatly this fits into what we were talking about earlier, the way in which people create negative self-definitions out of things that happen to them. It is circular and self-reinforcing: the more I negatively define myself, the more I will be inclined to distort and disrupt my ability to be in contact with that negatively defined self. And the more distortion and disruption of contact, the fewer resources are available and the more the value of self is diminished.

So here we are, with a dismal description of how people keep themselves unhappy, cut off from contact with self and others, and stuck. It is time to move on to something more hopeful. The therapy of contact-in-relationship is designed to reverse the cycle. Again, as we talk about the "phases" of such a therapy, please remember that the divisions are artificial: a real beetle uses all of itself, all of the time.

☐ Phase One: The Starting Point

Figure 6.4 highlights the most introductory ground level of psychotherapy, in which clients are likely to be disrupting contact at the *existence* level. They are often unaware of much that is going on, either internally or externally. Something is wrong, but they do not know what it is. More often than not, the problem that they bring to these first therapy sessions is far removed from what really needs to be fixed. Feelings of depression, or work stress, or an unhappy marriage, are real problems. But they are also symptoms of blocked and constricted relationships, of a self that has been fragmented and split off, of feelings and thoughts and memories and wants no longer available to consciousness but festering below the surface of awareness.

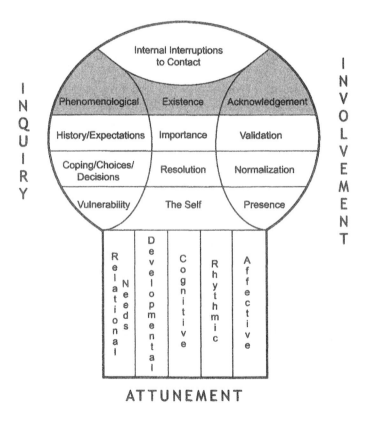

FIGURE 6.4. The first phase of a therapy of contact-in-relationship.

In this phase of therapy the focus of inquiry is *phenomenological*. "What is going on for you right now?" "What are you experiencing?" "Tell me your story; tell me what seems important at this moment in time." This focus makes sense for at least two reasons. First, it's where the client's energy is. Clients want their therapist to know what brought them to treatment, what their problem is. They want to know that the therapist understands and sees things from their perspective. They want their view of the world to be *acknowledged* by the therapist's interest, encouragement, and sympathetic understanding. To ask them to talk about anything else at this point would feel like a distraction or a discounting of their own sense of what needs to be discussed.

The second, and probably more important, reason for beginning the inquiry with phenomenology is that this is what is most readily available to awareness. Clients often do not know, do not understand, or cannot explain clearly (because of the very contact disruptions that lie at the root of their need for therapy) how they have learned to cut off internal and external awareness. They are not aware of the patterns of fixed gestalten that limit their flexibility and spontaneity and creativity. They do not have access to the buried and split-off parts of self. What they do have access to (but may not often attend to) is their immediate, ongoing experience. And that ongoing experience is what we ask them to tell us about.

We ask clients to tell us in detail. We inquire about every aspect of their experience. Attuned to their affect, their cognitive process, their rhythm, and their level of developmental functioning, we inquire about what they know, and feel, and believe, and imagine, right now. We *acknowledge* their responses with attention and with respect, letting them know that we are interested and involved and that we care about what they are telling us. And the questions and statements, the quirk of our lips or the interest in our eyes, all serve to lead clients into increasing awareness of themselves and increasing contact with us.

Eventually, if we are skillful and patient, the contact barriers will begin to melt. Awareness will broaden and deepen, and the client will begin to move from a focus on symptoms and story telling to a sense that something else is missing. He or she is now able to experience and acknowledge much more of what is happening internally, as well as to be more genuine and contactful in relationship with the therapist. It is time to move, gently and respectfully, into phase two.

☐ Phase Two: Making Connections

With a growing awareness of internal experience and an ever-increasing ability to be in contact with his or her emerging feelings, wants, and memories, the client is now ready to explore the *significance* of those experiences. Blocking awareness of importance is the second level of contact interruption, as Figure 6.5 indicates. "What's going on for you right now?" the therapist may ask. "Oh, I just felt kind of sad for a minute." "And what is that sadness about?" "I don't know; nothing, I guess." Even though the feeling of sadness is experienced and labeled, it is not connected to anything. In the client's experience, it exists in isolation, a curious and probably uncomfortable bit of emotion that will probably fade if we just wait long enough. "Everybody feels sad now and then," is the client's attitude. "There's no sense paying attention to it; just think about something else."

Another form of contact disruption at this level is that of making no connection between present experience and other parts of one's life, or making only a partial or even an inaccurate connection. "I'm sad because my 30th birthday is tomorrow; everyone feels sad about hitting that Big

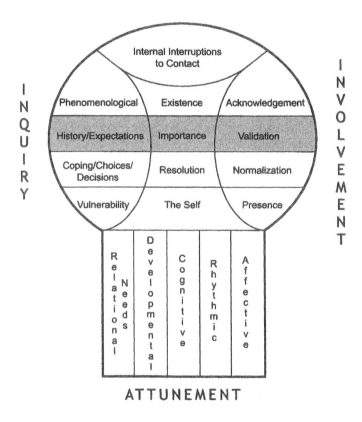

FIGURE 6.5. The second phase of a therapy of contact-in-relationship.

Three-Oh" or "You'd be upset too if you deserved a raise and didn't get it." A primary function of inquiry at this point is to explore all the possible connections between what is currently experienced and what else is or has been going on for this person. The therapist does not deny that thirtieth birthdays can invite sadness or that not getting a raise is indeed upsetting. But there is usually more than one determinant of any internal event, and the most therapeutically significant ones often have to do with past *history* and with *expectations* for the future.

Having mentioned expectations, let's take a moment's detour to look more closely at the notion of expectations and their close cousins, hopes and fears. We generally think of expectations and hopes and fears as having to do with the future. After all, that's where they point: I expect, hope for, or dread something that has not happened yet. But where do those expectations come from? How do we choose to hope for or be afraid about something that may be just around the corner? Expectations for the future are often echoes of the past. They derive from past experiences, and feelings about those expectations are important clues about what has happened to us and influenced us in the past. A person who has never seen a snake or read about or been told about snakes is unlikely to be afraid of finding one in the garden. Someone who has never experienced harassment generally does not expect it. And we hope for things that our past experience has led us to believe might happen (or has persuaded us will never happen, but we hope for it anyway). What all of this means for the therapist is that any expression of hope or fear or expectation about the future is an invitation to inquire about the past. That is where a connection may be, and that is the connection that is often blocked from awareness.

Nowhere is this past-to-future connection clearer or more important than in the context of the relationship between client and therapist. Transference is a statement about past relationships, about what has occurred and about what was needed in those relationships. What one expects, hopes for, or fears from one's therapist is an echo of what has happened before with important people. Even when memories of relational events are unavailable, affect about such events may be quite strong. Statements such as, "I'm afraid you're going to . . . " or "I hope you'll . . . " or "I know what you're going to say about this" may have much more to do with the client's parents, teachers, spouse, or childhood companions than with what has actually happened during the therapy. Again, it is important not to discount the part of the client's expectation that *does* relate directly to the therapist's behavior (remember, almost everything is multiply determined) and to acknowledge our own importance and responsibility. But don't stop there! Inquire about other relationships in which the same sorts of things happened, or the same sorts of feelings were experienced. Inquire about past *history* and its connection to *expectations*.

In Figure 5, you can see that the "importance" level of internal interruptions to contact is linked to the "history/expectations" level of inquiry. But how does *validation,* in the involvement column, fit in? Remember that we have defined validation in terms of acknowledging and valuing the significance of the client's experience. This is exactly what the other two columns of the diagram demand. If contact is interrupted at this level by denying that an experience is important or significant, then the therapist must find a way to counter the denial. The client may not understand, or even believe in, the importance of what he or she is reporting. But the therapist knows it is important. The therapist assumes that this experience is significant in the client's life: it is not a random thought, or a silly overreaction, or "just" something that popped into awareness. Validation, then, is about more than just acknowledging that an affect or a need or a memory is present. It affirms that the affect/need/memory is there for a reason and that the reason is significant and important.

As we move from simply acknowledging an internal event to validating its importance, we are helping the client to discover how he or she makes meaning and structure out of raw experience and how those meanings create a sense of continuity from past to present to future. Notice the wording here: we are not doing the discovering ourselves (or, if we are, it is of secondary importance). We are helping the client to do his or her own discovering. In the contactful environment of the therapeutic relationship, we are demonstrating our own interest in and commitment to the client's whole person. And that whole person is someone who exists in time and who has a past and a future as well as a present. We are inviting contact with the client at all of his or her times, past and present and future, because they are all important and are all a part of who that client is.

Therapists, too, are beings who live in time; our past and future must be available to us and (potentially) to the client. A physicist might say that in this second phase of a therapy of contact-in-relationship, there is a shift from three-dimensional to four-dimensional space, since physics has long considered time to be a fourth dimension of reality. Only with the addition of this fourth, temporal dimension can we truly validate, with our whole self, the importance and significance of what the client brings to us out of his or her whole self. With that dimension we will be ready to understand the decisions and choices that the client has made; with that dimension the client will be ready to develop his or her own meaningful life narrative.

☐ Third Phase: Choices and Decisions

Clients seek therapy because they do not believe that they can accomplish what they want on their own. The life situation they are dealing with, whether it is some sort of wound or trauma or dis-ease that needs to be healed or whether they want to make an already good life even better, has not turned out to be resolvable. In fact, it is the possibility of *resolution* that takes center stage in phase three. The client is now more fully aware of his or her internal experience and understands that this experience is important. Connections have been made between past events and expectations for the future. The client has a sense of the continuity of his or her perceptions, the ways in which early experiences shape later ones, and the ways in which meanings and structures here and now are founded on and grounded in what happened then and there. But all that does not seem to do any good.

If anything can be said to characterize this point in therapy, it is a sense of stuckness. "Yes, I understand. So what?" Awareness, at this level, does not seem to help. The problem does not go away; solutions do not magically appear. Sometimes it even feels worse than it did before therapy began. At least, prior to therapy, with all the client's defenses in place, he or she did not have to know about all this pain. And, if "stuckness" is the most common theme here, then the greatest challenge to the therapist is to help the client make the choice to move forward, out of the stuck place into contact with his or her ability to create new options, rather than to retreat into the old system of defenses and non-contact.

The significant word in that last sentence is "choice," because this is the phase in which the client becomes aware of *choices*, of *decisions*, and of how his or her experiences began as ways of *coping* (highlighted on the left, in Figure 6.6). The way in which one makes meaning out of experience is always based on choices. The choices may be about what part of awareness will be figure and what part will be background, choices about how to understand what is happening in one's life, choices about what to expect and what to hope for and what to give up on. Because the choices and decisions on which one's present perceptions are based have their roots in yesterday's needs, trauma, fears, and partial understandings, they are often not available to one's adult awareness. They do not feel like choices anymore; they feel like "that's just the way it is." Today's stuckness is the product of yesterday's decisions (Goulding & Goulding, 1979; Greenwald, 1973).

Perhaps an example will help clarify what we mean. Here is Anita, 32 years old, working as a receptionist in a small business. She is lonely, angry, and bitter. She has learned through painful experience that people cannot be trusted: her father left the family when she was a toddler; her mother (lonely herself, with little money and few resources) was abusive; and Anita had no real friends. She did have a boyfriend, once, for a few months, but he dumped her and started dating a cheerleader instead. It is easy to see where her belief, or her decision, about not trusting people

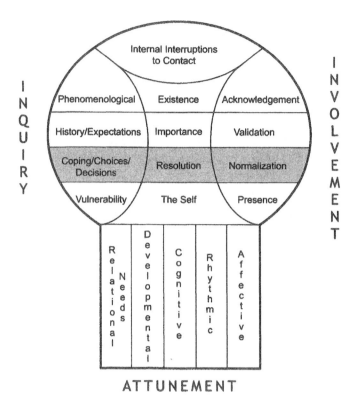

FIGURE 6.6. Third phase of therapy of contact-in-relationship.

came from. It was, for her, a matter of survival. If you don't trust people and don't let yourself expect anything from them, then you are less likely to get hurt. And now, as an adult, she has acquired a whole array of self-protective behaviors that serve to keep people at arm's length. She doesn't do it on purpose; she is not aware that there is any other way to be. She no longer has contact with the emotional decision-making, capable-of-choice part of herself. All that she knows is that people can't be trusted, life is hard, and she isn't very lovable. That's just the way it is.

Virtually all of our beliefs and feelings about people and our ways of being with them are born of our previous attempts to cope with relationships as we were growing up and (perhaps to a less significant degree) as adults. Like Anita, when we feel stuck in the ways we relate to others (and to ourselves, which is at least as important), that stuckness usually grows out of a lack of awareness of the choices we have made or the other choices that were possible. We build a whole life of relationships, good and bad, layer upon layer, but along the way we lose the plans that have guided our building. The relationship world that we know as adults does not feel at all like something we have constructed; it feels like something "out there," something that just happens to us.

In order to make changes that will allow more contactful and safe and positive relationships with others, clients need to recover their awareness of the existence of choices. It is a *resolution* issue. If one's current life situation is to be resolved, one needs to have access to one's choice-making, decision-making self. And this usually involves more than a rational, cognitive understanding of what has happened. To be fully aware and fully in contact, most clients need an emotional, experiential, feel-it-in-the-bones experience of the early decision-making processes. Only when the client reexperiences how it *feels* to make a critical life decision is that decision truly experienced as a choice rather than a necessity. Reestablishing contact with one's choice-making self empowers one to make new and different choices (Erskine, 1974/1997).

There is a danger here, though. As the client begins to understand, remember, and reexperience choices and decisions, he or she also begins to take responsibility for them. But responsibility is a two-edged sword: wielded carelessly, it can injure that which needs to be protected. Less metaphorically, responsibility can easily be twisted into feelings of guilt and shame. "It's all my fault that I'm so stuck and messed up. I really must be stupid/selfish/incompetent/unworthy. . . . " This is where *normalization* comes in. (In Figure 6, we see normalization to the right of the highlighted area, balancing out coping/choices/decisions on the left.) The client needs to know that his or her choices and decisions were made in the interest of coping and of surviving and that any reasonable person in a similar situation might have done the same thing. What the client did was normal, not stupid or crazy. Even more, it was often a brave or even heroic (and successful!) effort to keep that person alive and able to function in a difficult world. It is the therapist's job to help the client know this, believe it, and feel it.

Normalization is a function of therapist involvement. To simply reassure the client that his or her behavior was normal is not likely to be very helpful. Clients are experts at discounting such reassurances: "You're only saying that because you're my therapist, because you want to cheer me up, because it is your job to help me feel better." An involved therapist, meeting the client with full internal and external contact, does more than reassure. Such a therapist communicates, fully and genuinely, that the client has done the absolute best that he or she could, given the circumstances, and that anyone at this developmental level, with access to these resources, would probably have made the same sorts of decisions. And, believing it fully, the therapist *lives* that belief in his or her relationship with the client. What might otherwise be empty reassurance becomes a part of the bedrock upon which the whole relationship rests.

Phase three, then, involves inquiring in such a way as to help the client become aware of the choices and decisions that he or she has made, so that what has seemed carved in stone about self and others becomes changeable and resolvable. It utilizes the normalizing aspect of therapist involvement, which supports the client's ability to change and at the same time blocks his or her tendency toward self-blame and shame. And it prepares both client and therapist for phase four, that of full contact.

☐ Phase Four: Full Contact

Let us pause here for a moment to consider what the client's experience might be like at this point in therapy. He or she began the therapeutic process with a narrow and restricted sense of internal awareness, and a similarly narrow and restricted ability to be in contact with others. The therapist, sensitively attuned to all that the client is experiencing, has inquired about that experience and has consistently acknowledged whatever the client shared. Gradually, the client's awareness began to deepen. Old memories began to surface, and with them came connections between what was happening then and what is happening now, between past pain and present expectations. The client has come to understand and believe that what he or she now feels and thinks and does is always significant and that feelings and thoughts and behaviors link to learned ways of coping with life. And, perhaps most important of all, he or she has learned that these feelings and thoughts and behaviors are not something to be ashamed of; they are the result of a courageous and creative struggle to survive in a confusing and often frightening world.

Can you see how the connection between the self then and the self now is deepening, how the sense of continuity over time strengthens as repressed and denied and disavowed experiences are gradually welcomed back into awareness, and how defenses are melting in the face of growing appreciation of and compassion for all the parts of self that have been hidden away for so long? There is a tenderness about these moments, a feeling of awakening, almost of rebirth.

This is the moment that is highlighted in Figure 6.7. The client is becoming whole. Contact with the *self*, with all its complexities and capacities, so long split and fragmented, is being reestablished. Feelings and thoughts and perceptions rush in, often with surprising intensity. And each of those long-repressed, long-hidden parts of self has a kind of fragility, like a flower bud freshly opened or a butterfly newly escaped from its hard cocoon. This is *vulnerability*. But it is a new kind of vulnerability,

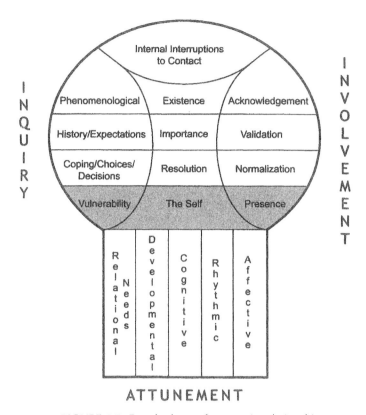

FIGURE 6.7. Fourth phase of contact-in-relationship.

different from the old, fearful vulnerability of a child in a hostile or un-caring environment. This is the vulnerability of safety in relationship, of contact with self and with a fully *present* and contactful other. It is a joyful vulnerability, filled with the excitement of achievement and discovery and possibility. It is the vulnerability of I–thou, two individuals being fully real with each other without pretense or self-protection (Buber, 1958).

In this phase of the work, the focus is on self and on self-in-relation-ship. There is no longer urgency to protect oneself from knowing and little concern with hiding or denying one's deepest longings. Somehow, incredibly, the client knows that he or she is valuable and worthy of re-spect, in spite of or even *because* of all of those needs and ways of being that were so unacceptable before.

Of course, this phase does not last forever. Peak moments are just that: moments. Every mountaintop requires a valley; every end must be a be-ginning or it is, literally, a dead end. With each venture into self-valuing

comes the possibility of a new area to explore, a new part of self to recover, or a new pain or problem to work through. Does it ever end? For
the client, we hope not. The journey of personal discovery is what keeps
one truly alive. For the therapist in this relationship, yes, it does end. At
some point the client must, like a fledgling bird, leave the therapeutic
nest and strike out on his or her own. He or she may return, or may seek
out a new therapeutic relationship, if the path again becomes too difficult
to travel without help. But, whether or not they meet again in the future,
this client and this therapist each share a part of the other. Each has been
touched by the other, and in that touching, has been changed. And each,
therapist as well as client, is the richer for it.

☐ Attunement

And what of attunement, the quality of relationship that we spent so
much time with back in chapter 3? As we said earlier, it is the basis for
everything else that happens in a therapy of contact-in-relationship. Contact is possible only through attunement; first, as the therapist attunes to
the client, and later, as the client becomes increasingly attuned to himself
or herself and to the therapist as well. Let us hasten to underscore, though,
what we have said many times already: the whole focus of the therapeutic relationship is on the well-being of the client. Even though the client
becomes increasingly attuned to the therapist (in a truly contactful relationship, increasing attunement is inevitable), the therapist's personal
experience is background, not foreground. In the therapeutic symphony,
the client's needs, fears, feelings, thoughts, and memories, are the theme;
the therapist's experiencing provides the harmony.

There is another, perhaps fortuitous, relationship that can be seen in
our keyhole diagram. Notice that the aspects of attunement that we detailed in chapter 3 (affective, rhythmic, cognitive, and developmental) lie
closer to the "involvement" side of the diagram and closest of all to "presence." Attunement is very closely intertwined with involvement: one
cannot be accurately and sensitively involved with another unless one is
attuned. And presence, that quality of "there-ness," of full and contactful
participation in the relationship, is so much a part of attunement, and
attunement so fundamental to presence, that it is difficult to distinguish
one from the other.

And on the other side of the "stem" of the keyhole is the category of
"relational needs," which were not discussed in chapter 3. They were so
important that they got an entire chapter to themselves (chapter 5). Awareness of relational needs is a part of attunement, and this awareness, like
the other attunement aspects, guides the therapeutic inquiry. As for the

client, his or her awareness of specific relational needs often emerges later in the therapeutic relationship, when it is safe to know about them and to share them—when he or she is able to be vulnerable. In a sense, the whole thrust of the inquiry process is to develop the ability to be vulnerable and aware of one's relational needs, and it is appropriate that these needs lie closest to the inquiry side of the diagram.

☐ But Wait . . .

As we, the authors, read over this chapter, we find ourselves uncomfortable with how neat and how linear it all sounds. It is logical, to be sure; each piece fits neatly into the next, and each, taken by itself, does reflect the way a therapy of contact-in-relationship progresses. But it is too tidy! In a real therapeutic relationship, things simply do not progress from "phase" to "phase." Clients move back and forth; they put one hesitant toe into the water of discovery and pull it back again; they may stay stuck for 15 minutes or several sessions and then make a great triumphant leap into new awareness. Progression from one "phase" to another, and back again, often happens in periods of minutes, not month to month or session to session. Overall, the pattern is more a spiral than a logical progression: ahead and then back, progress and then apparent regress, but always (and sometimes oh so gradually) the trend is toward health and growth, toward contact.

In the second section of this book, you will see some of those shifts, those back-and-forth-ings of the actual progress of therapy. Each of the chapters in this next section presents a complete segment of therapeutic work, rather than the short excerpts that we have been providing. Going back to our beetle metaphor, these transcripts represent the whole beetle, moving about in the real world, not cut up into parts. To help you see how the theory of integrative psychotherapy plays itself out in these real life interactions between therapist and client, there will be frequent comments about what is happening. It will not always (or even often) be neat and tidy, following exactly the progress of therapy as described in this chapter. We hope, though, that these chapters will help you to understand how the theory as we have described it does guide the development of contact-in-relationship and will enhance your ability to create and maintain such contact with your own clients as well.

Greta: "Mother, Come Home"

In psychology, the usefulness of a theory is measured by how well it helps us to deal with people. A theory that has no practical implications will at best become a building block for newer, more relevant theoretical formulations; at worst it will molder away in the pages of textbooks on the history of our discipline, or will be entirely forgotten. A theory of therapy is particularly bound by this imperative: here, if anywhere, the whole purpose of a theory is to guide the therapist in working with clients. A theory that helps us work more effectively will be remembered, used, and valued. Relevance to clinical practice is the ultimate test of all of our theories; the theory upon which this book is based is no exception.

No matter how clearly and logically a theory lays out the steps through which therapy must proceed and how those steps relate to the client's progress toward health and wholeness, though, that clarity tends to be lost in the real-life complexity of the actual therapy session. People (clients and therapists alike!) have a disquieting tendency to muddle things up, to do several things at once, to talk when we expect them to be quiet and to be quiet when we expect them to talk.

In this first of our major transcript chapters, we will sort through the in-the-trenches muddle by tracing the progress of one full integrative psychotherapy session. The client's journey will not be completed in this single session, of course, but we will be able to see how the therapist manages to simultaneously follow and guide her (a difficult balancing act, as all experienced therapists know) while being attuned to her natural process and recognizing the points at which she is ready for each next step.

Psychological health and wholeness, as we have said before, are based on contact: internal contact, with full access to feelings, thoughts, needs, wants, and expectations; and external contact, with full awareness of the environment that surrounds us. Newborn humans naturally make this kind of contact (although with limited capacity), but through the inevitable disruptions in relationship that result from living in an imperfect world, we often learn to dull, distort, or split off from some aspects of awareness. The "decision" to become unaware, to not-know about something in self or other, is usually made unconsciously and slowly over time through countless small adjustments and choices that seem at the moment to be desirable or even necessary to our survival. The result is a fragmented existence in which we are unable to know what we want, to fully utilize our resources, or to act spontaneously and creatively in our interactions with others.

Integrative psychotherapy provides a blueprint for interrupting this process of fragmentation. The "keyhole" model shows how inquiry, attunement, and involvement operate at the various levels of contact interruption, inviting the client to heal the distortions and restore contact with self, with therapist, and with others in his or her life. Often, this involves returning in fantasy to the relationship(s) in which the pattern of contact distortion was first developed, recognizing (at an affective as well as a cognitive level) that pattern and its implications for living in the present and experiencing the possibility of doing it differently. Once the pattern is broken in the context of the old, formative relationship, the client can break out of it in his or her adult life as well.

Greta, in the transcript to follow, is a 55-year-old woman who has survived a childhood replete with both passive and active abuse. Her father left the family when she was quite young, and her mother struggled to hold things together on her own. As a result of her mother's preoccupation and exhaustion and her father's absence, Greta was denied the kind of supportive and responsive relationships that a child needs. To cope with this lack, Greta learned to be stoic: she did not allow herself to know how great her pain was, how needy and angry she felt, or even what it was she wanted. Her relationships with others became increasingly superficial and unsatisfying, and her unhappiness eventually began to erupt in symptoms of anxiety and panic. It is these symptoms that bring her to therapy.

Greta: *I wanted to speak about my—that I'm so often frightened since I've started therapy. I feel so much more than I did when I was younger.*
Therapist: *Good.*

Acknowledging and normalizing the symptom. From the outset, the therapist is establishing that internal contact is a good thing, not a bad thing. This initial intervention also serves to capture Greta's attention, bringing her back into contact with the therapist rather than going off on a monologue. Once this has been accomplished, the next several transactions serve to explore the phenomenology of what is (and has been) going on for Greta and to find out more about how she is distorting or disrupting (or both) the contact with self and others—the first level in the "keyhole" diagram.

Greta: *Is it good? But I'm frightened so often and, you know, two days ago in the airplane I was really in a panic. I had to get out to change planes.*

Therapist: *Oh?*

Greta: *And I think, well, in this case, by changing the airplane I had control over a machine that was damaged.*

Therapist: *Damaged?*

Greta: *Well, twice they had to do something and the next day it still didn't work. There was something wrong with the engine. We started out and then we turned around and came back, and I went into panic. I didn't want to be over the ocean for eight hours not knowing what was coming next.*

Therapist: *Sounds like good judgment.*

What she is describing as a problem seems like an eminently reasonable behavior. But if Greta's decision to refuse to commit herself to a possibly damaged airplane is "good judgment," what is the problem? Although the therapist has a hunch about this, based on previous work with Greta, she will let Greta get there in her own way.

Greta: *It seems—I got to Amsterdam, got there and I was supposed to change to another plane, and it was there, but what was inside of me was something that didn't—I really couldn't handle it. My heart was pounding, and later on it was like a screw that couldn't unscrew until I got to New York or maybe even the next morning. That is too long for me, I think, to be screwed up.*

Therapist: *Screwed up—interesting choice of words.*

Greta: *Well, I will say my chest was so tight, and it wouldn't open, and that's what felt like panic—it's the beginning of a panic, I think. And I want to stop doing that. I want to be as normal as possible.*

Greta ties together the two meanings of "screwed up" when she equates "normal" with not keeping herself tight and panicky. There is another piece of her concern, though, that is not clear, and the therapist asks about it.

Therapist: *"That is too long for me," means what?*

Greta: *Like I said, in the airplane I didn't understand I was in a panic. Other people were in panic too, and I said, okay, I'll get out of this machine. But later on, until the next day, I was all tight inside. That's just too long for me. I want to be free. I want to . . .*

Therapist: *I thought you were talking about 50 years too long.*

Greta: *Pardon?*

Therapist: *I though you were talking about 50 years too long.*

Greta has talked before about fears and anxieties that go back to her earliest memories. The therapist's comment here may be based on an assumption that Greta is, in fact, connecting her airplane experience to those early experiences, or it may be an invitation for her to do so. In either event, she avoids that avenue, choosing instead to talk about how her old defenses against anxiety are no longer working.

Greta: *No—this feeling inside me that was, ah. . . . And I'm sensitive to other things that I feel more strongly now than I used to. I'm more frightened.*

Therapist: *Like what?*

Greta: *Darkness—if it's real dark, I feel anxious, and I let it out. Used to be I didn't show it. Like, going into a garage.*

Therapist: *Going into a garage? And when it's dark . . .*

Greta: *. . . and the door suddenly opens, I want to scream.*

Therapist: *Yeah.*

Greta: *And, I don't think that's normal. I want to get rid of this fear, this anxiety. . . . Plus, people tell me . . . sometimes, that. . . .* (her voice trails off)

Therapist: *People tell you what?*

Greta: *. . . that I'm more anxious than is normal, and besides, I don't feel well. I often have stomach pains—not in my chest, here, but in my stomach. This is a new symptom.*

Therapist: *There's much you don't want to remember. . . .*

All of the things Greta is talking about, including the panic feelings, the continuing sense of tension and tightness, the overreaction to darkness or sudden change, and the stomach pain, all are common responses to an effort to hold back emerging memories and awareness. The memories are painful, and Greta would rather not experience them. The cost of keeping them out of awareness, though, is very high.

Greta: *I want to.* (begins to cry)

Therapist: *You do?*

Greta: *If you ask me to, I . . .*

Therapist: *I just made a comment that there is much you don't want to remember.*

Greta: *There is much I don't want to remember.*

Therapist: *Yeah. . . .*

Greta: (long pause) *I think it was better when I didn't feel it and I didn't know that I was anxious. And now I'm so frightened of it. . . . It was better not to have it. It was better not to be so sensitive.*

Therapist: *Was it?*

Greta: *Yeah. I think I lived better.*

Therapist: *Better not to sleep?*

In a previous session, Greta had talked about insomnia—another common consequence of active repression. When we relax in sleep, we may dream, and the dream cannot be controlled the way waking thoughts can. Sleeping becomes threatening, frightening, dangerous; insomnia is a part of the cost of blocking internal contact. In this earlier work, Greta was able to recall a previously blocked-off incident and to work through the painful feelings surrounding it; subsequently, she has been able to sleep more normally.

Greta: *That's something else.*

Therapist: *Better to be physically tense all the time. Better to be driven.*

Greta: *Maybe . . . yes . . .*

Therapist: *Are you saying, "Yes, that was better?"*

Greta: *No, I see now what you mean.*

Therapist: *What do you think I mean?*

Greta: *If you mean it's better to have feelings and be able to sleep, instead of not sleeping very deeply and not having anxiety, then I prefer to sleep well and have anxiety. I do think they're connected.*

Greta acknowledges the connection between her physical discomfort and her desire to avoid painful feelings. With this acknowledgment comes a tacit signal that she is ready to proceed with the process of exploring those feelings and restoring contact with whatever she has split off within herself. The therapist's next question is an inquiry into her actual experience, her phenomenology.

Therapist: *And do you dream when you sleep?*

Greta: *Yes, sometimes.*

Therapist: *Um. Do you remember any of those dreams?*

Greta: *When I was a child I often had this dream about running away, running and running and never getting where I was going—just running and stopping or falling down.*

Therapist: *I meant since you started sleeping again.*

Greta: *I, I have good dreams—nothing to do with being . . .*

Therapist: (pause) *Do you remember the dreams?*

Greta assumes that if a dream is of therapeutic interest, it must be unpleasant; thus she devalues the possible importance of her current dreams. The childhood dream, though, is likely to have been related to the blocked contact that was restored in an earlier piece of work. The therapist is more interested in what is going on for her now, what underlies her stomach pain, her anxiety, and her feelings of being "screwed up." Even a pleasant dream may provide a useful starting place for exploring one's internal world; even the fact of remembering or not remembering may be important.

Greta: *I have to think about that . . . I dreamed at least two dreams. One dream about something as a family, I . . . and there was another dream I have to think about, because I don't understand it—it was just a short dream . . .*

Therapist: *So you started sleeping, and one of the two dreams you remember is about your family.*

Greta: *Um . . .* (long pause) *. . .*

Therapist: *Pardon?*

Greta: *I think this is good to talk about.*

Therapist: *Well, I think it's probably good, too. Are you feeling anything right now?*

Greta: *I feel tight in here* (indicates her upper chest) *and tears are coming up.*

Therapist: *Um-hmm. Let them come and tell me about them. Because I'd like to know.*

There is, of course, no way to know at this point what Greta's tightness and tears are all about; in all likelihood, she herself may not know precisely what has triggered this reaction. By inviting her to "let them come," the therapist hopes to short circuit her usual pattern of repressing the feelings and then experiencing the emotional and physical consequences of the repression. Letting the tears come, without choking them off, would not only allow her to escape those consequences, but it would also help her to know just what experience, hope, fear, or fantasy they are connected to.

Greta: *I'm just nervous, I think.*

Therapist: *Nervous?*

Greta: *I'm feeling real nervous.*

Therapist: *Well, your plane's not going to crash here. So your nervousness isn't about that. Is it possible that your reason isn't external? What if we just agree not to look for an external cause?*

Greta: *And what reasons do you think then?*

Therapist: *Perhaps not even searching for a reason, but just to honor that you're scared. . . .*

By searching for a logical reason for her internal experience, Greta is able to focus her attention on thinking rather than feeling. It can be much less uncomfortable to think about feelings than to actually feel them! The price she pays, though, is that the emotional reaction stays walled away, split off, and thus can never be worked through or discharged. The therapist will continue with a patient inquiry, allowing Greta to move at her own speed and gently encouraging her to attend to her immediate experiencing instead of analyzing and rationalizing that experiencing.

Greta: *I know I can find several reasons, because I was alone as a child; we were alone for three nights every week and I remember that.*

Therapist: *Tell me more about that.*

Greta: *Ah . . . when I was about 8, my mother worked in another town and she left us kids alone for three nights, in the apartment.*

Therapist: *You were 8?*

Greta: *Yeah, about 8, and my sister was 7 and my brother was 4. My younger sister was there, too. Because my mom knew that I was responsible and that I was strong and that I was, you know, she could trust me, and she didn't come home.*

Therapist: *And now you hold you breath—right this moment. Can you feel the holding of your breath?*

The memory is painful, and Greta automatically does what she has done for years in order to control the pain: she tenses her body and restrains her breathing. Disavowal of feelings is always accompanied by some sort of physiological holding back, and in Greta's case the holding back can actually be observed, even though she herself may be unaware of what she is doing. Calling her attention to it is, again, an invitation to focus on immediate experience and to begin to heal the broken internal contact.

Therapist: *Are you feeling anything?*

Greta: *Only here . . .* (indicating her chest)

Therapist: *And if you were to breathe all the way?*

Greta: *. . . I think my back itches a little bit . . .*

Therapist: *Now will you tell me that story again, about three nights alone—the same story, but try breathing while you're telling the story.*

Greta is not yet able to connect her held breath with her held-back anxiety; instead, she goes to a less threatening physical sensation. The therapist invites her into an experiment ("try" doing this) that will help her make the connection. The defense is well learned and well practiced: even with this direct suggestion, it is still hard for her to allow herself to understand what she is being asked to do.

Greta: *Without breathing?*

Therapist: *No, with breathing.*

Greta: *With breathing . . . uh . . .*

Therapist: *Yes. We know you can tell it without breathing.*

Greta: (her voice becomes tearful) *When I was about 8 my mother worked about 15 miles away in another town, and because it was too difficult for her to come back by bus after work, she left us alone at home.*

Therapist: *So this was about how it was difficult for her.*

Greta: *Um. . . .*

Therapist: *What's it like for you when mother says, "It's too difficult to come back and be with you at night"?*

A child needs a good, protective, caring parent. Children will go to great lengths to excuse a parent's bad or neglectful behavior and thus preserve the illusion that Mom or Dad is the kind of parent they need. Greta's focus on her mother's difficulty thus serves two functions: it allows Mom to be the good, loving mother she needs (in spite of the fact that Mom was not there for Greta) and it also distracts her attention away from her own pain and neediness.

Greta: *Now I think it was probably hard, but when I was a child, I don't know what I thought about it. . . .*

Therapist: *Let your body just respond* (Greta sighs deeply). *Just let that happen again. Yeah. Breathe. Will you just let your body do what it wants to, while you tell your story?* (pause) *Tell me that same story again.*

Greta: *When I was 8 years old, my mother worked in another town and we had to stay at home three days and three nights, all alone.*

Therapist: *Because it was difficult for her.*

The therapist supplies the explanation that excuses mother from responsibility; Greta does not have to protect her. Freed from this need, will she come back to her own experience?

Greta: *Because it was difficult for her.*

Therapist: *How was it for you?*

Greta: *It was . . .*

Therapist: *Tighten your chest up, now.*

Greta is already tightening up, breathing shallowly, and holding back the feelings. Suggesting that she let go of the tightness had little effect. Directing her to do what she is already doing may, paradoxically, allow her to do the opposite.

Greta: *It was painful.*

Therapist: *Say that to Mama.*

The invitation to talk to Greta's image of her mother, rather than to the therapist, marks the first major turning point in this piece of work. The therapist, developmentally attuned, sees that as Greta begins to let go of her muscular tension, she also begins to regress. She begins to think and to feel as she did when she was a lonely, abandoned little girl. The pattern of holding back in order to avoid emotional pain was developed back then, in her relationship with mother; it is in the context of that relationship that the pattern can be reversed and a new way of being can evolve.

Greta: *Oh. . . .*

Therapist: *Look at Mama the way she looked when you were 8.*

Greta: *Mama, it hurts. . . .*

Therapist: *Breathe right now. Just breathe, and talk to her.*

Greta: (beginning to cry) *I don't like this. . . .*

Therapist: *Keep going; tell Mama.*

Greta: (crying) *I know you have to work. . . .*

The old pattern emerges again, so the therapist moves quickly to refocus Greta's attention on her own experience instead of mother's problems.

Therapist: *Tell her what it's like to be 8 years old and to be defined as the responsible one.*

Greta: *It hurts. . . .*

Therapist: *Yeah. Trying so hard to be strong. . . . The 7-year-old was harder to take care of than the 4-year-old. . . . You have to have lots of control to take care of the 7-year-old.*

The therapist makes an assumption: it is harder for an 8-year-old to be responsible for a 7-year-old than for a 4-year-old. Controlling someone nearly your own age is harder than controlling a smaller child. Every threat to Greta's control was a threat to her survival; control was how she took care of herself and her siblings. She had to control them, and she had to control herself. When you are 8 and in charge of the family, you cannot afford to let yourself know how frightened and miserable you feel. The therapist continues to encourage Greta to explore the contradictions of that early experience, including the need to be in control and the yearning to be taken care of. Relaxing the muscular tension and the cognitive discipline that she still uses as an adult will make the exploration possible.

Greta: *Oh, it's hard to do!*

Therapist: *Just let it go . . .* (long pause) *being so strong—just what Mama wanted you to be. Wanted you to be strong. Wanted you to be dependable. Wanted you to just keep on going, keep helping her, keep the family going. . . .*

Greta: *She needed me to do that.*

Therapist: *Let's try something. Just look at Mama the way she looked when you were 8 years old. And try saying "Stay home, Mama."*

"Stay home" was the forbidden request. It was what Greta wanted and needed from her mother, but Greta's job was to protect mother. She not only had to protect her image of Mama as a good mother, but she also had to hide her feelings so as not to put additional pressure on an already stressed caretaker. Now, though, things are different. In the safety of the therapeutic relationship, she can have the experience of finally saying what could not be said back then.

Greta: (looking across the room) *Stay home, Mama.*

Therapist: *Right from your heart.*

Greta: (sobbing) *Stay home, Mommy.*

Therapist: *There you go. Breathe. Say it again.*

Greta: (continuing to cry) *Stay home, Mommy.*

Therapist: *Keep going.*

Greta: *I want you to stay home.*

Therapist: *Keep going.*

Greta: *Please, please come home on the bus tonight.*

Therapist: *Tell her why.*

Greta: *I don't want to be alone tonight.*

Therapist: *Keep going.*

Greta: *Don't stay there. Get on the bus tonight. . . .*

Therapist: *Tell her what it's like when she doesn't come home.*

In this and in the following series of interventions, the therapist focuses and deepens Greta's growing connectedness to her own experiencing. The tide has turned; instead of struggling against the current of Greta's defensive structure, the therapist can now provide gentle encouragement, support, and an occasional suggestion while Greta's own momentum carries her forward.

Greta: *It's so dark, and . . .* (she cries)

Therapist: *Keep going: "It's so dark. . . ."*

Greta: *It's so dark and I'm scared, and I have to run around into the other rooms, and I'm not supposed to cry. . . .* (she clutches her arms to her chest)

Therapist: *Yeah. Keep going. Do that with your body.*

Greta: *Oh. . . . It's so awful.*

Therapist: *Yeah. Tell her, "Mama, it's awful."*

Greta: *It's awful!*

Therapist: *Tell her what's awful.*

Greta: *It's dark everywhere. I'm looking for you and you're not home. I want you to come home.*

Therapist: *Tell her what you're feeling.*

Greta: (crying again) *I'm so scared; I need you!*

Therapist: *Yeah . . . "I need you, Mama. . . ."*

Greta: *I try to be brave, but I don't feel brave. . . .*

Therapist: *Running through all the rooms, and it's so dark.*

Greta: *Yes. . . .*

Therapist: *And tell her about what it's like to have to take care of those children.*

Deepening Greta's awareness, the therapist calls her attention to yet another part of the equation: she has to be strong to take care of herself, to take care of her mother, and also to take care of her siblings. The more responsibility Greta is given, the greater her sense of fear and abandonment, and the greater her need not to show or even feel those emotions.

Greta: *Um. They play. They always play, and then they go to sleep. They can sleep and I can't.*

Therapist: *You just held your breath again. Let that go now. . . . Keep talking to her.*

The reversion to breath-holding is a clue that Greta has stumbled into a new pocket of feelings, and she almost reflexively responds with her familiar protection. The therapy is working: she is reconnecting with the long-repressed and split-off parts of herself.

Greta: (crying) *Please come home. . . .*

Therapist: *"Because I need . . ."*

Greta: (softly) *I need you.*

Therapist: *Yeah. Tell her again, louder.*

Greta: *I need you a lot.*

Therapist: *Even louder now.*

Tapping first into her fear of being alone in the darkness and then into the fears and frustrations of being caretaker to the other children, Greta can now express aloud the need that has had to be hidden. Back then, her mother had to be protected from knowing how frightened Greta was; and Greta herself was not allowed to realize how much she needed her mother. Her first attempt to break this rule comes out softly, breathlessly, almost as if she expects to be punished for speaking out. Having said it once, and survived, she needs to say it again more forcefully. By turning her hesitant pleading into a clear demand, she will at last have the opportunity to be open and real in her relationship with mother and to make full external contact, just as she is learning to make full contact with her internal experiencing.

Greta: *I need you a lot!*

Therapist: *Scream it at her.*

Greta: (a bit louder) *I need you a lot!*

Therapist: *You've gotta scream it 15 miles.*

Greta: *I NEED YOU A LOT!*

Therapist: *Scream again: "Come home!"*

Greta: *Come home—I need you a lot!*

Therapist: *Now just let that go again.*

Greta: *COME HOME—I NEED YOU A LOT!*

Therapist: *Keep talking to her.*

Greta: *I want you to come home! It's too much for me. . . .*

Therapist: *Oh, say that again.*

Greta: *It's too much for me!*

Therapist: *Tell her about it.*

The therapist continues to help Greta explore and express what she discovers. It is very much like cleansing a festering wound: everything must be cleaned out and the deepest recesses probed; nothing of the old infection must be left undisturbed lest the whole wound be recontaminated and be unable to heal properly.

Greta: *It was all too much—all day, and the night and then again. I don't want this.*

Therapist: *"I need. . . ."*

Greta: *I need you, at least at night. And I want to sleep in your bed.*

Therapist: *Yeah. Tell her.*

Greta: *I want to sleep in your bed. I want you to be close to me. I want to hold onto you. I want to hold you!* (sobbing)

Therapist: *Keep talking to her.*

Greta: *Why don't you come home?*

Therapist: *Just make that a statement.*

"Why don't you come home?" is a dangerous question: it can again turn Greta's attention from her own feelings, and the opportunity to demand that those feelings be attended to, into a concern for her mother's problems. Her mother's "why" will not help this little girl get her needs met; it will only drive those needs underground. Typically, in integrative psychotherapy, we invite clients to turn this kind of question into a statement that refocuses on the client's experience.

Greta: *Please come home.*

Therapist: *Now, just make that louder.*

Greta: (slightly louder) *Please come home.*

Therapist: *Say it even louder.*

Greta: *Please come home!* (she is holding out her hand, in a pleading gesture)

Therapist: *Exaggerate that gesture, the way you're holding your hand.*

Greta: (gesturing again) *Please come home!*

Therapist: *Make that a demand now.*

Greta: *I want you to come home.*

Therapist: *Even louder now and harder.*

Greta: *Come home!*

Therapist: *Even harder now.*

Greta: *Come home!*

Therapist: *Just scream it at her.*

Greta: *Come home!* (her pleading hand has turned into a fist)

Therapist: *Even harder, with that hand now.*

Greta: *Come home—*

Therapist: *Now both hands.*

Greta: *Come home!*

Greta builds momentum as the therapist leads her through successive steps: she urges Greta to express the forbidden need/feeling/experience, express it to the person in the original relationship, express it as a direct request of the person, turn the request into a demand, and intensify the demand. Although she is much more fully involved in the experience than before, there is still a held-back quality in her voice and her gestures. The therapist continues to encourage her to break through into full and genuine experience and expression of her need.

Therapist: *Now, make a fuss.*

Greta: *Come home!!*

Therapist: *Keep going, keep going—even louder.*

Greta: *Come home!!*

Therapist: *Now, a big breath and keep going!*

Greta: *Come home. . . .*

The breakthrough has not come. Instead, Greta's last "come home" had a forced quality, a sense of "I'll say the words but it won't change anything." Her shoulders slump, and her face is sad.

Therapist: *Yeah. You keep stopping yourself, huh?*

Greta: *Because I know she won't come.*

Therapist: *Say that to her.*

Greta: *I know you won't come.*

The therapist's next intervention marks the second pivotal point of this session. Greta has stopped herself, closed down, and has spontaneously revealed the belief that underlies her inability to solve her problem: "There's no use in telling you what I need when I already know you won't give it to me." The next step is to explore the child's substitute solution of the problem: "Since I can't have what I really want, I'll . . . instead."

Therapist: *"So what I do is . . ."?*

Greta: *Oh, it doesn't make sense . . .* (beginning to cry again)

Therapist: *Just let that come—all that feeling. Just tell it to her.*

Greta: *. . . I'm so alone. . . . There's nobody. I don't know where my grand-mother, where she lives—some strange . . . and I can't call my Mom . . . .*

Therapist: *And you won't get mad at Mama. You start to get angry and then you stop.*

Greta: *I know . . . because I . . . she has to . . . all kinds of things. . . .*

Therapist: *So tell her what you do when you're angry.* (Greta silently huddles into herself) *Yeah, go ahead. . . .*

Greta: (still huddling, tapping her fist against her chest) *Ahhh. . . .*

Therapist: *Tell her what you're doing right there.*

Greta: *Right there it hurts. It's burning and hurting.*

Therapist: *Just increase that now—pull those shoulders closer together. That's it. Show her what you do instead of being angry.*

Greta has been acting it out, showing the therapist (and the fantasy of her mother) without words what happens as she feels the need that she knows will not be met. The reaction is so ingrained that she ordinarily does not even notice it. By asking her to exaggerate her reaction, to do it more, harder, longer, the therapist brings it to her attention; now she can put into words what has, up to now, been only in her body.

Greta: *. . . When I'm angry, then I'm so frightened.*

Therapist: *You're angry about being frightened?*

Greta: *No . . .*

Therapist: *Or you're angry at her that she's created the situation, and that you're frightened.*

Greta: *No, when I want to get angry but then I know she'll hurt us, or . . .*

As therapists, we are all highly sensitized to references to child abuse, and this certainly sounds like such a reference. The temptation is to abandon the regression experience and jump in to assess the extent of the early abuse and its effect on current functioning. The therapist resists that temptation, keeping Greta involved in the reconstructed relationship with mother while pursuing this new topic.

Therapist: *Tell that to her.*

Greta: *If I'm angry and I tell you, then you'll slap me or hit me with things and then I have to run away and hide or to try to get out of the house. And then I run around in the dark. . . .*

Therapist: *Because I need . . .*

As she reiterates her needs, voicing them rather than pushing them out of awareness, Greta can become increasingly aware of how she coped with the experience of need-not-met, and how those coping strategies are playing themselves out in her adult life.

Greta: *I need you not to threaten me.*

Therapist: *Yeah. And I need . . .*

Greta: *I need you to be kind to me.*

Therapist: *And I need . . .*

Greta: *I need you to come home in the evening.*

Therapist: *And I need . . .*

Greta: (crying) *I need you to be at home in the night, and me safe in your arms.*

Therapist: *And I need . . .*

Greta: *I need you not to slap me.*

Has Greta been using her growing awareness of feeling neglected and afraid as another defensive layer, to protect her from an even greater pain, that of active abuse? How does a child organize herself and her beliefs about how to survive in the world, when the person she looks to for protection is her persecutor? This is an essential piece of the puzzle, and the therapist will help her to fit it into its place.

Therapist: *Yeah. Say it again louder.*

Greta: *I need you not to slap me.*

Therapist: *Say it even louder: "Don't. . . ."*

Greta: *Don't slap me.*

Therapist: *Even louder.*

Greta: (somewhat louder) *Don't slap me.*

Therapist: *Now, make that a demand.*

Greta: *Don't slap me! Don't slap me when I'm angry or when I have broken something. If I do something wrong, don't slap me. . . .* (sadly, turning to the therapist) *There isn't anybody who tells her not to do it. There's nobody who tells her not to slap us children.*

It is extremely difficult for Greta to summon the energy and intensity to demand that her mother change. In spite of the therapist's directions, Greta's voice remains soft and reasonable; eventually, she interrupts her talking to her mother and addresses the therapist instead. Rather than continuing to push for more and risk Greta's feeling criticized, the therapist backs off, adapts to her pace, and helps her to reestablish the dialogue with mother. In that dialogue, she may discover what 8-year-old Greta needed back then and what she still needs, on some level, as an adult.

Therapist: *Keep talking to her. If you don't know what to say, just repeat.*

Greta: *Grandmother knows there's blue spots on us, but she doesn't say anything to you—nobody will tell you anything; I don't know why. . . .*

Therapist: *No wonder you're scared, little girl. You were just talking about being slapped. "Blue spots"—that's abuse—no wonder you're scared.*

Greta's statement, "nobody will tell you anything," is a child's yearning for help, for someone to intervene and solve the problem that she is too small and powerless to solve for herself. The therapist is quick to respond to the request, providing here in the therapeutic relationship the support that was needed but missing in Greta's childhood. Does this response allow Greta to use the therapist as she would have liked to be able to use her absent father?

Greta: *I wanted to. . . . I ran away and I thought . . . when my Daddy comes home, then I can go away with him. . . .*

Therapist: *What a wonderful hope—when Daddy comes home you can run away with him. . . . Did Daddy come back?*

Greta: *No. . . .*

Therapist: *Stayed away?*

Greta: *Yeah, he did.*

Therapist: *Did he die?*

Greta: *Yeah. But we didn't know until 11 years later.*

Therapist: *Eleven years waiting for him to come home. . . .*

Greta: *Yes. And then my mother married again.*

Greta has turned from her fantasied interaction with mother and is talking directly to the therapist about her absent father. Now she talks about her mother again, and the therapist immediately invites her to return to the fantasied interaction; this time, though, she will bring her feelings about her father into the conversation.

Therapist: *Tell Mama about that fantasy of running away with Daddy. "I want to run away from your hitting, Mama."*

Greta: *I wanted to run away from your hitting. And if Daddy comes back, I want to go away with him. We'll leave you. . . .*

Therapist: *Going to run away with a Daddy you don't even know, huh?*

Greta: *When she married this other man, I thought, where is my real Daddy? Where did he go? I want to go with him.*

Therapist: *Um-hmm.*

Greta: *Then I had the fantasy that perhaps he was living somewhere with another family. And then my mother married this other man; I was so—I wanted to jump out of the window, from the fifth floor. And then I had these fantasies about when I would be dead . . .* (her voice has begun to shake)

Therapist: *Just let that shake come.*

Shaking, of the voice and of the whole body, is often a signal that an old, well-established psychological pattern is breaking up. It may be caused by the body's reaction to the release of adrenaline and other hormones or by the confusion that occurs as the psychic system tries to find a new equilibrium. Whatever the cause, an integrative psychotherapist generally welcomes and encourages it as a part of the energy release that accompanies and facilitates an opening of awareness.

Greta: (crying) *I . . . there were many nights when I didn't sleep at all—just cried.*

Therapist: *Well, just tell that to Mama: "I cry at night, Mama."*

Greta: *I cry at night. I can't sleep, and you don't know.*

Therapist: *Tell her now so she can know.*

Greta: *I cry at night and I can't sleep. Sometimes I'm desperate at night.*

Therapist: *Yeah. Say that again, "I'm desperate."*

"Desperate" is an intense word, with many levels of meaning. Focusing on this word—Greta's own way of describing herself—is again an attempt to deepen her experience of all of the feelings, needs, and sensations that she has been blocking from awareness.

Greta: *I'm desperate at night.*

Therapist: *"Because I need. . . ."*

Greta: *Because I need you. And now this other man is lying in your bed, instead of me!*

Therapist: *"And therefore . . ."*

Again, the therapist invites Greta to look at the strategy, the small child's solution to her problem. When she cannot have mother's protection, what does she do? The therapist has a pretty good idea, but her understanding does not count. Greta needs to discover it for herself, right down in the muscles of her experience. But she is not yet ready to put it into words, so the therapist follows her rhythm.

Greta: (sigh)

Therapist: *"I need you, Mama. . . ."*

Greta: (crying) *I need you, Mama. I need you!*

Therapist: *"And without you . . . "*

Greta: *And without you, I don't want to live anymore.*

Here it is, the beginning of the old solution. Children solve insoluble problems by developing sets of thoughts, emotions, and behaviors that will help them survive and make sense out of their existence. Apparently one of Greta's sense-making conclusions was about the nature of life: it is not worth living.

Therapist: *Yeah. Tell her about that.*

Greta: (sobbing) *You know I wanted to jump out of the window, and Heidi called you, and you said you'd slap me again. . . .*

Therapist: *"And what I needed from you, Mama was . . . "*

Greta: *For you to take me in your bed, and hold me . . .* (crying hard)

Therapist: *Keep going, Greta. "Don't slap me, Mama, because I wanted to jump out the window. . . ."*

Greta: *Oh, don't slap me, because I want to die!*

Therapist: *"But instead . . . "*

Over and over, in all possible combinations, the therapist helps Greta to deal with the pattern-forming triad: "I need" . . . "but instead I expect" . . . "and therefore. . . ." Like a great, widening spiral, each iteration brings a new bit of information and a deeper awareness.

Greta: *Instead, take me in your arms—put me in your bed. I just want to be close to you!*

Therapist: *That's right, little girl. Keep talking to her.*

Greta: *And I want to stay with you, with you holding me. . . .*

Therapist: *Just tell her what you feel when she's not holding you.*

Greta: *Ohhh, when you don't hold me, I feel so lonely and so desperate. It hurts too much . . . too much!*

Therapist: *Of course it does. Too much pain, too much responsibility. . . .*

Greta: (long pause) *It makes me mad to hear you say it's easier for you to stay away from the family overnight. It makes me . . .*

Earlier, when she began to experience being angry at mother, Greta backed away, because it was too frightening and the threat of punishment was too great. Now, having experienced the therapist's support as she cried out her loneliness and sadness, Greta may have found the strength to come back to that anger.

Therapist: *Yeah, tell her that again.*

Greta: *It makes me mad to hear that it's easier for you—it makes me mad that you want to stay away from the family.*

Therapist: *Tell her what it's like for you when she stays away.*

Greta: *Oh, it's not easy! I'm scared, alone at night.*

Therapist: *Say that again: "For me it's not easy, Mama. . . ."*

Greta: (her voice sounds frightened, and she huddles again in her chair) *For me, it's not easy. . . .*

The fear in Greta's voice and her body language is a clear signal that she does not have access to the resources she needs to confront mother strongly and effectively with a statement about her needs and her anger that those needs are not being met. Without resources, she is likely to fall back into the old, familiar, "Don't feel it; don't show it" strategy that she has used for so long. To avert that, and to provide a new resource for Greta, the therapist steps in to confront Greta's mother with the therapist's own voice. This time, there *will* be someone to talk to mother and tell her that her behavior is inappropriate. This time Greta will not have to do it all by herself.

Therapist: (turning in the direction that Greta faced when she "talked to" her mother) *Now, listen to her, Mom! And don't slap her! She wants to talk to you, and you just listen to her. Fold your hands, and don't slap her, Mother!* (turning back to Greta) *Keep going, Greta.*

Greta: *It hurts . . .*

Therapist: *Keep talking to her. Tell her about your anger.*

Greta: (her voice is choked, and she struggles to get the words out) *I'm angry because you have a nice life over there where your job is. I don't know what you do after work, but your children are at home, and are waiting for you.*

It is safer, because it is less personal, to talk about her siblings or to disguise her own feelings by being just one of the "children." But the safety of impersonality does not make full contact; it impedes contact. Greta needs to talk about "me," not about "them" or even about "us."

Therapist: *Tell her about* you, *Greta.*

Greta: *And* I'm *waiting for you.*

Therapist: (very loudly and forcefully) *AND DON'T SLAP HER, MOTHER! Listen to her and respond to her, Mother!*

Greta: *I want you to come home, and I want you to talk to Heidi and to Grandma—it's all too much for me.*

Therapist: *Yes, now louder . . .*

Greta: *This is too much for me.*

Therapist: *LISTEN TO THAT, MOTHER—IT'S TOO MUCH FOR HER!* (to Greta) *Keep going.*

Joining Greta in confronting her mother serves several therapeutic purposes. First, because getting angry and confronting someone who is not really there is, in the world outside of therapy, a pretty odd behavior. Joining Greta in that behavior helps her avoid any sense of being ashamed or feeling crazy because of what she is doing. It models the kind of contactful anger that Greta needs to learn to sustain, and it also provides support, so that Greta can stay with the experience rather than close down in order to protect herself from her fear and desperate loneliness. Finally, it disconfirms Greta's belief that she will always have to do the important things on her own (which makes life not worth living). The therapist continues to alternate speaking to Greta's mother and encouraging Greta to "keep going."

Greta: *When the other ones go to sleep, I'm still awake. It's too much for me.*

Therapist: *SHE NEEDS YOU, MOTHER!*

Greta: (crying) *And, I need you, I need you to talk with me—someone has to talk with me. I'm so alone!*

Therapist: *AND SHE'S FRIGHTENED, MOTHER. SHE'S FRIGHTENED BECAUSE YOU ABANDONED HER. AND YOU MAKE HER TAKE CARE OF OTHER CHILDREN WHEN SHE DOESN'T HAVE THE SKILLS TO DO IT. . . . Keep talking to her, Greta.*

Greta: (choking up again) *I want you to come home and put me to bed. And kiss me good night, and give me hugs, and hold me tight. . . .* (cries softly)

Therapist: *Just let that come, now. And I'm going to talk to your Mama.* (loudly, to Greta's fantasied mother) *Mother, don't you dare slap her! That's no way to treat this precious little girl.* (in a more reasonable tone) *She's frightened of being alone and she's frightened of being with you because you hit her. She's frightened all the time. She pretends not to be, but she's frightened all the time.*

Greta: *Don't do it after this . . .*

Therapist: *Say that again.*

Greta: *Don't slap me after we're done talking here, in therapy.*

Therapist: *Oh, afterwards she'll slap?*

Greta: *Yeah. . . .*

Therapist: *So you must be scared now that if we stop she'll slap you afterward.*

Greta: *Once I ran away and slept at my girlfriend's house, and she found me. She pulled me out of the bed and I ran home and she ran after me and she hit me in the head with a wooden paddle, and I bled all over, and then she fainted. I don't know—she was crazy, maybe.*

A crazy parent is perhaps the most terrifying thing a child can live with, because craziness is unpredictable. When you have no way to predict what will happen, you cannot guard yourself or get ready for it. It is not safe to trust a crazy parent, because even when they seem to be doing nice things, it can all change in a heartbeat. It is no wonder that Greta decided it was safer not to deal with mother at all and to just be responsible and take care of the other children and not call attention to herself.

Therapist: *She was crazy?*

Greta: *I think she was crazy.*

Therapist: *And you're scared now if I go away, Mama's going to hit you again?*

Greta: *She's going to be furious.*

Therapist: *So it's real hard for you to tell Mama everything then, isn't it?*

Greta: (long pause) *I had to be nice.*

Another piece of the pattern emerges spontaneously: the way to survive and to take care of oneself is to "be nice" no matter how badly one is treated.

Therapist: *Had to be nice? Even when you're angry at her, huh?*

Greta: *Yeah. If I'm angry, then I have to apologize.*

Therapist: *And if you're scared?*

Greta: *If I'm scared and if I cry, then she gets mad.*

Therapist: *Hmm?*

Greta: (sounding small and frightened again) *When she gets mad, we all have to stand in a row, and I'm the tallest and my other sister next, and then my little brother. In that order. And so I'm at the end, and I get most of the slaps.*

Therapist: *Do you want me to tell Mama not to hit you after we stop talking?*

Greta: *Yes.*

Therapist: *MOTHER, DON'T YOU HIT HER WHEN WE'RE DONE HERE! YOU NEED THERAPY—NOT HITTING YOUR CHILDREN. SOMETHING'S GOING ON WITH YOUR LIFE, AND DON'T TAKE IT OUT ON YOUR CHILDREN, AND DON'T YOU HIT GRETA FOR TELLING THIS STORY! IT'S YOU WHO NEEDS THERAPY. SOMETHING'S GONE WRONG IN YOUR LIFE, AND DON'T YOU HIT GRETA FOR TELLING THIS STORY! YOU GO TO THERAPY!*

Greta: (long pause) *You say she needs therapy, but in those times, where we lived, nobody sought out therapy. You just figured out how to earn enough money to pay the rent and buy the food and keep going. Therapy—nobody thought of therapy.*

Therapist: *Does that mean she didn't need it?*

Greta: *I guess she needed my father coming home, or a man who earns money so things would not be so hard. Then she would not have to be so mean and angry. Maybe she would have felt ashamed if someone would have told her, "You mustn't do this to your children." Maybe . . .*

How subtle and persistent old patterns can be! Greta needed her mother to be a good mother, and to keep mother good she made excuses for her, protected her, took responsibility herself and learned how to get along on her own. Even now, she is uneasy with the therapist's confrontation and with her observation that Greta's mother needed therapy. A mother who needs therapy is crazy, and a crazy mother cannot be a good mother. Maybe she would have been all right if only someone had helped her out a little bit... but then she might have felt ashamed, and that would also have meant that she wasn't being a good mother. . . .

Therapist: *And I suppose you would like to protect her right now from that shame? You know, sometimes people deserve to feel their shame. She did something wrong against you and those other children by hitting you, slapping you, hitting you with a paddle. She needs to be ashamed of that. But you'd like to protect her from that shame. Right now you'd like to make excuses for her. How does that serve you, to make an excuse for her?*

The next therapeutic landmark is to identify the function of the problem response. We have seen Greta regress back to the original traumatic relationship by identifying the need that was not met in that relationship, and we have seen her explore what she did in response to the experience of her needs not met. Identifying the function of that pattern of responses will loosen one more coil of the tangle, freeing her to use her adult resources to find new and authentic ways to accomplish the same thing.

Greta: *It doesn't serve me.*

Therapist: *How does it serve you right now to make excuses for her? "It's the times," or "She can't help it, things are so bad," or "Nobody spoke to her about it . . . "?*

Greta: *She acted that way because she was sick.*

Therapist: *How does that affect you?*

Greta: *It makes it less. . . .*

Therapist: (pause) *It makes what less?*

Greta: *When you say she needs therapy and things like that, then I find myself coming up with all these excuses.*

Therapist: *You don't want her to go to therapy, huh?*

Greta: *No, it's not that. I think maybe we should just be taken out of this family, but I'm scared about that, too.*

Another fear emerges. If anyone were to find out what her mother does, they might take Greta away from her mother. No one helps Greta, and she cannot ask for help, because she might not like the kind of help she would get. Again, the only way to survive is to do nothing, say nothing, and feel nothing. Like a small animal, freezing in the face of overwhelming danger, Greta could only wait and try not to move. The therapist's question breaks the paralysis by allowing Greta to finally begin to examine and articulate her dilemma.

Therapist: *Scared of?*

Greta: *Of her—she changed so much. . . . I'm jumping in my head from one side to the other.*

Therapist: *Can you do the jump out loud so I can hear it?*

Greta: *Oh, on the one side I want to be taken out of this family; it's so awful here. But the other side is, sometimes she's— she takes us out, she makes it nice . . . she kisses us and she plays the piano and sings. She wasn't always so harsh—so awful.*

Therapist: *She wasn't always so awful.*

Greta: *Sometimes—you could never tell, and it was hard. Sometimes we got that punishment, but sometimes, I don't know why, it was like—there was, you know, it was different. . . .*

Therapist: *So you don't want Mama to go to therapy?*

Greta seems to be getting a bit confused and lost. She is trapped in the back and forth of her mother's kindness one minute and cruelty the next. The therapist brings her back to the more concrete question: "Do you want your mother to change?"

Greta: *I think so. . . .*

Therapist: *Is that yes or no?*

Greta: *Yes, from what I know now I say, "yes." As an adult I know she should go to therapy. But as a child, I couldn't have said that or even thought about it.*

Therapist: *So tell her as an adult—look at that woman the way she looked in 1945, 1946. . . . Tell her. Tell her what the adult knows.*

Earlier, the therapist intervened to confront Greta's mother when it became evident that Greta alone did not have the resources she needed to do so. Now she encourages Greta to access one set of her own resources: the knowledge and experience of her adulthood. Just as the child Greta could experience the protection of the therapist's earlier intervention, so she can now experience the presence of her own strong, competent grown-up self. Remembering the events of the past will be quite different when she recalls them with the resources of an adult rather than as a neglected, friendless, frightened child.

Greta: (toward the "mother" area of the room) *As an adult I know that if someone is like you, slapping children like you do, that person must go into therapy to learn not to treat their children like that. . . . And don't cry, now.*

Therapist: *Yeah—keep talking to her.*

Greta: *It's not my fault that you are out of your family.*

With access to her adult resources comes a new awareness, a new decision, and a different way of being in the world. Instead of desperately protecting her mother from criticism, Greta gives up the responsibility for her mother's feelings and behaviors. It is a very important shift, and the therapist encourages her to stay with it, to strengthen and emphasize what has just occurred.

Therapist: *Keep going. You just talk to her—say that again, and elaborate.*

Greta: *It won't help you to cry now.*

Therapist: *"And it's not my fault. . . ."*

Greta: *It's not my fault that you are out of your family.*

Therapist: *Tell her more about that.*

Greta: *It's your fault or it's your father's fault, but it has nothing to do with us children. We didn't make your parents treat you badly. You always try to be pleas-*

ant to your parents when they don't like you. Why do you bring them coffee and act so nice to them?

Therapist: *Make that a statement.*

Do you recognize the pattern? We saw it earlier in the work when Greta asked her mother, "Why don't you come home?" Here, again, the "Why" question takes the focus away from Greta's experience and into fantasies and rationalizations about her mother's experience. The therapist asks Greta instead to make a statement that will define Greta's own wants and needs.

Greta: *Don't bring them coffee. Grandmother doesn't deserve coffee. She only comes to visit in order to get something from you. She didn't look after us children. She does NOTHING for us. Why should she get coffee or something to eat from us? I can't understand why she acts that way, and why you don't . . .*

Therapist: *No, you can't understand it, and it's so frightening when you can't understand it. There's no control. You can't understand and you can't predict when Mama's going to be sweet and wonderful. And you can't predict when she's gonna be horrible and mean. 'Cause when she's good, she's very, very good, and then she changes and she's mean. Your Mama needs to go to therapy.*

This time it is more difficult for Greta to disentangle herself from the "Why." The contrast between how the mother treats the unpleasant grandparents and how she treats her own children is important to Greta; it is probably the opening of another avenue of exploration. But it is too late in the work to get into another major issue. Greta has come a long way, has tried out some important new behaviors, and has broken the protective rules that have been in place most of her life. It has been hard work; it is time to begin to close the session by giving her a chance to integrate all that she has accomplished. The therapist's intervention begins the final phase of the session, summarizing the problem of Greta's relationship with her mother and offering her own opinion about what was needed. With her support, Greta is now able to agree.

Greta: *Yes. She needs to go to therapy. She really needs something.*

Therapist: *And what do* you *need, right now?*

Greta: (long pause) *Protection.*

Therapist: *Protection. Do you want to try some?*

Greta: *Yeah.*

Therapist: *Well, we'll leave Mama over there. Come here, Greta. Just get behind me. Come here.* (Greta moves behind the therapist's chair, and they both turn toward the space where Greta has placed her fantasied mother)

Now she's got to hit me first. If she is going to hit, I'm the one who's going to deal with it. Do you like to hide back there? Greta, do you like to hide there?

Greta: *Sometimes. . . .*

Therapist: *Not for always. Not when she's giving kisses.*

Greta: *No.*

Therapist: *No. Shall we make a deal? When she's giving kisses you can come out and when she's giving hits you can go back there?* (long pause) *What are you thinking?*

The ambivalence is still a problem. Greta wants to be connected to a loving mother, but she needs protection when her mother is abusive. To a child's either–or logic, it has not seemed possible to have both. The therapist offers her exactly that, which is to "be with her mother when she's good, and I'll protect you when she's bad."

Greta: *I'm just trying to* (begins to tremble) . . .

Therapist: *Yeah—just let that shake come. Yeah. . . .* (pause) *Want to stay there? For a week or so, maybe?*

Greta: (giggling) *Hmm. . . .*

Therapist: *Hmm means what? Can you translate "Hmm" to English?*

Greta: *I don't know what she'll do when I come out.*

Therapist: (firmly, to mother) *Don't you hit Greta—not now, not later—not at any time, ever. Your troubles are not your daughter's fault. Your daughter did not make your life difficult. You're the one who decided to have an affair with another man while your husband was gone. You're the one who got pregnant by another man while your husband was away. You're the one who divorced your husband and gave up his pension. Your troubles are NOT your child's fault, and don't you ever hit her again!*

The fear of the unpredictable, reinforced over and over again in the experience of living with a crazy mother, is not melted away in a single therapy session. The therapist shows, both in her use of humor and with the utilization of information gained in previous work with Greta, that she is not afraid and that she will confront mother on Greta's behalf. She gives Greta, temporarily, the protection Greta is not yet able to provide for herself. The little girl will not leave this session terrified of her mother's retribution. She will, rather, leave with the memory of feeling safer than she has ever felt before.

Greta: *Yes, that's good—I'm not making excuses for her anymore. And I'm more relaxed.*

And so Greta's session ends. We can understand more clearly, now, the importance of her earlier comment, "It's too long for me." All the way from Amsterdam to New York was too long to have to stay anxious—but those lonely days and nights apart from her mother were too long and too anxious as well. Greta has begun to allow herself to remember, to get reacquainted with the frightened little girl she once was. In doing so, she has taken one more step on the way to healing the contact disruptions that keep her from being whole and distort her ability to relate to the world around her.

Greta's transcript is a good starting place in our examination of whole pieces of work, because it illustrates, perhaps more clearly than most, how the work progresses through a series of phases. As Greta first described her concerns, her feelings of panic, and the meanings she attached to them, the therapist inquired phenomenologically: she helped Greta to explore and elaborate on the quality of her experience. Phenomenological inquiry is nearly always the opening movement of a psychotherapy session; it helps client and therapist clarify what is foreground and what basic contact disruption the work may be leading into.

Greta is a psychologically sophisticated client, and the intellectual connection between present distress and early experiences with her mother was not difficult for her to make. Moving into the next phase of the work, in which Greta allowed herself to regress emotionally and reconstruct that relationship in fantasy, brought out and heightened its affective importance. As she experienced the quality of her responses to her neglectful and abusive mother, she became more and more emotionally contactful.

Of course, the reconstructed relationship was not identical to Greta's historical experience. If it were, no change would be possible. It is the *difference* between then and now that made it possible for Greta to respond differently this time around: the additional resource provided by the therapist's presence and by Greta's own growing and learning over the years. And a different response, no matter how tiny the difference may be at first, grows and creates its own momentum of change. Greta first allowed herself to know and feel what she could not know and feel back then. She allowed herself, protected by the therapist, to talk about the knowings and the feelings. She enacted actually talking to mother about them and discovered how her need to protect her mother had become a part of the system in which she had been stuck. Each new awareness and each fresh experiencing made possible the next, and the next, and the next...

Ideally, the growing awareness of the client culminates in a pattern shift. The interconnections that have maintained the old system are broken down to the point at which the system must reorganize itself in some way. The reorganization is often signaled by the client's talking about a shift, a change in the way he or she understands the world, a change in some old belief or behavior that is no longer needed. With Greta, the change came in her realization that she no longer had to be responsible for taking care of her mother, make excuses for her mother's behavior, and tense up her own body in order to keep herself from knowing how bad she really felt.

Psychotherapy is a reiterative process. Old perceptions and beliefs and decisions transform; the transformed ones themselves are revisited and revised; and the revisions are the subject of the next piece of work. Sometimes these spirals are executed in the therapist's office; often the client carries on with the work long after the session is over. We do not know what Greta will do with her new-found freedom from responsibility and with her newly reclaimed awareness of self. What we do know is that the process of splitting off and of restricted and distorted contact has been interrupted. Greta has begun to feel and to know more, rather than less; she has begun the journey back to the world of spontaneous responses to natural needs, the world of authenticity and genuineness in relationship.

In the chapters to come, we will follow other clients along their own unique journeys. Sometimes the path will seem simple, and the guideposts will be clear. For others, there will be backtracks, interwindings, tangles, and dead ends. We will try, in our interspersed comments, to share with you our understanding of the process as we travel together.

Sarah: Therapy
With a Regressed Client

Age regression is a common occurrence in everyday life. We have all experienced moments of high emotion or stress in which we found ourselves thinking, feeling, and acting as we did in earlier stages of our development. Psychotherapy, as it focuses on affect, on development, and
on phenomenological experience, can create such moments for the client, and it is not surprising that age regression occurs during psychotherapy. Integrative psychotherapists utilize such regressions in two major ways: diagnostically, as another indicator of the nature of contact and
relational disruptions and the strategies that the client has developed to
deal with such disruptions; and therapeutically, as a way to access and
work with the traumatized or split-off parts of the self in order to facilitate growth.

   There are a number of ways in which age regressions can differ, and it
is important to distinguish among them. First, the regression may take
the client back to different points in his or her developmental history:
clients may regress to the age at which a trauma occurred, to a time prior
to the trauma (in order to avoid the pain of the traumatic experience), or
to a time during which they experienced strong reinforcement. Second,
the client's level of awareness about the regression can vary: the age-
regressed client may be clearly aware of what is happening and have access to a simultaneously present observing ego; the regression may be out
of awareness and the sense of self fully (though temporarily) cathected to

the regressed state; or there may be a mixture of in- and out-of-awareness elements in the client's experience of the regression. This latter situation is most common when the client is experiencing a strong transference vis-à-vis the person with whom the regression takes place. (Often, but not always, this is the therapist.) Finally, a regression may be used, with or without awareness, to elicit needed or wanted responses from others with whom the client has current relationships. These regressive patterns are not mutually exclusive: the client may shuttle among several of them during a single regression experience.

The following transcript illustrates the clinical utilization of regression and the importance of developmental attunement. Developmental attunement is particularly critical in this piece of work, because the client shifts rapidly among three different developmental points: early childhood, early adulthood, and the present. Although she experienced trauma during both the first and second of these developmental periods, she has in previous therapy regressed to childhood as a defense against the pain of an incident in early adulthood and against the confusion of the present. Age regression, then, serves more than one function for her. It serves two major therapeutic purposes as well: it helps both therapist and client understand the nature of the traumatic events and the client's response to them, and it provides a means of working with parts of her self that would otherwise be inaccessible.

Age regression provides access not only to the client's internal experience and responses at earlier developmental stages, but also to relationships with significant others who have been introjected during those earlier stages. By enacting interactions with these significant others ("talking to" an important other person), the client can enhance internal contact and, again, gain awareness of thoughts and feelings previously unavailable to consciousness. In such interactions, clients demonstrate vividly how early decisions, conclusions, and survival reactions create a life script, a set of fixed gestalten, that directs and limits their adult responses.

In the transcript to follow, we will follow the client as she vividly remembers and reexperiences events in early childhood, early adulthood, and the present. We will see how the therapist, through sensitive developmental attunement, helps her to use the age regressions therapeutically, and how enhanced contact with self, with therapist, with perpetrator, and with husband (in fantasy), interact in a complex symphony of growth and healing.

Sarah, the client, is a 60-year-old woman who entered a convent in adolescence and was a professed Roman Catholic nun until her mid-thirties. She has worked with the therapist several times, and recently a consistent theme in her work has been her impaired sexual response since marrying at the age of 37. She has reported that as a child of 2 or 3 years she was sexually molested by her older brother; she has also described being a victim of date rape shortly after leaving the convent. Although she has done a considerable amount of therapeutic work around the early molestation, she has never dealt with the rape: each time she has gotten close to it, she has spontaneously regressed to the age of the childhood molestation. She has come to the present session with the explicit intention of dealing with the rape; she believes that her present sexual difficulties are, at least in part, a result of the rape and her reactions to it.

As this transcript begins, Sarah is huddling in her chair. She wears a frightened, yet determined, expression, similar to a child waiting for some unknown, but threatening, event.

Therapist: *Feeling little?*

Sarah: *Oh, up and down. I keep thinking about, um, what I was thinking, when I think of being raped I get very emotional. But like I said, how am I ever going to get to this rape if I keep getting little? And it's all confused.*

Therapist: *That's an interesting comment. Will you just take some time there before you rush on?*

There are several reasons for this intervention. For one thing, Sarah is not yet fully aware of all the ways in which the two sexual abuse incidents are connected. She knows that when she tries to address one, she invariably shifts to the other, but she sees this as an impediment to her work rather than a natural consequence of her problem-solving organization. The two incidents are "all confused," and allowing herself to experience the confusion, rather than trying to force her way through it, will help her to reestablish internal contact.

The intervention is also a phenomenological inquiry, a "What's-going-on-inside" implied question. As such, it conveys respect for Sarah's ability to figure things out and her courage in facing whatever she discovers; it also conveys cognitive attunement as it focuses on how she will unscramble her thoughts and create meaning from them. Finally, the therapist is expressing concern about a possible false rhythm that Sarah may be moving into, hurrying herself in order to "get into this." By suggesting that she "take time" before she "rushes on," the therapist invites her to find her own rhythm and her own best pace for exploring the difficult material to come.

Sarah: *Yeah. Thank you.*

Therapist: *'Cause you've just said something quite significant. Will you say it again?*

Sarah: *I said, "How am I ever going to get to the rape if I keep getting little? And that I feel it's all connected."*

Therapist: *So, is the "getting little" a way to avoid the rape?*

Sarah's way of phrasing her dilemma could suggest a kind of out-of-control avoidance mechanism, an almost reflexive shrinking from the painful emotions connected with being raped. The therapist's inquiry acknowledges this, but it also allows for the possibility that there may be more and that the "getting little" may serve other purposes as well.

Sarah: *No. It's connected. When I was raped, and, and after time had gone by and I was able to look at that rape, I remember that I was feeling the same way I felt when I was standing on that chair in the bathroom, and my brother was supposedly showing me how to give a proper bath to a little girl. And, and the feeling was, "Just get real still and let him do whatever he wants." Even though I knew it was wrong, I didn't have any power over it.*

It definitely is more than just avoidance, and Sarah knows it. The therapist could easily have intervened at this point to reinforce her connecting the phenomenology of the two incidents. But Sarah is very involved in her narrative and is invested in making sure that the therapist knows what really happened to her. Attuned to her need to relate the story, the therapist merely nods and continues to listen.

Sarah: *And then I was a grown-up . . . 35, 36, I had left the convent a few months before that. It was in that year, between leaving the convent and getting married. And, um, I was working at the university, working with the college kids at the Newman Center. And, um, I had gone out to dinner with this, um, this man. His name was Jerry. And we had come back to the, to the Newman Center, and the kids were watching TV, and they said, "Hey, Sarah, there's a movie on about a nun leaving the convent." I said, "Gee, I'd like to see it." But I didn't want to interfere with them and their fun, so I said, "Maybe I'll go home and watch it." So Jerry and I got in the car, and he dropped me at the apartment, but he didn't drop me at the apartment, he said, "I'd like to go in and see that movie, too." And, um, I was surprised at that, so, being naive and not terribly worldly, I let him in my apartment, and we started to watch the movie, and then his hands were all over me. And I was just pushing him away and trying to make light of it* (she talks faster and faster), *and get back to the TV, say my "no" that way.* (there's a catch in her voice; she sounds very frightened) *But . . . um . . . help me. . . . I'm afraid we might run out of time before I can get through this. . . .*

Therapist: *We're going to take your time.*

Sarah: *Thank you.*

Therapist: *If you go so fast, do you get to avoid feeling as intensely as you need to?*

A fundamental tenet of integrative psychotherapy is that every behavior has a function and that the intent of the function is to maintain the individual's well-being. No matter how obstructive or dysfunctional a bit of behavior may appear, we assume that it originated in some attempt to survive and to meet the person's needs. Acknowledging the behaviors and validating their function is a part of therapeutic involvement. Sarah's quickened rhythm is so obvious and so obviously interfering with her ability to process her experience that it must be serving some important psychological purpose. Asking her this question not only validates a possible function of her change in rhythm, but it also begins the process of shifting the function into the therapeutic relationship. As the therapist temporarily takes over whatever function her defenses have been providing, the therapeutic relationship becomes a place where she can let go, work through the old patterns, and develop new ones in their place.

Sarah: *Well . . .* (pause)

Therapist: *Your comment a few minutes ago, "I just want to get through this," you said it very quickly. And my experience is, if you go fast like that, we're going to have to do the work over again anyway.*

Sarah: *That's such good information. First of all, to give me permission to have time. That's very, very deep for me. Okay? And now, now I'll put that piece together, to let myself feel it.* (sighs; she begins to cry)

The therapist's rhythmic, affective and cognitive attunement have allowed her to provide exactly what Sarah needs at this moment: permission to slow down and feel her feelings and a valid and logical reason for doing so. She resumes her narrative at a slower, more reflective pace.

Sarah: (continuing) *And . . . didn't know the word "No!" . . . I didn't know that I could just kick him out of the apartment; I didn't know anything. I just knew how to do what I was used to doing . . . which was avoiding. Which was trying to . . . trying to . . . stop someone from doing something by either distracting them, or . . .*

Therapist: (pause) *The way you managed as a little girl, with your brother?*

Sarah: *I didn't know that with him. But later, I learned how to dance around things.*

Therapist: *So, with Jerry, you were relying on something you knew from many years ago?*

Sarah: *Yes. Yes.*

Therapist: *Either to go quiet and let him do it, or dance around . . .*

Sarah has described two coping strategies, passivity and distraction. As a child, she would "get real still and let him do whatever he wants"; later she learned to "dance around things." With Jerry she attempted to distract him by "trying to make light of it and get back to the TV." When that did not work, did she go to the even more primitive defense and just get still and let him do what he wanted? The therapist's inquiry and acknowledgment are helping Sarah to recognize the threads that connect the two experiences and that cause her to respond emotionally from a confused, everything-at-once kind of place. In the next intervention, below, the therapist's direction is a kind of inquiry, or a preparation for inquiry, as she both requests and gives permission for the first age regression of the session.

Sarah: *I tried to dance around. And it didn't work. And it . . . I remember that he had pushed me down on the couch. And that's when I . . . just let him do whatever. . . .* (her voice trails off and she looks sad and defeated)

Therapist: *Stay with that, Sarah. Just go right back to that experience. When you decided to just let him do whatever.*

Sarah: *I couldn't do the dancing; I couldn't make him stop. I didn't have the word "no" anymore. I didn't know how to do the "no."* (she cries)

Therapist: (pause) *What were you feeling towards him?*

After pausing to allow Sarah to continue, to finish her train of thought if it was still unfinished, the therapist makes a phenomenological inquiry. Asking Sarah to name and describe her feelings helps her to integrate her internal experience with the externalized narrative; it also explores the possibility of other, as yet unvoiced, feelings. Additionally, it intensifies the age regression: the core of a regression experience is experiencing the phenomenology of a past event, relationship, or time period.

Sarah: (crying) *Ohhh, ohhh. . . . I can't . . . revulsion was one.* (sigh) *Crazy thing—not wanting to hurt his feelings!* (crying hard again) *It sounds so crazy, when he's doing something to me and I'm concerned about his feelings. . . .*

Therapist: *You have to be nice?*

Sarah: *I've always been like that.*

And now we have three strategies, each one a bit more primitive than the last. When she was very young, her strategy was to do nothing, go quiet, and freeze. When she was somewhat older, she would distract and dance around. And at the most sophisticated level, her strategy was to "be nice." Sarah recognizes the historicity of this last coping mechanism, although she does not yet know when or how she acquired it. The therapist's response will acknowledge that she, too, has seen the strategy in operation over the time she has been working with Sarah. She next invites Sarah back onto the path that leads to therapeutic regression. Notice that she changes the tense of the verb (from "pushed" to "pushes") in order to transition from story telling to actual experiencing.

Therapist: *Yeah, I know.* (Sarah continues to cry) *He pushes you down on the couch. . . .*

Sarah: *I, I, I can't re-, I'm trying to remember . . . what I was wearing. I can't remember. . . .*

Therapist: *You won't remember if you go so fast. Your emotions are part of the memory. . . . I think you keep getting ahead of your own natural rhythm in order not to feel how devastating this is. Like many people, you may be believing that if you hurry up and go through it, maybe it'll go away.*

The therapist demonstrates her attunement to Sarah's process and gives a permission, wrapped around by an interpretation and some information. Sarah does need to slow down, and the therapist expresses her belief that the rushing along is a way for Sarah to protect herself from the pain of her memories. The therapist also offers her professional observation about the generality of Sarah's response. The two messages, "You're no different from lots of other people who choose this way to protect themselves from pain" and the invitation to slow down and allow the experience to develop, provide the validation and normalization Sarah needs. In her next comment, Sarah recognizes the defensive nature of her rhythm, but she does not yet begin to slow herself down.

Sarah: *I haven't gotten to the worst part yet; maybe that's why I'm trying to rush to get there, because I'm afraid I won't say it.*

Therapist: *I'll help you get there. But, Sarah, anything faster than your natural rhythm, and even if you get there you won't retain it over time.*

Sarah: *I guess I don't know what my natural rhythm is.*

Therapist: *Well, I don't know what it is either, but let's together find it out.*

In the last two responses, the therapist has emphasized the collaborative nature of this therapy work. "I'll help you," she says. "Let's together find out." As the work develops, notice the theme of aloneness, of nobody there to help that pervades the traumatic experiences Sarah is dealing with. It is not trauma alone, but trauma in the absence of relationship, that causes the most severe psychological damage. The therapist is underscoring the fact that, this time, Sarah will not be alone. This time will be different. Healing is in the contactful relationship, and this time there will be such a relationship.

Sarah: *Okay.*

Therapist: *My sense is that you've been going so fast, as a defensive process, not to feel the fullness of the feeling—not that you don't feel miserable in spite of it. . . .*

Sarah: *You mean all my life?*

Therapist: *I don't know. I'm referring to here, this morning.*

Sarah: *I always have a problem with time.*

Therapist: *I want to hear every single detail of this experience. And I think it's important for you not to overlook any of the details, including the emotional details.*

Sarah: *I think I shut my emotions down, because I was, like, in this nowhere place.*

Therapist: *Just take some time to know that nowhere place.*

A small child freezes herself into passivity. She goes inside, into her inner, fortressed being; she shrinks into no-feeling, no-thinking, and no-doing. Is this the "nowhere place" that Sarah is talking about? If so, it is no wonder she feels as if her emotions are shut down—because they are! By taking time to experience the nowhere place, those shut-down feelings can begin to reactivate. Also, the therapist's response helps to allay Sarah's earlier fear that there would not be enough time to finish her work. "Just take some (your) time"; "I'll be with you"; "Slow down"; "Let yourself be."

Sarah: (cries quietly; her crying gradually intensifies) *Ohhh. . . . Nobody's there to help me! There's people around and there's nobody there to help me!* (sobbing) *I—don't—know—how—to—cry—out!*

In this response, we see the importance of the therapist's earlier emphasis on working things out together. The trauma that Sarah experienced was bad enough, but even worse was her sense of aloneness. No one offered to help, and she did not know how to ask for help. This work is different; this time she will not have to deal with the problem all alone.

Therapist: *Can't make a noise loud enough?*

Sarah: *No, I can't even make a noise.*

Therapist: *Just like with your brother?*

Sarah: *Ohhh. . . . They were there. They saw him take me out of the kitchen sink when my sister was giving me a bath. And he lifted me right out of the sink . . . took me up to the bathroom . . . and nobody came to see what was going on! Ohhhh. . . .* (pause, then more quietly) *Nobody suspected anything. And I couldn't cry out, "Help me, somebody, help me!" I didn't know how to do it.* (crying again) *I don't know how to say, "Help me, somebody, pick me up and hold me, I'm scared. . . ." I don't know how to do it. . . .*

The therapist's inquiry has to do with defensive styles, or the way in which Sarah has learned to interrupt contact in order to protect herself from the pain of the failure of a valued relationship. Rather than recognizing the similarity of the two experiences, however, Sarah immediately regresses to the childhood incident. Although there is work to be done at that level, her explicit request for this session was to deal with the rape. The therapist will need to lead her back.

Therapist: *And on the couch, with Jerry?*

Sarah: *Oooohhhh . . . couldn't cry out. . . .*

Therapist: *Even if you had cried out, would somebody have heard you?*

Sarah: *I don't know. . . .* (pause) *I didn't even know that I needed . . . should . . . could . . . I didn't know. . . .*

Therapist: *It was as if no one was there, as if you were all by yourself with this man.*

Sarah: *I didn't know what he was going to do next.*

Therapist: *But you knew something when his hands were on you. Did you like it or dislike it?*

Sarah's repetition of "I didn't know," together with her description of the "nowhere place," suggests that she has lost much of her sense of self. She can no longer act, feel, or think. One of the first steps in recovering a sense of self is to return to a basic like versus dislike, want versus don't-want awareness. This is where self or ego begins, with the awareness of needs and wants (and don't-need and don't-want) as they emerge. Sarah had said earlier that she felt revulsion as Jerry began making advances, and this was certainly a strong experience of her own "don't want." Asking again whether she liked or disliked what he was doing may, on the surface, seem insensitive or even silly, but it is intended to recall that experience of revulsion and thus help her to move past her helpless, hopeless paralysis. As we will see, it does more: it brings her face to face with another painful aspect of the trauma.

Sarah: *Oh, that's the next part I have to get to. . . .* (crying hard) *That's the shame part. . . .*

Therapist: *You implied, a few minutes ago, that you didn't like his hands on you.*

Sarah: *No, it scared me. And I thought I could dance around and push him away and get back to watching . . .* (she makes a flicking-away motion with her hand)

Therapist: *Do that gesture again. That looks to me like a dislike gesture.*

Sarah: *Yes.*

Therapist: *Did you dislike his hands all over you?*

Sarah: *Yes, I did—yes, yes, I did! Because he—I didn't—it wasn't my idea—I didn't know what he was—I don't—No!* (crying)

Therapist: *Say that again—"No!"*

Sarah: *No! No! I didn't like my brother's hands on me, either. Get off!* (crying hard) *Not that way, no-no-no-no-no!*

The therapist's directions—to "do that gesture again" and to "say that again"—help Sarah both to move more fully into the age regression and to experience the old trauma in a new way. In neither the childhood nor the adult situation, as they actually occurred, was Sarah able to assert herself, protest, or say "no." She first "danced" and then went passive. Here, in fantasy, she begins to experience her own power and her ability to stand up and demand what she needs.

Therapist: *That's right, Sarah! Appreciate that "No!"*

Sarah: *NOOOOO!*

Therapist: *That's right! Push him away again!* (holds a pillow for her to push against)

Sarah: *NOT THAT WAY!*

Therapist: *Push him away—that's it!*

Sarah: *GO AWAY! Ohh, don't touch me like that!*

Therapist: *Again.*

Sarah: (pushing) *I don't want you to do that!*

Therapist: *"Don't touch me. . . . "*

Sarah: *DON'T TOUCH ME! DON'T TOUCH ME! I DON'T LIKE THAT!*

Therapist: *Yeah. . . . "I don't like . . . "*

Sarah is now doing exactly what she has always before held back from doing: standing up for her own needs and demanding that they be acknowledged. Even though it is not clear whether she is talking to her brother or to Jerry, she gains power with every "no," every "don't," and every push-away. The therapist continues to support and encourage her and will eventually help her to focus her new-found strength into the rape situation.

Sarah: *I—DON'T—WANT THIS! I DON'T LIKE THIS! SOMEBODY COME GET ME!*

Therapist: *That's right. "I need . . . "*

Sarah: *I NEED SOMEBODY TO HELP ME BECAUSE I DON'T WANT THIS! I'M TOO LITTLE, TOO TOO TOO TOO LITTLE!* (continues crying loudly)

The strength of the "don't want" is fully present, even though the scene is now revealed as that of the early abuse. The therapist directs her to bring that strength back to the rape scene.

Therapist: *Now look at Jerry and say it to him.*

Sarah: *Huh? Oh, my head . . . what did you say, look at who?*

Therapist: *Look at Jerry, and say it to him.*

Sarah: *Ohhh. . . . YOU FILTHY BETRAYING PIG!*

Therapist: *Keep going.*

Sarah: *YOU LYING BASTARD! I HATE YOU! GET OUT OF MY PLACE! GET OUT OF HERE!*

She makes the transition. Within the safety of the therapeutic relationship, trusting the therapist to support her venture into new and unexplored psychological territory, she lets herself feel the intensity of her rage toward the rapist. Again, the therapist's inquiry and direction will encourage her to strengthen her response, to fully experience what it is like to stand up, express her wants and needs, and take care of herself with strength and certainty.

Therapist: *"What I need to say to you is . . . "*

Sarah: (screaming) *OOOOOOHHHHHH! HOW DARE YOU? I never gave you any indication that I wanted this—YOU BASTARD!*

Therapist: *Try using "No."*

Sarah: *NO! NO! NOOOOOO!*

Therapist: *I don't want . . .*

Sarah: *I—DON'T—WANT—you to touch me like that. YOU DON'T EVEN KNOW ME!* (crying softly now) *You filthy pig. . . .*

Therapist: *Um-hmm . . .*

Sarah: *Just because you take me to dinner, you have rights?*

Therapist: *Make that a statement.*

Asking a question here, even though it sounds rhetorical, takes her a step backward into giving up her own power. What Jerry thinks is not relevant; what Sarah thinks and wants and demands must be foreground. The therapist's suggestion, "Make that a statement," invites her back to expressing herself, rather than asking questions.

Sarah: *YOU HAVE NO RIGHTS!*

Therapist: *"And furthermore . . ."*

Sarah: *And furthermore, I don't even like you; you're sleazy!*

Therapist: *Keep going.*

Sarah: *Ohhh. . . . Ohhh. . . . yeaghhch! Bleaghhhh!* (she makes disgusted, almost retching noises, then screams loudly)

Therapist: *"And I want . . . "*

Sarah's rage, while important in helping her recover a full sense of herself, is still noncontactful. In reexperiencing a trauma, anger (fully in contact with "I don't want," yet also clear about "I do want") is eventually more health-promoting and growth-promoting than rageful rejection.

Sarah: *Oh, I'd like a little respect, you blccchh! And I don't like people who lie to me—you lied and lied and lied!* (she sobs)

Therapist: *Tell him what you mean by that.*

Sarah: *You said you wanted to come in to watch the TV show. You slime bag! You slime ball! Oh, you knew what you were doing from the beginning! You knew you were taking advantage of me, you knew it, you knew it! Ohhh.* (crying) *I see that slimy face; I hate it!*

Therapist: *Yeah. . . . now look at that slimy face as he's pushing you down.*

This intervention serves two purposes. Primarily, it helps Sarah to move more deeply into the regressive reexperiencing of the rape scene, but this time with the chance to do it differently: to say no, rather than to go passive, and to do so with support rather than alone. Second, by looking specifically at Jerry, she can begin to undo the generalization that may have been interfering with her present sexual responsivity. Sex itself is not painful and revolting; *unwanted* sex *with Jerry* is.

Sarah: *Ohhh—I couldn't look at his face. . . .*

Therapist: *Do it now.*

Sarah: *Ooohhh—yccchhhh!*

Therapist: *Do it now so you know who it is. So it doesn't have to be generalized to everybody.*

Sarah: *Ycchh! Yccchhhhh!*

Therapist: *Look at his face.*

Sarah: *Ohhh, that awful face, that awful slimy lying face! The face of betrayal!* (sobs) *You're such a pig. 'Cause you're no different than my brother taking advantage of a little girl, and you knew it! I was naive, and you knew it! I was a virgin, and you knew it! Ohhh, you're despicable! You must have known; I was so naive; I look back now, I can see the signs that anyone could read. . . .* (cries for several seconds)

Therapist: *Mmmmm . . . and you said an important sentence there.*

Actually, *all* the sentences she just said were important: any one of them could be expanded on and could be used in working though the experience. Rather than choosing one, out of her own sense of priorities, the therapist invites Sarah to choose her focus. This also has the effect of helping Sarah recover her thinking; she has been in danger of losing herself in her tears and becoming helpless again.

Sarah: *You robbed me. You raped and you robbed me. And you've interfered with my sex life ever since! I hate you! I hate you!*

Therapist: *Yeah, tell him what he robbed. "You robbed. . . . "*

Sarah: *He robbed me of something so important . . . and I can't get to it now; I can't seem to get by this! I can't! I can't get there!*

Therapist: *"I was a virgin and you robbed . . . "*

By repeating Sarah's words and making more explicit the implied robbing her of her virginity, the therapist "primes the pump." The intent is, again, to increase the intensity of the affect and to fully wash out and cleanse this old, festering wound so that it can heal—so Sarah can "get there."

Sarah: *I was a virgin and YOU ROBBED ME!*

Therapist: *Tell him what* you *wanted to do with your virginity.*

Sarah: *Oh, I wanted to give it to someone in love. I didn't want someone to TAKE it and RAPE ME AND ROB ME!*

Here is a new theme: "I wanted to give it to someone in love." It is the first clear expression of a positive want, as contrasted with the "don't want" with which Sarah has been dealing. The therapist will help Sarah to expand and intensify this theme, enhancing both her sense of self and her valuing of that self.

Therapist: *Tell him how you'd like to give it to someone. Not him.*

Sarah: *Ohhh, I want to give it to someone special, who means something to me. Not some slimeball, who takes me out to dinner and thinks he has rights to my body!*

Therapist: *Tell him how you'd like it to have been. I bet there was a dream in there.*

Sarah: *Yes, I always knew that sex was something beautiful, and that it was an expression of my full personhood, and I didn't want someone to just go in there and just destroy that whole thing. . . .* (crying)

Therapist: *Tell him the dream of how it should have been. How you wanted it to be.*

Sarah: *It should have been something that just flowed from love—not this— oooohhhhh, not this! Not enough to get by my brother's poking and pinching and prodding, and . . . hard enough to get by that. That's bad enough. And then to have you come along, and just when—ooohhh!*

No matter how clear and logical the roadmap, the actual course of therapy seldom follows that kind of path. Instead, it goes forward and back; it detours and loops around. Sarah needs to go back to the negative, the "don't want"; some other piece must be picked up and woven into the whole before she will be ready to go on with rebuilding her dream.

Therapist: *Mmmm, tell him. . . .*

Sarah: *It's just like stamping that indelibly on my psyche or somewhere, my whole body! My mind, my spirit is just—Ohhh, my God. . . . Ohhhh, what you've done to me is NOT RIGHT!*

Therapist: *Yeah, say that again. "It's not right!"*

Sarah: *It's not right! And it's much bigger than I ever knew!* (wails) *Oh, I want to get by this. . . .*

As she is able to experience the old trauma and, simultaneously, contact and support from the therapist, Sarah's awareness of self is expanding. She now realizes the extent to which her whole selfhood has been infiltrated by the molestations and her response to them, and her wail is close to despair. The therapist acts quickly to provide her with a way to take action and to transform the despair into resolve.

Therapist: *Right, then tell your husband the dream. Put your husband right there* (indicating an empty chair) *and tell him the dream that got lost on the couch that night.*

Sarah: *Oh, Stephen, Stephen. . . . Ohhh, Stephen, my only love . . . you truly loved me, and cared for me, waited for me, pined for me, gave me space always . . . to this day . . .*

Therapist: *And if I hadn't gotten raped by Jerry that night . . .*

Sarah: *You wouldn't have had to wait so long. Even to this day, and you know, you must know, you're so sensitive, you must know, how I struggle, with all of this. . . .*

It is so difficult for Sarah to articulate what might have been and what she believes is forever lost. She has made a good beginning by experiencing her contactfulness with Stephen. Now she needs to take the plunge and to express, in words and in the context of the relationship with her husband, what she (and he as well) has lost. Only by doing so can she fully grieve the loss and then, in her words, "get past it."

Therapist: *Tell Stephen about the dream.*

Sarah: *Because, Stephen, my dream was . . . just to . . . give myself in love. To someone like you, and that one was you. Someone who really, really loved me, someone I really loved and respected and appreciated. And it got all . . . it got off to a disgusting start. . . . I couldn't get there . . . to love.*

Therapist: *Um-hmm . . .*

Sarah: *And it's been a performance with something missing; I haven't been able to get by . . .* (sobbing) *Oh, God, how I—Oh, Stephen, thank you for your patience! And your true love. . . .*

Therapist: *Tell Stephen what Jerry stole from you.*

Sarah: *He stole something so precious from me. . . .*

Therapist: *Keep going. Tell him what he stole.*

Directing Sarah to use language to actually name what was stolen gives form and identity to her loss. Clear and explicit language enhances contact with both self (Sarah needs to hear her own voice affirming and defining her experience) and with others (who cannot, after all, read her mind).

Sarah: *He stole my innocence; he stole my ability to, to let that flow—just jammed something right in the middle of it, a monkey wrench in the middle. . . .*

Therapist: *Tell Stephen what happened to your dream.*

Sarah: *My dream was shattered. My dream was totally shattered. I, I lost it somewhere. Ohhh. . . .*

Sarah's involvement in the regression and in the fantasy conversation with Stephen is genuine, and she has obviously experienced both new awareness and considerable relief. But there is still something missing that has not been dealt with. Like a surgeon probing for some small foreign fragment still left in a wound, the therapist picks up on an earlier remark of Sarah's.

Therapist: *Ready to go back and tell me about the "worst part" now?*

Sarah: *Well, it doesn't seem like the worst part anymore, but . . .*

Therapist: *Hmmm. . . .*

Sarah: *But, maybe I can get by the shame.*

Therapist: *Not too fast—*

Sarah: *Okay, okay, okay.*

Therapist: *You can't get by the shame, because that's what you hold.*

Sarah: *Say that again?*

Therapist: *You can't get by the shame, because that's what you hold inside, is the shame. Let's just go into it, instead.*

Sarah showed signs of speeding up again as soon as the therapist alluded to the "worst part." This time, however, Sarah is ready to name that "worst part." And as she does so, the dynamics become clearer: trying to get past her shame by moving quickly through her story or her memories is like trying to outrun her own shadow in a nightmare. Sarah must turn and face that nightmare and go into it in order to dispel the shadow once and for all.

Therapist: *He pushed you down on the couch. . . .*

Sarah: *And he put his penis inside me. I'm grateful that it wasn't big. 'Cause it would have really, really hurt. But when he came, then I got turned on, and it didn't make sense to me, because I was so angry with him.*

Therapist: *How biological.*

Normalization: Sarah's response wasn't weird or unusual; it is how people are. The core of a sense of shame is the belief that "something's wrong with me." Sarah has believed that something was wrong with her because of her sexual response. Until that belief is discarded, the sense of shame will persist, and with it the disruption in relationship: how could her husband Stephen, or anyone else, want to have real contact with such a flawed person?

Sarah: *And my body was responding, and I didn't push him away.*

Therapist: *How natural.*

Sarah: *And so I pulled that couch out, that turned into a bed, and I told him that he had, now that he had his way with me, he hadda give that back to me.*

Therapist: *What did you mean by that?*

Even though the therapist may have been quite sure she knew what Sarah meant, there are several reasons why it was still important for her to inquire. First, she could have been wrong. The statement was somewhat ambiguous and could have some additional meanings private to Sarah. Second, the question sends a clear signal to Sarah that the therapist is there, attentive, and caring about what Sarah is telling her. Moreover, the therapist's voice tone is matter of fact; there is no implied criticism that Sarah could use to reinforce her sense of shame. Finally, Sarah's own awareness is enhanced as she puts into words what has previously been only vaguely symbolized.

Sarah: *I meant that I was turned on, and now he had to satisfy me. Except that he laughed in my face, and he said, "You don't understand" with that sneer on his face. "I can't do that now," he said. I hated him!*

Therapist: *He wouldn't satisfy you, after he had his way with you?*

Sarah: *No, cause he—*

Therapist: *What a jerk!*

An involved therapist may find himself or herself responding sponta-neously with a personal reaction to what the client has said. In this case, voicing the spontaneous response was therapeutically helpful in that it was also a normalizing response: a woman naturally needs and wants to be responded to in a sexually satisfying way, and a man who satisfies himself and then refuses to be caring and responsive is a jerk!

Sarah: *Yes, but he was telling me I was a jerk because I didn't know that he couldn't get a hard on again. He was laughing at me, 'cause he got what he wanted. And you know what? This is so awful! I let him sleep in that bed with me that night. 'Cause this crazy thing goes on, like I didn't want to throw him out.*

In this response we see how Jerry reinforced Sarah's shame. Not only was she criticizing herself for her physiological arousal, but he also criti-cized her for her naiveté; now she had something wrong with both her body and her brain. She is also ready to criticize and feel ashamed of herself for letting him spend the night, not recognizing that her behavior may have grown out of a normal and natural need/hope/wish that some-how the trauma could be undone and that the rape could be transformed into an act of love and the rapist into a true lover. Can she become aware of such a hope, and so see herself as acting understandably, deserving of compassion rather than shame?

Therapist: *You didn't want to throw him out—what were you hoping for?*

Sarah: *I didn't want to throw him out of the house; it's like, I don't want to hurt his feelings, well, I don't want to kick him out in the middle of the night. Yeah, and maybe inside I was hoping . . . maybe I was hoping . . . that . . . that I would feel something.*

Therapist: *What a wonderful hope.*

Sarah: *Oh, it's. . . .*

Therapist: *Hoping that maybe you could recapture a little bit of the dream?*

Sarah: *No, not the dream, just the sex, and that's why it's so shaming. I started to feel something, but it was all mixed up and sullied and dirtied, and I just felt like a whore.*

Sarah is determined not to lie or to make excuses for herself, and she returns to the "something's wrong with me" position. Now she is not only biologically flawed and stupid, but she is also a whore. Sarah ap-peared, earlier, to accept the therapist's assertion that her response was "biological," but she has now gone back to shame. The therapist's next response is a confrontation: she points out the discrepancy between Sarah's acceptance of her response as a normal, biological one and her now feeling ashamed of it.

Therapist: *Will you back up for a moment? What is shaming about the natural thing you're describing?*

Sarah: *Oh, oh, oh. . . . Say that again, 'cause I need to hear that. Again, and again, and again. . . .*

Therapist: *What is shaming about the natural things you're describing?* (pause) *Like the rhythms of your body—as he gets excited to orgasm, your body wants to get excited to orgasm. I'm sorry, but I don't understand the shame.*

Sarah: *Because it was the wrong person in the wrong bed at the wrong time. It was wrong!*

Therapist: *Wait a minute, wait, wait. Your vagina didn't know who it was.*

Sarah: *Didn't?*

Therapist: *No.*

Sarah: *I did. I did.*

Therapist: *Yeah. The brain does, but what about your vagina?*

Sarah: *I don't know! That's, that's the disconnect that I can't get back into.*

Therapist: *Well, I suspect when you wanted him to satisfy you, at that point it was a vagina long overdue.*

Sarah: (giggles) *I'll say. Ohhh . . . you say that, and I can laugh, and then another part goes, "Ugh, you're disgusting."*

The split in her self, with one part criticizing the other, is very clear to Sarah at this point. She is no longer feeling her whole being as a shameful, disgusting thing, but is aware that the criticism is part of an internal dialogue; but she is not quite able, yet, to give up the shame and the self-criticism. The therapist continues with a gentle confrontation.

Therapist: *Now why would you disgust yourself with something that you know is so biologically natural?*

Sarah: *Because it was the wrong person at the wrong time. . . .*

Therapist: *But you tried to make it the right person.*

In integrative psychotherapy we focus on the psychological function of a behavior before attempting to change it. Was the function of Sarah's spending the night with her rapist to try to rebuild the dream by somehow making him be the right person and healing the pain of trauma in the absence of relationship? As the therapist comes back to this possibility, Sarah struggles. The shame reaction is stubborn; it will not let go easily.

Sarah: *I tried to make it the right person when it was the wrong person; that's the shame of it.*

Therapist: *Why?*

Sarah: *Because! Because I'm going after some sleaze ball that I hate, and that I'm so angry with, and then I'm trying . . .*

Therapist: *Were you trying not to hate him?*

Sarah: *No, I think I was trying to punish him.*

This is an unexpected twist; Sarah has not hinted at this before, and it is difficult to see at this point how her allowing Jerry to spend the night would punish him. An inquiry here is easy and natural, and it is certainly more appropriate than continuing to push at the "make-it-the-right-person" idea.

Therapist: *How were you going to do that?*

Sarah: *By humiliating him—except he twisted it around and he ended up humiliating me.*

Therapist: *Did you want him to satisfy you?*

Sarah: *My body did. My head wanted to punish him. It was all mixed up, don't you see?*

Therapist: *Yes, I see that. So let's take it one part at a time, 'cause you're feeling different things at the same time.*

Sarah: *Yes—yes—yes!*

Therapist: *Your body needed to be satisfied.*

Sarah: *That's why I needed to talk to you about it, 'cause I knew you'd say stuff like this. I need to hear it. I need to hear it, even if sometimes I get squiggly around it. . . . Am I making sense?*

It is hard to imagine a clearer statement of the need for validation: "I knew you'd say it, and I need to hear it." And of course the validation has to come from some external source, at least at first; how could you validate yourself with any conviction if at the same time you are getting "squiggly" about it? In fact, the "squiggliness" may have spread a bit, because in the last sentence Sarah seems to be expressing some uncertainty about her relationship with the therapist and asking for validation there as well.

Therapist: *You're doing just great. . . . Okay, so this man, although he disappointed you, and messed with your mind—*

Sarah: *Yes.*

Therapist: *He did stimulate your body.*

Sarah: *Yes.*

Therapist: *And you wanted more, then. Once having lost the dream, you might as well at least have a good orgasm.*

In this single sentence, the therapist summarizes the work of the last several minutes. She puts together what had been a confusing welter of contradictory feelings into a simple, logical, sense-making statement, one that normalizes and validates precisely what Sarah has been feeling shame about.

Sarah: *That's right. . . . Oh, God, I can't believe I'm saying this out loud!*

Therapist: *You, and a lot of other women having made the same choice.*

Sarah: *How? What?*

Therapist: *"All right, now that I've lost my dream, I might as well at least have something in compensation."*

Sarah: *Yes.*

Therapist: *Or hoping that you could still have at least part of your dream, that it could still be something good, that maybe, in the morning, he'd be wonderful.*

Sarah: *Bleaugggghhh!*

Therapist: *And not a sleaze bag.*

Sarah: *Oh, no, not that.*

Sarah has firmly and consistently rejected the idea of hoping that the relationship with Jerry could somehow become something good. There seems to be no point in pursuing it further; if and when it fits for her, she will come back to it. It is better, for now, to support what is currently in awareness and continue to inquire.

Therapist: *That wasn't going to happen.*

Sarah: *No, he was a sleaze bag, 'cause I felt betrayed. I felt the betrayal. I knew that his intentions—he would never—eagghhh!*

Therapist: *What happened after?*

Sarah: *So . . . as far as I can remember, he just fell asleep. And then I kicked him out in the morning. But what happened after that was hard, 'cause I didn't know* (begins to sob while talking) *who to talk to about it; I didn't know what to do; I thought it was my fault.*

Again, Sarah articulates this major premise of integrative psychotherapy: it is the absence of a supportive relationship following the trauma that causes the lasting damage. Being date raped was bad, but having no one to talk to and no one to reassure her that it was not her fault allowed the sense of shame to develop. And the shame, the belief that "something's wrong with me," is the true relationship rupturer, the core of Sarah's present contact difficulties.

Sarah: (continuing) *And then, and then he used to call the office where I used to work, next to the Newman Center. And he used to scare me, and he used to say things, "Don't call that rape," and, and then I remembered how I felt after, and I, I got really confused; maybe it wasn't, but I knew it was. And there was this guy who used to come, he was like a Mama's boy, he used to sit in the office and talk to me. And he was like, he wasn't like a manly man to me, he was just someone who needed someone to talk to. He was in the office when this guy called, and he saw my face was white, and I turned to him and I said, "There's someone on the phone; he keeps harassing me with these phone calls, and he won't stop calling, and I'm scared; can you help me?"*

Therapist: *Wow!*

Sarah: *And, and this little Mama's boy got up off the chair in the corner of my office where he used to sit and talk to me, and he got on the phone, and he turned into this unbelievable man, and he was saying things to this guy like you wouldn't believe: "And if you should ever call her again, I will blah-blah-blah-blah-blah-blah"—I never heard from Jerry again. He became my hero!*

Wow, indeed! Sarah finally asked for help at a time when she really needed it. And it worked. For the first time, she did not have to be alone and did not have to try to protect herself when she did not know how. It must have felt unbelievably good—and the therapist is quick to build upon that experience, using it to help Sarah construct a fantasy of being helped in the same way during the rape itself. Over time, fantasies can have the same sort of psychological effect as actual memories; once she has worked through the shame, a fantasy of calling for help and getting it can do much to relieve her remembered misery.

Therapist: *What would it have been like if he* [her hero friend] *had been your next-door neighbor?*

Sarah: *Yes! Oh, he was someone I needed. I needed someone like him.*

Therapist: *Can you just imagine what you would have done differently if he was living there?*

Sarah: *Yep.*

Therapist: *What would you have done?*

Sarah: *I would have screamed and hollered and called his name for help. He would have come in and he would have transformed into this macho man and he would throw this Jerry right out on his ass. Oh, that sounds good!* (laughs) *He did that, literally, on the phone.*

Therapist: *So the shameful part of all of this is your sexual feelings following the initial penetration?*

Sarah: *Yes.*

Therapist: *All right, now I want to ask you the most important, and probably the most embarrassing part. I want to talk about life today.*

Sarah: *Oh, God . . . yeah?*

Therapist: *Will you please talk about your life today?*

With this request, the therapist invites Sarah to deal directly with the concern that brought her to this session, her current sexual dysfunction. Healing the past and dealing with the shame of past memories will have little or no lasting effect if those changes are not carried into the present. If Sarah does not deal with the connection between how she shamed herself in the past and how that shame interrupts her present relationship(s), she will continue to create self-shaming situations and fantasies that will interfere with her ability to be contactful with others and with herself, and will certainly impair her sexual responsiveness. Sarah knows what is coming and expects that it will be difficult. But she wants relief, wants to make a significant change, and is willing to do whatever is necessary.

Sarah: *Yes.*

Therapist: *Having desired to enjoy your body following the rape, do you compensate for the rape and the desire for satisfaction by not fully enjoying your body with Stephen?*

Sarah: *I don't know if that's what I'm doing, but it would make sense. I've tried . . . (pause)*

Therapist: *Do you let yourself really relax and play with Stephen?*

Sarah: *It's like I try, and I can't.*

Therapist: (pause) *I understand that if you are falsely shaming yourself with something so natural, that you might compensate by holding back now.*

Sarah: *I do that! Oh. . . . whew. . . .*

Therapist: *It's been a long problem, hasn't it?*

Sarah: *Yes. I've tried to get help in a thousand different ways.*

The rape, and the absence of support and contact afterward, created a wound that has been festering for over two decades. Just as with a physical wound, it is critical to cleanse it well, not to close it up before all the infected material is gone. The therapist decides to go back, one more time, to see if anything remains to be cleaned away.

Therapist: *Do you need to say any more to Jerry? "You little . . . "*

Sarah: (turning toward the pillow that she pushed against earlier in her work) *You disgusting little shit. You certainly weren't much to look at, either.*

Therapist: *Tell him what you mean by that.*

Sarah: *You sleaze ball. Why did I even go out to dinner with you?*

Here is another apparently rhetorical question that nevertheless demands an answer. Unless the answer is made explicit, the question can go underground and become the fuel for another round of shame building. Answered and turned into a statement, it will enhance Sarah's emerging sense of self-discovery.

Therapist: *Make that a statement.*

Sarah: *Probably because I felt sorry for you, you stupid little shit.*

Therapist: *Tell him what was in it for you to go out with him.*

Sarah: *Just to go out and have a date.*

Therapist: *Yeah.*

Sarah: *Go out to have dinner with someone other than hanging out with the Newman Center kids.*

Therapist: *So you were lonely?*

Sarah: *Yes.*

Therapist: *So that was what was in it for you.*

More normalizing. It is natural to be lonely, natural to need the company of peers, and natural to want to be admired by a man. A central part of the therapeutic process is to facilitate Sarah's full awareness of her motivation, so that she can accept its normality.

Sarah: *Yeah.*

Therapist: *What else was in it?*

Sarah: *Nothing much more than that.*

Therapist: *Well, that's important.*

Sarah: *Yeah, that was important enough. Even though going out with people my own age didn't usually work out very well. Every single one I went out with back then, they were always either into their own problems, or like this guy had one thing on his mind. Oh, they were no fun. They were just pains in the ass, you know?*

Therapist: *Had you had too much to drink that night, Sarah?*

In past work with this therapist, Sarah has talked about her problems with alcohol. In early adulthood, she had abused alcohol for a time, had become sober, and at the time of the present work had not drunk any alcohol for several years. It is possible that alcohol abuse was another facet of the rape and may be another factor in Sarah's self-shaming. If so, it needs to be dealt with, lest it spoil the effect of the work she has done.

Sarah: *No. No, I wasn't. I had an incident years earlier when, the guy who was giving me driving lessons celebrated, the night before I was going to take my test, with how well I was doing, with wine, and had me in the back seat of the car, and I'm screaming "Don't take advantage. . . . " I knew that much, as he's pulling his dick out in the back seat. And I don't know what I said to him, but the next thing I know he was* (she laughs), *he was saying his Act of Contrition, and putting his dick away, and—and, he had, he had turned me on. He was rubbing my breasts, and he had turned me on, and, and then, I must have indicated, or he must have known that I was turned on, and then he was saying, "I can satisfy you in other ways." And I'm yelling, "Get out of this car!"* (laughs again) *Only it was his car, so he couldn't get out of the car. So he took me to my friend's house. And I arrived at my friend's house; I felt safe with her. And of course I walked in the house, and I must have been reeking with this wine, and, um, and I must have looked like hell, because he had pulled up my skirt, and I can imagine what I looked like after being in the back seat with all this going on. Oh, God—*(laughing)

Therapist: *Sarah, you're laughing about this, and this is like another rape.*

Sarah's laughter is her defense against the pain of this newly recalled incident of abuse and her shame about what happened. By laughing at it, she can deny its seriousness and how she uses it as another proof of her script belief that "something's wrong with me." The therapist's comment calls her attention to the inconsistency between her affect and the story she is telling. The intervention is a confrontation. Like all effective confrontations, though, it contains both acknowledgment and validation: it underscores the importance of what Sarah is talking about and signals the therapist's commitment to understand the function of both the behavior and Sarah's present way of dealing with it.

Sarah: (with no laughter; she sounds surprised) *It was. It was another rape.*

Therapist: *Here's another man with his hands all over you. Pulling your dress up . . .*

Sarah: *. . . taking advantage of me.*

Therapist: *Even if you were drunk, it's still . . .*

Sarah: *Never thought of that as a rape before.*

Therapist: *Maybe he didn't penetrate you, but it's using your body without your permission. Without your wanting it to be that way.*

This comment provides a connection between the three traumatic sexual incidents: brother's "poking and pinching and prodding" (without Sarah's permission), Jerry's using her sexually (without permission), and now the driving instructor's advances (without permission). Sarah no longer needs to deal with three separate traumas, and three separate pieces of evidence that she should feel shame; she can begin to replace "felt like a whore" with "was used without my permission."

Sarah: *Right.*

Therapist: *Without your consent.*

Sarah: *Without my consent. And I remember that, he had bought a glass of wine, and when I drank that I felt funny, and I had to go to the ladies' room, and I said, "Please, no more wine. Just take me home now." And I came back, and the second glass of wine was there. And I must have drunk it. I don't remember not drinking it. And I do remember getting really zonked. Whew! That was a tough one—how I escaped that—*

Therapist: *You yelled.*

Sarah: *I mean, doing this in the back seat—*

Therapist: *You said, "Get out of the car."*

Sarah: *Yeah, I did something different that time.*

This interaction brings Sarah's appropriate and effective action to foreground, rather than continuing to focus on her helplessness and shame.

Therapist: *That's right.*

Sarah: *And then I went to my friend's house. She asked me no questions. And then I think the next day I must have told her at least partially what had happened. And I must have just filed that away somewhere. That was too hot to handle.*

Therapist: *That was really serious.*

Sarah: *Very serious. Very, very serious. That was two years before I left the convent. It was after that that I left, went to a place to get my act together because I was falling apart. I thought I was falling apart for a lot of reasons, and I never thought of the significance of that. I wonder if that's also part of why I thought I had to leave the convent.*

Therapist: *How so?*

It is important to inquire at this point, because Sarah is beginning to relapse into nonspecific language. Notice how many times she uses the word "that" in her most recent response. What does "that" stand for? Is she being vague in order to avoid contact with her feelings and thoughts about her experience? The therapist's question is partly for her own information, more to encourage Sarah to reestablish full contact with her own memories and phenomenology.

Sarah: (pause, begins to cry) *'Cause I was a nun, doing things I shouldn't be doing.*

Therapist: *Like what?*

Sarah: *Drinking and ending up in the back seat of someone's car, and getting turned on.*

Again we see Sarah's confusion about her sexual response. In spite of (apparently) accepting the therapist's description of her response to Jerry as "biological" and normal, she reverts to feeling shamed by her sexual arousal in this earlier situation. If she believes that it is shameful to be aroused, it is no wonder she experiences sexual dysfunction in her marriage.

Therapist: *Does that mean something's wrong with you, 'cause he stroked your breasts and you turned on?*

Sarah: *The thing that's wrong is that I was there and I did it, not so much that my body responded.*

Therapist: *It's like—I'm trying to make a connection—it's like "you didn't deserve to be a nun," or "you weren't really a nun," or . . .*

Sarah: *Probably. Maybe I was scared, because I did get turned on, and maybe I shouldn't be a nun.*

Therapist: *See, a little while ago you said the worst thing about the other rape—which surprised me—was the fact that you got turned on.*

Sarah: *Yeah.*

Therapist: *That the worst shaming thing about that rape was that you were turned on. And that surprised me. I would* expect *you to be turned on. As well as turned off.*

Sarah: *Yeah, at the same time.*

Therapist: *At the same time.* (pause) *So I wonder if again, the worst thing that happened is the self-condemnation of being turned on.*

Although a great deal of foundation has been laid, this is the first time that the therapist has explicitly suggested that Sarah herself has created the "worst thing" about being abused. Is she ready to hear it?

Sarah: *Oh.* (pause) *And I thought something was wrong with me. . . .*

Therapist: *What did the Church tell you about it?*

Sarah: *Oh, the Church didn't teach me sex was bad. I didn't have that kind of thing. It was beautiful. And it was, it was a free gift that I was given.*

Therapist: *Is it beautiful for a nun?*

How much of Sarah's shame is a direct response to the teachings of her religion? The interface between spiritual and therapeutic awareness is a delicate one, and the therapist needs to know if the work is approaching that interface. More importantly, though, is the way Sarah's beliefs were acquired: were they understood and internalized with awareness, or were they simply introjected as whole, not-to-be-questioned chunks? Introjected materials are out of awareness and are often not available for examination or elaboration or revision; they keep the same childlike and often distorted form in which they were originally acquired and never become a fully integrated part of one's way of being as an adult.

Sarah: *Well, yes. If, if freely given. If freely . . . you know, and maybe because that happened to me, oh, this is beginning to make some sense. . . . (pause) It's like I didn't keep my vow, or something.*

Therapist: *Because you didn't keep it beautiful?*

Sarah: *A free gift, freely given. And I was spoiling it.*

Therapist: *It's beautiful if freely—*

Sarah: *It wasn't!*

Therapist: *I'm just, I'm just trying to make sure I get it right.*

Sarah: *Okay.*

Therapist: *It's beautiful, only if it's freely given.*

Sarah: (crying) *It wasn't freely given.*

Therapist: (pause) *So what happens between you and Stephen, if you know that the first one and a half times were not freely given?*

With the old belief now explicit, Sarah can begin to explore its implications for her present responses.

Sarah: *Ohhh, gets in the way. Gets in the way.*

Therapist: *So where's the beautifulness with Stephen, then?*

Sarah: *I don't exactly know what you mean, but I'll respond. . . . The beautifulness with Stephen . . . is that I give myself as much as I can, as freely as I can, but I can't get by this. I'm hoping . . . it's beginning to make some sense.*

Therapist: *Let's take our time. (pause) So we go at your rhythm. (pause) So you can have full sex.*

Sarah: (speaking quickly) *Help me not to feel shamed. All of a sudden I got this rush of, "Oh, my God, you told all, all these secrets." And I've held on to pieces of . . . I've told these stories, but I haven't gotten to what I hold secret. 'Cause I haven't been able to, but . . . but you're helping me get in touch with it. I think. . . .*

Like a fungus, shame thrives in the dark. Keeping the shaming bits secret (and the most shaming is always the most secret) allows the shame to continue. The imagined response of others is always so much worse than the reality, and that imagined other-response is a part of what Sarah uses to feed the shame. She has now let much of it out and has removed many of the barriers to contact that she has used in the past to keep her shame a deep secret. The "rush" she describes is a kind of last-ditch effort or a rear-guard action to restore her old familiar psychological balance.

Therapist: *Did you stop feeling beautiful after those experiences?*

Sarah: *Ohhhh. . . .* (cries painfully) *Oh, I guess I did. It wasn't who I ever wanted to be . . . and I do this thing, I tell other people it was my fault; it happened because I did this and I did that and I should have known and I could have and I didn't . . .*

Therapist: *And your experiences of sex were not beautiful.*

Sarah: *No. Not one of them, never, never since I was a kid even. And I wanted them to be! 'Cause I knew, I knew, I'd been taught well, I had a healthy . . . understanding, but my body didn't. I didn't have any good experiences. It didn't match what I knew it should be.*

Therapist: *So what happened to your dream?*

Sarah: *It got shattered . . . and it got funneled in all this kind of feeling of perversion. And then I take that to bed. Like it's my perversion, instead of . . .*

Therapist: *Like something's wrong with you, or you're not beautiful?*

Sarah: *And how can I freely give a beautiful thing if it's not beautiful?*

Therapist: *You can't freely give it to Stephen if it's stolen?*

Sarah: *No. It was stolen before Jerry, even. That thing in the back seat of the car. I didn't realize how big—I really buried that one. Even though I've told the story, I really buried the significance of that.* (she is sobbing)

Therapist: (long pause) *Now talk to Stephen.*

Sarah's experience of shame has persistently interrupted contact between Stephen and her, and made it impossible for her to relax into the kind of "free giving" that she wants their sex to be. With her new awareness—a phenomenological as well as an intellectual shift—she can now begin to restore that contact. Doing so in fantasy will help her to do so later in reality.

Sarah: *Stephen. . . .* (pause) *Oh, Stephen . . . when I say, "Stephen," I just see his arms around me, and he's just holding me. And I don't want it just to be like that.*

Therapist: *Tell Stephen how you want it to be.*

Therapist: *Oh. . . . I want it to be so much richer than it is, so much fuller. I don't want to get scared every time I get into bed.*

Therapist: *Tell Stephen the secret that's been getting into bed with you.*

Sarah: *Ohhh, Stephen. . . .* (turns back to the therapist) *It's almost like I felt like I violated him by . . .*

Therapist: *Tell Stephen.*

Sarah: *Stephen, it almost seems like I violated you by giving this away somewhere else. But I really didn't give it away; it was taken from me . . . by men who were nowhere close to you. Not your quality.*

Therapist: *Yeah, tell Stephen about his quality.*

Sarah: *Ohhh . . . Stephen . . . such deep love and respect . . . such a cherishing of me . . .*

Therapist: (pause) *Tell Stephen what it would have been like if you'd taken him home.*

Sarah: *I . . . I don't know . . .*

Therapist: *What about the dream that'd been shattered? Think we can put the pieces back together with Stephen?*

Sarah: *What I see is my wedding night, where it should have been so much better.*

Therapist: *Tell Stephen your dream.*

Sarah: *Yeah, this is the way I'd love it to have been, Stephen.*

Therapist: *Tell him how you were going to give away your virginity.*

Sarah: *After we say good-bye to all our friends then we go to our motel room before we go on to our honeymoon trip. . . .* (sigh) *Yeah, that's the way it should have been. . . .*

Therapist: *Tell him what you just pictured in your mind.*

The private fantasy may fade, become hazy, or be overwhelmed by a return of her old self-condemning beliefs. By saying it out loud and making it concrete and detailed, Sarah strengthens the new set of responses. In a sense, she inoculates herself against relapsing into shame.

Sarah: *I just pictured the fullness of my love for him and his for me. And that deep regard we have for each other, and respect for each other's needs and space and everything. And we just would have fallen into each other's arms, and it would have happened so naturally and so beautifully, in all the fullness and richness of that love.* (She is crying) *Yes. . . .*

Therapist: *Tell him what you would say to yourself when your body got excited.*

Sarah: *Yeah, this is the way it's supposed to be! Yes, this is all I dreamed of, this is . . . this is even better than I thought. 'Cause I can feel it; it's not just in my head!*

Therapist: *And rather than saying, "something's wrong with me," tell him what you'd think.*

In the remaining minutes of the therapy session, Sarah goes on to make specific plans for Stephen's return (he was currently away on a business trip). She reiterated that things were right, not wrong, with her, and she did so in fantasy conversations with both Jerry and the driving instructor. Her session ends as she comes back to Stephen.

Sarah: *Ahhhh . . . everything is right. This is so right. . . . I just need you, Stephen. Just need you. Just want you. And I'm going to kick those people out of my head, and my life, and be with you.*

In this piece of work, we have seen how a client can move rapidly from one age regression to another and how the therapist's attunement to those levels of regression helped her to shape responses that were appropriate both to the developmental level of the regression and to the problem focus originally requested by the nonregressed client. By exploring the script beliefs and other fixed gestalten that were constructed at the time of the early traumas, both Sarah and the therapist could understand more clearly the functions of Sarah's present problem behaviors as well as her responses to her brother's sexual abuse, the date rape, and the driving teacher's molestation. Although they happened at very different times in her life, and although her behaviors were superficially quite different, the underlying needs and survival strategies were the same.

Another important facet of Sarah's work was dealing with her sense of shame. As was pointed out earlier, the core element in the experience of shame is the belief that "something is wrong with me." As long as that belief persists, even though it may be deeply buried and unavailable to conscious awareness, the emotional responses associated with shaming will be elicited by any situation that is connected, affectively, cognitively, behaviorally, or physiologically, to the original shame experience. As Sarah regressed and reexperienced the responses that she had felt shame over, the involved, authentic, and normalizing presence of the therapist helped her to reorganize her beliefs and her memories so that she no longer needed to feel ashamed.

Sarah clearly experienced a number of traumatic events in her life, but, as she realized, it was not the events themselves that caused the lasting damage and the lasting sense of shame. It was the absence of a supportive relationship during and after the hurtful events that created the more serious trauma. In the absence of such relationships, Sarah had to figure out for herself the meaning of each event, the meaning of her emotional response, and a strategy for dealing with it and with its aftermath. As we saw, the meanings she assigned were self-blaming and self-critical: "There's something wrong with me," "I'm stupid," "I'm a whore." The strategies all grew out of the earliest trauma, the child sexually molested by her brother, with nobody available to call to for help or to provide comfort and understanding later. Strategy one: be nice; strategy two: dance around and distract; strategy three: freeze. These are the things the child Sarah figured out to do, and none of them was of much help when Sarah found herself alone with a rapist.

It was the quality of the therapeutic relationship, more than anything else, that helped Sarah find a way to change her well-rehearsed and by now automatic responses. She experienced not only the safety and comfort of an authentic and caring relationship—precisely what had been missing before—but also, within that relationship, the therapist took over the functions that had previously been served by Sarah's defenses, blocking her self-criticism and providing an understandable meaning for her behavior. As Sarah began to experience the therapist's taking care of those survival functions and to believe that the therapist could and would attend to her relational needs, it became possible for her to let go of the old defensive strategies. Not constrained to distract or freeze up or "be nice," she could experiment with new patterns. Instead of freezing, she could say, "No." Instead of distracting, she could be clear about her needs and wants. Instead of being "nice," she could express her anger toward an abuser. And, in so doing, she was able to experience her own strength and potential: no longer a woman who felt and acted like a powerless child, she became a woman who could feel and act like a woman.

Several months after this piece of work was done, the therapist received a letter from Sarah. We think her words are a fitting conclusion to this chapter.

> I took your hands and made myself look into your eyes as we worked our way though the details of each rape. . . . Hearing you reassure me that what I was feeling was normal, having you fill in the information I did not have at the time each rape was happening, experiencing your support of my efforts to make the only or best decision I could at those times, began the process of my letting go of some of the shame and guilt.
>
> In the telling of my stories I had related an incident that had occurred with my driving instructor the evening of my final test practice. . . . I ended up in the back seat of the car fighting off his advances. Telling this was so difficult. When you looked at me and said, "Sarah, that was rape," it was quite an awakening!
>
> My inability to enjoy a full and healthy sexual life with my husband . . . has always been troublesome to me. I accounted for it by blaming my early

incest experiences. Working specifically with my rape issues has been very powerful, enlightening and freeing. Thank you!

In the writing of this letter, I found myself getting slightly emotional but not being overwhelmed. For me this is a good sign. What had power enough to take me into regression, I can now look back on with a mix of sadness and acceptance. This is not a strange mix to me, but rather the resolution of grief. There is also a bubbling up of new life. I can now pursue a new dream—the fulfillment of my marriage.

Edward: Exploring the Function of Defenses

Psychotherapy is about resolving habitual interruptions to both internal and external contact. It involves the dynamic tension between one's natural tendency to grow and change and the equally natural pull to stay as one is and to remain with the familiar. Without both of these tendencies, to change and to remain the same, there would be no such thing as psychotherapy: without the urge to grow, psychotherapy would be useless; without the pull to stay the same, it would be unnecessary.

In this excerpt, we shall focus on the tension between growth and stagnation, between psychological expansion and contraction as it plays itself out in the therapeutic process. We will point out some of the ways in which the client strives to maintain his old, learned patterns of behavior and how the therapist validates the function of those patterns while simultaneously preparing the client for his next step toward full and healthy contact with self and others.

In order to keep the old patterns of thinking, feeling, and behaving, one must not allow oneself to change—a truism, to be sure, but a profound one. Not changing means keeping constant one's behaviors, one's values, one's fantasies, and one's beliefs about self and others. It means always responding in the same way to situations that are perceived as similar. It means applying old ways of organizing experiences to every new experience that comes along. It means, in short, defending oneself from the kinds of awareness that would lead to change—defending ourselves from the internal and external contact that would make our old patterns impossible to maintain.

Defenses are costly: not only do they bar one from the pleasures of contact and growth, but they also require energy to maintain. The more effort one spends on psychological defense, the less energy is available for anything else. So why do it? Why hang on to those old patterns? Why not relax, make contact, and be spontaneously oneself? Any response that is clung to so stubbornly, in spite of the cost, must have an important function or perhaps several important functions. In this chapter, we shall look at four of the most important of these functions as they are woven into a single therapy session.

First, *predictability*. If the world is unpredictable, we cannot prepare ourselves ahead of time for the bad things that might happen. In a predictable world, we know what is coming and we can get ready for it or perhaps even avoid it. One's pattern of beliefs about self, others, and the quality of life provides such predictability. We may not like what we believe to be true, but at least we will not be blindsided by it. We can brace ourselves to fight back, to run away, or to weather the storm.

Second, *identity*. This is, in a sense, a special kind of predictability: the predictability of one's own self, one's own being. Without such predictability, we would have no sense of continuity from one moment to the next, no sense that we are the same person as we move from one situation to another. And it is in the experience of continuity that identity develops and the self can be known as an ongoing entity. "I yam what I yam," says Popeye: "I" remains "I," the same "I," regardless of the changes that may occur around me. Hanging onto old ways of thinking, of experiencing emotion, and of interacting with the world around us, allows us to keep that sense of "I."

Third, *consistency*. Humans are organizing animals; without an organizing scheme, our lives would be a jumble of unrelated events occurring in a kaleidoscope of settings. Nothing would make sense, and nothing would relate to anything else. Maintaining our old patterns of thinking and feeling allows us to understand our reactions and put them into an organized context, to bring some kind of structure to our world. This structuring, in turn, makes predictability and identity possible.

And, finally, *stability*. Stability should, really, come first in the list: predictability, identity, and consistency are possible only if one can maintain some sense of control and some sense of being in charge of oneself. Without our defenses, we run the risk of being flooded by a rush of emotions, needs, memories—hopelessly confused, whirled away, drowning in our own ungovernable process. In popular parlance, this is being "crazy." Our defenses allow us to feel, actually to *be*, in control, and with that control comes the possibility of maintaining a consistent, predictable identity in a consistent and predictable world.

The task of the therapist is to help the client move out of his or her rigid patterns of perceiving and responding, of defending and distorting, and to find a new way of being in the world. But the functions served by those old defenses and distortions are necessary. The need for predictability, identity, consistency, and stability must be attended to. In integrative psychotherapy, we encourage the client to allow the therapeutic relationship to take over those functions temporarily, to fill in the gaps that are created as the client begins to abandon his or her old behaviors, beliefs, and reactions. Here is another of the "betweens" of therapy: the therapeutic relationship stands "between" the old way of being and the new kind of contact with self and others that is emerging.

The transcript presented in this chapter is taken from the third session that the therapist had with this client, Edward. The client is still somewhat tentative; he does not know the therapist well and does not yet fully trust her. His first step in changing will be to experience the therapist as a caring, trustworthy, and contactful other. As he begins to experience that relationship, so different from relationships of the past, he can also begin to recognize and appreciate himself and his defenses in a different way: he can begin to acknowledge and value himself as a creative and courageous survivor. Once that has been accomplished and the defensive patterns have moved into awareness, he will be in a much better position to create new options for himself.

Edward: *I'm a little bit intimidated, looking at you here, trying to . . . I come in and out of feeling serious and feeling playful . . .*

Therapist: *Intimidated?*

Edward: *Well, you suddenly look very . . . present, you know? Suddenly I'm here, and you're looking at me, and I'm . . . I don't have anything going on in my mind, particularly; I'm not here with any agenda at the moment, and suddenly I'm thinking "Now what is it that I was thinking about yesterday," and maybe I could be focusing on my life, and stuff like this, and . . .*

Therapist: *But if I am fully present, then you're intimidated?*

Edward experiences the therapist's presence, the core of the therapeutic relationship, as threatening. Since the therapist has given Edward no external reason to be threatened, the source of the intimidation must be internal. Edward may be defining the relationship between himself and the therapist transferentially, in terms of other important relationships that he has experienced. By exploring Edward's experience of the therapist, both he and the therapist will discover the significance and the implications of the relationships in which Edward learned to feel threatened and intimidated, as well as the psychological functions now served by continuing to feel that way.

Edward: *Like a sort of demand, yeah, that I sort of . . . come in and get serious, and try to* (laughs) *do something, or something like that, though I'm actually feeling a bit playful, which is all right.*

Therapist: *Can I be present without you being intimidated?*

Edward: *Well, it's getting that way now. I feel, you know, less intimidated, and . . . trying to find a way of getting at ease, um. . . . I feel you more, I know you more, I mean . . . it's like, I haven't had much, haven't had much time with you yet . . .*

Therapist: *But you're wanting to know something about me?*

Edward: *Yeah. I was thinking a lot about . . . while I walked this morning, I was thinking quite a lot about my mother, actually. . . .* (laughs) *As I walked, I was vaguely thinking about me in general, and . . . you know, um, thinking what am I doing, what do I want to do, where am I at . . . thinking about seeing you today. Very angry, and, um . . . what's the word—humiliating interaction that I used to have a lot with my mother. I mean, you know, she tried to humiliate me and in a way I'd try to do it back, you know. . . . We fought a lot. She was a very, um, very humiliating person, very dismissive, very . . .*

Therapist: *Humiliating like what? Can you give me a sense of how she would . . .*

This inquiry goes to Edward's personal history and by implication to his expectations of the therapist. It is a transferential inquiry. It assumes that whatever behaviors and responses Edward learned in his relationship with his mother were significant, served a significant function; that what he learned has implications for his present, adult relationships. In exploring how it was back then, with mother, both Edward and the therapist will begin to understand better how it is now, with the two of them.

Edward: *Oh, yes. She's, um . . . oh, she'd have, like a phrase: "Oh, I thought you'd understood." Stuff like that. Would be, like, um. . . . There was a lot going on between us, in general. Something that's come into my mind; it's one of the things I was thinking as I was walking—I was imagining talking about myself to you, and imagining saying to myself—imagining saying, "I don't want to talk about my mother anymore." Then also thinking, "No, actually, my life has definitely been constructed around this complicated, intense, rather sadistic relationship, and . . . it still goes on between the two of us, actually." And, um, it is important, then. It's not true. I want to say it clearly. It's not true that I don't want to talk about it anymore; it really is always there. It's always there in me, even though I'm 50 years old now, and I've done a lot of work on myself, it's still—it's an important part of my life. I feel like . . .*

Therapist: *Edward, can I assume a question unasked, as you look at me. Such as, "Are you, like my mother, going to humiliate me?"*

Here the therapist no longer simply follows her interest in Edward's expectations but addresses them directly. Her question implies, "Does your way of organizing the world require that I treat you as your mother did?" If true, this would certainly make things more predictable; and knowing ahead of time what was coming would allow Edward to avoid being disappointed by the therapist and to prepare himself for trouble.

Edward: *Well, I don't feel at all, you don't have at all that kind of energy. I do feel a kind of temptation to preemptively push you away a bit, you know. It's a kind of, um, "let me get in first before, before you do something to me" kind of feeling, which is a bit present, you know. Even though you seem to be really a nice person* (laughs) *in lots of ways, so it doesn't feel like it. . . .*

Therapist: *I wonder if that question always lurks half consciously and half unconsciously in the background.*

Edward: *Yeah. It's always, a bit of that going on. It's sort of . . . "Oh my God" here, and . . .*

Therapist: *Is humor a way to deal with that?*

Edward: *Yes, of course, that's . . .*

Therapist: *And what about your charm?*

Edward: *My charm?*

Therapist: *Is that spontaneous, or is that also to modulate potential humiliation?*

Humor and charm can both be coping skills, ways of defending against the pain of getting too close and then being humiliated. In the last three inquiries, the therapist has invited Edward to examine his interactional style in terms of its defensive possibilities. But humor and charm can also be spontaneous, authentic, and contact enhancing. The therapist now acknowledges both aspects, and Edward accepts the dual description.

Edward: *Both. I was also remembering this morning that somebody a few years ago said to me, "As a little boy you used to sing an awful lot." I still do, actually. I sing and whistle a lot. "And you seemed such a happy youngster." It was some older woman that I'd not seen for about 25 or 30 years. And, um, I was a lively little boy in a lot of ways. I've forgotten what the question was, oh, about the charm, that's right. . . . So I think it's both there naturally, but also, yeah, yeah, I like to . . . control people in certain ways, you know; I like to . . .*

Therapist: *Now you said very quickly that the humor was to control potential humiliation. Is it also natural, spontaneous humor? Or is it protective only? You* *see, I wondered, when you said that your charm was both natural and protective, if your humor would also naturally be there if you had a guarantee of protection.*

Edward's preadolescent years were a critical time in the development of his current ways of meeting the world, and this is the first of a number of references to that period of his life. Right now, though, the question of natural versus protective behavior is still on the table. The notion of humor and charm as *both* protective and natural opens the door to the "what if" question. How would Edward be if he did not have to protect himself? And would a different, nondefended way of being affect more than just his humor and charm? The therapist's suggestions act as a beginning probe into the vulnerability that Edward will experience as he becomes less defended. They also go to the identity-making function of Edward's defenses: "Who will you be, when you no longer have to protect yourself in this way?"

Edward: *I immediately feel "I hope so."* (laughs) *I mean, I'd hate to imagine . . . you know, not wanting to have the humor. But . . .*

Therapist: *Well, if you're going to have a defense, that's one of the nicest ones to have.*

Edward: *Yeah. Yeah, wouldn't like to, like to lose it. I do notice, you know, I overuse it. But I'm sort of finding myself thinking, " If I look at you a bit more, what is it I'd be looking for, what is it I'd be . . . that I'd like to key into?" I mean, is . . . there's a quality of wanting something . . .*

Therapist: *Wanting something?*

Edward is talking directly and specifically about his feelings toward the therapist. The more he does this, the more he explores the nature of his here-and-now experience in this relationship, the more contact there will be. Of course, we suspect that (in part, at least) he is not really relating to the therapist, but to the image of his mother that inhabits the in-between of many of his relationships. The therapist's simple repetition of Edward's last words encourages further exploration, without prejudicing or imposing a direction on that exploration.

Edward: *Yeah. . . . Soon as I say that I feel a bit wary and a bit, bit pissed off actually, you know . . . kind of surly.*

Therapist: *Any kind of impulse to depend on someone else would be met with a surly response in you?*

Edward allowed himself to feel (and talk about) "wanting something." This ran counter to his usual pattern, which is that wanting is a form of vulnerability, and vulnerability is not allowed. The next level of defense, after humor and charm, is surliness. Being surly protects both internally and externally: internally, it keeps Edward from feeling his neediness, and externally it maintains a safe distance between him and others.

Edward: *Well, underneath, yes. I mean, I'd probably pretend not, but there's a bit of surliness, you know. There's a bit of . . . well, it comes down to "Who do you . . . why would I trust you?" kind of thing, but it feels like, I mean, it feels, the words are there: "Who the fuck are you?" kind of thing. You know, this kind of, this angry . . .*

Therapist: *Will you turn up the volume on the surly? So I get to hear it too?*

Rather than fight with the defense, support it. Fighting with it, trying to break through it, might drive it underground, its function and characteristics disguised. It would be like pulling the top off of a weed: once you have done that, you cannot get at the root and it will just sprout again later, larger and more vigorous. Supporting the whole transferential process allows it to move more fully into awareness, be lived out, and be experienced in the context of a new relationship in which the other person will no longer act to affirm the old beliefs and expectations.

Edward: *Yeah, maybe. . . . Well, let me tell you about—it was so very fucking humiliating to be sent off to school with so much glee by my mother, you know. She really was fucking pleased to get rid of us, you know. I'd say that seems very clear to me. I was sent to boarding school at 12, and at the same time my younger brother was sent away at only 8. And he didn't see the family again for two months. You know, I mean, I was 12; I could sort of handle it. But at 8, my God! Anyway, no, so that does, and remains, rankles continually. I mean, you know, the sort of, the pleasure that she seemed to have felt in finding the solution to what to do with her children.*

Therapist: *Edward. When the person you are most dependent on, in this whole world, has glee in sending you away, something's got to happen in your heart.*

Even though it is not a question, this is clearly an inquiry: it is an invitation to move into the affective experience of the memory. It may elicit information about history and expectations, or it may move Edward into the "coping/choices/decisions" level of inquiry if what happened "in your heart" was a decision to harden that heart against future hurt. Another effect of the intervention is to normalize Edward's response to his mother. "Something's *got* to happen" translates to "anyone would respond intensely to that."

Edward: *Hmm. Oh, I really felt that way before I went. I mean, I, I, um, I was, I said to somebody, there were people, there were boys sitting around in class with tears rolling down their cheeks. There was one of my best friends called Kevin Martin who had a rash of boils, I remember, who was sitting there squeezing his* *boils out, and* (laughs) *with the tears running down his face . . . and I didn't cry at all. I remember saying, "I'm glad to get away from the old dump." But on the other hand, I'd just got pushed into a new dump, you know, it was, um . . .*

Therapist: *And inside, what were you really feeling?*

This intervention is a subtle invitation to therapeutic regression. It asks Edward to access the phenomenological experience of a younger version of himself, and that accessing is the essence of the regressive experience.

Edward: (pause) *I was glad to get away from it. I was . . . I didn't feel happy anymore; I hadn't felt happy anymore for at least two years; since I was about 10 or 11. I started feeling very unhappy about 10. Everything seemed to fall apart in a big way; I couldn't . . . I had a lot of very intense and preying fantasies, I mean they preyed on me is what I mean. Very intense sexual fantasies, very intense sexual activity; I . . . when my parents went out I'd take my clothes off and walk around the house naked; we moved when I was 11. I'd roam around in the woods and roll around in the leaves and hang on to trees, and stuff like that. Really had an enormous desire to get my clothes off.*

No true regression yet, although Edward may be dipping into it in order to retrieve these stories. He is certainly talking about the phenomenology of his preadolescent years, but he does not seem to be feeling the emotion that must have accompanied those experiences. His description of wanting to be naked has the flavor of a self-criticism, and the therapist responds to neutralize the criticism. Her words and her tone of voice acknowledge Edward's experience, normalize it, and validate its function.

Therapist: *Were you hungry for skin contact?*

Edward: *Oh, Jesus, I was just bonkers for it. But . . . I even got out on the roof* (laughs) *with no clothes on, fell off the roof; that was great. Middle of the night. Finally managed to find a window that I could crawl back in. The thought that I was going to be found in the morning, naked, outside the house, was just too horrible to be* (laugh) *imagined, so . . . finally found a window I* (laugh) *broke and got into . . .*

Therapist: *So you were hungry for skin contact.*

Edward has been speaking quickly and animatedly as he talks about his sexual fantasies; his other nonverbal responses indicate a great deal of energy. Immediately, though, he shifts into a quasi-humorous, self-denigrating anecdote as a way to defend against the intensity of his feelings. The therapist's repetitive comment invites him back to the internal experience.

Edward: *Oh, yeah, yeah, I was, um, seriously—*

Therapist: *Did anybody hold you on their lap? Did anybody lie down with you, and fall asleep, and cuddle you?*

This is a historical inquiry, and more. The images are intended to stimu-late affective memory, either of how it felt to experience these things or of the discomfort of not having them.

Edward: *No.* (pause) *I'm trying to think. We did have au pair girls. We always had au pair girls from when I suppose I was about 2 years old; there was one who was just wonderful. Woman called Renee. I was about 5 or so. She and I, I really liked her; she hugged me. But she went away, and she came back again, and I was really pissed off at her. Told everybody how fat she was, and things like that* (laugh). *'Cause she went away for a year and a half, and then she came back. Very hard to forgive her for having gone. It was difficult, too, because they'd leave every year, you know . . . again, there was some kind of triumph in my mother about that, too, you know. It's like, I had very close contact with some of these people, and then they were suddenly gone, you know—"say goodbye to Doris," you know, my mother would say.*

Here is more history supporting Edward's core script belief that "people can't be trusted." Renee and Doris abandoned him, and his mother engi-neered and enjoyed it. If he gets close and lets himself need, he'll just get hurt again. And he will be doubly hurt: by the abandonment, and then by mother's pleasure in his pain.

Therapist: *And was your father any sort of a balance to that, did he . . .*

Edward: *Not with me. 'Cause I was . . . we were four boys, and I was the one who was sort of . . . it was invisibly decided that I was like her, and therefore I was in her camp. How this decision was reached I don't know, but it was always said that I was "a Cooper," you know, like her, maiden name, you know, and I was therefore. . . . One of my big, um, my big fears was that they would split up, 'cause they had a very, very angry, rocky relationship; and they did split up a bit, when I was about 10, for about three months; they did talk about divorce. One of my fears was that I'd get left with her. Very strong fear about that. Really didn't want to be left taking care of her while the others—the other two—'cause the fourth one was born a lot later. . . .*

Therapist: *You keep coming back to that preadolescent time as significant for you. The friend who said you used to sing. When you talked about your life start-ing to fall apart after about 10 or 10 and a half. Getting naked. And you talked about your parents splitting up for a while at 10, and being afraid of being left with her.*

The focus on preadolescence is too pervasive to ignore. The therapist simply underscores it; if Edward wants to pursue it, he is welcome to do so. Apparently, however, Edward is most invested in what happened between him and his mother, and this is what he continues to talk about.

Edward: *Yeah . . . we went for a car ride once; she told me that my father was going to leave her. And we were driving around, somewhere near . . . somewhere near the river. And, um, I remember her saying with this sort of false kind of gaiety, "Well, we won't be able to do sailing anymore. But perhaps we can; perhaps we can all start skating instead." And I thought, "Oh fuck skates," you know. God, I hated skating. You just fall on your behind and hurt your elbows and so on. And I remember thinking very strongly I wanted the bottom of the car to just open and dump me out on the road and let her go on all alone, you know. Definitely wanted to be out of that. . . .*

Therapist: *To escape, or to punish her?*

Edward's "surliness" certainly carries a lot of anger. Edward has talked freely about his anger toward his mother. Was that anger conscious during preadolescence, and did it emerge in a desire to hit back? Or did it stay underground, replaced simply by a felt need to leave the field, get away, and escape from the pain?

Edward: *Oh, I don't think I felt, I just wanted to get out. I don't remember thinking of it as being a punishment; I just wanted the bottom to drop out.*

Therapist: *To escape.*

Edward: *I certainly felt like . . . not being a part of that fixed gaiety, of her phony gaiety, that "We'll be all right together . . . don't need your father," and I was thinking . . . oh, a feeling of, um, I felt something bad would happen. I felt something . . . I felt for a long time, and perhaps it's still there, this sense of "I don't want to be left alone with her," you know. I hated how she—you know, she was very brutal—Jesus Christ, she'd start—dry my hair, you know—God, bloody. . . . I was just really nuts, you know, crazy. I felt like belting her, you know? The sooner I could get her out of the bathroom and, you know, have no more to do with washing me or anything, the better it was. She'd clean our ears, kraaaaah! Just nuts, you know?*

Therapist: *I'm sorry.*

Edward: *Yeah . . . yes, I . . . she feels dangerous; she feels a little bit monstrous, you know?*

Therapist: *Um-hmm. I get that.*

Edward: *She feels, you know, a little—I don't trust her. Though what it is I don't trust her not to do, or to do, but . . .*

Here is Edward's first explicit statement of his script belief: "I don't trust." It starts with his mother and extends to people in general. It may also be an example of how a script belief can be both a perception/decision (a natural outcome of being treated badly) and an introjection from mother, who quite possibly had the same belief.

Therapist: *Well, would you trust her cleaning out your ears?*

Edward: *Whhhhhh. . . . I don't like people, uh . . .*

Therapist: *Would you want her washing you in the bathtub?*

Edward: *Whhh—it was* always *unpleasant. I mean, from the word go, as far back as I can remember. All that stuff was unpleasant. Washing in the bath, you know. There was something. . . . There was always a blaming thing going on. Blaming for being dirty—like somehow you could have avoided it, you know. "Look how dirty this is!" "Look at all this!" "Your ears are filthy!" You know, this kind of stuff. Oooghhh!*

Therapist: *Was that humiliating?*

Edward: *(pause) That's . . . that's, that's enraging, you know. That's not just humiliating; that's just, that's just . . . I mean that's where I felt surly, very surly indeed. "I'm not going to play the fucking game," you know. "I'm not going to clean the bathtub out afterwards; you're joking; not gonna put that towel back up or anything; I'm not gonna do anything." That was my feeling. In fact they used to call me Eeyore, because, you know, the Winnie the Pooh books—I was always the one who was complaining; I was always. . . .*

Enraging and humiliating, both. It was not safe to feel the humiliation (it hurt too much), and it was not safe to express the rage (he might have been punished), so to protect himself, Edward became surly. "I won't be nice," he seems to have been saying. "I won't try to bargain for good treatment; I won't let you like me at all because you'd just let me down in the end." This child had given up striving for attention or power, and was now acting out of vengefulness and a need to demonstrate his own felt lack of worth. It will be important for the therapist to notice and counter Edward's self-criticism, lest she (by omission) reinforce the despair of the little boy whose relational needs were so cruelly ignored.

Therapist: *Yeah, dour. . . .*

Edward: *"I don't like it," "There's something wrong," "This isn't the way it should be," you know, "It's not fair!" was what I said a lot. "It's not fair." Said it a lot. Felt it a lot. Something about it all wasn't fair; that's true.*

Therapist: *So you tried to protest.*

Edward: *Oh, I protested a lot. I got put down for it a lot; my father would tease me a lot.*

Therapist: *Tease you a lot?*

Edward: *Well . . . that feels unfair too, because I think that he was teased a lot by his father, and, you know, I don't think he was really a kind of teasing person, that much. He was actually potentially quite a kindly person. But he wasn't very kind with me. He tended to be kinder to my other brother who I think, in fact, needed it more, probably. But . . .*

Therapist: *Teased a lot?*

The therapist uses this sort of repeated phrase intervention frequently with Edward. Edward speaks quickly, often stumbling over his own words. His rhythm, particularly in the first half of the session, is a false one, developed probably as another way to protect himself. Simply repeating a very short phrase invites Edward to slow down, stay with his own process, and rediscover his natural rhythm.

Edward: *He teased me and he put me down. Said, "Edward," you know, it was this, "Stop doing," "Stop being. . . ." "Stop being Edward" or "Stop," you know, "We don't want to hear any more of your typical kind of. . . ." Whatever it may be. Yes, just plain teasing me about it, you know. He took photos of me when he was . . . a series of photos on holiday when he'd asked me to go and get something from the hotel, and I didn't want to 'cause we were already half a mile out on our walk; and I'm sitting on a gate getting more and more . . . upset. . . . He took a whole series of photos, while he was trying to force me to go back to the hotel and pick up his binoculars or whatever. And I ended up crying. I think I probably went up, I probably ended up probably going back to the fucking hotel. . . . Well, you know, I mean every child has these experiences. . . .*

Therapist: *No, every child does* not *have that experience.*

This therapist response is a normalizing intervention. Edward's comment, "Every child has these experiences" could easily extend to "and they don't all respond like I did; therefore, there's something wrong with me." The therapist's contradiction implies that, since Edward's experience was not universal, his response to it would necessarily be different from the responses of a child who had a different history.

Edward: *Yeah, probably don't. Well . . . it certainly happened a lot.*

Therapist: *But that is probably a very wonderful way to sort of defend against intensity, to homogenize, and to make yourself common.*

This is a direct appeal for Edward to respect and value his defensive system. He needs to learn to appreciate his defenses, to understand their function, and to be able to recognize his own courage and creativity in learning how to survive both the attacks from without and the pain from within. As he learns to acknowledge what he is doing, he can begin to let go, just as someone with a clenched fist must first notice the clenching before being able to consciously relax the hand. The therapist is beginning to expose the defensive process, always in the context of validating and normalizing it.

Edward: *Well, also, I must say that I felt that in some sort of indefinable way I got out of it all rather better than my elder brother and my younger brother. I put my younger brother down a lot, of course. We get along very well now, but I think I, I mean, I'd make up games and of course he'd always lose, you know, what can you say, I was five years older. Had to win somewhere. . . . But, um, I feel bad about it. And I feel with my elder brother even more so. I mean, I tried really, really, really hard to . . . get the . . . what's the word—get the upper on him, get over . . . win out on him, which I think I did from about the age of 7 or 8 onward, you know? I think I became more, more intense than him. It was, you know, I would go further than him. I'd fight harder, you know; he was, I made him, kind of a loser. We'd all pick on each other in turns, in a way. Mmmm. . . .*

Therapist: *What a wonderful momentary relief. To be the picker on someone else. I would imagine for those few moments, a sense of relief.*

"They had it worse than I did; I picked on them." Here comes the self-criticism. The therapist quickly normalizes ("What a wonderful relief") and then uses the normalization to invite even further exploration of that young boy's phenomenological experience.

Edward: *I do remember giggling about that kind of thing. It was like, you know, what I do remember feeling is (a) that it was totally unfair; (b) that I enjoyed giggling about it, . . . and (c) wondering how Hughie was going to cope with it— as my younger brother. You know, wondering. And I was, I did try and make up to him in certain ways, you know. I took him round with me a lot; he was quite a lot younger. I tried to make up to him in various ways 'cause I felt that he was really, I mean, it was even less fair on him, because he was even less able to protect himself, defend himself. And it wasn't true that he was stupid, you know; this was really—oh, it's certainly true that—it was a relief, as you say; it certainly was a relief that around the house, somebody else's turn, you know. Oooofff. . . .*

Therapist: *How wonderful the release for those few minutes.*

The therapist is acknowledging the cognitive content of the story but at the same time directing the focus to the phenomenology and to the function of the behavior. Edward has showed us another layer of his defensive structure: charm and humor, then surliness, then aggression. Each brings its own kind of protection and its own kind of relief.

Edward: *It's hard for me to feel that way now. I feel . . . (pause) I mean . . . yeah. Well . . . yeah.*

Therapist: *Edward, may I venture an interpretation?* (Edward nods his permission) *You said a moment ago that you wanted to see how Hughie would cope* *with it. And I wonder if also—in addition to the relief of picking on someone, there was the hope that he would teach you something, that you could then use with your Mom and Dad. If by picking on him, and he taught you how to handle humiliation, you would have a new skill.*

Interpretation is always risky. Here the therapist's question, preceding the interpretation, serves to establish a minicontract; it also reassures Edward that this therapist is not trying to sneak something past him—all interpretations will be clearly labeled as such. The interpretation itself, of course, invites exploration of another function for the defensive behavior.

Edward: *Well, that's not how I felt. What I really felt was, this is a life and death fucking thing. You know, it's like, I felt like I could probably just—and I often feel this way in my dreams, as well—I can probably just about handle it. And I wasn't sure if the others could. And it's still the way I feel. I mean I, I had a dream about a year ago where . . . police came round to visit me and went into the farm next door, and they dug up a body, a dead body, which I'd apparently killed. And I remember sort of saying, "Oh, well, it seems like there's no way around this; I obviously have killed somebody, some time back. And, uh, well, you know, maybe I can get away with 10 years of prison, you know, maybe I can handle that; I'm sure I can, you know, I can read," and stuff like this. All this stuff was going on in the dream; very clearly, "I can live through it." Very strong feeling, I can live through it, I can manage that . . . (softly) But I'm not sure I always can, you know. . . . Um, and again quite recently a dream where, I mentioned I've just had a few dreams about aging, and I, I dreamed that I suddenly noticed that my hair was mainly white. And I thought, oh, shit, that was quick, you know. . . .*

Although he rejects the interpretation, Edward goes on to reveal some rich new information. Dream material is typically full of possibilities, suggestions, and multiple meanings. A therapist can never be completely sure of understanding what these meanings are or where they may lead; we file them away to be checked against what emerges as the work moves on. Here, for instance, the therapist wonders about Edward's statement, "I obviously have killed somebody." Has he killed his need to depend on other people? His ability to be intimate? His awareness of body sensations, so vivid in his preadolescent relish of nakedness? The number 10, previously associated with preadolescence, comes up again and may connect in some way to those early years. The prison dream is also almost surely about how he protects himself, endures, and gets through pain. And the white hair dream? Is this a warning not to go too quickly with this therapy?

Edward: *And I thought, um, well, shit, that's the way it is, you know; you get used to it quite quickly . . . so I'm very, feel I can survive . . .*

Therapist: *So a lot of pride in surviving, too.*

This is the first authentically self-affirming thing Edward has said. He is proud of himself for surviving. The pride in survival may be extendable to the defenses he developed in order to survive; valuing and respecting the defenses opens the door to deeper exploration of them, and ultimately to appreciating and valuing their psychological function.

Edward: *Yeah. Quite a lot of pride in surviving I used to think that all I could do was survive. I quite strongly felt that way, that if I could survive that was already not bad, you know. Now I'm noticing that I can do a lot more; that's nice. Nice perception. But certainly that was my main assignment. Let's try and get through.*

Therapist: *In this conversation, right now, Edward, do you get a sense of what percentage of this is survival mode and what percent of this is just spontaneous and natural?*

The therapist draws an implicit parallel between Edward and his mother, on the one hand, and Edward and therapist, on the other. The intervention weaves together Edward's initial comments about feeling intimidated, the later discussion about fearing humiliation, and whatever Edward is experiencing at the present moment.

Edward: *Is there a difference?* (he chuckles, and then becomes serious again) *I don't think I'm feeling like I have to survive this time with you, you know; I'm quite, I'm enjoying—enjoying talking to you.*

What a reaction! Is Edward in "survival mode" so constantly that he truly does not know the difference between guardedness and spontaneity, or are his transactions with the therapist free of those "survival mode" strategies? Although his question may have been intended to sound like a joke, that joking may still serve to provide stability and predictability, and it may reflect the degree to which he is unaware of his self-protective behaviors.

Therapist: *And my question is for your discovery. It's not so much that I need the answer to it.*

Edward: *Well, I'm trying to get it, trying to get a handle on what you, what your question means. Um, what do you mean by "surviving" rather than spontaneous, or, if there's a choice between one or the other . . .*

Therapist: *Yeah, I guess I'm making an assumption, that the survival is sort of a secondary level to you, even though it might be an automatic pattern.*

Edward is an intelligent, well-educated man. The fact that the therapist has to explain to him the difference between natural, spontaneous behavior and self-protective behavior suggests that he may be on overload right now.

Edward: *Mmm.* (pause) *The question throws me a little bit, in the sense that, I still don't quite understand what you're saying—the comparison between authentic and survival mode, you know.*

Therapist: (pause) *Does my question feel humiliating?*

One reason that Edward does not understand the question might be that it triggered a very intense, archaic defensive pattern. Like an animal that freezes when caught in the headlights of a car, a regressed Edward may be too frightened to be able to think about or understand what the therapist is saying. Asking about humiliation suggests this possibility, both in direct content and in the implied connection between this interaction and those early ones between Edward and his mother. Edward, however, continues to be confused.

Edward: *Not particularly, actually. Um . . . I feel pretty open to what you're saying; I don't feel defensive particularly. I'm trying to, I know you're trying to say something; I'm not sure if your words are actually saying, or at least I'm not able to hear it. Um, I know you're asking me something, but I'm not, the question's not coming through. I know there's a question there, but I'm not catching it.*

Therapist: *Well, I think it's related to your earlier question: "Are you going to humiliate me?"* (pause) *And what would be different if you had an absolute, provable guarantee that I wasn't going to humiliate you? Would you be able to not be in survival mode?*

Edward: *Yeah, I don't feel in a potentially humiliating position. I do feel I have the choice of letting go into something or not letting go into this, little hard to exactly grasp what it is. It's something about abandon—abandoning. I mean, letting go, surrender kind of thing. Um, which is where it gets difficult, you know. It's like, you know, kind of, sort of in the direction of asking you for something, but what would it be anyway, you know? I mean, I can at least, in my life I've certainly got as far as knowing that I can ask people to desist from humiliating me, you know, this, I mean, this, I can lay it out, I can define my space, and I can certainly feel very comfortable when I think that we now agree that you're not going to humiliate me. That's all right. But it's like—well, that's just—well that's a bit "survival" actually; it's like, we've got to a point; well that's okay, I'm sitting here, you're sitting there, and, you know, I'm aware that you, that I'm not going to get humiliated here—*

Therapist: *A pretty complicated thought . . .*

Edward: *However, I could, I could . . . maybe . . . want something more.* (laugh) *This is where it gets a little complicated, you know . . .*

Therapist: *But can you trust me with that next part of your vulnerability?*

All the confusion, the unfinished sentences, the stepping on his own words, suggest that, in spite of his protests to the contrary, Edward is feeling very anxious. The therapist's question both inquires and provides information: it asks about Edward's trust level and it reassures him that he is not being expected or invited to become totally vulnerable. He need only deal with the "next part," and he himself is in charge of deciding just what that "next part" will be. Can the therapist be trusted? In the affect of Edward's transference, she cannot. Caught in the conflict between his rational adult self and his threatened, anxious, regressed self, Edward is wordless.

Edward: *Mmmph . . . well,* (sigh)—

Therapist: *Can I answer for you, Edward?* (Edward nods) *"No. No, I can't trust you. You haven't proven yourself."*

Defenses attacked tend to go underground, where they are even more difficult to deal with. The therapist eases off, supports the defense, and normalizes it: of course Edward cannot trust her, since he does not know whether she is trustworthy.

Edward: *Well, it's not quite that, it's more like . . . it's me, really. I know it's me. I mean, it's, you're a very warm person, I can feel all that, you know, and you've got a lot of capacity to be . . . insightful and affectionate and supportive, I mean this is sort of self-evident to me—at the rational level. But, of course, at another level it's like . . . ummph . . .*

Therapist: (long pause) *"I'd like to trust you,* but . . . *"*

Again, the therapist supports Edwards defense. All this about "warm person" and "insightful" and so forth are socially acceptable and are certainly true at an adult level. But the phenomenological reality of the preadolescent (which Edward has told us repeatedly is the critical age) lies in the word "but," and that is where the therapy needs to go.

Edward: *Yeah, I mean, what is this—*

Therapist: *I'd like to attend to that younger level . . . who does not think like a grown-up.*

The phenomenology of the preadolescent boy is now an even more explicit focus.

Edward: (pause) *It's not you I can't trust, exactly. It's where, it's where it all might go. It's where . . . it's the meaning it might have; it's something to do with . . . what happens then, you know. It's kind of. . . .* (sigh) *What does that make me, and if I do it, if I do say, if I do ask something from you, then what's going to be asked back, you know, this kind of thing. It's, uh. . . .*

The written transcript fails to reveal an abrupt change in Edward's rhythm and voice pattern at this point. This is the first time he has not talked over himself, talked quickly, or stepped on his own words. In contrast to his earlier pattern, this response is slow, with long pauses. He is exploring now, rather than reacting. When the pressure to take the next step into vulnerability was released, he took that step smoothly and naturally.

Therapist: (whispering) *"What's going to be asked back?"*

Repeating Edward's own words, the therapist echoes another possible facet of Edward's self-protective belief system: there is always a payback, always a demand, always strings attached. It was that way with mother; that that's the way it is with everyone; the way it is with you. The belief provides predictability: "I may not like that there is always a price to pay, but at least I know it is coming."

Edward: *Well, first of all, that I'd have to live up to it, which I'm not sure I want to do.* (pause) *Oh, it's all right for 5 minutes, 10 minutes; you know, but then, will I have to live up to it forever, you know?* (pause) *I mean, you know, as they say* (laugh)*, there is no free lunch, you know. . . .* (sigh) *And then, a sort of, way, it's in here, something like . . .* "But you said that. . . ." *You know,* "You needed something from me, and now look what you're doing!" *You know.* "I was so nice to you and now look . . . " *you know, sort of. . . . That's why I feel surly about you.* (pause, sigh)

Therapist: *There'll be a price to pay. . . .*

The price to be paid is a complex one. There is the standard tit-for-tat exchange, the "now I'm in your debt and must repay you" kind of price. There is also a life-long "have to live up to it" price. And, underneath all the rest, there is the specter of a gleeful, vindictive "Gotcha!" that represents the truly terrifying price: the price that a defenseless child must pay simply because he exists in a world of people who, like mother, cannot be trusted.

Edward: *I'd like to know that you don't think that I'm, you know, sort of deep down a bit of a jerk, really. And I worry about that, sort of check that out.*

Therapist: *Ouch. What an uncomfortable fantasy.*

Another bit of the self-protective belief system, this time contributing to Edward's sense of identity by imagining what others think about him. It all fits together neatly: others cannot be trusted; they always exact their price; Edward protects himself by being charming (and incurs no debts), and when that does not work he gets surly, and then people must think he is a jerk, which proves that they cannot be trusted. The therapist's label ("uncomfortable fantasy") joins an adjective that Edward will easily accept (uncomfortable) with a noun that he probably would not have chosen (fantasy). He agrees with the adjective and describes his fantasy.

Edward: *Yeah, it is a little uncomfortable. Feeling I maybe could screw up right at the beginning, in a big way, just leaving a rather unpleasant aftertaste in your mouth; then it feels like an uphill struggle, where you kind of get back into some kind of normal exchange, you know . . . Feel, feeling sad at the moment. Feeling kind of . . . it's been a life of this, you know, there's no question, it's been. . . . (sigh) I mean, it's gotten surprisingly easier in the last 10 years or so, to my amazement. And yet, you know, it's all in there; it's all sort of, it just happens quicker now, in a way. I sort of run through it quicker. It disturbs me less. I compensate much better than . . .*

From "feeling sad" he bounces quickly into a kind of pseudoheartiness: it is not so bad; he doesn't really mind it; he can compensate.

Therapist: *Are you in a loving relationship?*

If things really are getting better, this should be reflected in his primary relationships. The therapist's question invites an examination of one of these relationships—will it too be contaminated by Edward's need to protect himself?

Edward: *Heh! That was a . . . I have a . . . Michelle and I get on a bit like a cat and a dog, but* (laugh) *we like each other. We like each other a lot, but we quarrel a lot. But we get over our quarrels very quickly now; we laugh about them. But we certainly can't help quarreling. This is definitely true; we quarrel a lot. No, I experience it as being an affectionate relationship, more than a loving one; I experience it as being . . . um, a, a dynamic relationship, I'd say it's been like we shake each other quite a lot. It's, um, loving seems to me . . . you know, not the word that came to my mind . . .*

Therapist: *Edward, I don't know you well enough yet to do this, but I'm going to try it anyway. . . . I would guess that your fears about the price you're going to have to pay, and what's going to be required of you—that's sort of familiar, and that's where you get stuck. I would guess that the "what if," which is a bit more frightening, is "What if I would really love you?"*

"What if I would really love you?" is ambiguous; it may refer either to Edward's partner or to the therapist herself. Either way, for Edward it may translate to "What if I would really let you in, let myself experience my need for you, and allow you to be you rather than the transferred image of my not-to-be-trusted mother?" The question is, of course, unanswerable: Edward cannot know what life would be like without his defenses. But it suggests that such a thing is possible, and it invites him to explore the fertile but frightening ground between the known and the unimaginable.

Edward: *Oh, I . . .*

Therapist: *"What if I would really want you?"*

Edward: (pause) *Yeah. . . .*

Therapist: *Perhaps that question is a bit more frightening.*

Edward: *It is. It is, definitely.* (pause) *Feels like jumping off a cliff, sort of, doesn't feel. . . .* (pause) *It's not, not easy to imagine.*

Therapist: *That's the world you don't know. That's the sense of your self you have no idea about.*

Edward heard the questions and took it seriously: it served its purpose. The therapist moves quickly to forestall self-criticism: "You don't know that world, you have no sense of that self, and therefore you couldn't possibly answer what I asked." In doing so, she also underscores the importance of this line of exploration: "*Here* is what you really do not know about and (by implication) need to know about."

Edward: *Oh, yes, no, I, I, yeah, I'm connecting to what you're saying. Got no idea about, but it's . . . I can certainly accept conditional loving; I certainly can*not *accept unconditional loving; there's no way at all; even the words sound vaguely mocking in my ears—*

Therapist: *Um-hmm.*

Edward: *There's no question that it doesn't . . . and it feels a part of what I want to hang onto is this—I mean, I, as, again, the same age, you know, 9, 10, I had a lot of angry sexual fantasies about my mother too. And I, still feels like I want to hang on to that. It's like I don't, it's like we're going to, might, sense is, we're going to sort of, well, we'll erase all that, then. Erase all that, so everything's nice. And then I'm sort of looking around thinking, "Yeah, but this is still here;* (patting his chest with both hands) *this is still me." You know, and I haven't, I mean, I haven't agreed to get rid of it.*

Therapist: *Now we're back to what you said before, when you said, "But . . . " and you talked about those defenses. And I asked you, "Can I trust that defense?" 'Cause it's there for an important purpose. Maybe to keep you organized, to make sense of your world—*

Edward is beginning to experience much more deeply the importance of his defenses and the lack of continuity, the void, that would be left if they were to be dissolved suddenly. The therapist's validation is intended to reassure him by communicating that she, too, understands how important Edward's defenses are, and how much Edward needs them right now. Edward's defenses are there for a purpose: they provide consistency and stability in an otherwise chaotic world. The therapist will not criticize Edward for having them, and she will not push Edward to give them up.

Edward: *Well, apparently yeah. . . . I certainly feel frightened by the idea of letting . . . I mean . . . when you say, like, um, what if I just, you know, I mean,* (he begins to shake) *I can hardly even say the words, you know, "just want you, want you," whatever your words were. . . .* (sigh) *It feels like I would have to be just tremendously . . . tremendously good, I mean, you know, tremendously . . . whhhhhhhw. . . .*

With this last reassurance that he will not be criticized, humiliated, or forced into something he is not ready for, Edward takes the risk of letting himself go another step into the vulnerability of his needs. It is so frightening that he cannot even say the words out loud.

Therapist: *So you would have to pay the price of being tremendously good?*

Edward: *Yes, there's no question, I mean, feels inconceivable . . .*

Therapist: *You can't even imagine what that would be like—that you wouldn't have to pay for it.*

Edward: *I'd probably have to spend most of the rest of my therapy on my knees, you know, to avoid* (laugh) *any potential fucking up.* (laugh)

Therapist: *Or you could go back to being surly.*

The protective function of Edward's surliness is now clear. "Going back" to it, with the conscious awareness of how it fits into his defensive system, would be a very different experience from acting it out without realizing its psychological function. It does not matter whether Edward chooses to accept the therapist's suggestion or whether he rejects it; he wins either way.

Edward: (laugh) *Surly. . . . You're right; it's not a very good game to play.*

Therapist: *Sounds agonizing—that you can't even conceive of someone caring for you, without your having to pay the price of being very good, all the time, forever. And that imagining being wanted is so frightening. And so important.* (pause) *So all that surliness and humor and pushing people away, that we've been talking about, is to protect yourself from that eventual abandonment.*

Edward spoke of "abandonment" in a rather detached, story-telling way early in this piece of work; he has not referred to it since then. He has talked about humiliation, and pleasure at his discomfort, and withholding of affection, but the core fear, the survival issue, has been avoided. Now, with the trust that has grown between them—due, in part at least, to the therapist's consistent validation and normalization of Edward's defenses—Edward can acknowledge this basic issue.

Edward: *Oh, yeah. Oh, yeah, no question.*

Therapist: *And I think to rush and try and change that too rapidly would be like cutting your legs off at the knees.*

The therapist makes it explicit: I won't try to break down your defenses, and I don't want you to do so either.

Edward: *You know, at times I look at Michelle like she's a stray dog, trailing in off the street or something. You know, that's how she feels. I can tell she's feeling that way; she says something to me and I just look at her with this same look that my mother had, you know; I know I do that, you know; I don't want to do it, but I do. So . . . (sigh) she feels totally put down. . . . Anyway, that's the way it is (sigh). . . . Yeah, I'd like—*

Therapist: (pause) *Now we come back to how much it hurts to even want . . .*

The cues for this intervention were the sighs, Edward's sad face and slumped posture, and his words. He has realized that he treats his partner the way his mother treated him and is on the brink of going into self-criticism again. Instead, the therapist refocuses on the pain of his unmet needs.

Edward: (sigh) *Yeah. Yeah. It hurts more to want it than to get it in small doses. I've organized myself with most people, people I interact with, nice comfortable exchanges. . . . I'm a reasonably giving person, so I get something back, and then, that's okay . . . not too much, not too little, you know. . . . It's true that imagining a lot is . . . I get frightened at the idea of getting more—it's not for me. (pause) I don't want to get that, not for me, I don't want that much from anyone. Really don't. (pause) And it feels a relief to me to have stopped, mostly, desiring that. And, paradoxically, it becomes a little bit more accessible.*

Therapist: *Um-hmm.*

Edward: (pause) *'Cause it used to be, I'd go, you know, I'd fantasy about some amazing love or something and immediately feel "What an asshole I am," you know—Good Christ!—All this kind of stuff. But, so, I've let go of that, over the years. . . .*

Therapist: *When you give up that fantasy you become a little less abrasive?*

If he does not have the fantasy, he does not feel the need so strongly. When he does not feel the need, he does not have to protect himself from the pain. When he does not have to protect himself, he does not have to keep people so far away by being abrasive.

Edward: *Absolutely, yeah.*

Therapist: *Right, and suddenly here you are—pow, right up against it.* (Edward laughs) *You are in a tough spot, Edward.* (Edward laughs, sighs)

For the last several minutes, Edward has not been behaving according to his script belief, "People can't be trusted." He has not kept the therapist at arm's length; he has not been surly; he has not tried to charm and entertain. Instead, he has allowed himself to talk and feel about his neediness. He is in a "tough spot" because, if he allows himself to experience the therapist responding authentically to his needs, he will inevitably feel the contrast between how things are now and how they were back then. This is the essence of juxtaposition, and another function of the defensive system is to guard against the pain of experiencing it.

Therapist: *Perhaps part of the tough spot is when we stop soon. What's going to happen in the quiet time after this piece of work? Is it going to feel like a mini-abandonment, like more of the same?*

A bit of therapeutic preplanning. The session is drawing to a close, and ending the session is a made-to-order opportunity for Edward to snap back into his old patterns of experiencing himself as rejected and abandoned. By predicting this, the therapist creates a win–win situation: either Edward does not feel abandoned and takes positive feelings away from the session, or he does feel abandoned and can explore that feeling as a now-conscious facet of transference.

Edward: *I don't think so. When you were saying that, what's going to happen afterwards, I feel . . . I feel pleased I've talked about it. And actually, my life's a little about that, you know; it's sort of, slowly coming out in the wash like a, like a strange dye that, you know . . . has to come out, has got into the fabric and needs to come out slowly . . .*

Therapist: *Like perhaps the color of your hair?*

Edward: (laughs loudly) *It's not Grecian Formula #5. . . .*

Therapist: *I'm talking about that dream. . . .*

Edward: *Yeah, yeah, yeah. . . . Right. Maybe, yeah.*

Therapist: *Didn't the color of your hair change very rapidly, in that dream?*

Edward: *Yeah, very rapidly there, yeah.*

Therapist: *And I don't think that this work happening rapidly would be good for you.*

Edward: *Yeah, that's the big thing—*

Therapist: *And I need, for your sake, to take time to appreciate your defenses.*

Emphasizing the "I" in this sentence signals the therapist's genuine involvement. It is not just that Edward needs to go slowly; the therapist needs that, too. To be sure, she qualifies the expressed need ("for your sake"); nevertheless, the overall impact is one of the therapist's authentic caring about and involvement with Edward's well-being.

Edward: *Yeah, I do hear that.*

Therapist: *And that together we really look at how those defenses have provided stability. What I mean by that is, keep you from going absolutely nuts. . . .*

Edward: *Yeah, absolutely.*

Therapist: *And how they've provided the continuity with your Mom's nondependability—how your defenses are the most dependable thing you've got. Your humor, your ability to adapt, your survival. . . And as you talk about it, almost with a sense of affection—who would you be if you weren't a man who could take anything that came your way? What would you feel if you weren't the guy that could handle every humiliation?*

Edward: *Yeah... (sigh) You've got a point; yes, that's true; I'm quite, I'm quite proud of it. I can beat you, kind of roll with the blows, you know, kind of—*

Therapist: (pause) *Well, maybe I need to share in that pride with you, lest this become a pushy therapy to make you be something different, before we've really had a chance to value how stabilizing, what continuity, what sense of identity, all of these defenses have provided, to say nothing about how you've maintained them. You've got predictability for the future.*

Moving Edward back to his preferred, cognitive comfort zone is another way of preparing him for the end of the session. And providing the theoretical rationale for the direction this work has taken (reiterating the psychological function of his defensive "surly" behavior and his script belief that "people can't be trusted") gives him a framework with which to remember, revisit, and continue exploring what he has uncovered.

Edward: *Hmm. Hmm. I like what you're saying to me. I like what you're saying about time . . . something I've perhaps gradually become aware of in myself, but it's not something I've said in words like that. I, I think it's . . . very clearly important for me to allow myself to be . . . a slow person in that respect. . . .*

There is little need for a final wrap-up of this chapter: the therapy itself and the annotations say it all. In this piece of work, the therapist has provided Edward with a great deal of explicit cognitive structuring. Therapy with another client might well have ended with a behavioral suggestion/ assignment, something that would allow him or her to experience self or others in a way that runs counter to the old familiar expectations. That, however, would encourage change. The paradox of Edward's work is that helping him to change requires helping him not to change; helping him break free of his defenses requires staying with and valuing those defenses.

In this piece of work, the therapist concluded with a cognitive focus, helping Edward to understand clearly the function of his defenses. Explaining what is happening and making sure that Edward understands each step is a way of building trust. As he learns to trust this therapist, to believe that the therapist really means what she says, Edward will be able (slowly!) to find stability, consistency, predictability, and identity in a different way, in the authenticity experienced within the therapeutic relationship. That relationship, in turn, can become the bridge to more authentic and trusting and contactful relationships in the world outside of therapy.

10
CHAPTER

Loraine: Therapy
With an Introjected Other
(Part I)

As integrative psychotherapists, we believe that the conflicts clients bring to therapy are interrelated and self-reinforcing. They form a pattern or a life script, and they grow out of survival reactions, conclusions, and decisions made in response to traumatic or ongoing relationship failures. "Decisions" may not be precisely the right word in this context, however. A "decision" is usually a choice, consciously made, among a number of alternatives. Conclusions and survival reactions, and often early decisions as well, are generally constructed out of awareness and are also usually accreted over time rather than set in place at one particular moment. They feel like inevitable, unavoidable, necessary reactions to ongoing events, and as components of one's life script they become patterns of beliefs and feelings and ways of reacting to the world. They are the cumulative result of thousands of small, often-unnoticed choices about how to believe, act, and feel. Over time, the choices become habits, and the habits become necessities. No longer available for conscious evaluation, they affect our perceptions, our expectations, our beliefs about self and others, and our quality of life. They are both consequence and cause of contact disruption: challenging and replacing them is the essence of therapy.

But not all such patterns arise as a direct result of an individual's response to life events. Some come from unconscious defensive identification with significant others. In the absence of full contact with needed persons, we do the next best thing: we introject them, making them (or our perception of them) a part of our own self (Perls et al., 1951). We acquire the psychological characteristics of our caregivers, teachers, or even abusers. We internalize, without realizing what is happening, the attitudes and response patterns that characterize the other person, including *their* self-limiting beliefs and decisions; and these introjected patterns are, again, out of our awareness and therefore often unavailable for editing or updating in the light of adult learning and experience (Guntrip, 1968, 1971; Fairbairn, 1952). They sit within the individual much like an alien army in an occupied country, unintegrated and in control.

Integrative psychotherapy has developed a method for working directly with psychological introjections. A therapist assists the client to *cathect* the introjection, to take on its characteristics, its beliefs and feelings, its memories, its hopes and fears and needs. The client temporarily sets his or her sense of self aside and assumes the character of the introjected person, making it available for therapy (McNeil, 1976). Similar to the Russian "matrushka" (a doll within a doll), therapy with the introjected other is nested within the client's own therapeutic work; healing the splits and distortions of the introjected other paves the way for the client to dissolve the introjection and go on to heal his or her own splits, defenses, and distortions (Dashiell, 1978; Mellor & Andrewartha, 1980).

The client who works with an introjected other is not "pretending" or "role-playing." For the space of time in which the work is being done, the person *is* that significant other, just as the other was internalized and preserved, out of awareness yet influencing much of what the client thinks and feels and does. The therapist helps the client to assume and maintain the persona of the introjection by directing the client to talk, gesture, and hold his or her body as the introjected other did, and by frequently using the other's name. Although the client often begins this kind of work with a sense of play-acting and artificiality, it seldom is long before the introjection is fully cathected and psychologically present. Yet at the same time the client usually has a clear, present awareness that this entity is not really "me"; it is an other who has had a major influence in shaping his or her life.

In earlier chapters of this book, you met one such significant other: Alice, whose work was quoted in chapters 2, 4, and 5 to illustrate aspects of inquiry, involvement, and relational needs, is in fact an introjection. In the next two chapters, you will meet Loraine, the actual (physical) client whose work has been transcribed. Loraine herself begins and ends the work, but in the central and major portion the therapist is working with Alice, Loraine's introjected mother. In the first of the two sessions to be presented, Loraine accepts the contract to identify and treat the introjection and moves into the persona of Alice. As Alice, she struggles to maintain a split between unacceptable (to Alice) feelings and her conscious awareness. The session ends as Loraine/Alice finally acknowledges, accepts, and values what she has been denying for most of her life.[1]

Loraine has been working with this therapist for several sessions and has gained a great deal of self-confidence from her previous work: she can now say "No" and "I don't want" and mean it, both emotionally and physiologically. She has talked before about the tensions between herself and her mother, which often center on Loraine's being overweight. Loraine begins this session, though, with a complaint not about mother, but about the therapist.

Loraine: *I want to work on something in me that feels very violated. And I want to start with, when I left my wallet here and you looked inside it.*

Therapist: *Yes, to find out who it belonged to.*

Loraine: *I know that. But I didn't like it.*

Therapist: *Why?*

Loraine: *Well, that's just what came to me when I thought about it. . . . This is not a grown-up thing.*

Loraine realizes that her response (from an adult perspective) is unreasonable. She also knows that the response is important to her; it is intense, and she recognizes it as part of a familiar pattern. By labeling it as "not a grown-up thing" she signals her willingness to go into archaic material: she knows the therapist and trusts the therapeutic relationship enough to be able to dispense with preliminaries and move quickly into the work.

Therapist: *So help me to understand the significance to you, with it.*

Loraine: *It's like you, you. . . . It's like you came in and you. . . . It's like it's my stuff.* (pause) *I'm just working with what I got here. And I got it about the wallet.*

Therapist: *What did you get?*

---

[1]Describing a therapy session with an introjected other presents some unique problems. Is the other to be referred to by his or her real name, or as the physical person who is speaking? (You see, even writing this footnote coherently is difficult!) How do we indicate a conversation between the original client and the introjection? In this book we have chosen the following conventions: transcript "speeches" of the introjection are labeled with Loraine's actual name, followed by "as Alice" (the name of the introjected other). In comments about the work, we use Alice's name if we are speaking of what Alice did, thought, or felt in the past, and we use "Loraine/Alice" when we are talking about the behavior of the introjection here in the therapy session.

Loraine: *And I got it last week when you came out into the waiting room and set that big bunch of stuff on the table next to me. Those books and papers, all dusty, and you didn't have to put it right next to me.*

Therapist: *Oh. Yeah, I can see how that would be offensive.*

Loraine: *And it was, it was just like my mother's anger when I eat. And that's what all this is about. Having somebody . . . in me. Or . . .* (long pause) *I don't want it, I don't want it near me.*

Therapist: *That makes sense.*

In these very early statements, we can see a prefiguring of Loraine's work. Loraine's mother is an angry woman, and Loraine may well have introjected her mother's anger (and much more of her mother, as well). That anger is emerging in uncomfortable and inappropriate ways; Loraine recognizes that it is not truly her own ("Having somebody . . . in me"), but she does not know what to do about it.

The nature of an introjection is that it requires disrupted contact. The introjected other is split off from the rest of the self; it is a psychic foreign object, isolated and embedded and unintegrated. In developing an introjection, people deny, distort, and disavow aspects of the self. They use the whole repertoire of defensive maneuvers that allow them to take in and yet maintain a split. Healing, then, involves reversing the process by giving up the defenses and the lying-to-self, feeling what has not been safe to feel, thinking the unthinkable, so that the barriers to internal contact can be dissolved and the introjection decommissioned or discarded.

As this long piece of work unfolds, we shall see such a reversal occurring. It does not happen evenly, step by step, but in spurts and in pauses, in divergences and reiterations, and in moments of rest. But through it all, the therapeutic plan remains: reveal the distortions, experience the contact, bring wholeness to that which has been split apart, and restore internal and external awareness, all within a respectful relationship with both the actual client and the personification of the introjected other.

Loraine: *I just want to say, "No! No, I don't want it." * (pause) *I want to say what I don't want.* (pause) *And I don't really care about the wallet and the pile of stuff, but that's how it came to me.*

Therapist: *The things that you "don't want."*

Loraine: *That's right, and my space. I did what I had to do about the pile of stuff. I moved it. But I didn't say to you that I didn't like it next to me. And that's what I do. I can take care of myself and put away the things that I don't want, but I can't always talk about why I don't want them.*

Therapist: *I imagine it would be unpleasant to have something dirty like that right next to you.*

Loraine: *Yeah. Like, with my mother I told her I don't want to eat with her if she's angry. But I didn't tell her why. I just said it's not good for my digestion.*

Therapist: *And the other "why" is . . .*

Loraine: *I feel like I have to eat it—her stuff.*

Therapist: *Eat her anger.*

It would be easy to jump in with an interpretive comment at this point, because Loraine's metaphor of "eating it" is so closely related to the concept of introjection: taking another person's thoughts, feelings, and beliefs into ourselves without "digesting" or assimilating them. Interpretation, though, would tend to encourage Loraine to analyze her response rather than explore it; analysis would be a way to not-feel and would be more likely to hinder than to encourage Loraine's exploration. Instead, the therapist chooses to inquire, first by simple reflection (as in the above statement) and then by phenomenologically directed questions that encourage Loraine to delve further into the experience she is reporting.

Loraine: *Eat her anger. I don't want it. It gets all over me. I don't want it anymore.*

Therapist: *How do you experience her anger all over you?*

Loraine: *Like I digested it, and it's just in my body.*

Therapist: *Do you experience yourself as being angry? Like her?*

Loraine: *No, I don't experience, I experience myself being angry at her, for feeding it to me. But in me it's not anger, it's just, it's just weight. Just something I didn't know was hers, before. Before, in the work I did, you remember, I got in touch with her fear and it was, it used to be in me, but it was out there; it was like a balloon. And it wasn't mine. It was hers. And for a while I felt like it was tied to my ankle, like a helium balloon. But then it just flew away. Wasn't mine. And I feel like the anger is the same thing. It's not mine. It's, it's turned into fat. It's her energy, and it turned into my fat.*

Therapist: *Would you like me to talk to her about that anger?*

Loraine: *You could; you don't know her. You could. . . .*

Therapist: *That's never stopped me before.*

Loraine: *Oh, yeah. . . . I need practice talking to her about her anger. I don't know if I really want to talk to her for real about it. But I could talk to her for pretend.*

Therapist: *Loraine, I'll talk to her for real. Then, maybe for the first time, you won't have to be forced to take charge.*

Several important things have happened in these last few exchanges. First, the therapist has offered Loraine a minicontract: shall we talk with your mother? Loraine's counteroffer, to have a dialogue between her mother and herself, did not convey much enthusiasm. The tentativeness of the offer ("I could" do it "for pretend") suggests that she may have already realized that this sort of work is not likely to be real or meaningful. The therapist restates the proffered contract and affirms one of the important dimensions of what is about to take place, that Loraine will not have to be in charge. As we shall see in the second part of this piece of work, the need to be responsible, in charge, and a caretaker, is one of Loraine's major issues.

Loraine: *Okay. I won't have to keep having the, all those, I work hard at those boundaries.*

Therapist: *Well, how about if I take over the boundaries, and you get a little vacation? What do you think of that?*

Loraine: *I just, I feel all like a slug. Like I don't have anything around me now.*

Here is another choice point for the therapist. Loraine's phenomenological metaphor is a rich one; the image of the defenseless, tender-skinned slug carries with it a sense of both vulnerability and self-denigration. Moreover, she suggests a growing awareness of how she uses her fat to protect herself. The therapist chooses, however, not to go in that direction, but to stay with the contract that has just been established. Loraine has agreed to deal with the introjection, and to do anything else right now would simply take her away from what the therapist suspects is most beneficial.

Therapist: *I'm going to get a special chair for your Mom.* (she pulls another chair over, opposite herself) *Come sit over here, Mom.* (Loraine moves into the new chair) *Now just close your eyes as you sit down. And see if you can sit right into her posture. Right into the way she would sit. And see if you can get your back just like Mom's. That's it, the same facial expression, just like Mom's.*

Loraine: *Has to be mournful.*

Therapist: *All right, get mournful.*

Loraine: *I don't think I can be mournful.*

Therapist: *Well, you do the—*

Loraine: *I'll just pretend.*

Pretending again. Apparently it is important for Loraine to hang onto this layer of defense: if things get too bad, "just pretending" can be an escape hatch, a way to make it not so threatening or painful. Loraine has taken care of herself most of her life by being in charge, and this is a way of keeping the control that seems so necessary for her. The therapist will not challenge it; getting into a tug-of-war at this point would not be helpful. Instead, she trusts the developing momentum of the work to take Loraine where she needs to go.

Therapist: *That's right.*

Loraine: *I don't like this.*

And yet another choice point. Is Loraine protesting the therapist's method? This would require a respectful acknowledgment of her concern. On the other hand, she may be describing the discomfort of experiencing her mother's sensations, which is a signal that she is cathecting her introjected mother and the work is on track. The therapist decides to continue to explore the introjection. If Loraine complains again, the complaint will provide an opportunity to explore Loraine's experience of a therapeutic error. Therapeutic errors are inevitable and necessary. They are inevitable because the therapist cannot possibly share a client's exact phenomenological experience. And they are necessary because they allow the client to experience the healing of a ruptured relationship (the rupture between client and therapist). Without this experience, the client's ability to extend his or her newly gained interpersonal contactfulness into the outside world would be fragile and undependable.

Therapist: *What's your name, Mom?*

Loraine: *Alice.*

Therapist: *Alice. That's a pretty name. Where do you come from, Alice?*

Loraine (as Alice): *New York. But I didn't like that, so we moved to Kansas when the kids were little.*

Therapist: *What didn't you like about New York, where you came from?*

Loraine (as Alice): *That's where I was born, and I didn't like it. I wanted to get away from it. It's a very painful city for me to be in.*

Typically, work with an introjected other begins with several minutes of relatively inconsequential chitchat (which often, of course, proves to be anything but inconsequential later on). It is the same thing that any good therapist does with a new client as they get to know each other. Loraine/Alice, however, does not seem to need this warming-up time; she moves immediately into a series of important memories.

Therapist: *How come, Alice?*

Loraine (as Alice): *Well, reminded me of my parents, and my father . . . dirty.*

Therapist: *Your father's dirty?*

Loraine (as Alice): *My father was drunk. I don't know if he was dirty. He was just drunk and abusive.*

Therapist: *So you're trying hard to get away from that which reminds you of your past.*

Loraine (as Alice): *And I wanted to have my kids live out in the sunshine, and where they could play in the dirt and have a good time, have swings . . .*

Therapist: *And were you successful at getting away from your past, Alice?*

Loraine (as Alice): *No. I have it all wrapped up in a big tablecloth behind me, and it's like . . . bunch of pots and pans. And as I walk from room to room, it rattles.*

Therapist: *You mean, you sort of carry it around with you?*

This is another striking metaphor. This time it is Alice's metaphor, rather than Loraine's, and so it can be explored without diverting the work from the issue at hand.

Loraine (as Alice): *You bet.*

Therapist: *In this tablecloth.*

Loraine (as Alice): *Solid tablecloth. Yes.*

Therapist: *Now, why in a tablecloth?*

Loraine (as Alice): *I don't know.*

Therapist: *Well, I just wondered—*

Loraine (as Alice): *Noisy.*

Therapist: *If the tablecloth was something—*

Loraine (as Alice): *And domestic.*

Therapist: *—something special from your childhood.*

Loraine (as Alice): *Well, I never got, we never probably had a tablecloth in my childhood.*

Loraine/Alice gives so much information that the therapist's problem is not what to ask about, but what to let go of! "Noisy" and "domestic" could both be inquired about, and both probably carry important information. Instead, however, the therapist chooses to follow Loraine/Alice's apparent readiness to talk about her early experiences. Not only will this help both of them to make sense of Alice's overall pattern of responses, but it also is respectful of the need to be in control, shared by both Alice and her daughter.

Therapist: *Oh. What do you mean, Alice?*

Loraine (as Alice): *I never had, even sheets.*

Therapist: *How come?*

Loraine (as Alice): *'Cause my parents were drunk all the time.*

Therapist: *Oh, both parents.*

Loraine (as Alice): *Yeah, both of them. And I slept with coats and stuff over me, in the cold. I still can't bear to get cold.*

Therapist: *Alice, it sounds like you carry a lot of things left over from your childhood.*

While this may appear to be a rather obvious and even superfluous comment, it serves to emphasize the important connectedness between Loraine/Alice's past and present, as well as to convey respect and empathy for how presently burdensome that past must be. Notice, too, that "Alice" has become truly the client; Loraine's observing ego may be watching, but it is Alice who speaks.

Loraine (as Alice): *Yes, I do.*

Therapist: *Tell me more about it.*

Loraine (as Alice): *My brothers and sisters got taken away by the cruelty society. And my mother lied, that she was still nursing me, so they left me at home. I was two-and-a-half.*

Therapist: *And was she drunk while nursing you?*

Loraine (as Alice): *I don't know. I don't know if she was still nursing me. She lied to keep me, 'cause she loved me.*

Therapist: *And did you feel loved, Alice?*

Loraine (as Alice): *Yeah. My mother loved me. She wasn't very easy to live with, but she loved me.*

Therapist: *Now how do you know she loved you? What were the loving things she did?*

Children who grow up with abusive or neglectful parents can hardly avoid being confused about "love." The "loving" parent is also the hurting parent; the one who must be trusted is also the betrayer. To protect the necessary illusion that the parent is good and will act appropriately, the child lies to himself or herself, distorts reality, and even takes responsibility for the bad things that happen. Out of conscious awareness, it is as if the child reasons, "If I believe hard enough that she really loves me, then it will turn out to be true" or "If it's all my fault, then it cannot be Mom's fault and so she can still be a good Mom." This illusion, this lying-to-self, protects the child from pain, but at the cost of splitting that child off from his or her own experience. In order to avoid pain, the child must avoid contact with self.

The therapist's question to Loraine/Alice, "How do you know she loved you?" is the opening wedge into that pattern of distortion, denial, and broken contact. She will return to it again and again in this early part of the work.

Loraine (as Alice): *She would tell me that she loved me . . .*

Therapist: *So, she'd verbalize it.*

Loraine (as Alice): *I guess.*

Therapist: *What else, Alice?*

Loraine (as Alice): *She had red hair. Long red hair. And I would comb it; she liked that.*

Therapist: *So you knew she loved you, because you would comb her long red hair.*

Loraine (as Alice): *Yeah. And it shone in the sunshine.*

Therapist: *And does it seem loving to you to put you to bed with no sheets, just covering you with a blanket?*

The therapist raises a general question: "How do you know she loved you?" Why would a loving mother, even one with beautiful hair, put her child to bed with no sheets? Revisiting the happiness of combing mother's hair gave Loraine/Alice a short respite; now it is time to dip back into the hard part.

Loraine (as Alice): *Coats.*

Therapist: *Uh, coats . . .*

Loraine (as Alice): *Or, newspapers; I don't know what it was. Laundry.*

Therapist: *Coats and newspapers and laundry . . .*

Loraine (as Alice): *Junk. Like I was trash.*

Therapist: *Yet you know she loved you. . . . You say you were cold?*

The therapist continues to play upon the contrast between Loraine/Alice's assertion that her mother did love her and the memories of being cold, covered with coats and newspapers. The therapist wonders whether Alice's mother was dealing with desperate poverty or whether she was neglectful because of her alcoholism. So she inquires, phenomenologically and historically.

Loraine (as Alice): *Yeah, I was cold a lot. And hungry.*

Therapist: *Was she sober then?*

Loraine (as Alice): *I don't think so.*

Therapist: *But you know she loved you.*

Loraine (as Alice): *I loved her.*

Earlier, Loraine/Alice said that she knew her mother loved her because she (Alice) combed her mother's long red hair: the *child's* behavior is used as evidence of the *mother's* feelings. Here she makes the same sort of switch by responding to the therapist's probe about her mother's loving her (Alice) by reiterating that she loved mother. Was Alice doing the loving *for* her mother as well as for herself? Did Alice believe that loving her mother had some magical ability to make mother love her back? There are many possible hypotheses; all we know for sure is that loving her mother served a very important function. That function is what the therapist inquires about.

Therapist: *Tell me about the importance of loving your mother.*

Loraine (as Alice): *She was all that was really there 'cause my father would come home drunk. . . .*

Therapist: *So your mother was less drunk than your father?*

Loraine (as Alice): *Yeah, I think maybe my mother wasn't drunk until later; I'm not sure. But she went out to work. She cleaned houses. And I was by myself all the time.*

Therapist: *And your brothers and sisters were taken away by the cruelty society?*

Loraine (as Alice): *Yeah, I really missed them. That was really hard.*

Therapist: *Tell me about that, Alice.*

The therapist tends to pay particular attention to Loraine/Alice's affect-oriented comments. This not only helps to keep Alice fully cathected and present (and to keep Loraine in the background), but also takes Loraine/Alice deeper into her experience and her phenomenology. And every step taken into that experience makes it harder to maintain her contact disruption, her defensive "not knowing."

Loraine (as Alice): *Especially my brother, my brother, Jack.*

Therapist: *Yeah. . . . Tell me about Jack, Alice.*

Loraine (as Alice): *I went to see him once, and he gave me roller skates. He lived with my aunt. I don't remember which aunt. My aunt something, I don't know. . . .*

Therapist: *So he lived with a relative. And he gave you skates?*

Loraine (as Alice): *Yeah, he gave me skates.*

Therapist: *And did you skate with them?*

Loraine (as Alice): *I skated—Oh, I skated! Up and down the street, and the man at the grocery store yelled at me to stop skating; he would give me a penny or something to go away, and then I'd come back later and skate again* (she chuckles).

Therapist: *How wonderful it must have felt to have the, the freedom that skates have!*

Loraine (as Alice): *They were from my brother.*

Therapist: *Oh, and that made it even more special.*

Loraine (as Alice): *Right. 'Cause I didn't have anything from anybody.*

Therapist: *Even Mother, who loved you so much?*

Loraine/Alice finds another happy memory, and the therapist enjoys it with her for a moment. Again, this is a rest and a breather before plunging back into the work. This time, Loraine/Alice returns without prompting: "I didn't have anything from anybody." The therapist comes back immediately to the central issue, Alice's need for a loving mother.

Loraine (as Alice): *No.*

Therapist: *Didn't buy you gifts?* (she shakes her head "No") *So the skates from your brother were important. What else was important to you, Alice?*

Loraine (as Alice): *Deciding I would never be like them.*

Therapist: *Tell me what you mean.*

Loraine (as Alice): *Decided when I was little that I would never, ever, ever be like them. Wouldn't raise my children like that. Wouldn't be like that. Wouldn't marry a man like my father. I wouldn't be like my mother. I wouldn't be drunk. I wouldn't fight. I wouldn't have violence.*

A child's decisions, especially those made under stress, often become highly significant guidelines for how that child will live out his or her life: they are the basis for the life script. How one experiences the world, the responses that one calls forth from others, the parts of self that one may and may not acknowledge, all are affected if not determined by these decisions. Alice's decision to "never, ever be like them," recalled here with such intensity, has been significant in her own life and in her daughter's life as well. Recognizing this, the therapist begins to explore the details of that decision.

Therapist: *Wouldn't marry a man like your father, and you wouldn't have violence, you would never fight. . . .*

Loraine (as Alice): *That's right.*

Therapist: *There would be no anger, or anything like that—*

Loraine (as Alice): *That's right. We would never raise our voices.*

Therapist: *Hmm. What an important decision!*

This is one of the segments that was presented in chapter 2 as an example of the importance of inquiring about decisions. In the context of the full transcript, we shall see how central this decision was and how it has permeated Alice's life. Although (unlike many clients' early decisions) this one was held in awareness, easily available for consideration and discussion, its ramifications and permutations were not. Attending to it and inquiring about it takes Loraine/Alice one step further along the road to full internal and external contact.

Loraine (as Alice): *Yes, it was. Kept me from killing myself. 'Cause I almost did that a couple of times.*

Therapist: *So to be different from your parents is an important survival decision.*

Ordinarily we think of a "survival decision" as a decision the child comes to as a way of protecting himself or herself from a threatening environment. "I will believe that mother loves me," for instance, allows the child to have a good mother even when the mother is abusive. Here, though, there is an additional and quite literal meaning: the decision was also a conscious choice to live rather than to die.

Loraine (as Alice): *That's right.*

Therapist: *Congratulations. How did you do with that, once you moved to Kansas?*

Loraine (as Alice): *Well, I had my two little girls, Loraine and Ellen. And my husband.*

Therapist: *A husband whom you never fought with?*

Loraine (as Alice): *We never fought.*

Therapist: *So you kept your decision.*

Do you see how this decision becomes a part of Loraine/Alice's pattern of splitting and of disrupting contact? "I won't be like them" becomes "I will never be angry," which in turn requires "I must not have angry feelings." "Any experience of anger must be distorted or denied; any part of me that gets angry is unacceptable." Sensing, through her cognitive attunement with the Alice introjection, that Alice is not yet ready to think about changing the pattern, the therapist continues to probe and highlight how that decision was carried out.

Loraine (as Alice): *That's right. We had peace and quiet in our house.*

Therapist: *And no anger.*

Loraine (as Alice): *Well, Loraine has a different opinion about this. . . .*

Therapist: *What's your opinion, Alice? You're the one who counts right now.*

Loraine (as Alice): *We never raised our voices. We never raised our voices. I would get irritated . . .*

One of the great problems about denial and splitting is that the split-off part fights back, leaks out. Then the leaked-out part must in turn be distorted or denied. Loraine/Alice's angry feelings cannot be just waved away; even when sternly suppressed, a residue remains. But "irritation" is tolerable, perhaps, as long as she does not call it "anger." Being careful to avoid any interpretation, the therapist patiently traces this new thread.

Therapist: *Tell me about that, irritation.*

Loraine (as Alice): *My husband would start projects and he wouldn't finish them.*

Therapist: *Then you would get irritated?*

Loraine (as Alice): *I'd get irritated. Sometimes I would have to resort to raising my voice to get attention. So he would finish the project.*

Therapist: *So you sort of broke your commitment once in a while.*

Loraine (as Alice): *Only when it's, only when it was the last resort.*

Therapist: *Now what do you mean, the last resort?*

Loraine (as Alice): *Sometimes you have to put your foot down.*

Therapist: *Um-hmm . . . and how did it feel to you, to break your decision that you were never going to—*

The decision was not irrevocable, was not all-encompassing. There were some situations (perhaps more than Loraine/Alice cares to recognize) when it could be broken. And it is at such moments, when the defense-preserving decision is broken and Loraine/Alice expresses a forbidden aspect of self, that she is most fully accessible, most fully available to contact. An attuned therapist is alert to the possibility of reconstructing such moments, and this therapist senses such a possibility in Loraine/Alice's response:

Loraine (as Alice): *Terrible.*

Therapist: *—get angry, and never be violent?*

Loraine (as Alice): *Terrible. I hated it. I hated to have to come to that.*

Therapist: *So did you wind up having to say violent things?*

Loraine (as Alice): *No, I would just. . . . No, I didn't say violent things, I would just . . .*

Therapist: *Nag?*

Loraine (as Alice): *Yeah, nag. Yeah. . . .*

Therapist: *Nag, and yell?*

Loraine (as Alice): *Nag, kinda nag. I guess that's true.*

In the last few transactions, Loraine/Alice's voice has grown a bit edgy and a bit defensive. Sensitive to the possibility that she may feel criticized (after all, she has just admitted to breaking a very important rule that she made for herself and has accepted a negative label for her behavior), and to her need to be valued and supported, the therapist offers a normalizing response.

Therapist: *Well, how else are you gonna deal with a husband who sorta gets lazy in the middle of a project? I mean, doesn't it seem normal to you, to nag him?*

Loraine (as Alice): *Yeah. . . . and to be sarcastic. Say "Well, that looks nice!"*

Therapist: *Sarcasm.*

Loraine (as Alice): (sarcastically) *"I really like the way that closet looks without the door on it."*

Therapist: *Ouch. Did he get it? Or was he thick-headed?*

Loraine (as Alice): *He, he wasn't thick-headed. He knew I wanted the door fixed. He just ignored me.*

Therapist: *And how'd you deal with your kids when you were irritated with them? Or did you make sure they, that you were never irritated with them?*

If Alice were the primary client, the therapist would probably not have introduced the topic of her children at this point. It would be more important to follow her lead and to let her find her own way into the focus of her work. Because she is an introjection, however, residing within her daughter, the relationship between Alice and Loraine is of central importance. Exploring it will illuminate the way in which the introjection was formed in the first place and will also help client and therapist experience, understand, and work through Alice's rules and responses so that they no longer distort Loraine's relationships.

Loraine (as Alice): *I would lecture them.*

Therapist: *"Lecture." Now what's "lecture"?*

Loraine (as Alice): *And I would tell them, tell them, what it was like for me when I was a kid.*

Therapist: *Give me an example, Alice...of telling them what it was like for you when you were a kid.*

Loraine (as Alice): *I'd tell them "You don't, you've never gone to bed hungry. And you should be grateful you have a nice bed to sleep in, and a good hot meal. And I want, I don't like you not to like that."*

Therapist: *And your kids weren't grateful, were they?*

Loraine (as Alice): *They weren't always grateful. Loraine was grateful. Ellen wasn't so grateful.*

Therapist: *Loraine was grateful that she didn't know what it was like to be hungry and cold?*

Loraine (as Alice): *She was a good little girl. She was very good. Sort of quiet . . .*

Therapist: *Hmm. So you never had to ever get irritated with her.*

The art of therapy lies in keeping track of all the strands of the work, tugging at first one and then another, making sure that none gets lost or out of balance, and eventually weaving them together so the intricacy of their relationship becomes clear. Here the therapist brings together two of the important strands of this piece of work: Alice's relationship with Loraine, and Alice's anger (relabeled as "irritation"). It was the introjected "Alice irritation," remember, that opened this session. We have spiraled back to the same issue, but how different, how much richer, it has become!

Loraine (as Alice): *Almost never. I guess I must have, though, 'cause once when she was real little she asked me why I was mad all the time. I told her I wasn't mad.*

Therapist: *Now that's interesting, because you're gonna confess to—*

Loraine (as Alice): *I guess I lost patience with her.*

Therapist: *You lost patience. What do you mean?*

The therapist is about to confront the discrepancy between Alice's vow never to be angry and her admission that little Loraine asked why she was "mad all the time." Loraine/Alice interrupts, though, with a new thought (losing patience) and the therapist decides to follow her lead. Looking at how Alice violated her decision can be done later. The confrontation can wait.

Loraine (as Alice): *I think it was about the laundry or something. Dropping things . . . I was tired, I had all these men to take care of all the time. Ironing, had to iron—*

Therapist: *All these men? All what men?*

Loraine (as Alice): *My husband, my husband's brother came to live with us, and then my nephew came to live with us for a while. And they all needed their shirts starched all the time. . . .*

Therapist: *So how come you took on the job of taking care of all these men?*

Loraine (as Alice): *Well, I think it was just . . . we lived in a big house in the Depression with 13 people, and it was just, just take people in. . . . I never want anybody to be without a home.*

Therapist: *No one should ever feel what you had to go through.*

The therapist's statement here resonates with Alice's old decision even though the words are quite different. Alice originally decided "I will never be like them." From that decision, it is a tiny step to "I will never treat anyone the way they treated me;" and this transposes easily to "No one should be treated as I was treated. No one should suffer as I suffered." And with this final transformation, Alice has created a litany that feeds the flames of the very anger she has vowed never to express.

Loraine (as Alice): *That's right. It was so horrible.*

Therapist: (pause) *Tell me again about being irritated and lecturing your kids, and sarcasm and all that stuff. 'Cause that seems like a violation of your decision never to get angry.*

Having emphasized the contrast between what ought to have been and what was, between how Alice was treated and how she vowed to treat others, the therapist now returns to the issue of the broken decision.

Loraine (as Alice): (with energy) *Well, it really griped me when people didn't appreciate what I did, and that I made the effort to have good food on the table—*

Therapist: You *would have been more appreciative—*

Loraine (as Alice): *And they turned their nose up at what I cooked. That's right!*

Therapist: *You would have been real appreciative if your mother cooked* anything.

Loraine (as Alice): (animatedly) *Nobody ever made me breakfast; there was one time I went to my girlfriend, Libby Jenkins' house, and she had this breakfast and I'll never forget it. I hadn't had any breakfast, and she wouldn't eat it. It was oatmeal, and orange juice, and snowflake rolls. And every time I eat oatmeal I talk about this breakfast that I didn't get to eat.*

Another indication that the introjected other is fully cathected and that the client is experiencing and interacting as the introjected other is the use of specific, concrete details in describing memories. Alice's use of her childhood friend's name and her description of the breakfast menu affirm that the work is on target and that "Alice" is the client now.

Therapist: *And every time your kids don't eat their breakfast, what do you tell them?*

Loraine (as Alice): *I tell them about Libby Jenkins' oatmeal.*

Therapist: *Were your kids ungrateful?*

Loraine (as Alice): *Can't help it! I don't, I can't help it. They just, that just comes up out of me.*

Alice's anger is triggered not so much by the memories of her own experiences as by her children's failure to recognize and reward her for being a good mother. It was not safe for Alice to be angry with her mother, back then, because she needed a protective and nurturing parent. She has kept the buried anger smoldering all these years and has finally found a target for it. Will exploring the anger toward her children lead her back to the original source? If so, this is yet another reason for keeping the focus on her parenting of Loraine.

Therapist: *Yeah. So what's it like when kids aren't appreciative of the warm coats you buy them? Or they're not appreciative of having their own room?*

Loraine (as Alice): *They just don't understand.*

Therapist: *What don't they understand now?*

Loraine (as Alice): *They don't understand what it was like for me. I don't want them to understand that. I don't want them to know that.*

Therapist: *But you do want them to be grateful.*

Loraine (as Alice): *Yeah.*

Therapist: *But they can't possibly be grateful unless they have a contrast.*

Alice does not want her children to know, even vicariously, the pain she had to suffer. But how can they appreciate how much better it is for them, without knowing? This creates more conflict, more frustration, and more opportunity for the anger to feed upon itself. And there is more opportunity to feel guilty and ashamed of both her wants and her anger, as she tells her story. The therapist will be very careful to avoid any hint of judgment or evaluation; sensing criticism from the therapist would only add to Loraine/Alice's shame, strengthen her defenses, and widen the gap that separates her from her disavowed and unaccepted parts.

Loraine (as Alice): *Maybe that's why I tell them so much.*

Therapist: *Explain that to me.*

Loraine (as Alice): *Maybe if they know what it's like, what it was like for me, they'll know how different it is for them and how hard I worked to make it different.*

Therapist: *You mean how hard you still work.*

Loraine (as Alice): *What it took—that's right, what it took out of me.*

Therapist: *What did it take out of you?*

Loraine (as Alice): *The courage, and determination, and praying, and . . . fighting . . .*

Therapist: *And sort of ignoring your background.*

Another theme is introduced. From her previous work with Loraine, the therapist knows that Loraine/Alice is a very "proper" woman for whom appearances are extremely important. The fact that her parents were alcoholics and that they were poor and ignorant would be a source of shame, which is another thing that must be kept separate from the way she wants to see herself and be seen by others. All of that background, too, must be reclaimed and owned if she is to be able to be authentic and whole—with herself and with her daughter.

Loraine (as Alice): *That's right.*

Therapist: *Tell me about that, ignoring your background.*

Loraine (as Alice): *Ignoring my background. I don't know about that.*

Therapist: *Well, sounds like your family was pretty low class.*

Loraine (as Alice): *Yes. Lower than low.*

Therapist: *Tell me about lower than low.*

Loraine (as Alice): *Just in . . . I don't know, when I see children . . .*

Therapist: *It's called drunk class, right?*

Loraine (as Alice): *Drunk class, yeah, drunk.*

Therapist: *Lower than low class.*

Loraine (as Alice): *No coal in the stove on Christmas morning, let alone a tree. I gave my kids every toy imaginable on Christmas.*

Therapist: *Now what was it like—*

The "lower than low" designation, and the associated memories and feelings, are too much; Loraine/Alice comes back to how different things are now. It is an urgent, intense sort of coming back, with a flavor almost of desperation: "I must tell you *this,* to keep you from asking about *that.*" The therapist, allowing herself to be interrupted, respects the urgency of the unspoken request and follows Loraine/Alice's lead.

Loraine (as Alice): *And Easter, let me tell you about Easter.*

Therapist: *Oh, tell me. I like Easter.*

Loraine (as Alice): *We had a candy store down in the middle of Emporia that made special candy. And I would go weeks ahead, and I would order candy, big coconut eggs and stuff covered with . . . other stuff, white chocolate and jelly beans, and bunnies, and I would, my kids never woke up on Easter morning without an Easter basket.*

Therapist: *And your kids were never going to be skinny, were they?*

Loraine (as Alice): *No, never. My Loraine was skinny when she was a baby. I was so ashamed. I went to the doctor's with her, and I thought the doctor would think I wasn't feeding her.*

Therapist: *Yeah. Like, she would be so skinny somebody would think her mother was a drunk, huh?*

Always suggesting connections, never insisting on them, the therapist has now brought together Loraine/Alice's need to be different from her own parents and Loraine's weight problems. It is another faint allusion to the damage that may have resulted from Alice's way of dealing with her feelings. And in the background, like a somber, distant theme in a symphony, is the forbidden topic of Alice's shame about her origins. Again, though, Loraine/Alice defends herself. This is one thing she is definitely not ready to discuss.

Loraine (as Alice): *I guess; well, nobody would think I was a drunk; I was very well dressed, I took very good care of myself, I made my clothes, and . . . was always clean.*

Therapist: *Uh-huh. So what was your feeling when your kids would get these wonderful Christmas presents, all the toys they could imagine, and the wonderful Easter baskets? And you saw your kids with all that stuff . . . what happened in your heart?*

Loraine (as Alice): *I was really sad about myself.*

Therapist: *Will you tell me about that sadness?*

Loraine (as Alice): *Just a big emptiness. Big, dark, cold, hungry emptiness.*

"Sad," "low class," and "angry" are all connected; exploring one affective response fully will nearly always lead to the next experience. The therapist follows Loraine/Alice's energy into the "big, dark, cold, hungry emptiness." What happens to that emptiness when it is not fed?

Therapist: *Dark, cold, hungry . . .*

Loraine (as Alice): *Just remembering all those years . . .*

Therapist: *So even while you were making it good for your kids, there was a dark, cold, hungry emptiness.*

Loraine (as Alice): *That's right.*

Therapist: *So didn't buying all those presents at Christmas, didn't that fill the emptiness?*

Loraine (as Alice): *No.*

Therapist: *Buying the white chocolate, and the coconut eggs. . . . Did that fill the hunger?*

Loraine (as Alice): *No.*

Therapist: *And what happens when you see your kids and they are not grateful for all that candy?*

Loraine (as Alice): *I don't know if they were grateful or not. I think they ate it. They opened their presents. . . .*

Therapist: *Did they love . . .*

Loraine (as Alice):   (sharply) *We had a* nice Christmas. *And we had a nice Easter.*

The nonverbal part of this exclamation is so clear that she might as well have said it aloud: "I *will* believe it!" Something has touched a nerve and brought out the old defenses in full force. It is an important reaction, one that will need to be attended to.

Therapist: *Tell me about your tone.*

Loraine (as Alice): *We had, nobody was drunk.*

Therapist: *You just changed tones there.*

Loraine (as Alice): (determinedly) *We had a* nice *holiday. That's what I wanted. I wanted to have a nice holiday. I wanted a nice Mother's Day.*

Therapist: *Did you get it?*

Loraine (as Alice): *Sometimes.*

Therapist: *And other times?*

Loraine (as Alice): *Wasn't what I wanted, I don't know . . . wasn't what I expected. I never, it was nice. I mean, at the end of each time I think, I would always think, it's kind of a relief to have a nice holiday. Get to the end of it and nothing bad happens. And when I go to weddings I'm always relieved at the end of a wedding reception. I always say, "That was nice, nobody got drunk. Nobody misbehaved."*

A "nice holiday" is one that does not evoke the painful memories, one that allows her to maintain her respectability and not be reminded that she came from a "lower-than-low," drunken family. To the first two painful emotions—anger, that must not be expressed, and cold, empty sadness— we can now add fear: fear that the old family will emerge within her own, fear that her hard-earned respectability will be destroyed, fear of what she and her family might really become if she let herself relax. Here is another strand for the therapist to keep track of and to eventually weave in with all the others.

Therapist: *So the best thing for you is in the relief that there's nothing violent happening.*

Loraine (as Alice): *Right.*

Therapist: *But then there's still the dark, cold, hungry emptiness.*

Loraine (as Alice): *Yeah. . . .*

Therapist: *That isn't filled up with all the Christmas decorations . . .*

Loraine (as Alice): *Nope.*

Therapist: *And what happens when somebody like Loraine can't play with all the toys at once?*

The therapist invites Loraine/Alice to put the emptiness and the anger together: the emptiness that no amount of frantic Christmas ritual can fill and the anger when a child does not appreciate the effort of those rituals. This time, Loraine/Alice seems more willing to look where the therapist is pointing.

Loraine (as Alice): *I don't mind if she doesn't play with them; I just want her to take good care of them.*

Therapist: *Oh. Tell me about the importance of taking good care of everything.*

Loraine (as Alice): *I never had a doll. (pause) If I had had a doll I would have taken care of it.*

Therapist: *And she probably just plays with the doll, takes its clothes off, throws it around, doesn't brush the hair, right?*

Loraine (as Alice): *Yes . . . but I'm not so worried about the toys, I let them play, make messes; I let them, they dug in the backyard; we had, called it the dirt pile, they were always out there covered with mud, and . . .*

Therapist: *Sounds like you were a great mother!*

Loraine (as Alice): *Well, thank you.*

Therapist: *Giving all the opportunities that any child should have.*

Loraine (as Alice): *That's what I wanted to be.*

Again, sensing Loraine/Alice's need for validation and approval, the therapist supports and applauds her attempts at parenting, even though she was often out of contact with her children's needs. The supportive statements have another function as well: they are leading up to an inquiry in which Loraine/Alice will be invited once more to acknowledge how much she envied and resented her own children because they had, and did not appreciate, what was so painfully missing for her. With that acknowledgment, she may be able to reclaim her anger and direct it appropriately, rather than let it leak out onto her family.

Therapist: *Did you ever miss any opportunity? Anything you wish you'd done over?*

Loraine (as Alice): *No.*

Therapist: *So you did everything perfectly.*

Loraine/Alice: *I did everything. Well, I'm far from perfect, but I did everything I knew how to do.*

Therapist: *And then I bet you did things you didn't even know how to do.*

Loraine (as Alice): *I did. I did. I didn't know. I learned how to make slipcovers and stuff for the house. . . .*

Therapist: *Slipcovers!*

Loraine (as Alice): *Yeah.*

Therapist: *Tell me about the slipcovers.*

Loraine/Alice has been working hard, dealing with quite painful memories and doing so with a great deal of courage. She needs another respite, a chance to breathe and recover. By her genuine and contactful interest in sharing Alice's memories, the therapist will create a space in which Alice can take in support and respect and celebrate some of the things that she has done well.

Loraine (as Alice): *Well, I learned how to make them during the Depression. I learned how to make slipcovers.*

Therapist: *Why'd you make slipcovers?*

Loraine (as Alice): *'Cause the furniture would start to look old, and I didn't want to get, I couldn't afford always to get new furniture, so I would make slipcovers. And if I wanted the living room to be green, I would make green slipcovers.*

Therapist: *Uh-huh.*

Loraine (as Alice): *It was good; it was fun for me.*

Therapist: *So you could really decorate with slipcovers.*

Loraine (as Alice): *Right, and curtains.*

Therapist: *And that way it was freer to let the kids come in and jump on the furniture, too.*

Loraine (as Alice): *Well, kids didn't jump on the furniture; I wouldn't let them jump on it. They could go jump around outside.*

Therapist: *So you didn't let them jump on it.*

Loraine (as Alice): *I didn't want them to get hurt.*

Therapist: *Did they play in the living room?*

Loraine (as Alice): *They played in the living room, yeah.*

Therapist: *Just, don't jump on the furniture.*

Loraine (as Alice): *Don't jump on the furniture, yeah. I didn't want them to get hurt.*

Therapist: *Your kids must have been sure lucky having you as a mother.*

Loraine (as Alice): *Well they were certainly luckier than I was.*

The side trip has done its job, and Loraine/Alice is ready to get back to business. But it was more than a side trip; in addition to giving her a chance to rest and recover a bit, it has highlighted even more vividly the contrast between Alice's childhood and what she provided for her own children. It is to this contrast that she returns, and the therapist is quick to respond.

Therapist: *Tell me about the contrast.* (Loraine/Alice sighs deeply) *That's hard, isn't it, Alice?*

Loraine (as Alice): *Yes. . . .*

Therapist: *But tell me about the contrast* (she sighs again)—*that contrast that only you can appreciate.*

Loraine (as Alice): *I was there. I was there when they got up in the morning; I was there if they got up at night.*

Therapist: *Now make the contrast.*

Loraine (as Alice): *My mother wasn't there all day. I would wander around the neighborhood. Three or four years old. It's a wonder I never died, or something horrible happened to me. . . . Just playing on people's cellar doors, and just . . .*

Therapist: *And you were there every morning for your—*

Loraine (as Alice): *I was; I was there for my kids. I made breakfast every day.*

Therapist: *And your kids don't ever have the capacity to appreciate it, 'cause they don't know what it's like—*

Balancing and exploring, first one strand and then another, the therapist weaves in and out of the pattern that Alice has created. Here she touches once more on the contrast between Alice's experience and that of her children, and then moves smoothly into how the children do not notice. This, in turn, allows her to invite Alice into more description of what they do not notice, a description of the difference, and a new and deeper awareness of how it was for her.

Loraine (as Alice): *No, they don't know the difference.*

Therapist: *—to have a mother with a hangover.*

Loraine (as Alice): *Right.*

Therapist: *Cause what's it like to have a mother with a hangover?*

Loraine (as Alice): *It's very empty. Very scary. Scary.*

Therapist: *Because when she was irritable all the time . . .*

Loraine/Alice is much more in contact now with her experience of and emotional reaction to the early trauma. With this growing awareness, is she ready to take the next step, to explore how she had to organize her internal world in order to cope with the neglect and abuse? Is the rigid defensive structure beginning to soften?

Loraine (as Alice): *I don't know. . . .*

Therapist: *Just think about it, Alice. People with hangovers are irritable. And you gotta be very careful around them, or they blow up in your face.*

Loraine (as Alice): *I don't know about that. . . . My mother was awful when she was an old lady. But . . .*

Therapist: *Well, I can expect some things from your childhood you'd want to not remember, so we can just pass by that; I'm just pointing out that, if she was waking up with a hangover she's gotta be irritable.*

The therapist backs away, with a clear statement that there is something important here even though Loraine/Alice is not ready to remember. Loraine/Alice is not quite ready yet. It will emerge in its own time. In exploring the contrast between her childhood and the experiences she provided for her own children, Loraine/Alice seems most able to expand her awareness and to reclaim the feelings that she has been denying. With each cycle back into these memories, she gains a bit more.

Loraine (as Alice): *Well, she usually didn't get up.*

Therapist: *Mmm. But you were up for your kids.*

Loraine (as Alice): *I was up for my kids. I was up before they got up and had their school lunches packed.*

Therapist: *Did you ever wish, while you were packing the kids' lunch, that it would have happened for you?*

Loraine (as Alice): *I wish somebody would have packed me a lunch.*

Therapist: *And do you ever wish somebody would greet you with a warm "Good morning"?*

Loraine (as Alice): *Yes. . . .* (sharply) *It's not gonna happen!*

Therapist: *What just happened to your voice tone there, Alice?*

Loraine (as Alice): *It's not gonna happen. There's no point in crying over spilled milk.*

It was too much, too painful, and Loraine/Alice slammed the door shut. She uses the old familiar defense: if it cannot be repaired, don't even think about it, don't feel the feelings, and don't let yourself know how much it hurts. This time, relying on the therapeutic alliance that has been established between them, the therapist confronts her defense head on.

Therapist: *Your voice wasn't a voice of crying, Alice.*

Loraine (as Alice): *It's in the past. . . . I don't talk about this much. I really, I'd really rather not. It's all, what's gone is gone.*

Therapist: *I know you'd rather not. And yet I think I could help you with all that tension in your body. You do suffer from a lot of tension, don't you?*

Acknowledging her preference, the therapist suggests a concrete and immediate benefit that Loraine/Alice might gain if she tried a different way. Her answer is a tacit acceptance of the bargain.

Loraine (as Alice): *I'm scared a lot. I'm real tight.*

Therapist: *Well, you probably wouldn't agree with me if I told you what I thought you were scared about.*

Loraine (as Alice): *You could tell me.*

Therapist: *Would you give it some serious thought? Or would you just dismiss me right away?*

By predicting Loraine/Alice's resistance, the therapist engages her in two ways. First, she appeals to Alice rationally: you will not like my ideas, but would you think about them before you reject them out of hand? It is the sort of proposition that is difficult to refuse, especially for someone who prides herself on being sensible and fair. Second, at a deeper level the therapist has challenged Alice's whole defensive structure. If Alice does reject the therapist's idea, then the therapist has successfully predicted her behavior and demonstrated that Alice is really being understood in this relationship, which is a new and script-contradictory experience. And, of course, if Alice does not reject it she will also be moving into a new area of awareness. Either way, Loraine/Alice wins.

Loraine (as Alice): *I'll think about it. Tell me, and then I'll try.*

Therapist: *Well, Alice, I was watching when you said, "That's all in the past." And just moments before that, I was watching your mouth and your jaw. I was watching your fists. . . .*

Loraine (as Alice): *I'm tired—ooh. . . . Yeah, go ahead. . . .*

Therapist: *And I was thinking . . . that your body was having such a different reaction than your decision never to be angry. And I was thinking that just for a fraction of a moment there, you were angry at your mother. . . . And then you said, "It's all in the past."*

Loraine (as Alice): *I was angry with her. I pray a lot about that.*

When the acknowledgment comes, it is so easy that it is almost as if the denial had never happened. Loraine/Alice has moved from "I'm not angry" to "I wish I weren't angry," and this is a giant step.

Therapist: *Pray not to be angry?*

Loraine (as Alice): *Can't forgive my parents.*

Therapist: *Do you pray not to be angry?*

Loraine (as Alice): *I pray for forgiveness. 'Cause I never followed the commandment, "Honor thy father and thy mother."*

Therapist: *Well, your parents didn't follow a different commandment.* (pause) *You know there was a commandment, long, long, a thousand years before Moses? Not the commandments given to Moses, one through ten, but the one given to Abraham when he was about to kill Isaac. A thousand years before Moses.*

Loraine/Alice's religion is important to her both as a source of comfort and stability and as another way to appear respectable. Framing this intervention within the Judeo–Christian tradition gives it credibility and demands that Loraine/Alice consider it seriously.

Loraine: *What is that?*

Therapist: *Parents, honor thy children. The life of a child is holy and should never be sacrificed.*

Loraine: (softly) *I was sacrificed.*

This comment marks a pivot point in Loraine's work. Until now, the focus has been on helping Loraine/Alice to reclaim the split-off and denied parts of herself and to access her feelings and memories fully, so that Loraine, in turn, can have access to what she has introjected. Loraine/Alice has gradually come to experience and acknowledge how angry she has been and how that submerged anger has spilled over onto her children. As her acknowledgment of anger emerged, with it came self-condemnation and shame: "I shouldn't feel that way; I pray every day for forgiveness." Now, in contrast, there is a tenderness in her voice and a true accepting and taking back into self of that angry and abused child. It is a good place to end the session, an ending place that will allow Loraine to take away a new sense of self-awareness and self-comforting.

There is much yet to be done before Loraine will be able to dissolve the Loraine/Alice introjection. As the work with Loraine continues in her next session, we see Loraine/Alice slide back into her old habits of denial and defense and then emerge to make full and authentic contact with the memories and the feelings of the past. And we shall see Loraine begin to deal with Alice differently: to experience the internalized Loraine/Alice differently and to make plans about interacting differently with her living, flesh-and-blood mother.

Therapy with an introjected other is impactful in several ways. Most obviously, it can effect changes in the introjection itself, so that the intrapsychic restrictions and internal demands of the introjected other are modified. And, equally important, it provides the client a chance to observe those changes as they happen. How wonderful for Loraine, both as child and as adult, to be able to see her mother emerge from that straight-jacket of tight-lipped disapproval and of rigid and bitter and demanding criticism! How different it would have been to be in relationship with an authentic and contactful mother!

Often, work with an introjected other ends where we have left Loraine in this chapter. There are, of course, some necessary closing activities: the client must be helped to leave the persona of the introjection and reconnect with himself or herself and may want to talk about the experience with the therapist or with the fantasized other. The immediate focus of the therapy session shifts back to the client, and there is no further therapeutic conversation between introjected other and therapist. In this example, however, the work with Loraine/Alice did not stop, but continued into the next session of therapy. So, instead of speculating about what might happen next, we shall see for ourselves in chapter 11.

11

Loraine: Therapy
With an Introjected Other
(Part II)

In the previous chapter, we followed the first of two sessions of therapy with an introjected other. The client, Loraine, began the work by expressing anger and irritation, which she identified as being not so much her own as that of her mother. She had "eaten" her mother's anger and swallowed down her mother's feelings and reactions and expectations, and those introjected patterns were now getting in the way of Loraine's living and relating to others as she wanted to do.

Loraine and the therapist entered into a contract to work with the introjection of Loraine's mother, Alice. Loraine agreed to put her own sense of self to one side and assume the persona of Alice; the therapist's commitment was to work with "Alice," so that Loraine would no longer internally experience or act out "Alice's" anger and pain.

This first session with "Alice" involved a great deal of patient inquiry, as the therapist helped her to explore her memories, her beliefs, and her feelings, and to begin to overcome the defensive patterns that she had used for so many years to deal with her unmet needs. At the point at which chapter 10 ended, "Alice" had gained the courage to look squarely at her own childhood and to acknowledge its effect on her way of being in the world. She recognized that her joy had been sacrificed to her parents' alcoholism and that she had never stopped being angry about what had been done to her. Loraine returned for the next session ready to continue her work with her introjected mother. The transcript begins a few minutes into the session. Loraine and the therapist have reviewed the previous piece of work and Loraine has cathected "Alice" again. After a few moments to reestablish the contact between "Alice" and the therapist, "Alice" is invited to pick up where she left off in the previous session.

Therapist: *Last week, Alice, you said you were sacrificed. Tell me about the sacrifice—on an altar of booze.*

Loraine (as Alice): *Stayed home with my parents. My brothers and sisters got taken away and . . . at least they were taken care of; at least they were clean; at least they were fed. And I stayed there with my parents like a scapegoat, or a sacrifice, or. . .* [1]

Therapist: *And tell me about your prayers, Alice, when you prayed to be forgiven for being angry at them.*

Loraine (as Alice): *I am angry at them!*

How different from the Alice we met at the beginning of chapter 10, the Alice who loved to comb her mother's hair and who made a vow that she would never, ever be angry at anyone. Her anger, always simmering under the surface, is now strong and clear. Alice may even be ready to value it, and in so doing value herself in a much more authentic way than before.

Therapist: *Yeah. Just feel that bitterness in your mouth right now.* (pause) *You see, Alice, I think your folks broke the earlier commandment. Remember the one we talked about last week—the one that was so basic that by the time Moses went up Mount Sinai he didn't even have to write it down. Your parents didn't honor their children.*

Loraine (as Alice): *Well, I didn't survive because my parents honored me; that's for sure. I survived because I honored me. Wasn't gonna be like them.*

Therapist: *Would it be okay with you if I respect how angry you are? Even if you try to pray it away? Even if you try to push it into the past? Value that, for you, each Easter egg is, just for a fraction of a second, an angry reminder? And each toy at Christmas, each bowl of oatmeal, each clean-smelling sheet on the bed is a moment of anger that has to be shut off? Okay if I understand that and value it?*

Loraine (as Alice): *I'm ashamed of that.*

---

[1] We shall follow the same convention in this chapter as in the previous one: transcript "speeches" of an introjection are labeled by Loraine's name, followed by "as Alice" (the name of the introjected other). In comments about the work, we use Alice's name if we are speaking of what Alice did, thought, or felt in the past, and we use "Loraine/Alice" when we are talking about the behavior of the introjection here in the therapy session.

Therapist: *I'm not going to put you down for being angry, Alice. So you don't have to be ashamed in my presence. Now I understand that you're going against your decision. But I wonder if that vow was there because you are so angry at them that you've got to make sure you don't kill them.*

Early in the previous piece of work, Loraine/Alice told of her life-shaping decision: she would never, ever, be like her parents. She would not fight; she would not have violence. She is now ashamed of her anger, both because as a child she would have been humiliated and punished for it and because it seems to her to violate her decision, the promise she made to herself. In order to dissolve the shame, both the punishment and the promise must be undone. But it would not be helpful for her to simply shift the sense of shame and now be ashamed of making the decision in the first place. The therapist acknowledges both Loraine/Alice's need to be angry and the importance of her vow. She is helping Loraine/Alice to understand that her promise to herself was indeed protective, not in the way she thought, but at a much deeper level—a level she is gradually beginning to understand.

Loraine (as Alice): *That's why I wanted to kill myself.*

Therapist: *Tell me about that, Alice.*

Loraine (as Alice): *I went into the bathroom to mix up some medicine for my mother. I had to take care of her; she was real sick. And I stood there. And I had the bottle up to my lips and I was gonna drink it 'cause I didn't think I could go on.*

Therapist: *How old were you?*

Loraine (as Alice): *Couldn't go on. . . . I was a grown-up. Didn't have kids yet. I didn't have kids until later. I didn't marry until I was 35.*

Therapist: *Um-hmm. Weren't gonna get yourself into that old kinda crap your Mom got into, were you?*

Loraine (as Alice): *My husband didn't want to get married, and he wouldn't until I finally put my foot down.*

Therapist: *Um-hmm. You mentioned putting your foot down the last time we talked together, too.*

Notice how the therapist consistently abandons her own line of inquiry in order to stay attuned to Loraine/Alice's process. She begins to ask about the circumstances of Alice's attempted suicide; then she follows Alice's reference to how late in life she married. When the therapist asks about the "put my foot down" metaphor, Loraine/Alice is ready to answer. Putting her foot down will take her back to being angry, and that is where her energy is.

Loraine (as Alice): *That's right.*

Therapist: *You good at that?*

Loraine (as Alice): *Yeah. Put my foot down.*

Therapist: *Tell me about that.*

Loraine (as Alice): *Well, when I have, I'm patient, but when I have enough, I have enough.*

Therapist: *And how's it show up?*

Loraine (as Alice): *Put my foot down.*

Therapist: *You ever wish you could put your foot down hard, right on Dad?*

Gestures and actions are often physical metaphors for impulses that are inhibited from being acted out in transaction with others. The clenched fist that hides the wish to hit, or the swinging foot that expresses a desire to kick, are examples of metaphoric gestures. In Loraine/Alice's statement, the metaphor is in words that describe a physical action. The therapist makes both translations: from the words to the action, and from the adult meaning to the more archaic one. And Loraine/Alice seems to have no trouble in understanding and accepting the translation.

Loraine (as Alice): *Kick him a good one!*

Therapist: *So how do you kick somebody a good one, when you've made a vow never to be violent and angry?*

This, of course, is the problem that Alice struggled with for so many years. The therapist frames it neatly and concisely and invites her to discover how she has been trying to solve it. An interpretation would be easy to make—we, outside the system, can see how she transformed her anger into criticism and rigidity—but it is Alice's problem, Alice's solution, and Loraine/Alice must work her own way back to the core of it.

Loraine (as Alice): *Well, it doesn't work.*

Therapist: *How do you do it? I mean, how do you manage to keep the vow and keep your foot grounded?*

Loraine (as Alice): *All goes right here.* (indicating the center of her chest) *It burns, right there.*

Therapist: *Burns . . .*

Loraine (as Alice): *Anger. Burns. Burns me up. I say that all the time. "It burns me up." "This really burns me up."*

Another metaphor—in fact, a metaphor of a metaphor! The first substitution occurs when Loraine/Alice transforms her desire to kick and punish into a burning in her chest: the anger, which needed to be expressed outwardly, was instead turned inward and became a physical sensation. That sensation, in turn, engenders the verbal metaphor, "It burns me up," which elegantly expresses both the sensation and the anger.

Therapist: *Um-hmm! So that means you're pissed off.*

Loraine (as Alice): *I don't use language like that, but yeah, it burns me up.*

Therapist: *You're gonna do everything different than that family you grew up in.*

Loraine (as Alice): *That's right.* (pause) *I forget what we were talking about.*

It is no accident that Loraine/Alice "forgot" the subject at this moment. Just as happened in the previous session, when Loraine/Alice almost frantically interrupted to divert the therapist as she began to inquire about Alice's family, here Loraine/Alice "forgets" what she was talking about. The need to keep the illusion that her parents loved and cared for her, to avoid thinking about how awful her family life was, is too strong to risk following this line of thought. Rather than challenge the defense (and risk damaging the relationship that she has established with Loraine/Alice), the therapist gently refocuses her.

Therapist: *We were just talking about the most important topic here of all: Alice, and Alice's feelings. And the quality of your life, Alice.*

Loraine (as Alice): *My life is good now.*

Therapist: *And how misunderstood you are. That is one of the things that's irritating in your family, isn't it? I'll bet no one really understands you.*

Loraine (as Alice): *Nobody knows what's in my memory.*

Therapist: *And the contrast between what's in your present reality, and your memory, must be great.*

Loraine (as Alice): *I thank God every night for my bed.*

Therapist: *But at that same moment, I bet you continue to be angry at how bad it was for you as a child. You don't dare ever forget it.*

When the inquiry is about Alice's family, Loraine/Alice defends; when it is about her own experience, she is able to respond. Yet the two are intimately connected; they are two sides of the same coin. It is as if she must hold them apart in order to hold herself together. But holding them apart prevents her from being truly "together" and truly whole. The therapist continues to inquire, following up each new thread as it emerges.

Loraine (as Alice): *I can't forget it.*

Therapist: *Tell me about that experience, Alice.*

Loraine (as Alice): *I can't let go of it.*

Every behavior has a function. If Loraine/Alice has to hang on to her anger, there is a reason for that hanging-on: exploring the function of the behavior will help her discover new options and alternative ways to meet the need.

Therapist: *Because what happens if you would let go of how secretly angry you are at your drunken parents? What would happen to you? I believe you. I believe that you have needed to hang on.*

Loraine (as Alice): *Just . . .* (helpless gesture) *I'd just be nothing.*

Therapist: *So in order not to be a nothing . . .*

Loraine (as Alice): *Oh, I feel like I'm floating.*

The feeling of "floating" may be a signal that Loraine/Alice is beginning to dissociate, which is the ultimate defense against unbearable pain or anxiety. Her anger really has been a survival tool; even the fantasy of giving it up takes her into the realm of not being. She needs to come back, be grounded, and reexperience the protection of the therapeutic relationship. The therapist's next invitation, though confusing to her at first, brings her back.

Therapist: *Let's come back to what you're angry about.*

Loraine (as Alice): *Be angry?*

Therapist: *So you don't float away. Tell me. What thought just came to your mind, just now, Alice?*

Loraine (as Alice): *What did he do to me . . .*

Therapist: *And would you like to put your foot down right on his face? So he can't stick another drink in his mouth? You said you wanted to put your foot down on him, and somehow I feel you'd like to put your foot right down on his mouth, so he couldn't drink. Just imagine being a young woman. At the time you first wanted to commit suicide, or back when you were a teenager. What would have happened if you'd kicked the bottle out of his hand?*

"What did he do to me . . . " could refer to a wide range of possible behaviors, and it would be tempting to find out exactly what did happen between Alice and her father. The therapist, however, chooses to stay with what is known: her father's drinking and its effect on his daughter. Rather than paralyzing and burning herself with anger turned inward, the therapist invites Loraine/Alice to fantasize the experience of expressing her anger, of making a natural and spontaneous and need-meeting response. Loraine/Alice's answer sheds more light on the self-protective nature of her decision to never show anger and never "be like them."

Loraine (as Alice): *Would have felt good. He would have killed me, but it would have felt good.*

Therapist: *He would have what?*

Loraine (as Alice): *Killed me, or something. He would have . . .*

Therapist: *So that's a good reason not to show your anger, huh?*

Loraine (as Alice): *Yeah.*

Therapist: *And what would happen if you kicked Mom's bed in the morning and said, "Get up and make me oatmeal, like my friend's mother does."*

Loraine (as Alice): *I don't want to do that.*

Therapist: *Why not?*

Loraine (as Alice): *She probably got beat up by my father the night before when he came home. I could hear them. I slept in their room for many years.* (her voice is shaky) *I don't even want to talk about that; it was horrible.*

The need to protect her mother (and to protect herself from the memory of what she saw and heard in her parents' bedroom) is stronger than the need to experience and express her anger. Loraine/Alice's distress is evident in her quivering voice, and the therapist responds to her distress.

Therapist: *Okay. You don't have to do it all in this session. Shall we postpone it now? Or do you just want to give me a brief outline?*

Loraine (as Alice): *He'd just come in drunk, and he'd say, "Get your skirt up, Mary." No love, no tenderness. My husband was tender with me. I didn't know anything about sex when we were married. And he was patient and tender.*

The therapist's response again demonstrates that Loraine/Alice is in charge, and Loraine/Alice's anxiety dissipates. When it's her choice, she can talk about it. No doubt there is much to be explored here, more self-protective decisions made as the young girl was forced to witness her parents' sexual behavior. Rather than follow up this new area of content, though, the therapist chooses to relate it to the theme that has been developing: the difference between the two families, the one with Alice's parents and the other with her own husband and children.

Therapist: *Another contrast.*

Loraine (as Alice): *Yeah. . . .*

Therapist: *What's it like inside, Alice, to live with all these contrasts? Every place you turn around. You walk in the living room and you see the pretty slipcovers. What a contrast! You see how well dressed your kids are, on the way to school.*

Loraine (as Alice): *They have their education. Everything.*

Therapist: *You see the food on the breakfast table.*

Loraine (as Alice): *Ohhhhh. . . .*

Therapist: *Smell the clean sheets. . . . What's "Ohhhhh" mean?*

Loraine (as Alice): *I'm* proud *I did it.* (her hand tightens against her leg)

Therapist: *And your right hand is saying something too. Do it again. "I'm proud. . . . " That right hand is saying something.*

The therapist does not know what the gesture means and does not need to know; all that is needed is that she notice and ask Loraine/Alice to attend to it. As Loraine/Alice repeats and exaggerates her hand's movement, the feelings intensify and the meaning of the gesture emerges spontaneously.

Loraine (as Alice): *I'm angry I never had it. Why couldn't it have been like that? It was never like that.*

Therapist: *"Angry that I never had it."*

Loraine (as Alice): *Never had it.*

Therapist: *"Proud" that you give it to them, and at the same time inside angry that you "never had it" yourself.*

Loraine (as Alice): *God forgive me. Yes.* (pause) *I'm angry every day of my life.*

Therapist: *Well, see, I don't think God can forgive you until you really own it—"angry every day" of your life. And you get angry at your kids, because they failed to appreciate it.*

Loraine (as Alice): *They don't know what it's like.* (pause) *I don't want them to know what it's like.*

Again, Loraine/Alice spirals around to where she has been before: I want them to know, and yet I don't want them to know. And again, she comes back to the old conflict with new awareness and self-acceptance. The therapist's next question builds on that awareness, taking her further into exploring how, hungry for contact with her children, she still keeps them at arm's length.

Therapist: *And yet, then* you *don't get known, do you?*

Loraine (as Alice): *I try not to bring it up.*

Therapist: *And yet you tell them stories all the time.*

Loraine (as Alice): *Yeah, I guess I do. I stop myself, though; I never get into the really bad stuff. They don't know the half of it.*

Therapist: *Sort of like you stop yourself here today with me, too, huh? But you've got a lot of stuff on your mind, don't you, Alice? Lots of stuff.*

Loraine (as Alice): *Keep it to myself.*

Therapist: *That will probably kill you.*

Loraine (as Alice): *Well, I'm almost 86; you gotta die with something.*

Therapist: *Would you like to die with an eased mind?*

This question marks the transition into the final phase of the work with Loraine/Alice. Throughout the session presented in chapter 10, and up until now in this session, the focus has been on exploring, and the change in Loraine/Alice has emerged primarily in response to her increased awareness and her growing trust in the therapeutic relationship. Now the therapist will begin to assess whether she is available for more intense affective work.

Loraine (as Alice): *I don't know if that's possible.*

Therapist: *Well, how's it then telling me today about how angry you are, and your jealousy toward your own kids?*

Loraine (as Alice): *I didn't say I was jealous.*

Therapist: *You didn't? I thought that's what you were describing.*

Loraine (as Alice): *I said they'll never know. And I don't want them to know.*

Therapist: *Didn't you tell me that you were angry whenever you saw the beautiful slipcovers, the oatmeal on the table, . . .*

Loraine (as Alice): *Angry? I wasn't angry at my kids. . . . Wasn't ever their fault I grew up like that.*

Have things moved too fast? Have the therapist's questions triggered Loraine/Alice's old self-criticism, her need to protect herself from the danger of feeling angry, and the shame over being jealous of her children's good fortune? She certainly seems to be backpedaling and reerecting the old defenses. The therapist's response puts her pain into words; the understanding in the therapist's voice normalizes Loraine/Alice's reactions.

Therapist: *But they don't really understand you, do they?* (pause) *And they're not as grateful as you would be. Had all the dolls you never had.*

Loraine (as Alice): *That's what I want them to have.*

Therapist: *Yes, I understand that part of it. I understand your generosity. But what happens after they get it?*

Loraine (as Alice): *I just don't have anything more. I don't, nothing can fix it for me. All I can do is make it better for them; I can't fix it for me.*

Therapist: *But then you feel the cold, empty hunger.*

Loraine/Alice is starved for relationship; she desperately needs contact, but equally desperately she must keep her inner, unacceptable part from being known. The choice is between rejection and shame, on the one hand, and cold empty hunger on the other. It is this false dichotomy that must be resolved in order to restore contact and free Loraine from the burden of Alice's conflict.

Loraine (as Alice): *Yeah. . . .*

Therapist: *And then do you tell them how grateful they should be? Or at least do you think it?*

Loraine (as Alice): *No, I tell them stuff; I probably shouldn't. Tell them stuff . . .*

Therapist: *So maybe jealousy is too strong a word. Would envy be a better word for you? You wish you had it for yourself? And every time you see them with it, it opens that old wound of not having. And be angry at those parents for choosing alcohol over you. . . . Oh, Alice, what a sad life to bear this all alone.*

The therapist is not just a technician; she too feels the dilemma. Even though she is working with an introjection, an entity that exists only in Loraine's head, there is pain, and the therapist's compassion is genuine.

Loraine (as Alice): *Well, my husband understood, 'cause he came from the same kind of background. We understood each other. I really miss him.*

Therapist: *Tell me what you miss, Alice.*

Loraine (as Alice): *I miss him next to me in the bed at night. Like it's so cold . . . . I miss knowing that there's somebody there who understands how it was for me. 'Cause I met him when I was 16 years old, and he knew what my life was like. He knew what a struggle it was.*

Therapist: (pause) *Keep going, Alice.*

As Loraine/Alice talks about her husband, she describes getting the kind of contact that she had been longing for all her life: someone who really knew her, really understood, and still loved her. Losing that interpersonal contact and support must have thrust her back into the cold emptiness, worse even than before because she had finally experienced being warm and full. Here is another part of what she aches to have others know—the depth of her loneliness.

Loraine (as Alice): *We weren't married that long. We didn't get married until I was 35, until I finally said I want to have kids, and if you won't marry me I'm going to give up on you and go get somebody else. And then he went to Reno or some damn place and got a quick divorce, and then he married me. And then he wasn't really well a lot of the time.*

Therapist: *But he understood you.*

Loraine (as Alice): *He understood me. And he used to sing to me . . .* (crying) *Oh, and every time I go to a wedding . . .* (wailing) *And they sing "Daddy's Little Girl." That's what he sang to me. . . . Oh, I can't stand it! Ohhhhhh. . . .*

Therapist: *Because what does it remind you of from your childhood?*

Loraine (as Alice): (crying) *Ohhhh, I never had a Daddy who sang to me. Ohhhh! He's been gone 22 years now, and I still miss him so much. . . .* (more quietly) *He was gentle. . . . And he was good to me, and he was good to the kids. He worked hard. . . .* (pause) *See, this is just what happens; what good is this?*

The loneliness of no-husband blends into the loneliness of no-Daddy, and for a moment Loraine/Alice abandons herself to it. Then she catches herself and wraps the shreds of her defenses back into place: "What good is this?" Talking about your hurt just makes you hurt more; crying just makes you feel worse. Perhaps Alice's crying, like that of many people who cry alone, brings no relief because of the absence of contact-in-relationship. To cry while experiencing the therapist's attuned response of compassion allows the grief to be shared and to dissipate. The therapist takes Loraine/Alice's question seriously and gives two truthful answers. Loraine/Alice responds to both.

Therapist: *This crying with me is perfectly good. This will help you die easier. And it's good for your daughter.*

Loraine (as Alice): *I told her what I want at my funeral. She's good to me; she listened.*

Therapist: *Well, she's been trying to understand you all her life.*

Loraine (as Alice): *She takes good care of me now.*

This is dangerous ground. As Loraine/Alice talks about her daughter's caretaking, she risks falling back into shame or denial or both about being angry at that daughter. Believing that her anger is bad, she allows it to break rather than to build relationship. The therapist must help her to turn that pattern upside down, to experience her anger as natural and as potentially contact-making. She decides to use a similar experience of her own to support and normalize Loraine/Alice's mixed feelings toward her daughter: a response to the relational need for mutuality.

Therapist: *But there's something your daughter can never understand. Alice, can I tell you a little story about how you and I are alike?*

Loraine (as Alice): *Sure.*

Therapist: *One day, back when my daughter was in kindergarten, I had a lot of things to do. But she had, the week before, complained that I hadn't taken her to the park. So I rushed to get my work done so I could take her to the park. And then she said, "I don't want to go. I want to watch television."*

Loraine (as Alice): *Yeah.*

Therapist: *And I said to a friend, who was visiting us, "Look at that! Doesn't she know what it means to have somebody take her to the park?" And my friend's* *comment was, "Nope. She doesn't know what it's like* not *to have somebody take her," because I'd been taking her to the park several times a week for several years. Nobody ever took* me *to the park. And my daughter will never, ever understand that, Alice.*

Loraine (as Alice): *That's right.*

Therapist: *My daughter will never understand how sad I felt when she wasn't grateful that I wanted to take her to the park. So there are things that your daughter will never be able to understand and appreciate about you. And I bet you get irritated with her when she doesn't understand.*

Loraine (as Alice): *I just stop.*

Therapist: *Stop what?*

Loraine (as Alice): *I just go to my room.*

Therapist: *But inside?*

Loraine (as Alice): *Burning.*

Given Loraine/Alice's comments about missing her husband and withdrawing to her room, the therapist assumed that the relational need for mutuality—to be in the presence of someone who understands Alice's sadness because she has had a similar experience—was now foreground. Sharing her own story served not only to respond to this need, but also normalized Alice's emotional response. The strategy appears to have had the desired effect: in that single word, "burning," Loraine/Alice expresses a world of feeling. This may be the moment the therapist has been waiting for, the moment when the introjected Alice has softened enough to be ready to begin the process of integration. Is Alice ready to talk to Loraine, really talk, about what really matters?

Therapist: *Burning? Oh, Alice, all that praying your anger away . . . might be just what's burning you up. Rather than saying, "I'm angry at the neglect. And I'm angry at the pain. And no amount of making it good for my kids is ever going to take my own history away."*

Loraine (as Alice): *Yes. . . . That's right. . . .*

Therapist: (pause) *But I think there's something you might want to tell Loraine now. Just imagine her sitting right here at your feet. Just the way she looked when she was young. Just look at that young Loraine. . . . Instead of praying things away right now, instead of pushing things in the past, talk to her from your heart. . . .*

Loraine (as Alice): (looking at an imaginary child Loraine) (pause) *You're so serious. . . . You ask so many questions . . . so many questions I don't know the answers to. I wish I knew all the answers.*

Therapist: *But you do know your experience.*

Loraine (as Alice): *I wish I could keep you from every hurt in the world. I love you so much. . . .*

Here is another facet of Alice's contact-disrupting decision. Keeping Loraine from hurt meant keeping her from knowing the self-defined "bad" parts of Alice, and that meant distance and distortion in the relationship.

Therapist: *Well, Alice, by keeping her from every hurt in the world, you've added some hurts. Sort of like raising a child in a germ-free environment, then when they go to school they get sick.*

Loraine (as Alice): *I didn't mean to do that; I'd never do anything to hurt her.*

Therapist: *I believe you. Say that to Loraine.*

Loraine (as Alice): *I would never have done anything to hurt you; I've done my best. You know I love you. I remember rocking you when you were little . . . and how wonderful it felt in the bathtub, your slippery skin, and then to say prayers together . . .*

Therapist: *Just like your mother never did with you.*

Loraine/Alice needs to come to grips with that contrast and to finally talk openly and honestly to her daughter about it. The Alice introjection is like a time-release capsule, swallowed down with all its bitterness and anger and shame closed within. Honesty now can melt the capsule and allow Loraine to integrate what is inside, washing away the toxins and absorbing the nourishing and enriching parts.

Loraine (as Alice): *Just like my mother never did for me; I never wanted you to have that emptiness. I never wanted you to wake up on Christmas morning to a cold house. I never wanted you to be hungry or ashamed of being dirty.*

Therapist: *But the problem, Alice, has been she never fully understands you.*

Loraine (as Alice): *I can live with that.*

Therapist: *But you do get irritated about it.*

Loraine (as Alice): *Well, yes I do.*

Therapist: *And that irritation hurts your daughter.*

What Alice will not do for herself, she will do for Loraine. She held back her anger and transposed it into an internal burning in order to protect her daughter. Now, trusting the therapist's wisdom (and her own emerging sense of self) she risks sharing what she has tried so long to disguise. It is still tentative, partial, guarded...but it is a beginning.

Loraine (as Alice): *(pause) I had a terrible life. And you don't know the half of it. And you don't need to know. It wasn't your life, it was my life.*

Therapist: *Now tell her about your anger.*

Loraine (as Alice): *It burns me inside, every day of my life. It's like a fire that will never, ever go away.*

Therapist: *And tell her how you act it out.*

Loraine (as Alice): *And I go around with my jaw set . . . and I snap at little things that don't matter.*

Therapist: *"In order to cover up . . . "*

Loraine (as Alice): *In order to cover up the big things. . . . And I never want to feel that way again.*

Therapist: *"And what I do to you, my daughter . . . "* (pause) *Want me to help you out?*

Loraine/Alice has been speaking with a new kind of honesty, but here she gets stuck: she cannot quite make the connection between how she has dealt with anger and how her daughter has been affected. Sensing her genuine confusion, the therapist is ready to help her understand, but only if Loraine/Alice wants her to. Loraine/Alice is still in charge of the process. Her response provides the therapist with permission to give an interpretation that will clarify the pattern for her.

Loraine (as Alice): *I don't know what I do. Help me know.*

Therapist: *Your anger invades her psyche. It violates her inner space. She's not in charge of the vibes between you and her. The anger you pretend isn't there, and pray away, invades and violates your daughter's psyche. And the more you try to cover it up, the more violating your anger is. . . . And your daughter who's so loyal tries to take it on and carry it for you. Like many loyal kids, whatever the parents deny, that's what the children bear. Now I heard your commitment never to hurt her.*

Throughout the work with Loraine/Alice, the therapist has been careful to stay neutral and to avoid any sense of partisanship in the conflict between mother and daughter. Now, as contact begins to be reestablished between Alice (introjected) and Loraine (as a child), the therapist can allow her core commitment to show: the work with Alice is for Loraine's benefit. While she will continue to respect and support Alice, the primary relationship is with Loraine, and the ultimate goal is to help Loraine to grow and heal.

Loraine (as Alice): *Yeah. . . .*

Therapist: *Then you must be honest about how angry you are. 'Cause to deny it is what will hurt her. . . .*

Loraine (as Alice): (pause) *I don't know how to do that.*

Therapist: *Why, Alice, you've been doing it fine for almost an hour. What you've done is superb. You might think you don't know how to do psychotherapy, but you've just been marvelous. So just say to her—*

Loraine (as Alice): *That's such a relief to me! To know I can do that right!*

Therapist: *Just talk to her right from your heart. Right—*

Loraine (as Alice): *I want to do what's right for you, Honey!* (crying)

The combination of reassurance, support, and encouragement strikes exactly the right note. As Loraine/Alice continues, her voice has a genuineness that has not been here before. She is finally able to share the depth of her pain, her anger, her fear—to share it with Loraine and to accept it herself.

Therapist: *And what's right is to be honest with her. No coverups at this moment.*

Loraine (as Alice): (crying) *Oh, I hated my parents; I never wanted you to hate me like that!*

Therapist: *Tell her what happens when you deny.*

Loraine (as Alice): *It poisons me. It poisons you! It's everywhere.* (sobbing loudly) *It's in the dishes, it's in the sofa! It's everywhere, it's in everything I make!* (wailing) *It's in everything I touch. . . . Ohhhhhhhh. Ahhhhhhh! It's everything! Ahhhhh* (screaming) *Ahhhhhh! Ahhhhh! Everything! Ahhhhhhhhhh!*

Therapist: *What a crazy house you grew up in as a kid! What a crazy house you grew up in, Mom!*

Loraine (as Alice): *Ahhh, God, it was awful!* (continuing to wail) *Oohhhhh! Ahhhh, so awful! Ahhhh, Oh, God, Oh God, help me, it was so awful! Ohhhh. . .*

Like a boil that has been lanced, the poisons finally come pouring out. Alice's wails and screams are an expression of years of accumulated misery. She sounds younger now; the cry is that of a lonely, needy child. The therapist invites her to put into words what has been buried far out of awareness and could never be experienced until she had reached this point of internal contact.

Therapist: *Try "Oh, Loraine, help me."*

Loraine (as Alice): *Oh, Loraine!* (sobbing)

Therapist: *'Cause that's what you've been saying for 40 years, isn't it?*

Loraine (as Alice): *Oh, Loraine. Oh, Loraine, help me* (deep sobs) *Help me feel better, ohhhhh! Make it okay! Ohhhhhh.* (wailing)

Therapist: *Yeah, keep going. Tell Loraine what her job was. . . .*

The little girl who was so neglected, but who could not get angry, never outgrew her deep need to be loved and cared for. This need that could never be acknowledged, much less expressed, was at the core of her way of being with others and permeated her relationship with her daughter. That relationship can be summarized in a few words: "I want you to take care of me, but we must both pretend that it isn't so, just as we must pretend that I'm not angry and afraid." The angry pretending that brought Loraine to the beginning of the previous session is now being replaced by contact. Creating a dialogue between the two parts, the introjected Alice and the contact-deprived child Loraine, allows them to be externalized, an important step in the integration process. The introjection is beginning to dissolve.

Loraine (as Alice): *Make it okay! For me!*

Therapist: *Tell her how she was supposed to make it okay!*

Loraine (as Alice): (sobbing) *Love me! And be there! For me! And . . . oh, God, hold me!* (wails)

Therapist: *Like a good Mama?*

Loraine (as Alice): *Ohhhhhhh! Ohhhhhh, God. . . .* (gradually calms) *Oh, God. What did I do?*

Therapist: *Tell her what you did. Tell your daughter what you did.*

Loraine/Alice has come through the emotional storm. Affectively, she has experienced and acknowledged her pattern, faced the forbidden parts of self, and reestablished internal contact. Without cognitive understanding, however, this is likely to be a transient phenomenon, an emotional catharsis that drains away after a few days or weeks, leaving the system essentially unchanged. The therapist now urges her to crystallize her experience by expressing it in words that Loraine can hold onto and use to guide her future growing and changing.

Loraine (as Alice): *I wanted you to make me okay. I wanted you to give my life a center and a purpose. I wanted you to make me warm. I wanted you to fill up the empty place. Oh, God, I wanted you to be healthy, I wanted you to shine. . . .*

Therapist: *"So that I . . . "*

Loraine (as Alice): *. . . so that there was something I did in this world that was right, so that I fixed it, so that I proved it, so that it was really, I really beat it, I really beat em!* (her clenched fist beats the arm of her chair)

Therapist: *Yeah, come on, show me with your hand.*

Loraine (as Alice): (pounding the chair) *I really beat em! I really beat em! I really got away from them, I really made it!*

Therapist: *Oh, Alice, what a wonderful hope! What a wonderful victory.*

Loraine (as Alice): (softly) *I really made it.*

Therapist: *The only problem was that by not talking about it straight and honestly, and with a good therapist, you invaded your daughter's psychic space.*

Loraine (as Alice): *I'm so sorry.*

Therapist: *Well, it's pretty easy to fix, Alice. If you're willing to fix it. Can I tell you how?*

Emotions, thoughts, and behaviors all interact, and each must shift into a new pattern if a piece of work is to be truly effective. Loraine/Alice has experienced major changes in affect, and has begun thinking about herself in new ways. The therapist is now about to suggest a way to translate the thoughts and feelings into behavior that will carry the therapy process out beyond the walls of the room in which they are working.

Loraine (as Alice): *Yeah.*

Therapist: *You've been fixing it here, in this room.*

Loraine (as Alice): *Yeah.*

Therapist: *You've been talking straight. And you've got a lot of straight talking to do before you die, lady. Instead of telling her she doesn't know the half of it, tell her the whole of it.*

It may seem odd to categorize Alice's "telling" Loraine as a behavior, since this "telling" is in fact an internal event for Loraine. To the extent that Loraine can reorganize her thought patterns to include a conscious reiteration of this work, psychologically experiencing her mother's active contact-making, though, the internal event will have the same sort of effect as an actual, externally observable conversation. In the weeks to come, this may facilitate the 49-year-old Loraine to fully engage the real-life, 85-year-old Alice in a genuine dialogue while there is still time to build a caring and intimate relationship that will be healing for them both.

Loraine (as Alice): *Yeah, I'll tell her.*

Therapist: *And maybe even tell her how you were jealous every Christmas. And every morning at breakfast. Or envious, or whatever word you want to call it.*

Loraine (as Alice): *Yeah. . . .*

Therapist: *Maybe "contrast" is a better word. When you would see what you would give to her, it would always be that painful, angry reminder of what you didn't get.*

Loraine (as Alice): *Yeah. . . .*

Therapist: *You're really a fine woman, Alice.*

Loraine (as Alice): *I do my best.*

Therapist: *I can feel that. And now you got a new best.*

Loraine (as Alice): *Yeah. . . .*

Therapist: *A new way to do it.* (pause) *Alice, are you open to hearing what Loraine feels?*

The final movement of therapy with an introjected other comes as the client in his or her own persona addresses the introjection. The client (who has been observing the work with the introjection throughout the session) now has an opportunity to express his or her feelings about the work, his or her own opinions and needs and understandings and point of view. This last shift also reestablishes the client as the person with whom the therapist is in relationship and allows for any needed mending of the therapeutic alliance.

Loraine (as Alice): *Yeah.*

Therapist: *'Cause perhaps she's angry at you too, which is going to be hard for you to understand. Probably even impossible for you to understand, when you think about how good she had it and how bad you had it. But at least will you listen to her experience?*

Loraine (as Alice): *Yeah. . . . I know I didn't listen to her.*

Therapist: *Well, maybe that's the one thing. . . . And I think you didn't talk enough.*

Loraine (as Alice): *Yeah, I don't talk.*

Therapist: *You didn't say, "I am angry today," or "I am jealous today." "Every time you get three dolls for Christmas, it's a reminder that I didn't have one doll in three years."*

Loraine (as Alice): *Or in all my life. Yeah. . . .*

Therapist: *Okay. You stay there, Alice; we're gonna bring Loraine over here.* (moves Loraine back to her original seat, facing "Alice's" chair)

Although not absolutely necessary for this sort of work, switching chairs is very useful in helping clients to establish a sensory ground for each of the entities or personas that they assume. From the "Alice" chair, Loraine sees Alice's view of the room, sits with Alice's posture, and feels the chair against Alice's body. When she moves back to her own chair, all of that changes, and the change makes it easier to "get out of Alice's skin."

Loraine: (deep sigh)

Therapist: *Just get out of Alice's skin. . . .*

Loraine: *Whhhhhhh. . . . Oh, God.*

Therapist: *That's a lot to carry.*

Loraine: *Oh, God. Ohhh.* (sigh)

Therapist: *What's behind that "Oh, God"?*

This is a perfectly neutral, open-ended inquiry. The therapist may guess at some of what Loraine is feeling and what her "Oh, God" is intended to convey, but she cannot know all of it, nor can she know what parts Loraine most needs to talk about. The inquiry expresses her wanting to know and gives Loraine freedom to begin wherever she wants.

Loraine: *Just how tight that was. Ohhh. How closed up and . . . whhhhh. . . .* (pause; she seems to be searching for words) *Oh, Mom. . . .* (sigh) *Don't know where to start. . . . I knew all this, but I didn't really know it, not until now . . . . I think I need some help. . . .*

With this request, the therapist is given permission to suggest an entry point; her suggestion is not an intrusion now, but rather a response to Loraine's request for help.

Therapist: *Try "Oh, Mom, you are a pretty angry woman. . . . "*

Loraine: *Oh, Mom, you are one angry woman.*

Therapist: *Now elaborate.*

Loraine: *You are so angry that . . . you're so angry that your skin burned. You do, it burns you up; you are burning up. All that skin you have, all around your neck and in your ears and . . . skin on your legs, like it's burning, burned. So burned.*

Therapist: *And tell her what it's like, living with that kind of burning anger.*

Alice has had her opportunity to talk about her experience. Now it is Loraine's turn; she needs to tell Alice what *her* experience was like, with no holds barred, free at last from the constricting demand that she take care of Alice, never hurt her, and make everything all right again.

Loraine: *It's really scary; it's really confusing. It's really . . . it's really sickening, it's really nauseating. It really nauseates me.*

Therapist: *Yeah.*

Loraine: *It's like when hair burns. Ugh. Smells. I never knew who you were mad at. I knew you were mad all the time, and you never . . .* (her voice trails off into silence)

Therapist: *And tell her what you know now.*

Loraine: *I know you were mad all the time. I know your burning anger, and I know it's not about me, and I know it's probably not even about Dad—and all the sarcastic little remarks you make and all that, that was just . . . little safety valves all the time, a little steam. And that's kinda exhausting.*

Therapist: *Um-hmm. It's exhausting.*

Loraine: *I don't want it. It's yours. I, I feel, I feel such compassion for you; there are parts of you in me that I love and value. The warrior. You don't know what a warrior you are.* (crying) *You don't know what a warrior you are! Don't even see the courage that it took to live what you lived. And how I have that, and what that means to me.* (cries) *But I can't do what you do. I can't do the anger. I can't do it. I just can't do it for you anymore.*

With the dissolving of the introject, the monolithic other becomes three-dimensional, human, someone with both good and bad qualities, and Loraine is free to pick and choose. She can value and be nourished by the parts of her mother that are loving and admirable, but she need not take with them the held-in anger. By asking her to talk more about her feelings toward her mother, the therapist will help her to sort through what she loves and what she resents, what she will keep and what she will reject.

Therapist: *Tell her about the part of her anger that you resent.*

Loraine: *Ahhh . . . well, I resent thinking it was my problem. I resent you not clearing that up for me. I resent you not owning that. Uhhh, I resent you letting me think that it was my job. I resent the anger in that house. I don't want to eat that anymore. I don't want it: the anger in the creases in the towels. I don't want that anymore. All the work, work all day, work, work, work, work, work, to make it okay. It is okay. It's been okay. I'm okay. . . . You don't have to work at that anymore. You could even fall apart if you wanted to.* (pause) *I'm not gonna hold you together, but you could fall apart. We'd be okay if you fall apart. Nobody really falls apart.* (sigh) *I resent you picking on my sister. I think she really got the shit end of the deal. I really resent that. Blame it on menopause; I don't know. I see women in menopause all the time; they're not nasty and sarcastic. I think you were too hard on her. I think that's why she had to move to California. Makes it hard to see her sometimes because we're so far away. I resent that. I think you pushed her away. She had to save herself. I don't like that.* (pause) *I don't know what else to say. I need help again.*

Therapist: *What are you feeling, Loraine?* (long pause) *You feel like you're holding—to me it feels as if you're holding something down.*

Loraine: *I guess I'm just sad. Feel caved-in, sad.*

Therapist: *Sad about . . . will you say more about that?*

Loraine: *I'm sad I can't fix it. 'Cause I love you.*

Giving up an old system, an old set of beliefs, is not without cost. The responsibility of being her mother's caretaker, the one who had to "fix" mother, was a terrible burden for Loraine to bear, yet giving it up means also giving up the possibility that it might just be accomplished. As long as Loraine could keep herself invested and involved in making Alice's life all right, she didn't have to feel the pain of knowing that it could never be fixed. Now, giving up the responsibility, she feels the sadness for Alice and for herself.

Therapist: *Yeah, tell her about being sad that you can't fix it.*

Loraine: *I'm sad that you're sad. I'm sad that . . .*

Therapist: *Tell her about the job she assigned you. The impossible task.*

Loraine: *Oh, yeah. Make Mom's life okay.*

Therapist: *Did you want to do that job?*

Loraine: *I think I wanted to, originally. Yeah. It was . . . gave me a way to be with her.*

Therapist: *Tell her.*

Loraine: *I thought the only way I could be with you was to take care of you, to carry your shit.*

Alice believed that the only way to be in relationship with Loraine was to hide her feelings, her neediness, her "shit." And Loraine, introjecting Alice's view, swallowed the "shit" as if her mother were some sort of Trojan horse, welcomed at the gate but carrying a deadly enemy hidden within. Loraine is realizing that the bargain was a sham and that the promise of relationship as a reward for keeping the pact was a promise made to be broken. Taking in Alice's way of being in relationship guaranteed that the relationship would never satisfy either mother or daughter. Now Loraine has come to the very edge of rejecting the bargain and of refusing to try to do Alice's impossible job. The therapist recognizes the approaching decision point and underscores what Loraine is moving toward.

Therapist: *Yeah, say that sentence again.*

Loraine: *To carry your shit. I don't want to carry your shit. I can't do it anymore.*

Therapist: *So return it to her.*

Loraine: *Well I am grateful to you. You gave me a lot. But I'm not grateful for that. You can have it. I feel like I filled up your buckets all the time, and you just dumped them out. You said, "Here, this is empty again." And I can't, uh, I can't do that anymore.*

Therapist: *"So what I'm gonna do is . . . "*

It is not enough for Loraine to declare that she's done with the old job. One cannot simply stop doing something; one must do something else instead. If this new decision is to be solid, if it is to make a difference, Loraine needs to be specific about how her behavior will change.

Loraine: *What I'm gonna do is . . . take care of myself. And I'm gonna tell you when, when you're coming in on me, when your expectations are not real. When I can't meet your expectations. I don't know if you're gonna get it. I don't care if you only did have an eighth grade education; I think you're smart as hell.*

Therapist: (pause) *Anything more you want to say to her?*

Loraine: *I don't think I need to say anything else right now. I think I need to do it for real—in life. I need to sit at the kitchen table with you and just be clear. And not cave in. And not go away.*

Loraine did go back and talk with her mother in a different way. The contact was not perfect, and the relationship was not miraculously transformed. After all, there is a real, flesh-and-blood Alice with whom Loraine must interact even after the Alice introjection has been dealt with. But the conversations with another were qualitatively different for Loraine: she was no longer constricted by the distorted views of her introjected mother, Alice, and no longer bound by an unspoken (and unspeakable) pledge to take care of mother by pretending that mother's deepest feelings did not exist. For the first time in her adult life, Loraine could be real in the presence of her mother.

As we have noted, therapy with an introjected other is impactful in at least two ways. Most obviously, it can effect changes in the introject itself, so that the intrapsychic restrictions and demands are modified. And, equally important, it provides the client with a chance to observe those changes. For Loraine, it was almost as if her mother had really gotten therapy, had really been able to connect with a caring therapist. Imagine what it would have been like for Loraine, as a little girl, to experience her mother softening and opening as her relational needs were appreciated and responded to in therapy, no longer using Loraine as both savior and scapegoat, and you can appreciate the intensity of this sort of process.

There are several elements that must be attended to if therapy with an introjected other is to be successful. First, the client must experience a strong therapeutic alliance with the therapist. Observing the understanding, empathic interaction between therapist and introjection, the client may feel abandoned, as if the therapist is somehow "taking sides" against the client and with the introject. The initial contracting (in Loraine's work, the clear understanding that the therapist is going to talk to Alice in order to help Loraine) helps to mitigate this danger, but that contract is believable, over the entire piece of work, only in the context of a strong initial therapeutic relationship.

Second, the therapist must be able to suspend his or her own knowledge of "reality" and allow the client to truly become the other. The therapist's ability to respond to that other with full contact and authenticity makes it possible for the client, in turn, to fully take on the persona of the introject. Without this suspension of "reality," the deliberate choice to believe the unbelievable, therapy with an introjected other would be mere playacting; it might possibly lead to some intellectual insights, but it could not have the profound intrapsychic and behavioral influence that we have seen in the work with Loraine.

Third, the client must have an opportunity to respond to the introjected other after the other has completed its work. The client always gets the last word. Failure to follow this guideline can seriously rupture the relationship between client and therapist; it can also weaken rather than strengthen the client's sense of self as separate from the introject.

Finally, the therapist must keep in mind the loyalty of a child toward its caregiver. This childlike loyalty is a fundamental part of a person's experience of an introjected other, no matter what the chronological age at which the introject occurred. However demanding, rejecting, or abusive caregivers may be, children still need them. Even if a client is ambivalent about the person who was introjected, confronting the introject too strongly or being in any way disrespectful is likely to evoke resistance, protectiveness, and a return to the old self-defeating pattern.

At the close of a successful piece of work with an introjected other, the client may feel a combination of relief and freedom as well as a deep sadness and compassion for the experience of the other. This is how Loraine seems to have reacted. With other clients, the effect of the work may be muted and held in abeyance while the client takes time to mull over and fully integrate the changes that have taken place. No matter what the initial reaction, however, the experiences arising from the work cannot be undone; the insights cannot be unlearned. Therapy that creates a shift in the psychological system of an introjected other is real. Often it is the next best thing to travelling back in time and providing therapy for the actual person who is the template for the introjection.

Some two years after Loraine had done the work described in these chapters, she wrote a letter to us describing her experience. Here, in part, is what she said:

> It was very important to me that my therapist treated "her" [Alice] with kindness and respect. Feeling this happening enabled me to surrender to the experience. I was amazed by the intensity of the sadness and anger

that erupted from me, and by the knowledge even as it happened, that it was not "mine."

The work had an immediate effect on my body. After the work, I experienced about a half hour of deep body tremors which seemed to me to be some kind of reorganization of my insides. The next morning I awoke peaceful and refreshed, and lay in bed a long time. Something was gone from me. I patted my body up and down. I had the sense of an energy body that had occupied the same place as my physical body for as long as I could remember and only now knew about because it was gone. I felt lighter. I have continued to lose weight slowly and permanently with no special effort since then.

But the real value of the work was in my relationship with my mother, who lived with me at that time until her death more than a year later. Her emotionality (anger and sadness about her early life, frustration about aging, reactions to daily living) no longer felt invasive to me; I no longer needed to deny my own tenderness for her that I felt so easily towards others but had not been able to express to her. I could feel my own feelings *and* be present to hers without feeling swamped, or trumped. I relaxed into loving her as I always wanted to, but had been too defensive to express fully and gently. Both the immediacy and the enduring quality of these changes in me led me to conclude that the parent interview had been a truly transforming experience. She, too, softened. Her last year was one of the best and her death was peaceful. I will always be grateful for the opportunity to do this work while she was still living.

Integrative Psychotherapy With Couples

Integrative psychotherapy utilizes a broad range of theoretical bases. It differs from a general eclecticism ("if it works, use it!") in that it synthesizes each idea, each technique, and each treatment plan into its own carefully developed framework. At the core of that frame of reference is the concept that interpersonal contact, as experienced in relationship, is a primary factor in psychological well-being. If there is a deficit in someone's psychological health, integrative psychotherapy assumes that damaged relationships are a part of that deficit. Similarly, we assume that healing damaged relationships and providing stable and healthy new ones helps clients to recover their psychological well-being. To the degree that one experiences contact in relationship, psychological health will be enhanced. And this principle holds for all relationships: for therapists and their clients, for parents and children, for friends, and for couples.

The notion of healing through relationship is particularly relevant for couple therapy, where the couple relationship is accepted at the outset as the focus of treatment. Although it is often the case that one or both members of a couple can benefit from individual psychotherapy, and an ideal treatment plan for couples includes opportunities for individual work as well, the third "client" in couple therapy is always the relationship itself. As couples learn how to be increasingly contactful, how to listen and respond to and nurture each other, their relationship changes; over time, these changes may significantly diminish the need for ongoing individual therapy.

314

In chapter 5, we introduced the concept of relational needs, and discussed in detail how attending to these needs is a major part of the therapist's task. Relational needs, though, are not exclusively, or even primarily, a phenomenon of psychotherapy. They are a part of every relationship, and the health of a relationship is largely a function of how and how well such needs are met. Relational needs are not "abnormal" or "pathological" or "immature"; they are a part of being human. Our relational needs are a constant in the background of our experiencing; when one of them emerges into awareness and is satisfied, it naturally returns to the background again. If the need is unsatisfied, however, it remains in the foreground until something is done about it; over time, such an unsatisfied need can impact nearly every aspect of our way of being in the world.

In a committed couple relationship, consistent failure to acknowledge and respond to one or more of a partner's relational needs will inevitably affect the whole relationship. Like an itch that cannot be scratched, the unmet need becomes more and more demanding. It transforms from annoyance to pain and from pain to fixation. The partner experiencing this pain tries to solve the problem, using the sorts of strategies that have worked in other situations. If these strategies prove ineffective, the partner is likely to resort to older and more childlike coping mechanisms based on the script beliefs that, out of awareness, govern our behavior and limit our spontaneity, our flexibility, and our creativity. The partner may experience frequent psychological regressions, exhibiting more and more archaic behaviors. His or her perceptions of the other partner, and responses to that partner, will be increasingly a function of his or her own need, frustration, and projections.

And what is the partner doing while all this is going on? Why, experiencing that his or her own relational needs are not being met, feeling frustrated, trying to cope, going through the same process. Together, the partners create an interactive downward spiral, with each partner reacting to the ineffective behaviors of the other. It is a familiar pattern for every therapist who works with couples, and the challenge is to reverse the pattern: to help each partner to recognize and respond to the other's relational needs, replacing self-protection with trust, trading fixed gestalten for spontaneity and contact.

Our model of a troubled relationship suggests that dysfunctional relationships have two primary characteristics: one or both partners tend, when trouble arises, to *project* (that is, to define the other partner in terms of past relationships) and to *regress* (to use increasingly primitive problem-solving strategies). It stands to reason that anything that will replace these kinds of responses with more satisfying and effective ones is likely to reverse the deterioration in the relationship. In order to accomplish this, we utilize four major therapeutic processes with couples: (1) observing the system to identify the contact disruption, the nature of the projection, and the archaic patterns; (2) "individual" work with each partner, in the presence of the other, to uncover and bring to awareness old, no-longer-useful patterns of perceptions, beliefs, and behaviors; (3) teaching the partners to identify and respond to relational needs; and (4) teaching the partners to use therapeutic inquiry with each other. Taken together, these processes can reverse the downward spiral so that partners can begin to support and lift each other rather than dragging each other down; in effect we use the relationship to heal the relationship.

Throughout our work with couples (and with individuals as well) we are particularly attentive to the ways in which relational needs are expressed and are responded to. You will remember (chapter 5) that we identified eight major relational needs: the need for *security*; for *valuing* of the function of one's affect, behavior, and mental processes; for *acceptance* from a protective and dependable other; for *mutuality*; for *self-definition*; to make an *impact* on the other; to have the *other initiate*; and to *express love*. These needs, and the responses to them, form a rich background to whatever the ostensible content of the therapy session may be. In couple work, expression of and responses to relational needs intertwine among the three participants: partner to partner, partner to therapist, and therapist to partner. (Yes, the therapist also experiences relational needs. Awareness of them is essential; expressing them may sometimes be therapeutic; noting how the client/partner responds to them can help all participants to understand the patterns and processes of relationship.)

In this chapter, we will present you with two transcripts, each taken from work done in an intensive couples' therapy group. While the overall process of the group involved much sharing and discussion among the couples, each piece of work presented here focuses on a single couple, with the group serving as audience and witness rather than actively participating in the work (although all group members participated in a discussion of the work, and how it applied to their own situation, after it was completed). The first transcript illustrates what we have described above as "individual" work with one partner in the presence of the other. The transcript begins with the couple discussing their problems, their wants, and their hopes in a rather general way, but it quickly focuses in on a central problem in the relationship: the amount and quality of contact between the partners. From that focus emerges a perceptual distortion of one of the partners, a projection based on the cumulative trauma of his early relationship with his mother. Typical of our work with couples is the way in which the therapist weaves the "individual" work, dealing with this partner's archaic issues, back into the couple's current relationship, and how this weaving-in opens the door to the next chapter of the overall therapy process.

Lois and Lester came to this session in the midst of a family crisis: Lois's father was ill and not expected to live. However, they do not begin by talking about Lois's father, but rather about the stresses and strains in their typical daily routine. Lester has said that he is bothered by Lois's constant working around the house; he cannot get her to relax and just enjoy being together. At the therapist's invitation, Lois talks to Lester about what prompts her to keep herself so busy:

Lois: *I can remember trying to be open, many times, with you. Then when I'm open, you get scared, and put the wall back. And that's so painful! So that I go into my work, 'cause it's safe. And then you say you want to be with me, and how come I go away, when you want to walk with me and be together. And then, it's like you want to just be with me and at work at the same time.* (pause) *Does that make any sense?* (pause) *Many times we'll be there together, and I share something with you. And I'm trying to get close, and it doesn't work, and it's painful; then I go away, do my own work. I enjoy it, too.*

Therapist: *So when he sees you, what he calls "overworking"—which I don't really know what that means, but you know what it means—when he sees you doing those activities, what do you want him to think about?*

Lois: *I would like it if he would just grab me and say, "Let's go and do something. I would like to be with you."* (pause) *I could easily be taken away from the working.*

Therapist: *So touch becomes important.*

One of the relational needs is the need to have the other initiate. Lois seems to be asking that Lester meet this need by coming to her and suggesting that they do something together. But she has just said that Lester does come and want to be with her. How is it that his behavior leaves her need unmet? It is possible that she is unable to fully take in Lester's communication, or to fully experience his contact, when it is only expressed in words. Depending on one's overall communication style and on the particular needs of the moment, one may be more receptive to auditory messages (spoken words), to visual information (seeing someone do something), or to kinesthetic stimuli. The therapist suspects that Lois's use of the phrase "grab me" is significant, that being physically touched may, in the situation she is describing, be the best way for her to experience contact.

Lois: *Yes.*

Therapist: *Because you emphasize the grabbing more than the words he might say.*

Lois: *Yes. And I want him to ask me, too, and be interested in where I am. Emotionally.*

In addition to having Lester initiate, Lois wants him to "be interested" in her and how she feels. She is expressing her need both for validation (of the significance of her emotions) and for self-definition (for Lester to help her know and express her individuality and uniqueness). The therapist puts all this together, along with Lois's preferred channel of communication, in the context of her need for contact.

Therapist: *So touch and emotions are where you're open for contact.*

Lois: *When you shut yourself in, with a newspaper, or going off to the bathroom, Lester, giving yourself that kind of space, I know in my head it's for taking care of yourself. But still. . . .*

Therapist: *You experience it as being left out?*

Lois: (to Lester) *And the cigarettes, and all that. I am so jealous of your cigarettes! I'm very jealous. Really. That's another level. They get between us.*

Therapist: *I want to know how that works. But something is happening right now with Lester. Lester, are you feeling ashamed right now?*

The therapist has been focusing on Lois and helping her to tell Lester specifically what she wants from him. Lois has responded by becoming more clear, more definite, and more emphatic. The danger, though, is that Lester may interpret the therapist's interest in Lois's needs as taking her side, sympathizing with her and blaming Lester. To forestall this, as well as in response to an abrupt change in Lester's facial expression, the therapist turns to him with a phenomenological inquiry.

Lester: *Yes, I do. I'm, uh, I recognize all those things. . . .*

Therapist: *But I was wondering if each time Lois says it, rather than hear it as useful information, it becomes one more piece of evidence that "something's wrong with me," which I think is at the core of most people's sense of shame. Do you hear this as criticism or a put-down of you?*

Lester: *I hear that, too. And I also hear a wish and a longing that she wants more of me. And, um . . .*

Therapist: *And does that feel shaming? Or does that feel interesting to you?*

Lester: *Scary, because I'm scared; I'm very, very scared to be rude to Lois. And I'm scared not to be able to, well, defend myself somehow. Or . . . well, define my integrity.*

This is the third time the therapist has inquired about Lester's sense of shame, and each time Lester has acknowledged it but immediately moved to something else. The message is, "I'm not ready to deal with this yet, even though I know it's there." To press the issue at this point would be to devalue the self-protective function of Lester's behavior and thus fail to respond to his relational need for security. Instead, the therapist accepts

Lester's change of focus, implicitly acknowledging that Lester knows best what he needs to explore.

Therapist: *Let's talk some more about that. How does that become frightening to you?*

Lester: *One is that I did notice how when Lois talks, I got defensive. So I think one thing is that I hear a lot of what she says as demands and expectations. And if I meet those expectations, there would be more expectations. So that's one thing.*

Therapist: *So part of it is the fear of getting interwoven. It's like . . . there'll be more and more.*

Lester: *Yes. More and more. And also it's like, if I had something that would, might give her what she wants, I should give it to her. And sometimes I just don't want to do that.*

Lester fears the unendingness of Lois's demands. One thing leads to another, and he protects himself by creating space between them. But the problem is not this simple; if it were, two intelligent people of good will would have solved it long ago. The fact that Lester and Lois's difficulties persist is ample evidence that there are many layers of meaning here. The therapist, however, makes no interpretation and does not hurry the work; she patiently continues to inquire.

Therapist: *So sometimes that paper really is to create the space for you.*

Lester: *And also the cigarettes. I know them. I trust them. I know I can't control them, in a way, but still, I can have them. I know they are there. And they control me in another way, but . . .*

Therapist: *But right now, let's talk about how those cigarettes provide a smoke cloud for you to be alone in. We can deal with the medical aspects later. I think what's really more important, and one of the reasons people go to something like the cigarettes, is you find some psychological comfort in them.*

To have the function of one's behavior, or one's psychological process, valued is a major relational need. One of the consequences of not getting this need met is a sense of shame: "I'm doing this thing that nobody approves of or sees any reason for, and therefore there must be something wrong with me." This could easily be happening to Lester with reference to his smoking, a behavior that is increasingly being characterized in our culture as unhealthy, inconsiderate, and offensive. By attending to the function underlying Lester's smoking, the therapist not only responds to Lester's relational need, but also moves to counter his sense of shame.

Lester: *Comfort. . . . Maybe, too, it helps my hunger. I mean, I also want . . . more closeness, more intimacy, and more emotional involvement. So in another way I'm also longing to be intimate, to let go, and to . . . puncture that control.*

Therapist: *So if each time you wanted a cigarette you went to Lois and said, "Hug me," what would be different?*

Lester: *Yes, you're right. I'm . . .*

Therapist: *Wait, I can't be right with a question.*

Lester's agreement is quick, and he seems about to move into self-criticism. Does he understand the parallel that the therapist has drawn, and, if so, does he agree that it fits for him? This is too important to slide past, and the therapist asks for clarification.

Lester: *What's different is, it's the same need, really. It's just a different. . . .*

Therapist: *But there's one thing the cigarette won't do: say "No."*

He did understand, and he does accept the interpretation: he uses his cigarettes as a substitute for contact with Lois. This pattern has all the characteristics of a fixed gestalt, in which one learns, over time, how to distract or pacify oneself in the presence of a need that is unmet in one's relationships. But why must the need be unmet? What does Lester use to keep himself from asking Lois to provide what he really wants? Continuing to value the function of Lester's behavior, the therapist suggests one possibility, which Lester expands on.

Lester: *"No?"*

Therapist: *Lois could say, "No."*

Lester: *Yes. That's right. And also, the cigarette could awake more hunger, of course, but then I have more cigarettes. And also Lois's attention could awake more hunger, and that scares me. I mean, what I, I notice now when I'm talking about it, I'm afraid. I probably have experienced, somehow, I don't know, but, um, responding to expectations creates more expectations. And that's what I, I think that's what I'm afraid of, too.*

Therapist: *You're afraid of it in her and you're afraid of it in yourself?*

Lester: *In me. That if I go, instead of taking a cigarette, I go and ask for a hug, and when I get that hug I want more. . . .*

Lester's initial fear, that Lois would ask for more and more, has now been transformed: it is Lester, not Lois, who is likely not to be satisfied. Lester was projecting his self-perception onto Lois and is now reclaiming that projection. He may be on the edge of discovering where the self-perception came from and how it protects him. This is delicate ground, and the therapist is careful to maintain her rhythmic and affective attunement, staying precisely at the point of Lester's growing awareness.

Therapist: *And then what?*

Lester: *Then she gives a "No." She's too tired; I'm asking too much, "you are too much."* (his hand makes a warding-off gesture) *Or . . .*

Therapist: *Do that again.*

Lester: (gesturing again) *"You're too much." "Don't disturb me."*

Therapist: *That's old. That's even before Lois.*

Attunement again: developmentally attuned, the therapist recognizes that Lester's gesture does not fit, somehow, with the comments of a mature adult. It is more a child's imitation of an adult response, suggesting Lester's expectation that his wishes will be disregarded rather than respected. The feelings that Lester is experiencing are likely to have more to do with old relationships than with current ones, and the therapist points this out.

The written words of the transcript give the impression that Lois, here and for the next several minutes of the work, is being ignored and left out. In fact, she is very much a part of the process. Both Lester and the therapist are keenly aware of her presence, and she in turn is attentive and involved in what is going on. Being able to watch while someone else deals with Lester, in a way that is still respectful of her, is meeting her relational needs for security and for acceptance by a strong, competent other.

Lester: *Yes.*

Therapist: *Who's doing that? "You're too much, Lester." "Your needs are too much."*

Lester: *Well, I think it's, uh, my hunger was more for Mother, I think. I think it's my mother who did it. Both Mom and Dad did, in different ways. But, uh, I think it's my mother.*

Therapist: *And are you feeling that now? That message from Mom?*

Lester: *No, I don't think so.*

Lester's response here is surprising, given the intensity of his gesture. Suspecting that he has automatically protected himself by repressing his painful affect, the therapist invites him to recapture it through fantasy.

Therapist: *Just close your eyes, and be her for a moment. Just imagine little Lester down there. And say that sentence again: "You're too much."*

Lester: *You're too much.*

Therapist: *Just imagine that little boy down there. What else do you want to say to him, Mother?*

Lester: *If I'm my real mother?*

Therapist: *Or at least the mother in your head.*

Lester: *Yes.* (his voice changes pitch and cadence) *Well, I . . . I'm too busy with myself. I don't have time for you like that. You're disturbing me. Now. . . .* (pause) *And also, you bring up too much in me.*

"You bring up too much in me"—is the mother in Lester's head saying that she, too, is never satisfied? Is the way that Lester characterizes himself, as always wanting more, a projection of mother's characterizations onto him? It does seem possible, but it is not certain; the therapist will be careful not to suggest the interpretation herself, but will let Lester find his own way to it.

Therapist: *Keep going, Mother. Tell little Lester. . . .*

Lester: *Too much. And I, I feel guilty. I feel very guilty, doing that. But I, um, I know I should pick you up. I should listen more to you. But there are all the other kids, and, uh, it's also me.* (he gestures again) *Too much, just for me.*

Therapist: *Now look at the little boy—just be that little boy . . . oh, that little boy who's gotta cope with Mama's hand gesture.*

Having recaptured the scene in fantasy and intensified it by putting his mother's refusal into words (and into gesture), Lester can now begin to bring into awareness the part of himself that needed more contact with mother and could not get it. Fully experiencing that need-not-met will, in turn, allow him to recover the coping pattern that he developed over time in order to survive the pain of relational deprivation. Lester's story is typical of cumulative trauma, in which there is no single dramatic event but rather a repeated deprivation of contact that, over months and years, creates the expectation that this is how people are and how life is. Why ask, when the answer is always "No"? Why try, when the outcome is always failure? Leading Lester into this regression provides a way for him to experience a "Yes," a successful outcome, and thus challenge the expectations that he has held for so long.

Lester: *Yes, I don't need to be with you, very long. I just want you to be there for a while, not a whole lot. I don't need a lot. Just a while.*

Therapist: *Keep going, Lester.*

Lester: *To be there, too . . . to be seen with my needs, and my . . . my longing. My love.*

In refusing to attend to him, Lester's mother failed to satisfy not just one but probably all of his relational needs. He did not feel security with her; she did not value the function of his responses. She was not accepting, and she chose to project her own self-image onto him rather than to explore honestly the ways in which they were the same. She did not support his individuality and did not allow him to have an impact on her. She certainly did not initiate contact. And, as Lester reveals here, she did not allow him to express his love.

Therapist: *Yes. Say that again: "I want you to see, Mama. . . ."*

Lester: *I want, just want to be received. And not be—I am not too much.*

Therapist: *Louder.*

Lester: *I am not too much.*

Therapist: *Keep talking to her.*

Lester: *I, really, I, I'm very used to small pieces. And I'm also pretty satisfied with that. So I wouldn't swallow you. I'm scared to death of swallowing anybody I wouldn't take all of you.*

With his declaration, "I am not too much," Lester seems to be breaking though the old pattern and experiencing himself in a new way. His next response, though, has an apologetic cast to it, an almost a pleading quality, as if he were promising, "Please, I won't ask for much. Just give me a little bit and I'll try to be satisfied with it." That's the old pattern, the disavowal of what he really feels, and the therapist is quick to counter it with a direction to express the opposite.

Therapist: *"But I want—"*

Lester: *I want some time to hold on. I want some pieces.*

Therapist: *Without being interrupted.*

Lester: *Without, um, something else being more important.*

Therapist: *"Hold me for the length of time it takes to smoke a cigarette."*

This is not exactly an interpretation, but it is certainly an invitation. By calling attention to one way in which the cigarette smoking is similar to what Lester wants from his mother, the therapist subtly suggests that one may be a substitute for the other and invites Lester to consider the possibility.

Lester: (chuckle) *Yes, about that. Or maybe two cigarettes.*

Therapist: *And how many cigarettes do you have a day?*

Lester: *About 20.*

Therapist: *So if she held you 10 times a day, the length of time it took to smoke two cigarettes . . .*

Lester: *Yeah, but I wouldn't want her 10 times a day.* (pause) *I also enjoy it. I really enjoy, also, being alone.*

Lester has made the connection. At a deep affective level, he has sensed his longing for contact and how he expects rejection and turns to self-comfort instead of reaching out. His last remark, made in a quiet, reflective voice, suggests that he is seriously reexamining his need for alone time and separating that which is his own from that which he adopted out of the need to deal with the cumulative trauma of contact deprivation. With this new awareness, he is ready to come back to his life partner to renegotiate how they can now be together. The therapist directs him to begin this next phase of the work.

Therapist: *Now look at Lois, Lester. And see if what you've said to Mom, you need to say to Lois.*

Lester: *Yes. I only want small pieces of you. And . . .* (pause) *But I'm afraid that you want big pieces of me. That's what I would say to my mother. But I don't think, I don't . . .*

Lois: (pause) *What do you mean by "big pieces of me"?*

An excellent inquiry. Lois may have begun to learn the importance of inquiry from her observation of the work between Lester and the therapist. The safety and protection of the therapist's presence may also allow her to feel secure enough to inquire, rather than assume that she understands what Lester means and leap to defend herself. By inquiring, she not only enhances the accuracy of their communication, but by valuing his meaning enough to ask about it she also meets Lester's need for self-definition.

Lester: *That my life will be used up, that I would have to really fight to get away.*

Therapist: *"So if I come to you for a hug, instead of smoking a cigarette . . . "*

Lester: *You might catch me.*

Therapist: *Ask her, "Would you please let me go afterward?"*

With couples, the old patterns exert an almost hypnotic pull. It is easy to fall back into old misunderstandings, old expectations, and old ways of trying to get relational needs met even while expecting that they will not be met. Couple therapists often find it necessary to coach and remind partners of what they have just learned, as they begin to put that learning into practice. Implicit in this suggestion from the therapist is the reminder that Lois is not Lester's mother, that he can risk being direct about what he wants. "Try it," the therapist is saying. "Experience for yourself that this is different. And let Lois experience the difference in you, as well."

Lester: *Well, if I ask you, Lois, I get what I want. But, um, what I'm afraid of is when you ask me. I'm, I'm afraid that you won't let go afterwards.*

Lois: *And I am also afraid. . . . For me, you never stay where we started. And I remember when you told me, "You'd better change or I'll just go live with Stuart* [one of their grown children], *and we'll see if you can manage that." And that was sort of what I was used to. I'm afraid to be dependent, or, anyhow, I used to be.*

Lester: *I know that.*

Therapist: *And it sounds as if you're ready to depend on him more.* (pause) *Tell him about that, Lois. Out of your own words, your own experience.*

Lois's recollection of being hurt and rejected by Lester signals a rising relational need in her. The focus has been on Lester long enough; Lois now needs to be acknowledged and attended to. The therapist responds to her need, but does so by affirming the positive changes Lois is making, rather than her remembered pain. Her tears, in response to this intervention, appear to be tears of relief, not sadness. Someone does understand; someone will listen; someone does value her experience and accept her for who she is. This is the security she needs in order to respond to Lester with new behaviors of her own.

Lois: (pause; her words are unintelligible; she is crying)

Therapist: *"And when my father dies, what I need from you, Lester, is . . ."*

Lois: (sobs; long pause) *And when my father is dying, what I need from you is that you understand . . . and are with me. Not saying, "You're making a big thing of it."*

Lester: *You don't—you don't take care of yourself around that.*

Therapist: (pause) *Did he just miss you, Lois, or did he connect with you?* *(pause) Did you just get missed?*

Lois's nonverbal response to Lester's comment was incongruous: rather than accept his concern about her taking care of herself, she drew back and quite visibly closed herself in. Both the therapist and Lester need to know what has happened and what new or old wound has been opened.

Lois: *I felt hurt. . . .*

Lester: *By what? What hurt you? How did you hear me?*

Lois: *I heard you saying that, um, me being so ambivalent about maybe going to be with Dad . . . and you're saying I can go, it's all right . . . and it's like when I'm trying to fight for what I need, I'm too strong for you. And suddenly I thought of a dream I had last night. There were two bowls for cat food under the table, and one of the cats wanted food and the other one just went away so the first one got both. . . . I need you with me, and when I come under the table, you give up your need, and you come and take care of me. I keep on fighting nowadays, and I do try to win. But I don't want your bowl to be empty. I need to keep on fighting, but I don't want to be too strong for you.*

Lester: *I'm fighting for my bowl, too. And, um, what I, what I am angry at is not the ambivalence. . . . Yes, it is the ambivalence, but it's not that—your father dying is a big thing, of course it is. There's a lot of emotional . . . and you did say* *goodbye; you said what your father wanted was not to, he wouldn't want you to go to him. And where I get angry is that I believe, I think, as a daughter, that you go home because you're mad at your sister. And that's where I get . . .*

Another door opens, and another sequence begins. Lester and Lois will now begin to unravel their differing perceptions of Lois's entanglement in her family of origin and will use the gains they have already made to make that unraveling a different kind of interaction than it has been in the past. Lester has recognized a pattern in himself that leads him to believe that others (especially Lois) think he's too demanding, too needy, too much. Acknowledging that self-perception, and how he projects it onto Lois, frees Lois to talk more freely about her own ambivalence: her desire to be dependent and her need to stand up for herself; her need to fight and her equally strong need not to dominate.

When a pattern that has been out of awareness is recognized, alternative possibilities can be recognized as well. The client no longer experiences his or her reactions as inevitable and necessary, but sees them as old solutions and decisions that may now need to be updated. For a couple, this kind of shift brings the possibility of new ways of relating and new freedom to see and respond to one's partner in a different way.

The hours and days following such a new awareness are critical in the development of a healthier couple relationship. There is often a kind of exhilaration and a sense of renewed hope and optimism that follows a major therapeutic step, and this positive energy can fuel significant changes in the pattern of interaction between the partners. Also, the best time to learn and practice new responses is when the old patterns have just been brought to awareness, when the log jam has shifted and a new tangle has not yet formed. Teaching the skills of inquiry, described at the beginning of this chapter as the fourth facet of integrative psychotherapy with couples, is perhaps most easily accomplished during the "window" that follows a major therapeutic gain for one or both partners.

Even at the most optimal moment, learning to replace old, self-protective behaviors with an attuned and involved process of inquiry is not easy. Couples bring a lot of baggage into their therapy: their own childhood history of needs-not-met, their accumulated resentments toward their partner, their fears of being abandoned or controlled or of being found unacceptable in some deep, too-awful-to-contemplate way. Working individually with each partner in the presence of the other, as we saw in the Lester and Lois segment, allows the therapist to model the inquiry process while exploring these issues. The individual work serves two purposes: it helps each member of the couple to understand both self and partner, and it demonstrates the skills that they will both need when the therapist is no longer available to them. Often, the therapist will invite the couple to practice inquiring of each other, rather than listening while the therapist does the inquiring. At this point, the therapist may become a coach, suggesting, correcting, and intervening to teach this couple what they will need to do in order to continue the inquiry process on their own.

In teaching couples how to inquire of each other, it is necessary to bring them back, over and over, to the basic focus of the inquiry: the partner's internal experience. Whether inquiring directly about the partner's phenomenology, about his or her relationship history, or about the ways in which he or she learned/decided to cope, it is the partner's own unique experience that is central to the inquiry process. Most couples find it very hard, at first, to maintain this focus. The inquiring partner may stray into establishing "reality" ("But it didn't happen that way!") or into self-defense ("I never said that!"), or he or she may switch from a focus on the partner to an expression of his or her own views about the issue. The inquiree may become anxious, may misunderstand the questions, and will often shift from internal experience to external events. And each of these sidetracks is a potential topic of inquiry in itself: "What happened for you just then?" "What was it like for you to have me say that?" "What are you wanting from me right now?"

Assisting a couple in the inquiry process is a demanding task. There are so many strands to keep track of—being attuned to each partner's emerging experience, staying in touch with one's own feelings and imaginings and sensations, tracking the pattern that is being created between the partners, attending to the technical details of effective inquiry, making decisions about if and when to encourage the partners to describe their own phenomenological experience or to move back into inquiry about the other. In the next transcript, you will find first one and then another of these strands coming to the foreground.

Betty and Sally, a lesbian couple, have come to this group therapy session asking the therapist to help them learn to "communicate" with each other. After some discussion of what each partner hopes to gain from the work, the therapist begins to talk about the concept of "presence" and its importance in the inquiry process. This discussion is partly for the benefit of all the group members, and partly to set the stage for the work that Betty and Sally are about to do.

Therapist: *Presence is really twofold and almost contradictory. I talk about "presence" as decentering yourself. It's a way of making your own needs, your own desires, your own outcomes, your own knowledge, unimportant for a period of time. At the same time, however, to be present requires all the richness of our history, everything we've ever learned, everything we've ever read, all of our experiences, our own pains and agonies as well as our joys and pleasures. And it's a*

combination of going back and forth between the two, tapping into all of our expe-
riences as a rich resource library, and then almost forgetting it and being totally
interested in the other. And then coming back to our own experience and using it as
a resource to connect with the other. So it's that combination of free-associating
within ourselves, to everything we've ever experienced, and then dropping it and
focusing on the other.

I particularly wanted to emphasize that, Betty, because I think you have a his-
tory of forgetting yourself. Part of presence is knowing yourself fully, but then, for
the moment, dropping it, as you center on the other. So with you I'm also going to
emphasize the richness of your own history that you bring to this relationship.
Keep in mind, now, that if you're going to really inquire about her phenomeno-
logical experience, it's not about the content. It's about how she experiences it, the
meaning she makes, what she feels, what she remembers . . . all the stuff that goes
on inside her head that we cannot observe. That we can only get by inquiring. (to
Sally) *Are you ready? For her to know you?*

Sally: *Yeah.*

Therapist: *And for you to know you, through her knowing you?*

Sally: *Yeah, okay.*

Betty: (pause, then softly) *Where would you like me to begin knowing you?*
What part of you—

Therapist: (interrupting) *One question at a time! Your first question was just*
fine.

Beginning inquirers often string several questions together in an effort
to get it just right or as a way of talking to themselves about what they
want to say. Too many questions at once do not meet the relational need
for security. They can confuse and derail the partner, who may get caught
up in trying to keep track of all the questions, and then not know which
one to answer first.

Sally: *Uh, where would I like for you to start knowing me. . . .* (pause) *I'm*
wondering if I'm confusing "where" with "when"?

Betty: *Hmmm.* (to the therapist) *I think that's why I started to rephrase the*
question.

Therapist: *Okay.*

Now that Betty has characterized her double question as "rephrasing,"
the therapist does not object. Sally's comment suggests that Betty may
indeed need to come up with a better way to help Sally begin to explore
her inner experience.

Betty: (pause, still very softly) *Let me try another question. What part of you*
do you want me to get to know first?

Therapist: (pause; Sally stares at her hands) *Sally, what's really important here is your discovering your answer. It's not about a "right" answer. It's about your discovering of yourself, with her stimuli.* (to Betty) *Ask her the question again.*

Sensing that Sally's cognitive processing is getting in the way of reporting on her experience, the therapist coaches her on how to be an inquiree. The therapist's comment not only gives Sally information about what is expected of her, but it also gives her permission to let go of her need to be "right" and to look good. Even a "wrong" answer is valued.

Betty: *What part of you do you want me to get to know first? Right now?*

Sally: (pause) *I just go blank.*

Betty: *Can you tell me what was in your hand when you were looking at it just now?*

Sally: *I think it's the young part of me.* (somewhat sharply) *'Cause you only see the grown-up.*

Sally's tone of voice lends an accusatory quality to her statement, and Betty reacts nonverbally as if she has been criticized. Her body stiffens, and her expression is one of surprise and hurt. To forestall a defensive response, the therapist suggests a new line of questioning.

Therapist: (to Betty) *Now focus on what you do in your behavior, that she only gives you the grown-up.* (pause) *Just start, "What's my behavior that I only get the grown-up part of you?"*

Betty: (carefully) *What do I do that makes you only want to give me the grown-up part of you?*

Sally: *Whatever it was you just did then . . . tone of voice, I'm not really sure, feels a bit patronizing. Feels a bit not sure what's going to happen next. Not sure whether you're going to be attacking, or turning . . .*

Betty: *Sort of like, what comes over in my voice isn't clear?*

While Betty has not quite captured Sally's exact meaning, she is focusing on trying to capture it, rather than on defending herself. She is learning how to inquire!

Sally: *Intonation.*

Betty: *How does my intonation—*

If Betty continues along this line, though, she may switch the focus from Sally's experience to her own. To keep this from happening (and to keep Betty from feeling criticized), the therapist shares her perception and makes a suggestion.

Therapist: (interrupting) *Can I help you?*

Betty: *Yes.*

Therapist: *I think what she's saying is the way you're cautious with her. I think if you'd just talk much more matter-of-factly, and directly. . . . I know you're trying to be empathetic, right?*

Betty: *Yeah.*

Therapist: *And you're trying to be protective.*

Betty: *Yeah.*

Therapist: *I think when you get protective, she thinks something must be wrong, that you're being protective. And so she gets more scared. Try just a matter-of-fact way of talking to her.*

Betty: (laughing) *Yeah. . . .*

Therapist: *Have you noticed that when I talk to her matter-of-factly, she relaxes more? I think sometimes people who are used to protectors trying to protect them from some terrible danger, um, respond to somebody's protective voice as though a danger must exist. See what happens if you talk to her matter-of-factly.*

Sally: (to the therapist) *Boy, that feels so much better! It's like, I was waiting for the ax to fall. . . .*

Betty: (pause; to the therapist) *Yeah, I don't very often . . . but I think I forgot the question.* (she chuckles)

Therapist: *So what is it in my behavior that you don't like?"*

Betty: (in a more conversational tone) *What is it that I do, the way I say things—*

Sally: (interrupting) *Well, you talk in intellectuals all the time. And it's like you're creeping around. And then I think, "What the heck is she creeping around for? Does she think I'm going to explode, or something else is going to happen? Do I need to creep around?" And I don't want to creep around. Um . . . and it's like, like I don't know whether you're going to shoot me or become a tiny baby. Or that 2-year-old that stiffens her legs and goes, "I-want-I-want-I-want-all-of-you-I-want-all-of-you!" And you can't have all of me. I don't want to give all of me to you.*

The "matter-of-fact" tone worked: Sally is much more animated and more forthcoming than she has been earlier, almost too much so for Betty, who now looks tearful. The therapist invites her to continue inquiring, rather than reacting emotionally.

Therapist: (pause, then prompts Betty) *"What do you want to give me?"*

Betty: *What . . .*

Therapist: *Matter-of-fact!*

Betty: *Yeah. Okay. So what do you want to give me, then?*

Sally: *I want to give you* what *I want to give you* when *I want to give you!*

Betty: *And that—what is that?*

Sally: *I want to give you my excitement, and my creativity, and my craziness, and my sadness, and my anger; and I want, I want to give you . . . whatever I want to. But there has to be that bit that sometimes I don't want to give you all of me. I want to give to other people, too.*

By inquiring, rather than defending, Betty has met Sally's relational need for self-definition, which is the opportunity to express who she is as a unique individual. She responds by expressing herself fully and strongly. In helping her to do so, however, Betty must temporarily ignore her own needs. These needs, for security (Sally's demandingness is not security-making for Betty) and acceptance, have now intensified to the point where Betty may not be able to maintain her focus on Sally. Betty may also be believing that she is being criticized and attacked, while Sally has become more comfortable and spontaneous. It is time for a switch and time for Betty to be given a chance to explore and express her own phenomenology.

Therapist: (to Sally) *Now, you make an inquiry. . . .*

Sally: *Uh. . . . So how is that for you?*

Betty: *I'm really struggling to stay adult and stay in there.*

Sally: *Right. . . .*

Therapist: (prompting Sally) *"Tell me more about it. . . . " This is decentering from* you *now.*

Sally: *Yeah, yeah.*

Therapist: *And making her the center.*

Sally: *Um, so . . . tell me more about that.*

Sally's willingness to switch to a focus on Betty, rather than engaging in the usual struggle about whose experience is more valid or important, encourages Betty to move more fully into her affect.

Betty: (close to tears) *When you get big, and you start doing all those things . . .* (pause) *I think I become unimportant then. And I want to be important to you.*

Sally: (whispers) *And you* are. . . .

How difficult it is to stay with a partner's process rather than jumping in to ease his or her pain! Sally's response to Betty's tearful longing is almost reflexive. But pain-easing here is like the aspirin that masks the symptoms of a disease: it can get in the way of discovering what is really happening. Betty's primary relational needs here are for acceptance and self-definition, and the therapist invites Sally to attend to them.

Therapist: (to Sally) *Too much reality, too soon. Go three or four more inquiries about being important.*

Sally: *Okay.* (to Betty) *So, what does being important. . . . So tell me about what being important means.*

Betty: (sigh) *It's taking time with me. And sharing an interest in what I do. Showing that I can do things, so that you can see that I can do things. And then it's getting all mixed up, because I'm getting all mixed up now between you and my mother. I know it. That's why I want you to do it, because she didn't do it.*

Sally: *So tell me what it is that I'm doing to make you get mixed up.*

Betty: (pause) *I really like that question. I wish to God I could find the answer.*

Sally: *Just keep looking at me. My body? My voice? My eyes? My hands? Check me out.*

Betty: *It could be your voice. . . . It could be your voice. It's not your hands. It's not things like that.*

Sally: *Okay.*

Betty: *You do what she does to me. You say, "Right, Betty, pull yourself together, and give me the right answer. Stop being a child and give me the right answer, 'cause you know what it is really." You do that to me. That's what I hear you doing to me. That's when I say, "You're criticizing me."*

Sally has been doing very well, but here she finds herself stuck. She looks at the therapist with a "What-do-I-do-now" expression, and the therapist helps her to move Betty from "You do it" into "I need something."

Therapist: (prompting Sally) *"So are you saying what you need from me is . . . "*

Sally: *Ah. So you're saying you need for me not to say to you, "Pull yourself together"?*

Betty: *I need for you not to expect me to get it right. 'Cause I don't always do it your way.*

Sally: *No, you don't.*

Betty: *That doesn't mean to say I'm wrong.*

Sally: *No, no. There is a "your way" and there is a "my way."*

Betty: *Yeah.*

They are stuck again. Sally may be sliding into searching for a solution to the problem, or she may be struggling with her desire to talk about her own experience or defend her behavior. Whatever is going on for her, it is taking her attention and her focus away from Betty. Even the therapist's prompt does not really bring her back.

Therapist: (prompting Sally) *"So are you saying . . ."*

Sally: *Yeah—God, this is hard! So are you saying . . . Uh . . . I don't know what to say here.*

Therapist: *What is she saying to you? You've got to stay focused on her. What is she saying to you?*

Sally: *Uh . . . I'm going to get this wrong, wait a second. . . . So are you saying to me that—*

As the inquirer, just as when she was the inquiree, Sally is concerned with getting "it" right. She is reluctant to venture a guess that might not be correct. And her struggle to find that "right" answer is interfering with her focus on Betty. The therapist gives the needed permission.

Therapist: (interrupting) *It's all right to get it wrong. 'Cause she'll correct you.*

Sally: *Yeah, I get it.*

Therapist: *The question built into it is "Am I wrong?" So "Are you saying . . ." and let her correct you. Assume you're wrong, and say it.*

Sally: *I don't know what the question is, though. I haven't got a question.*

Therapist: *"Are—you—saying—"* what did she say to you?

Sally: *That sometimes she's going to get it wrong, and there's a "her way"—and no, she's not going to get it wrong. Her way isn't wrong.*

Therapist: *"So are you saying that you want me to value your way? Even when it's different from mine?"*

Sally: (to the therapist) *And it's really interesting, 'cause right now there's a little fight going on in me, saying, "But I do do that."*

This response is virtually inevitable; if it is not made out loud, it is experienced internally by most partners somewhere in the inquiry process. When our partners describe an experience that is contrary to our own, we almost automatically move to argue with or correct them. Arguing or Correcting, though, is destructive of the inquiry process, and the therapist urges Sally to decenter and refocus on Betty.

Therapist: *Drop it! Get out of your own experience. Get into hers.* (pause, then softly) *Get out of your own experience. This is not about reality; this is about her experience. Here is what doesn't make the relationship work. Get out of your experience, Sally. Right now make Sally not count.*

Sally: *But I've spent so long saying I do count!*

Therapist: *I know. That's the first half of psychotherapy. This is the second half. Go ahead, and keep it a question.*

Sally: *So, what you're saying is, what you're asking me to do is, to value your way.*

Therapist: *"Is that right?"*

Sally: *Is that right, or is that wrong?*

Betty: *Yes. I want you to do that.*

Sally: *Right. So, what would I be doing or saying so that you knew that I was doing that?*

Therapist: *Beautiful question!*

It *was* a beautiful question. Moreover, Sally has handled the therapist's confrontation very well indeed, and the therapist's appreciation here is also an acknowledgment of Sally's willingness to put herself to one side and focus on Betty.

Sally: (to the therapist) *See, I can do it!*

Therapist: *I know you can! You've just got to make yourself not important for the time being.*

It looks so easy—and appearances are so deceptive! Beginning therapists have a difficult enough time learning to be effective inquirers with their clients. It is enormously more difficult to keep the inquirer focus when you are talking with someone with whom you are emotionally involved. Moreover, the skills of inquiry, as we teach them to partners in couples therapy, are in sharp contrast to what a client often learns in individual therapy. Individual therapy teaches clients how to be more self-aware and how to enhance their intrapsychic contact. It does so, of course, within the context of enhanced interpersonal contact between client and therapist, but the therapist is doing the lion's share of the work in maintaining that interpersonal connection.

Now, in the couples work, everything is turned around. Instead of focusing on what goes on inside, on the thoughts and feelings and expectations that have been long buried, the client is invited to put all that aside for a period of time and focus fully upon his or her partner. An inevitable correlate of putting oneself aside is that one's own relational needs must be set aside as well. As we have seen, when a relational need is not responded to, one tends to fall back on archaic and often childlike coping behaviors. Such behaviors, and the narrowing of awareness and contact that they always include, are antithetical to the process of inquiry.

So here, in a nutshell, is the dilemma of partner-to-partner inquiry: somewhere in the process, sooner or later, the inquiring partner will experience a need-not-met and must either shift focus to take care of it (thereby abandoning the inquiry) or risk sliding into old relationship-destroying behaviors. What makes the situation even more hazardous is that, at the point when the break is most likely to occur, the inquired-of partner may well have allowed himself or herself to become more open and vulnerable, so that the effect of being abandoned or attacked is even greater than it would be otherwise.

It sounds like a recipe for disaster, and without the kind of therapeutic structure and safeguards provided by the integrative model, it might well be. We outlined that structure at the beginning of this chapter: (1) observing the system to identify the contact disruption, the nature of the projection, and the archaic patterns; (2) individual work with each partner, in the presence of the other, to uncover and bring to awareness old, no-longer-useful patterns of perceptions, beliefs, and behaviors; (3) teaching the partners to identify and respond to relational needs; and (4) teaching the partners to inquire with each other. The therapist's diagnostic observations help him or her to anticipate where the affective triggers may be for each partner and to respond effectively to signals of distress before the partner's relational need-not-met becomes unmanageable. The individual work helps partners to loosen the grip of their archaic coping patterns, to recognize those patterns in self and in partner, and to begin to develop alternative responses. One of which, of course, is to recognize the partner's relational need, as well as his or her own, and to inquire about that need.

Inquiry, in fact, is a highly effective alternative to most of the contact-disrupting responses that people develop in order to deal with the pain of unmet needs. It can only be used, however, if the automatic, knee-jerk quality of the old protective pattern is interrupted. Sally's protest, toward the end of our transcript, voices it well: one of the defenses she has learned over the years is to fight back, to become the aggressor, and to spit and snarl and demand attention. This has been her way of saying "I *do* count!" and it is frightening to give it up, especially when she feels threatened.

In this chapter on couples' therapy, we have presented the work with Lois and Lester first because the kind of work done with them generally precedes the kind of inquiry coaching done with Betty and Sally. Only after clients have at least begun to deal with their projections and recognize their patterns, and only after they have experienced the therapeutic relationship, in all of its richness, and feel safe and supported by the therapist, will they be able to risk "not counting" and making their partner's experience more important than their own.

13
CHAPTER

The Keyhole Revisited

In the transcripts presented in the previous five chapters, you have seen a wide variety of interventions. The therapist's inquiry, informed by attunement and involvement, has followed the clients' own exploration and has focused on many different aspects of their thoughts and feelings and memories. There has often been so much going on that it has been difficult to keep track and to find a framework that will provide a pattern for it all.

One of the things that makes real-life, "in the trenches" psychotherapy so complicated is the variety of entry points that the therapist may use in working with a client. Because integrative psychotherapy values an integrated approach, an approach that takes into account the whole array of arenas within which people relate to self and others, we are able to move among different focuses, taking advantage of the client's shifts from one kind of contact to another. And clients do shift, from a willingness to examine behaviors, to a greater interest in affect, to an exploration of relationships, or bodily awareness, or cognitive understandings. As you saw in the transcripts, there is a broad range of possibilities, and the attuned therapist uses them all, at one time or another. Indeed, "using them all" is an important guideline, for a facet not attended to will tend to become isolated and inaccessible, remaining as a kind of hardened knot in the gradually untangling skein of the client's development.

At the end of the first section of this book, we discussed the "keyhole" model. This "keyhole" represents, in some sense, the progress of therapy through time—the movement from one level of contact-making to another. In contrast, the facets of therapeutic intervention (Figure 13.1) are the various aspects of the client's experience that can be explored at any level of the keyhole. We have found it convenient to think in terms of seven major facets of intervention: affect, physiology, cognition, fantasy, behaviors, family and social relationships, and the therapeutic relationship itself. We place the first six around a circle, each connected to all of the others. "Affect" and "physiology" are paired, joined by a thicker line; they are the two facets most concerned with nonverbal internal processes. Similarly, the two facets most concerned with making sense of our experience, "cognition" and "fantasy," are joined. The third pair is "behaviors" and "social systems"; they are most involved in external contact. Finally, a special aspect of social relationships, the "therapeutic relationship," surrounds and supports all the others: the quality and texture of the therapeutic relationship pervades all of the work, all of the other facets, all of the time.

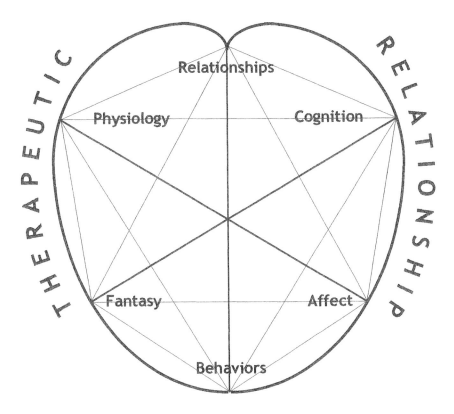

FIGURE 13.1. The facets of a therapeutic intervention.

For a therapy of contact-in-relationship, maintaining the contact between therapist and client must be the therapist's most central and overriding concern. We may put cognition or fantasy aside for a while; we may choose to postpone dealing with affect or physiology; we may temporarily acquiesce to the client's avoidance of behaviors or relationships in general, but we must never lose sight of what is going on in the therapeutic relationship. It is both the door to what will be and the mirror of what has been in the client's life.

Expanding beyond the therapeutic relationship, relationships in general are of primary importance in integrative psychotherapy. In fact, it would be difficult to overemphasize the importance of retracing, reexperiencing, and reshaping old relationships within the therapeutic context. From the infant's earliest, inchoate experiencing of self-in-the-world, through the ever-present relationships that form the patterns of one's life, up to and into the therapeutic relationship itself, contact with others is the very stuff of one's sense of self and one's ability to function as a human being. In its most archaic form, the sense of self-in-relationship is largely unverbalized and unverbalizable; by the time one has acquired language, relational identity is already so much a part of the self-concept that there seems simply no other way to be. Like the proverbial fish that does not realize that it is wet because it has no concept of "dry," we have no conscious concept of the relational basis of our sense of self because we have nothing with which to contrast it. No matter how much a client may have added to his or her store of relationship experiences, no matter how significant that neighbor lady or scout leader or first love or trusted colleague, the archaic, preverbal sense of self-in-relationship is the foundation upon which almost everything else rests, the pattern that must be taken into account if fundamental and lasting change is to occur.

Just as early relationships are the ground upon which the sense of self is built, the therapist's attention to relationship is the ground upon which the therapeutic work is built. The therapeutic relationship may be dealt with directly, as client and therapist talk about how they are dealing with each other. Edward's work in chapter 9 opened with this kind of exploration:

Edward: *I'm a little bit intimidated, looking at you here, trying to . . . come in and out of feeling serious and feeling playful . . .*

Therapist: *Intimidated?*

Edward: *Well, you suddenly look very . . . present, you know? Suddenly I'm here, and you're looking at me, and I'm . . . I don't have anything going on in my mind, particularly; I'm not here with any agenda at the moment, and suddenly I'm thinking, "Now what is it that I was thinking about yesterday," and maybe I could be focusing on my life, and stuff like this, and . . .*

Therapist: *But if I am fully present, then you're intimidated.*

With the therapist's encouragement, Edward went on to make the connection between his feelings toward the therapist (and his projections onto the therapist) and his relationship with his parents. The therapeutic relationship served as a mirror of the past and a new context within which he could explore old experiences.

A client's initial concern about the therapeutic relationship is often a bridge to exploring older and more historically significant relationships. We saw this in Loraine's work, in which she tells the therapist about being irritated with her. Loraine has an unusually clear understanding of the parallel between current and historical relationship issues and reminds the therapist that she needs the therapist to be attuned to the developmental level at which she is working.

Loraine: *I want to start with, when I left my wallet here and you looked inside it.*

Therapist: *Yes, to find out who it belonged to.*

Loraine: *I know that. But I didn't like it.*

Therapist: *Why?*

Loraine: *Well, that's just what came to me when I thought about it. . . . This is not a grown-up thing.*

Even when the explicit focus is elsewhere, though, the therapeutic relationship is always present, always serving as both a mirror of and a contrast with the relationships of the past. It is like the deep, rich supporting instruments of the orchestra, providing a constant background to whatever voice may be carrying the melody. Let us look, briefly, at these other melodic voices, the other six facets of therapeutic intervention.

Cognition

Out of the preverbal and all-pervasive experience of early relationships emerge the core cognitions, the primary belief system. These are the firmly established, usually out-of-awareness beliefs about the self, about others, and about the quality of life. They are the schema that one uses to make sense out of the shifting and varied elements of one's experience. Based on the earliest, primary me-in-world interactions, balanced between pleasure and pain, the belief system is relatively malleable during the first years of life. The child is essentially questioning, "What does a person like me do in a world like this with people like you?" With the acquisition of language, the core belief system begins to form, and later to harden. With repeated experiences of relationship disruptions, many of which reinforce previous learning, the child's conclusions become confirmed and set into a relatively permanent structure: a life script. Details and embellishments may be added, but by adulthood the basic pattern is strongly resistant to change.

Cognitive processes cover the whole continuum from conscious to out-of-awareness. At one extreme, clients can explain their perceptions and their decision-making processes cogently and convincingly, even though they may be focusing on the affect that accompanies those perceptions and decisions. Greta, for instance, while describing feelings of panic, is still quite clear about her decision to get off the airplane: "And I think, well, in this case, by changing the airplane I had control over a machine that was damaged. . . . I didn't want to be over the ocean for eight hours not knowing what was coming next."

At the other extreme, many core beliefs about self (something is wrong with me), others (people cannot be trusted), or quality of life (things eventually go wrong) are not consciously known and may even be strongly denied; only after the completion of a piece of work does the client come back to acknowledge what was out of awareness before the work was done. Sarah, toward the end of her work, is realizing that she is now accessing areas of cognition that were previously unavailable:

All of a sudden I got this rush of, "Oh, my God, you told all, all these secrets."
And I've held on to pieces of, I've told these stories, but I haven't gotten to what I
hold secret. 'Cause I haven't been able to, but . . . but you're helping me get in
touch with it. I think.

Dealing with a client's cognitions requires, first of all, cognitive attunement. Sensing the core beliefs that may underlie what the client is telling us, we allow ourselves to reverberate to those beliefs. We put ourselves into the client's cognitive context and vicariously experience how that context forms and frames the client's view of the world. We construct our interventions so as to invite clients to venture outside of their frame and to experiment with new conceptualizations and explanations of their experience. We explore with them the ways in which they make meanings and how they translate objective data into subjective "facts." We may teach new ways of thinking about the events they describe to us or suggest behavioral experiments that will provide new experiences to think about. And, mindful of the constant interweaving of experience among the various therapeutic facets, we are careful to offer them a cognitive framework within which to understand the affective, behavioral, physiological, fantasy, and relationship facets of their work.

Affect

Affect is, in a sense, on a parallel with cognition. Thinking and feeling are the twin processes of our internal life. Like cognition, our affective patterns emerge from our earliest experiences of identity in relationship. Unlike cognition, however, we tend to experience affect as happening *to* us, rather than as something that we *do*; and we develop whole sets of defenses as a way of protecting ourselves from the pain of negative affect.

Emotion and cognition are inextricably intertwined. Each has an effect on, and is affected by, the other. Most of us tend to "lead" with one or the other; that is, some people are generally better at and more comfortable with thinking, while others prefer feeling. To some degree, though, we all do both: we think about our feelings, and we feel about our thoughts. To the degree that we can do both easily, we are aware of and in contact with our internal experience; to the degree that we cannot, contact is broken and dis-ease is likely to result.

Integrative psychotherapists maintain affective attunement, support affective exploration, and encourage clients to recognize and use both affect and cognition to experience fully the richness of their internal experience. From an integrative psychotherapy perspective, affect is transactional–relational in its intent, naturally seeking a corresponding affect with which to resonate. Affect is not just what one person feels; it is a form of communication among two or more people. Because it is transactional—two way—a client's affect can be genuinely experienced and expressed only when the therapist is involved as well as attuned. Therapist involvement is a necessary counterpart of attunement; together they complement the client's process and allow for full affective expression. Attunement and involvement give depth to the exploration of affect, making possible a rich, human encounter rather than a mechanical application of technique.

Behavior

Observable behavior is the acted-out result of one's internal cognition and affect. Cognition and affect are the internal consequences of one's external activities. They can be talked about separately, but in real life they are inseparable; they twine themselves through all our waking hours. These three (thoughts, feelings, and behaviors) are the building blocks of human experience. People behave in ways that will maintain the structure of their cognitions, the predictability, identity, continuity, and security provided by their belief system, and will protect them from emotional pain. They think so as to make sense of what they do and feel. And their emotions both respond to and direct their thoughts and their behaviors.

Behaviors can serve to establish and maintain contact with others or to defend against such contact. At best, one's behaviors allow one to meet the world openly and relate to it with spontaneity and creativity; to be sensitive to one's own and others' needs and wants and to act so as to meet those needs. As defenses arise, however, one's range of behaviors tends to become more restricted. One begins to fall back on older, more archaic behaviors and on strategies that may not be appropriate for today's situations. Contact is interrupted through failing to utilize all the available options and failing to recognize one's ability to behave in new and different ways. Yet, more serious interruption occurs when one has learned to defend against even noticing one's needs, wants, feelings, and beliefs: here the appropriate behaviors cannot be engaged in because even the need for them is out of awareness.

Clients' stories are most often about behaviors. Greta tells of getting off the airplane; Edward talks about acting "surly"; Sarah describes what she did and what she did not do to protect herself from a rapist. Stories about behaviors, though, will remain only stories, unless the external behaviors can be connected to the rich internal world of thoughts and feelings that support those behaviors. It is through exploring these interconnections that awareness can be expanded, rigid patterns broken through, and contact restored.

Again, in dealing with behaviors, the context of the therapeutic relationship is all-important: the therapeutic relationship becomes the medium within which behavioral exploration can occur. Integrative psychotherapists encourage clients to examine old behaviors (or to consider behaviors that have been avoided) and to experiment with alternative possibilities in the safety of the therapeutic relationship. Enactments of interactions with others—in the past or in a possible future—allow the client to try out new patterns and options. Sarah, regressed to childhood and reexperiencing being abused, pushes her abuser away and says an important "No":

Therapist: *Push him away again!* (holds a pillow for her to push against)

Sarah: *NOT THAT WAY!*

Therapist: *Push him away—that's it!*

Sarah: *GO AWAY! Ohh, don't touch me like that!*

Therapist: *Again.*

Sarah: (pushing) *I don't want you to do that!*

Finally, clients are invited to continue their experiments outside the session and to be aware of the interaction between their internal and external experience as they do so. Here Loraine is planning this kind of new behavior as she finishes her work with the introjection of Alice:

Loraine: *What I'm gonna do is . . . take care of myself. And I'm gonna tell you when, when you're coming in on me, when your expectations are not real. When I can't meet your expectations. I don't know if you're gonna get it. I don't care if you only did have an eighth grade education; I think you're smart as hell.*

Therapist: (pause) *Anything more you want to say to her?*

Loraine: *I don't think I need to say anything else right now. I think I need to do it for real. In life. I need to sit at the kitchen table with you, and just be clear. And not cave in. And not go away.*

Fantasy

Fantasy is the imagined interaction among thoughts, feelings, and behaviors, remembered from the past and projected into the future. It is the world of "as if" and "may come to be," and it, too, grows out of the underground of archaic self–other experience. Many repeated negative fantasy experiences, from niggling worries to outright nightmares and anxiety attacks, involve either experiencing or barely warding off catastrophe; to the degree that the catastrophe is actually avoided in real life, the fantasy creates its own self-reinforcement.

Clinically, the fantasy facet is utilized when we help clients to follow through with their fantasies, to explore them to their outmost edges, and then to take them even further. The classic example of fantasy work, of course, is working with dream material. Edward tells of a dream, and even the brief telling of it brings him to the next stage of awareness:

I had a dream about a year ago where . . . police came round to visit me and went into the farm next door, and they dug up a body, a dead body. Which I'd apparently killed. And I remember sort of saying "Oh, well, it seems like there's no way around this; I obviously have killed somebody, some time back. And, uh, well, you know, maybe I can get away with 10 years of prison, you know, maybe I can handle that; I'm sure I can, you know, I can read," and stuff like this—all this stuff was going on in the dream; very clearly, "I can live through it." Very strong feeling, I can live through it, I can manage that. (softly) But I'm not sure I always can, you know.

Moving into a fantasy, choosing to experience the whole thing, even (especially!) the parts that one usually avoids, helps one to discover the connection between one's fantasy and one's reality. Greta, for example, is encouraged to explore her childhood fantasy of Daddy's coming home:

Therapist: *Tell Mama about that fantasy of running away with Daddy. "I want to run away from your hitting, Mama."*

Greta: *I wanted to run away from your hitting. And if Daddy comes back, I want to go away with him. We'll leave you. . . .*

Therapist: *Going to run away with a daddy you don't even know, huh?*

Greta: *When she married this other man, I thought, where is my real Daddy? Where did he go—I want to go with him.*

Therapist: *Um-hmm.*

Greta: *Then I had the fantasy that perhaps he was living somewhere with another family. And then my mother married this other man, I was so—I wanted to jump out of the window, from the fifth floor And then I had these fantasies, about when I would be dead.* . . . (her voice has begun to shake)

Through fantasy, the thoughts and feelings and behaviors of internal imagination, we approach the thoughts and feelings and behaviors of external relationships. And, as always, the attuned, involved presence of the therapist makes it all possible.

Physiology

As therapists we take delight in working with a client to uncover and explore internal experience and in discovering together how that experience connects to the client's external behaviors and relationships. In that delight, there is a danger: we sometimes forget that the client is not just a container for psychic activity but is also a physical being. People do not "have" bodies, they "are" bodies. And physiology, too, provides a facet of therapeutic change. People maintain defenses through body tension, muscular holding in, which eventually becomes habitual and may even be converted into relatively permanent bodily structures or malfunctions; changing those structures or malfunctions can significantly impact the defensive patterns.

One's physiology (like all of the other facets of therapy) is both cause and effect. Thoughts and feelings and interactions with others have a significant effect on how the body functions and what sensations it experiences. Conversely, physiology has a significant effect on internal and external behavior: remember what lack of sleep or chronic pain does to your ability to think, feel, and relate to other people?

The body is a sensitive and powerful instrument of communication. It is the interface between internal and external awareness; it is the tool that transforms that which is private to that which is shared experience, and that which is shared to that which is private. The body is the beginning, the end, and the ground against and within which everything else is done. It is the vessel in which our psychic patterns are carried and into which we deposit the accumulated consequences of living out those patterns.

Integrative psychotherapists use their awareness of the client's body and their attunement to his or her physiological rhythms to help them understand and access the other facets of therapy. We also make direct use of physiology. We may invite clients to experiment with moving or holding their bodies in a different way. We call their attention to their gestures, their tension, their breathing. "Let your body just respond," says the therapist to Greta, who immediately sighs deeply. The therapist continues, "just let that happen again. Yeah. Breathe. Will you just let your body do what it wants to, while you tell your story?"

The therapist's body, too, is a part of the equation: we feel muscular tensions, notice changes in our breathing, and attend to the physical sensations that accompany our attunement to and involvement in the client's experience. We sometimes touch clients, hold them, or invite them to physically push or pull or struggle with us. Part of therapeutic involvement is the willingness to enter into a real and personal relationship as real and physical beings. Within the ethical guidelines of our profession, and always maintaining our commitment to put the client's needs first, we do exactly that.

Relationships

We have come all the way around the circle, back to family and social relationships. We have already said quite a bit about the importance of relationships (in this chapter and throughout the book!). And we make no apologies for this emphasis. All of our thoughts and feelings and behaviors and fantasies (and, yes, our physiological experience) take place in the context of relationships. As important as one's interactions with a mountain or an automobile or a T-bone steak may be, interactions with other humans have infinitely greater psychological significance (unless the mountain or the steak symbolizes some quality of some relationship, and that would take us back to relationships again).

In our diagram, the therapeutic relationship is a special case of the "family and social relationships" facet. The therapeutic relationship circle flows out from relationships in general to surround and encompass all the rest, just as the therapeutic relationship enfolds and supports the work done in each of the other areas. These two aspects of relationship, family and social in general and therapeutic in particular, underscore the significance of relational needs and the basic urge in all of us for contact-in-relationship. Experiencing contact with the therapist, experiencing the therapeutic relationship as qualitatively different from all the other relationships (real and fantasized) that have helped the client to maintain his or her life script, is the single most critical element in our approach to therapy. Whatever else we may do, whatever strategies and techniques we may have developed or adapted from other theoretical frameworks, tending the relationship is our central responsibility.

☐ Putting It All Together

In chapter 6, we described how inquiry and involvement, supported and informed by attunement, follow the client's pattern of contact interrup-

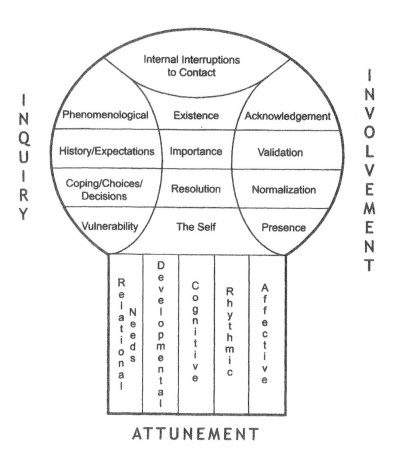

FIGURE 13.2. Contact-in-relationship Keyhole.

tion. The keyhole diagram showed four levels of contact interruption, beginning with lack of awareness of the existence of an internal or external event and proceeding through lack of awareness of an event's importance or significance, lack of awareness of the possibility of change, and lack of awareness of one's own personal, individual, and unique ability to deal with the feelings and resolve the situation. In this section, we shall revisit those levels, discussing the seven therapeutic facets as they may be used at each level and using excerpts from the transcripts of chapters 7–12 to illustrate the concepts.

The First Level: Phenomenology

At the top level of the keyhole, inquiry is phenomenological: "What's happening internally?" "What are you sensing, feeling, wanting, and remembering?" At this level, the client is sorting through a jumble of internal experiences and trying to figure out what is going on inside and in the world around, and, of course, at the same time using all those tried-and-true protective patterns to *avoid* feeling or knowing. Phenomenological inquiry helps the therapist attune to the developmental level of the client and to the meanings, affects, and rhythms of his or her experiences; as the therapist's involvement grows the story becomes richer, fuller, more three-dimensional. With the sensitivity to relational needs that comes from attunement, and the genuineness of involvement, the therapist can acknowledge, validate, and support both sides of the struggle and can help the client to explore whatever aspect of experience comes to foreground. And that foreground experience moves, sometimes very rapidly, among the seven facets of therapeutic intervention. Just as we focus first on one thing, then another, as we look around a room, so the therapeutic focus shifts and segues among different areas of experience.

Relationships

Lois and Lester, for example, began by talking about their relationship with each other. Lois talks to Lester about wanting to be close:

Lois: . . . *it's like you want to just be with me and at work at the same time.* (pause) *Does that make any sense?* (pause) *Many times we'll be there together, and I share something with you. And I'm trying to get close, and it doesn't work, and it's painful; then I go away, do my own work. I enjoy it, too.*

Therapist: *So when he sees you, what he calls "overworking"—which I don't really know what that means, but you know what it means—when he sees you doing those activities, what do you want him to think about?*

Lois: *I would like it if he would just grab me and say, "Let's go and do something, I would like to be with you."* (pause) *I could easily be taken away from the working.*

Therapist: *So touch becomes important.*

The therapist, in a single response, acknowledges Lois's concern with her *relationship* and her experience of relational needs, ties in a reference to *behaviors*, and inquires about her *fantasy* of what she would really like from Lester. She next responds to the *physiological* reference contained in that fantasy: "Touch becomes important." This rapid shifting, following the client's attention to first this facet of experience and then that one, keeping track, and making sure that each facet that emerges in the work is attended to and that every facet is eventually included, is a hallmark of the integrative approach. Throughout the whole piece of work with Lois and Lester, we can see the way in which exploration of each of the other facets is connected back to the initial relationship focus.

Cognition

Attending to cognition means attending not only to the client's thoughts, but also to how the thoughts arise: how the client makes meaning, understands, and decides what causes what and why it happens that way. Greta, for example, has been talking about her anxiety and her physical symptoms. The therapist, mindful of the way in which people tie themselves in physiological knots in order to avoid thinking painful thoughts, acknowledges her need to protect herself from her thoughts:

Therapist: *People tell you what?*

Greta: *That I'm more anxious than is normal, and besides, I don't feel well. I often have stomach pains—not in my chest, here, but in my stomach. This is a new symptom.*

Therapist: *There's much you don't want to remember. . . .*

Greta: *I want to.* (begins to cry)

Therapist: *You do?*

Greta: *If you ask me to, I . . . .*

Therapist: *I just made a comment that there is much you don't want to remember.*

Greta: *There* is *much I don't want to remember.*

The therapist's recognition of Greta's need to block some things from memory brought a surge of affect and a promise to try to do better. Attuned to Greta's cognitive process, the therapist recognizes that this is part of Greta's "good girl" pattern, a pattern that emerges when she tells herself that she has been wrong or bad in some way. The therapist reiterates her earlier statement, and this time Greta hears the acknowledgment, rather than translating it into a criticism.

Cognitive inquiries, too, trigger awareness of other aspects of experience. Loraine, in the following excerpt, is trying to explain why she responded so strongly to the therapist's "invasion" of her space. When the therapist acknowledges both Loraine's thoughts and feelings, she jumps to a memory of an incident with her mother. The next inquiry brings her back to her cognitive process, to how she makes meaning out of her experiences, and, of course, it is also an inquiry into relationships with both mother and therapist.

Loraine: *That's right, and my space. I did what I had to do about the pile of stuff. I moved it. But I didn't say to you that I didn't like it next to me. And that's what I do. I got, I can take care of myself and put away the things that I don't want, but I can't always talk about why I don't want them.*

Therapist: *I imagine it would be unpleasant to have something dirty like that right next to you.*

Loraine: *Yeah. Like, with my mother I told her I don't want to eat with her if she's angry. But I didn't tell her why. I just said it's not good for my digestion.*

Therapist: *And the other "why" is . . .*

Affect

Affect, of course, is what most clients expect to talk about in therapy. The early part of the therapeutic process nearly always touches on affect: painful feelings are what clients most often want relief from. Inquiring about these feelings phenomenologically requires careful attention to what is happening with the client *now*, in response to the here-and-now situation with the therapist as well as to the story the client is telling.

Sarah: *And I was just pushing him away, and trying to make light of it* (she talks faster and faster), *and get back to the TV, say my "no" that way.* (there's a catch in her voice; she sounds very frightened) *But . . . um . . . help me. . . . I'm afraid we might run out of time before I can get through this. . . .*

Therapist: *We're going to take* your *time.*

Sarah: *Thank you.*

Therapist: *If you go so fast, do you get to avoid feeling as intensely as you need to?*

As Sarah recounts the experience of being raped, she automatically engages the defenses she has learned to use to protect herself from being emotionally overwhelmed. While the defenses do help her to stay in control, they also keep her emotions buried, split off, and unavailable to be worked through and made less toxic. The therapist's inquiry, based on her attunement to Sarah's shift in rhythm, acknowledges the function of Sarah's defensive speeding up as well as the intensity of the feelings she is trying so hard to keep in check. And it gives Sarah the support she needs, as we see a few transactions later:

Sarah: *That's such good information. First of all, to give me permission to have time. That's very, very deep for me. Okay? And now, now I'll put that piece together, to let myself feel it.* (sigh; she begins to cry)

Behavior

Behavior is the outward manifestation of the affect, cognition, fantasy, and physiology of relationships. In integrative psychotherapy, an inquiry about or acknowledgment of behavior always carries with it, implicitly or explicitly, a concern about the relationship(s) within which it occurs and the accompanying internal experience. This exchange with "Alice" (Loraine's introjected mother) provides an example of how behavioral inquiry can be used as an entry into that internal experience:

Loraine (as Alice):   *. . . I was tired; I had all these men to take care of all the time. Ironing, had to iron—*

Therapist: *All these men? All what men?*

Loraine (as Alice): *My husband, my husband's brother came to live with us, and then my nephew came to live with us for a while. And they all needed their shirts starched all the time. . . .*

Therapist: *So how come you took on the job of taking care of all these men?*

Loraine (as Alice): *Well, I think it was just . . . we lived in a big house in the Depression with 13 people, and it was just, just take people in. . . . I never want anybody to be without a home.*

Alice is talking about behavior (taking care of the men and starching their shirts), but she is also talking about her relationship with them, with herself, and with her parents. Her story is about behavior, but behavior in the context of relationships—as all behavior, ultimately, must be.

Fantasy

Fantasy includes our "what if's," our "might have's," our hopes, our fears. It is the vehicle through which we deal with all the things we can imagine, the things that are not now but may have been or may come to be. And it is our fantasies, our metaphors, and our stories that tell the important things we do not know how to say any other way. These stories and metaphors are nearly always worth attending to, because they carry so much meaning and so much emotion for the client. They are born out of experiences too rich to fit into ordinary words.

Therapist: *And were you successful at getting away from your past, Alice?*

Loraine (as Alice): *No, I have it all wrapped up in a big tablecloth behind me, and it's like . . . bunch of pots and pans. And as I walk from room to room, it rattles.*

Therapist: *You mean, you sort of carry it around with you?*

Loraine (as Alice): *You bet.*

Therapist: *In this tablecloth.*

Loraine (as Alice): *Solid tablecloth. Yes.*

Therapist: *Now, why in a tablecloth?*

Obviously, the therapist is not interested in an imaginary tablecloth for its own sake. It is the symbolism of the tablecloth, the meaning and the emotion that it represents, that is important. But asking about this meaning in a straightforward way is not likely to be useful; if straightforward talk could explain it, there would have been no need for the metaphor in the first place. Staying within the framework of the fantasy and maintaining cognitive, rhythmic, affective attunement with the client acknowledges the symbolic importance of the metaphor (or the daydream, or the hope, or the fear) without demanding an impossible translation.

Physiology

Sigmund Freud (1900/1938) maintained that dreams are the "royal road to the unconscious." Similarly, physiology may be thought of as the royal road to the out of awareness. What one feels in one's body and does with one's body is affected by interactions among all the other facets of experience; and those body responses and sensations in turn affect everything else. Calling a client's attention to what is going on physiologically can help him or her to access and appreciate other aspects of experience.

In integrative psychotherapy, we ask clients to attend to their physical sensations, including feelings of tension, of shakiness or agitation, of pain or discomfort. We invite them to notice how they are moving their bodies—their gestures, their swinging foot, or the position of a cocked head or a drawn-in arm. And we suggest experiments: "Let that shake come" or "Breathe into your tight chest." Such interventions may be suggested by what we see happening in the client's body; our own bodily responses, as well, sensitize us to the physiological components of the client's experience.

Sometimes clients themselves will make the connection between physiology and other aspects of their being-in-the-world and will tell us about it. These connections may be noticed and described as a part of the evolving work or after a piece of work has been completed. Or the client may bring them to us at the beginning of the work, as Loraine did:

I experience myself being angry at her [Alice], for feeding it to me. But in me it's not anger, it's just, it's just weight. Just something I didn't know was hers, before. Before, in the work I did, you remember, I got in touch with her fear and it was, it used to be in me, but it was out there; it was like a balloon. And it wasn't mine. It was hers. And for a while I felt like it was tied to my ankle, like a helium balloon.

But then it just flew away. Wasn't mine. And I feel like the anger is the same thing. It's not mine. It's, it's turned into fat. It's her energy, and it turned into my fat.

Notice, again, that Loraine is not talking just about her body. She is making a connection between her weight and her anger, between physiology and affect; she also uses a fantasy figure (the helium balloon) to convey a quality of her experience. Everything is connected; each aspect of the self exists in the context of all the others. Even when a client appears to be focusing on one thing—behavior, affect, physiology, whatever— we must keep in mind that all of the other facets are background, coloring and underscoring and giving dimension to whatever is foreground.

Therapeutic Relationship

The therapeutic relationship is a special case of relationships in general. It is a special case for at least two reasons: first, it is the medium through which the client can begin to experience something different, someone who refuses to confirm the old beliefs and expectations, someone with whom he or she can begin to develop a new and more contactful way of being with self and others. Second, it provides a kind of therapeutic laboratory: it is right here, available for examination and testing and digging into. There is no need to try to recall exactly what did happen in that argument yesterday or at the dinner table Tuesday night—here client and therapist can look directly at how the client's relational needs are being acknowledged or met and how the client responds in their experience with each other.

In every phase of the therapy work, then, the integrative psychotherapist will be particularly attentive to how the client is responding to him or her and to how he or she reacts to that client response. This concern with relationship is an important aspect of therapeutic involvement: it requires a willingness to be present as a fellow human, with our own thoughts and feelings and vulnerabilities, always guided and undergirded by our therapeutic intent. Comments and questions about the therapeutic relationship are likely to have first priority and to be dealt with immediately. Often, an exploration of the therapeutic relationship at the outset prefigures the theme for the whole piece of work. In Edward's case, the work began with his commenting about feeling "intimidated" by the therapist; the sense of intimidation and potential humiliation turned out to be the cornerstone of his relationship with his mother. Loraine talked about her irritation with the therapist, and that irritation led her first to a recognition of her own anger at her mother, and then to a new level of contact with the mother she had introjected into her own person. For both of these clients, and, in less obvious ways, for all of the others who have walked through our pages, acknowledging the quality and the importance of the therapeutic relationship at the beginning of the work paved the way for using that relationship later for the client's benefit.

The Second Level: History and Expectations

At the beginning of a piece of work, the therapeutic relationship surrounds and supports the client's attempts to sort out what is going on, to find a focus, and to make sure that this therapist can be trusted to listen, to care, and to understand. As we move to the next level of the keyhole (and, of course, this is a gradual, back-and-forth process that is seldom clearly marked by a single transaction), relationships, and particularly the therapeutic relationship, take on a new significance. For here the focus is on discovering the connections between one's past relationships and those of the present. This level is about how the client sees the world of here-and-now through the glasses of then-and-there. It is about transference, experiencing and understanding and playing out present relationships as if they were the same as old ones. In a very real sense, all of this second-level work is about relationships and about validating their significance, whatever else the client may be specifically talking about.

Family and Social Relationships

It is almost impossible to pull out an example of work with a particularly "relationship" focus; it is rather like trying to find a cupful of ocean that is particularly "wet." All of the clients whose long transcripts have been presented (and all the earlier ones as well) are dealing with relationships. In the couples' work with Lois and Lester and with Betty and Sally, relationship is the explicit focus throughout the work.

Betty tells Sally how she brings her past responses into their relationship:

Sally: *So tell me about what being important means.*

Betty: (sigh) *It's taking time with me. And sharing an interest in what I do. Showing that I can do things, so that you can see that I can do things. And then it's getting all mixed up, because I'm getting all mixed up now between you and my mother. I know it. That's why I want you to do it, because she didn't do it.*

Lester, too, finds his responses to Lois colored by how he experienced his relationship with his mother: "Well, I think it's, uh, my hunger was more for mother, I think. I think it's my mother who did it. Both Mom and Dad did, in different ways. But, uh, I think it's my mother."

Sarah explores her childhood relationship with her brother, and her later way of relating to the man who raped her, and the therapist helps her to make connections between those relationship experiences:

Sarah: *I just knew how to do what I was used to doing . . . which was avoiding. Which was trying to . . . trying to . . . stop someone from doing something by either distracting them, or . . .*

Therapist: (pause) *The way you managed as a little girl, with your brother?*

Edward and Greta and Loraine all deal with mother: Greta in a regression experience, Loraine through work with the "Alice" introjection, and Edward through his memories. With each of them, the therapist's inquiry, attunement, and involvement help the client to fill in the gaps, to recall what has been pushed out of awareness, and to take seriously the importance of these relationship experiences. Here is Edward, for instance:

Edward: *Very angry, and, um . . . what's the word—humiliating interaction that I used to have a lot with my mother. I mean, you know, she tried to humiliate me and in a way I'd try to do it back, you know. . . . We fought a lot. She was a very, um, very humiliating person, very dismissive, very . . .*

Therapist: *Humiliating like what? Can you give me a sense of how she would . . .*

The therapist's response is not merely a clinically correct intervention; it is an expression of honest concern and genuine wanting to understand. Her unverbalized message reciprocates Edward's relational need for valuing and acceptance: "Your relationship with your mother, with all of its meanings for and effects on you, is very important. I want to understand it as clearly as possible, because I care about you." This message is implicit in all of our inquiries about relationships. And, ultimately, all of our inquiries *are* about relationships, because relationships are everywhere: they are what a therapy of contact-in-relationship is all about.

Cognition

Attuned to the client's emerging recollections and aware of our own involvement in the process, our work with cognitions at the level of history and expectations and transference can take many forms. We may help clients to explore how they thought about and made sense of early experiences at that time. We may ask them about their current thoughts about those early experiences. We may invite them to use their adult cognitive abilities to re-form or reshape old patterns of meaning-making or give them information that will help them to think about their experiences in a different way.

Sarah: *But, maybe I can get by the shame.*

Therapist: *Not too fast—*

Sarah: *Okay, okay, okay.*

Therapist: *You can't get by the shame, because that's what you hold.*

Sarah: *Say that again?*

Therapist: *You can't get* by *the shame, because that's what you hold inside, is the shame. Let's just go into it, instead.*

Shame is a complicated response, weaving together cognition and affect (what I believe and how I feel about it) as well as past and present (my previous experience of relationships and how I now respond to the memory of them). There is probably no other issue in which being attuned to the client's cognitive process, acknowledging all of the meanings that the client has created around his or her relationships, and validating the function of the experience is more important.

Affect

Clients often find it relatively easy to relate their memories. They tell us what happened, what the other person did, and what they did in response. They may even tell us the story of how they felt about it. But telling the story of how one felt—that internally rehearsed, constructed-over-the-years story—is very different from being in direct contact with the feelings. At the level of historical exploration, the therapist's response to and inquiry around affect is most often focused on enhancing direct contact with affect, in all its dimensions.

Edward: *I was sent to boarding school at 12, and at the same time my younger brother was sent away at only 8. And he didn't see the family again for two months. You know, I mean, I was 12, I could sort of handle it. But at 8, my God! Anyway, no, so that does, and remains, rankles continually. I mean, you know, the sort of, the pleasure that she seemed to have felt in finding the solution to what to do with her children.*

Therapist: *Edward. When the person you are most dependent on, in this whole world, has glee in sending you away, something's gotta happen in your heart.*

Edward's story was ostensibly about his anger with his mother, that she could be so cruel to him and his brother. The affect was real; he had been angry and he felt anger again in recounting it. Another dimension, though, the pain and loss of being abandoned, and of her taking pleasure in abandoning him, was not present in his story. The pattern of behaviors he developed in order to protect himself from the pain became his life script; helping him to recover and recognize his affective response will help him to weaken the influence of that script.

Behavior

Behavior is the raw material of conscious memory. When we recall something from our past, it is most often in the form of behavior, either our own or someone else's. Exploring those behaviors and inquiring about them helps the client to make the memory concrete and detailed, so that its significance can be drawn out. Most of the behavioral inquiries we make are intended to help (or perhaps to prepare) the client to expand his or her awareness of some other facet of experiencing. In the "therapy within therapy" of the work with Loraine's introjected mother, for example, the therapist asks "Alice" about her behavior during the early years of her marriage:

Therapist: *How did you do with that, once you moved to the suburbs?*

Loraine (as Alice): *Well, I had my two little girls, Loraine and Ellen. And my husband.*

Therapist: *A husband who you never fought with?*

Loraine (as Alice): *We never fought.*

As "Alice" begins to paint the picture of what she did during those years, she is less and less able to deny the feelings and beliefs and wants and needs that surrounded those behaviors. Awareness is growing and internal contact is enhanced; she comes closer and closer to re-owning the denied and distorted parts of who she is.

Fantasy

The fantasies of the past are a window into the needs, the fears, and the protections that a client carries into the present. Whether daydreams or metaphors, hoped-for imaginings or dreaded catastrophes, fantasies tend to take us to the place where our defenses are not so strong and where the forbidden thoughts and feelings are most accessible. As Sarah recounts the story of being raped, it becomes clear that the real trauma of that experience was not so much the physical rape, but the loss of a dream that had defined a very deep part of her being and without which she could not (or so she believed) be the person she wanted to be.

Sarah: *He robbed me of something so important . . . and I can't get to it now; I can't seem to get by this! I can't! I can't get there!*

Therapist: *"I was a virgin and you robbed . . . "*

Sarah: *I was a virgin and YOU ROBBED ME!*

Therapist: *Tell him what you wanted to do with your virginity.*

Sarah: *Oh, I wanted to give it to someone in love.*

Therapist: *Tell him how you'd like to give it to someone. Not him.*

Sarah: *Ohhh, I want to give it to someone special, who means something to me.*

Not some slimeball, who takes me out to dinner and thinks he has rights to my body!

Therapist: *Tell him how you'd like it to have been. I bet there was a dream in there.*

Telling the dream, and reexperiencing the thoughts and feelings and sensations of the still-able-to-dream Sarah, helps her to recognize that the dream is not lost after all and that it can again be a central part of her selfhood. The therapist's attunement to the nuances of Sarah's dream allows her to focus and deepen the work. Her involvement, her genuine and personal response to Sarah's loss, makes it possible for Sarah to feel her presence: to feel acknowledged, validated, and safe as she moves through her pain and into new possibilities.

Physiology

As we revisit our history, we also re-create the physiology of that history. Our bodies begin to respond in the same way that they did back then, when those things were happening. Integrative psychotherapists use those re-created responses to help the client recover more full memories; we also encourage clients, while they are remembering, to notice what they are doing physically.

Greta: *[I was] about 8, and my sister was 7, and my brother was 4. My younger sister was there, too. Because my Mom knew that I was responsible and that I was strong and that I was, you know, she could trust me, and she didn't come home.*

Therapist: *And now you hold you breath—right this moment. Can you feel the holding of your breath?*

Often, the encouragement takes the client beyond "noticing" to actually changing. Changing one's physical response to a situation allows one to experience it differently; changing what our body does as we reexperience an old event can literally change the memory and the meaning of that event.

Therapist: *Let your body just respond* (Greta sighs deeply). *Just let that happen again. Yeah. Breathe. Will you just let your body do what it wants to, while you tell your story?* (pause) *Tell me that same story again.*

Greta: *When I was 8 years old, my mother worked in another town and we had to stay at home three days and three nights, all alone.*

Therapist: *Because it was difficult for her.*

Greta: *Because it was difficult for her.*

Therapist: *How was it for you?*

Greta: *It was . . .*

Therapist: *Tighten your chest up, now.*

Greta: *It was painful.*

Therapist: *Say that to Mama.*

Greta: *Oh. . . . .*

Therapist: *Look at Mama the way she looked when you were 8.*

Greta: *Mama, it hurts. . . .*

Therapist: *Breathe right now. Just breathe, and talk to her.*

The Therapeutic Relationship

Often, what the client does and feels and thinks vis-à-vis the therapist is colored by past relationships. The quality of the contact between client and therapist is our best and most direct route to the whole pattern of relationships that frames the client's experiencing. For this reason, no comment about or indication of the client's response to the therapist should be ignored. A great deal of what goes on between client and therapist is, at least in part, a reenactment of the kinds of contact (and lack of contact) that the client has developed over time.

Edward's work provides an unusually clear example of this kind of re-enactment and how it can be used therapeutically. Edward focuses on his feelings about the therapist from the beginning of his work: "Well, you suddenly look very . . . present, you know? Suddenly I'm here, and you're looking at me, and I'm . . . I don't have anything going on in my mind, particularly; I'm not here with any agenda at the moment."

As we have seen, Edward goes on to talk about his feelings toward his mother and his reluctance to discuss them, and his narrative is interspersed with oblique references to similarities between his response to his mother and his response to the therapist. Finally the therapist asks directly about the connection: "Edward, can I assume a question unasked, as you look at me. Such as, 'Are you, like my mother, going to humiliate me?'"

From this point, the work takes on a new sense of direction, as both client and therapist recognize the pervasiveness of this expectation and its effect on Edward's ability to engage in any kind of contactful relationship.

The Third Level: Coping, Choices, and Decisions

An exploration of history, of memories of events and relationships, inevitably blends into an exploration of how the client coped with those events and relationships. So this happened—What did you do about it? How did you survive? What did you conclude, figure out, decide? The choices and decisions of the past, and the survival patterns that those choices and decisions set up, are the out-of-awareness framework upon which our present behaviors and reactions are built.

As the work of therapy turns to those old coping styles and choices and decisions, clients begin to see how they are truly the architects of their own lives, how their present pain and dis-ease grows out of the patterns of the past. Here, more than anywhere else, normalization of those coping decisions is essential. "I can't keep on blaming other people for my problems," the client begins to realize. "I did it to myself, and I keep on doing it." So far, so good, but that awareness can so easily turn into shame: "I must be really bad/stupid/worthless to have gotten myself into such a fix." The therapist's job is to point out how important and how self-protective those old choices were, when they were first set in place, and to firmly support the normality and the courage of the younger person who made them.

Family and Social Relationships

Relationships are the context of all behavior, the surround for all beliefs and decisions, the very stuff of human experience. Invariably, the most important choices that people make as they go through life have to do with relationships with self and with others. Resolving disruptions to contact and healing relationships in the present often requires an exploration of old relationship decisions and old beliefs about self and others. Sarah, for instance, searched through several sets of beliefs and decisions as she dealt with the trauma of being a rape survivor. One of the most painful of these was her sense of shame, arising from her belief/decision that her physiological response to the rape was unacceptable. The therapist challenges this belief, setting it in its relational context:

Therapist: *Now why would you disgust yourself with something that you know is so biologically natural?*

Sarah: *Because it was the wrong person at the wrong time. . . .*

Therapist: *But you tried to make it the right person.*

Trying to "make it the right person" is appropriate and understandable. Never mind that it may not have been wise—mistakes are normal, too. What feeds Sarah's shame is the belief that what she did was *bad*. As she comes to understand and accept her response for what it really was— a traumatized woman's desperate attempt to hold onto a precious part of herself—that sense of shame will lose its intensity, freeing her to take back the parts of herself that she has been hiding away for so many years.

Cognition

Cognition, the making of meaning, is particularly important during this phase of the therapeutic process. It is the meanings that we assign to events, the ways in which we understand what is happening and predict what may happen next that motivate our choices and decisions. In fact, figuring out what will probably happen next *is* a decision, one that powerfully affects what we do and think and feel.

Edward: *And I thought, um, well, shit, that's the way it is, you know; you get used to it quite quickly . . . so I'm very, feel I can survive . . .*

Therapist: *So a lot of pride in surviving, too.*

Edward: *Yeah. Quite a lot of pride in surviving. I used to think that* all *I could do was survive. I quite strongly felt that way, that if I could survive that was already not bad. You know. Now I'm noticing that I can do a lot more; that's nice. Nice perception. But certainly that was my main assignment. Let's try and get through.*

Believing that the best thing that could happen would be simple survival, "getting through," would make it foolish to try for something better, to risk a contactful relationship, to hope for understanding or comfort or joy. Why waste energy working for the impossible? And so, for Edward, the expectation becomes a self-fulfilling prophecy, in which close relationships are forever out of reach because they are not reached for.

For "Alice," Loraine's introjected mother, early decisions became a rigid scaffold upon which her adult life was constructed:

Therapist: *What else was important to you, Alice?*

Loraine (as Alice): *Deciding I would never be like them.*

Therapist: *Tell me what you mean.*

Loraine (as Alice): *Decided when I was little that I would never, ever, ever be like them. Wouldn't raise my children like that. Wouldn't be like that, wouldn't marry a man like my father. I wouldn't be like my mother. I wouldn't be drunk. I wouldn't fight. I wouldn't have violence.*

Therapist: *Wouldn't marry a man like your father, and you wouldn't have violence, you would never fight. . . .*

As the therapist quietly and patiently reflects Alice's decisions, Alice begins to see how their rigidity has kept her from being real with her daughter, and at the same time has leaked a much more toxic "realness" into the mother–daughter relationship. She can think, now, with the support of the therapist, the thoughts that could not safely be thought in the absence of that support; she can question her old decisions and begin to consider how they might be revised.

Affect

Nearly all important decisions, enduring coping styles, and script beliefs are born out of intense affective experience. We hang onto them: we developed them in order to survive bad experiences or to sustain wonderful ones, and they (to some degree) worked. Who would give away something that works, especially when it works in an important and emotional situation? As therapists, we help our clients to revisit those affective experiences and to learn that they can be survived (or sustained or re-created, if that is the intent) in other ways, using other resources that were not available back then. The purpose of revisiting strong emotional experiences in psychotherapy is not simple catharsis; it is finding a way into a new perspective, a new decision, a different way of being.

Greta: *It's so dark, and . . .* (she cries)

Therapist: *Keep going: "It's so dark. . . ."*

Greta: *It's so dark and I'm scared, and I have to run around into the other rooms, and I'm not supposed to cry. . . .* (she clutches her arms to her chest)

Therapist: *Yeah, keep going. . . .*

Why would any well-intentioned person encourage someone to reexperience this kind of pain? It is certainly not because the pain itself is beneficial. Rather, it is a means to an end, a way of enhancing awareness of and contact with all the parts of oneself, so that all those parts can be accepted and reintegrated with new understandings and decisions that are affirming and life-enhancing. Sometimes this shift comes cognitively, with recognition of an old decision; sometimes it comes affectively, with recognition of an emotional response long kept out of awareness:

Greta: (to mother) *Ohhh, when you don't hold me, I feel so lonely and so desperate. It hurts too much . . . too much!*

Therapist: *Of course it does. Too much pain, too much responsibility. . . .*

Greta: (long pause; to mother) *It makes me mad to hear you say it's easier for you to stay away from the family overnight. It makes me . . .*

"Lonely and desperate" leads to one set of survival decisions; "mad" can lead to a very different set. Greta can now look at both emotions and learn what it is like to have a full range of affective responses available— as well as to develop the kinds of beliefs and decisions that are possible for an emotionally whole person.

Behavior

Like thoughts and feelings, the behaviors of the past are the raw materials of coping decisions. As we help clients to explore their behaviors, we are also helping them to explore the beliefs that support those behaviors and result from the behaviors. Edward, for example, becomes increasingly clear about how his behaviors and his beliefs are intertwined as he talks about how he coped as a child:

Edward: ... *I mean that's where I felt surly, very surly indeed. "I'm not going to play the fucking game," you know; I'm not going to clean the bathtub out afterwards; you're joking; not gonna put that towel back up or anything; I'm not gonna do anything. That was my feeling. In fact they used to call me Eeyore, because, you know, the Winnie the Pooh books—I was always the one who was complaining; I was always. ...*

Therapist: *Yeah, dour. ...*

Edward: *—"I don't like it," "There's something wrong," "This isn't the way it should be," you know, "It's not fair" was what I said a lot. "It's not fair." Said it a lot. Felt it a lot. Something about it all wasn't fair; that's true.*

Therapist: *So you tried to protest.*

Greta, too, begins to realize how she set up a pattern of behavior based on beliefs that, out of awareness, could not be questioned:

Therapist: *Being so strong—just what Mama wanted you to be. Wanted you to be strong. Wanted you to be dependable. Wanted you to just keep on going, keep helping her, keep the family going. ...*

Greta: *She needed me to do that.*

Some minutes later in the work, Greta returns to this theme: she talks about what she "had to" do in order to take care of mother (and, by taking care of mother, take care of herself).

Greta: (long pause) *I had to be nice.*

Therapist: *Had to be nice? Even when you're angry at her, huh.*

Greta: *Yeah. If I'm angry, then I have to apologize.*

Therapist: *And if you're scared?*

Greta: *If I'm scared and if I cry, then she gets mad.*

Fantasy

Fantasies, too, shed light on people's choices and decisions and beliefs. Whether they are the fantasies of the past or of the present, they express one's dreads and one's longings, and they are hedged about by the restrictions created by the old, well-worn script beliefs that shape one's life. As we help clients to explore their fantasies, we encourage them to follow the fantasy, the daydream, the metaphor, the wish or the fear, out to its furthest extreme, not to cut it off and swallow it down.

Greta: (to mother) *I need you, at least at night. And I want to sleep in your bed.*

Therapist: *Yeah. Tell her.*

Greta: *I want to sleep in your bed. I want you to be close to me. I want to hold on to you. I want to hold you!* (sobbing)

Therapist: *Keep talking to her.*

Later in this piece of work, Greta explores another fantasy, this time having to do with her absent father:

Greta: *I wanted to . . . I ran away and I thought . . . when my Daddy comes home, then I can go away with him. . . .*

Therapist: *What a wonderful hope—when Daddy comes home you can run away with him. . . .*

The session continues with more discussion of Greta's father:

Therapist: *Tell Mama about that fantasy of running away with Daddy. "I want to run away from your hitting, Mama."*

Greta: *I wanted to run away from your hitting. And if Daddy comes back, I want to go away with him. We'll leave you. . . .*

Therapist: *Going to run away with a daddy you don't even know, huh?*

Greta: *When she married this other man, I thought, where is my real Daddy? Where did he go—I want to go with him.*

Therapist: *Um-hmm.*

Greta: *Then I had the fantasy that perhaps he was living somewhere with another family. And then my mother married this other man, I was so—I wanted to jump out of the window, from the fifth floor And then I had these fantasies, about when I would be dead . . .*

As Greta relates these fantasies, with the acknowledgment and validation and normalization provided by the therapist, she becomes more and more fully in contact with the feelings of longing and loneliness that she has been carrying for so many years. And with that contact comes an awareness of how she learned to cope as a child, by caring for mother, making excuses for her, and blaming herself. It is this coping pattern that interferes with her ability to make spontaneous, genuine contact with others as an adult, and with herself as well.

Physiology

There are two primary ways in which body responses are focused on in the exploration of choices, decisions, and coping strategies. The first we have already met: inviting clients to continue or exaggerate a physical action or both in order to take them more deeply into their internal experience. Sarah was encouraged to physically push at a pillow, so as to *feel* her ability to reject and repel her abuser. Greta, in a kind of mirror image of that work, is invited to enact her old pattern of holding in—to feel it, know it, experience it as intensely as possible, in order to eventually break out of it.

Therapist: *That's right! Push him away again!* (holds pillow for her to push against)

Sarah: *NOT THAT WAY!*

Therapist: *Push him away—that's it!*

Greta: (silently huddles into herself)

Therapist: *Yeah, go ahead. . . .*

Greta: (still huddling, tapping her fist against her chest) *Ahhh. . . .*

Therapist: *Tell her what you're doing right there.*

Greta: *Right there it hurts. It's burning and hurting.*

Therapist: *Just increase that now—pull those shoulders closer together. That's it. Show her what you do instead of being angry—*

A second kind of physiological focus is seen toward the end of Sarah's work. Here the emotional and cognitive learning of the work that Sarah has just done are connected to her present physical complaint. As she experiences her body's response as a logical, perhaps even necessary consequence of her old belief system, that response begins to lose its power, its sense of inevitability:

Therapist: *Did you stop feeling beautiful after those experiences?*

Sarah: *Ohhhh. . . .* (cries painfully) *Oh, I guess I did. It wasn't who I ever wanted to be . . . and I do this thing. I tell other people it was my fault; it happened because I did this and I did that and I should have known and I could have and I didn't. . . .*

Therapist: *And your experiences of sex were not beautiful.*

Sarah: *No. Not one of them, never, never since I was a kid even. And I wanted them to be! 'Cause I knew, I knew, I'd been taught well, I had a healthy . . . understanding, but my body didn't. I didn't have any good experiences. It didn't match what I knew it should be.*

Therapist: *So what happened to your dream?*

Sarah: *It got shattered . . . and it got funneled in all this kinda like feeling of perversion. And then I take that to bed. Like it's my perversion, instead of . . .*

Therapist: *Like something's wrong with you, or you're not beautiful?*

The Therapeutic Relationship

Just as people play out their old decisions in the context of their present relationships, so they are played out with even more intensity in the therapeutic relationship. Part of the artistry of therapy is knowing when to allow this playing out to continue unremarked upon, when to encourage it, when to verbalize one's own involvement, and when to confront it or turn it in a different direction.

The authenticity of the therapeutic relationship, the genuineness of our involvement, gives impact to our interventions. These interventions may acknowledge clients' growth-enhancing decisions, may validate the ways in which they update their belief systems, or may support their choices to keep some defenses in place until the time is right to make a change. Again, we turn to Edward's work for an example of the latter:

Therapist: . . . *And how they've provided the continuity with your Mom's nondependable—how your defenses are the most dependable thing you've got. Your humor, your ability to adapt, your survival. . . . And as you talk about it, almost with a sense of affection—who would you be if you weren't a man who could take anything that came your way? What would you feel if you weren't the guy that could handle every humiliation?*

Edward: *Yeah.* (sigh) *You've got a point; yes, that's true, I'm quite, I'm quite proud of it. I can best you, kind of roll with the blows, you know, kind of—*

Therapist: *Well, maybe I need to share in that pride with you, lest this become a pushy therapy to make you be something different, before we've really had a chance to see how stable, what continuity, what sense of identity—all of these defenses have provided. To say nothing about how you've maintained them. You've got predictability for the future.*

Edward: *Hmm. Hmm. I like what you're saying to me. I like what you're saying about time . . . something I've perhaps gradually become aware of in myself, but it's not something I've said in words like that. I, I think it's . . . very clearly important for me to allow myself to be . . . a slow person in that respect. . . .*

The Fourth Level: Vulnerability

This phase of therapy is the breaking-through phase, the moments at which the client experiences the "Aha!" of a shift in perceptions and beliefs and the possibility of something new and different. It celebrates the vulnerability of defenses no longer needed, of willingness to be in full contact with self and with other and of valuing that self and that other. It encompasses the awareness of relational needs, the expression of those needs to another person, and a reliance on the other for need satisfaction.

It is the level at which the other work is aimed and the outcome that makes the rest of the work worth the pain and effort.

Relationships

Vulnerability is an essential part of contact: to the degree that we protect ourselves from another person, we distort or disrupt our contact with them. As clients begin to reclaim themselves, reown all of their parts, shed their defensive structures, and reach out to the world, their relationships change. Occasionally, the therapist is fortunate enough to share some of the joy of such moments.

Therapist: *Tell Stephen.* (Sarah has been "talking to" an imagined husband, represented by an empty chair.)

Sarah: *Stephen, it almost seems like I violated you by giving this away somewhere else. But I really didn't give it away, it was taken from me . . . by men who were nowhere close to you. Not your quality.*

Therapist: *Yeah, tell Stephen about his quality.*

Sarah: *Ohhh . . . Stephen . . . such deep love and respect . . . such a cherishing of me . . .*

Cognition, Affect, Behavior

We have combined these three categories because one client, Loraine, provides us with a beautifully clear picture of how all three can come together during the final phase of a piece of therapeutic work. Loraine has completed "Alice's" work and is now in her own persona, talking to "Alice" about what has happened:

Therapist: *And tell her what you know now.*

Loraine (to Alice): *I know you were mad all the time. I know your burning anger, and I know it's not about me, and I know it's probably not even about Dad and all the sarcastic little irritation and all that, that was just . . . little safety valves all the time, a little steam. And that's kinda exhausting.*

Therapist: *Um-hmm. It's exhausting.*

Loraine: *I don't want it. It's yours. I, I feel, I feel such compassion for you. . . .*

Loraine's knowing, understanding, and being able to think about her relationship with Alice in a different way clears the path for a different affective experience as well. For perhaps the first time, Loraine experiences an upwelling of compassion for her mother. A few minutes later, the new affective and cognitive experiencing of the relationship lead to a determination to make a behavioral change and to be contactful and genuine (and vulnerable) with Alice in real life.

Loraine (to Alice): *Well, I am grateful to you. You gave me a lot. But I'm not grateful for that. You can have it. I feel like I filled up your buckets all the time, and you just dumped them out. You said, "Here, this is empty again." And I can't, uh, I can't do that anymore.*

Therapist: *"So what I'm gonna do is . . . "*

Loraine: *What I'm gonna do is . . . take care of myself. And I'm gonna tell you when, when you're coming in on me, when your expectations are not real. When I can't meet your expectations. I don't know if you're gonna get it. I don't care if you only did have an eighth grade education; I think you're smart as hell.*

Fantasy

The fantasies that accompany increasing contactfulness and vulnerability are not always delightful. Nothing comes without cost, and the cost of emerging into a new way of being is the loss of predictability, of familiarity, of the safety of those old defenses. Edward, as usual, is quite direct about this discomfort:

Edward: (pause) *It's not you I can't trust, exactly. It's where, it's where it all might go. It's where . . . it's the meaning it might have; it's something to do with . . . what happens then, you know. It's kind of. . . .* (sigh) *What does that make me, and if I do it, if I do say, if I do ask something from you, then what's going to be asked back, you know, this kind of thing. It's, uh. . . .*

Therapist: (whispering) *"What's going to be asked back?"*

Edward: *Well, first of all, that I'd have to live up to it, which I'm not sure I want to do.* (pause) *Oh, it's all right for 5 minutes, 10 minutes; you know, but then, will I have to live up to it forever, you know?* (pause) *I mean, you know, as they say* (laugh), *there is no free lunch, you know. . . .* (sigh) *And then, a sort of, way, it's in here, something like . . . "But you said that. . . . " You know, "You needed something from me, and* now *look what you're doing!" You know. "I was so nice to you and now look . . . " you know, sort of. . . . That's why I feel surly about you.* (pause, sigh)

Therapist: *There'll be a price to pay. . . .*

Edward: *I'd like to know that you don't think that I'm, you know, sort of deep down a bit of a jerk, really. And I worry about that, sort of check that out.*

Therapist: *Ouch. What an uncomfortable fantasy.*

The Therapeutic Relationship

Actually, the above excerpt is also an example of dealing with the therapeutic relationship in a new and contactful way. Most often, however, clients do not focus on their contact with the therapist as a piece of work draws to a conclusion. They are more likely to be focused on their life outside of therapy, on the possibilities for change in their ongoing relationships. Later, perhaps, clients may talk about their feelings toward the therapist as they found themselves being open and vulnerable in a new way. Sarah did so in her letter to the therapist, written several months after the work upon which chapter 6 is based: "Hearing you reassure me that what I was feeling was normal, having you fill in the information I did not have at the time each rape was happening, experiencing your support of my efforts to make the only or best decision I could at those times, began the process of my letting go of some of the shame and guilt."

So there they are, the levels of our "keyhole" and the focus on various facets within each level. And as we write these words, we feel a curious sense of incompleteness, of "not quite right." It is the beetle phenomenon again. We have torn it up, presented it part by part, and in so doing we have robbed it of the wholeness that gives it life.

Psychotherapy, like all relationships, is an indissoluble whole, a series of interrelated contact experiences with self and with other. Handled well, it builds synergistically, leading the client into a spiral of ever-broadening awareness of internal and external events. Each time an idea, a memory, an emotion, or a belief is revisited, some new richness or interconnection is revealed. Back and forth, addressing first this facet and then that, relating one thing to another, attuned to client and to self, maintaining both the involvement of genuine presence and the professionally honed skills of therapeutic inquiry, the therapist is responsible for keeping it all in balance.

Because therapy *is* a kind of spiral, coming back again and again to visit the same concerns (which are, of course, never quite the same), it is perhaps fitting that we end this book by going back to the beginning, or at least to the end of the beginning, to sum up all that we mean by "beyond empathy." Here is what we said as we closed chapter 1:

Inquiry, attunement, and involvement comprise the essence of a successful therapeutic relationship. With careful inquiry, sensitive attunement, and authentic involvement, the therapist will be experienced as dependable, consistent, and trustworthy. Experiencing such a relationship, clients can begin to reintegrate the parts of self that were split off in response to trauma and neglect; and with reintegration comes the possibility of full contact with self and with others, of true relationship, of being in the world as a whole person again .

REFERENCES

Adler, G., & Myerson, B. G. (1973). *Confrontation in psychotherapy*. New York: Science Press.

Ainsworth, M. D. (1969). Object relations, dependency and attachment: A theoretical review of infant-mother relationship. *Child Development, 40,* 969–1025.

Ainsworth, M. D., Blehar, M. C., Waters, E., & Wall, S. (1978). *Patterns of attachment: A psychological study of the strange situation*. Hillsdale, NJ: Laurence Erlbaum Associates.

Andrews, J. (1988). Self-confirmation theory: A paradigm for psychotherapy integration. Part I. Content analysis of therapeutic styles. *Journal of Integrative and Eclectic Psychotherapy, 7* (4), 359–384.

Andrews, J. (1989). Self-confirmation theory: A paradigm for psychotherapy integration. Part II. Integrative scripting of therapy transcripts. *Journal of Integrative and Eclectic Psychotherapy, 8* (1), 23–40.

Arlow, J. (1969a). Unconscious fantasy and disturbances of conscious experiences. *Psychoanalytic Quarterly, 38,* 1–27.

Arlow, J. (1969b). Fantasy, memory, and reality testing. *Psychoanalytic Quarterly, 38,* 28–51.

Bach, S. (1985). *Understanding psychotherapy: The science behind the art*. New York: Jason Aronson.

Baker, E. (1982). The management of transference phenomena in the treatment of primitive states. *Psychotherapy: Theory, Research and Practice, 19,* 194–197.

Balint, M. (1959). *Thrills and regressions*. London: Maresfield Library.

Basch, M. F. (1988). *Understanding psychotherapy: The science behind the art*. New York: Basic Books.

Bergman, S. J. (1991). *Men's psychological development: A relationship perspective*. Works in progress (No. 48). Wellesley, MA: The Stone Center, Wellesley College.

Berne, E. (1961). *Transactional analysis in psychotherapy: A systematic individual and social psychiatry*. New York: Grove Press.

Berne, E. (1966). *Principles of group treatment*. New York: Grove Press.

Berne, E. (1972). *What do you say after you say hello? The psychology of human destiny*. New York: Grove Press.

Bettelheim, B. (1967). *The empty fortress: Infantile autism and the birth of the self*. New York: The Free Press.

Bollas, C. (1979). The transformational object. *International Journal of Psychoanalysis, 60,* 97–107.

Bollas, C. (1987). *The shadow of the object: Psychoanalysis of the unthought known*. New York: Columbia University Press.

Bowlby, J. (1969). *Attachment. Volume I of Attachment and loss*. New York: Basic Books.

Bowlby, J. (1973). *Separation: Anxiety and anger. Volume II of Attachment and loss*. New York: Basic Books.

Bowlby, J. (1980). *Loss: Sadness and depression. Volume III of Attachment and loss*. New York: Basic Books.

Bowlby, J. (1988). Developmental psychology comes of age. *American Journal of Psychiatry,* *145* (1), 1–10.

Brandchaft, B. (1989, October). *Countertransference in an intersubjecive perspective: A case presentation.* Panel discussion, 12th annual conference on the psychology of the self, San Francisco.

Brisser, A. R., (1971). The paradoxical theory of change. In J. Fagan & I. L. Shepherd (Eds.), *Gestalt therapy now: theory, techniques, applications* (pp. 77–80). New York: Harper & Row.

Buber, M. (1958). *I and thou.* (R. G. Smith, Trans.). New York: Scribner. (Original work published 1923)

Cashdan, S. (1988). *Object relations therapy: Using the relationship.* New York: W.W. Norton.

Clark, B. D. (1991). Empathic transactions in the deconfusion of child ego states. *Transactional Analysis Journal, 5,* 163–165.

Dashiell, S. (1978). The parent resolution process. *Transactional Analysis Journal, 8,* 289–295.

Dinkmeyer, D. C. (1965). *Child development: The emerging self.* Englewood Cliffs, NJ: Prentice-Hall.

Efran, J. S., Lokens, M. D., & Lokens, R. J. (1990). *Language, structure & change: Frameworks of meanings in psychotherapy.* New York: W.W. Norton.

Epstein, S. (1972). The nature of anxiety with emphasis upon its relationship to expectancy. In C. C. Spielberger (Ed.), *Anxiety: Current trends in theory and research* (Vol. 2). New York: Academic Press.

Erikson, E. H. (1950). *Childhood and society.* New York: Norton.

Erskine, R. G. (1995). A Gestalt therapy approach to shame and self-righteousness: Theory and methods. *British Gestalt Journal, 4,* 108–117.

Erskine, R. G. (1980/1997). Script cure. Behavioral, intrapscyhic and physiological. *Transactional Analysis Journal, 10,* 102–106. Republished in *Theories and methods of an integrative transactional analysis: A volume of selected articles* (pp. 151–155). San Francisco: TA Press.

Erskine, R. G. (1993/1997). Inquiry, attunement and involvement in the psychotherapy of dissociation. *Transactional Analysis Journal, 23,* 184–190. Republished in *Theories and methods of an integrative transactional analysis: A volume of selected articles* (pp. 37–45). San Francisco: TA Press.

Erskine, R. G. (1994/1997). Therpeutic intervention: Disconnecting rubberbands. *Transactional Analysis Journal, 24,* 7–8. Republished in *Theories and methods of an integrative transactional analysis: A volume of selected articles* (pp. 172–173). San Francisco: TA Press.

Erskine, R. G. (1994/1997). Shame and self-righteousness: Transactional analysis perspectives and clinical interventions. *Transactional Analysis Journal, 24,* 86–102. Republished in *Theories and methods of an integrative transactional analysis: A volume of selected articles* (pp. 46–67). San Francisco: TA Press.

Erskine, R. G. (1997). Trauma, dissociation and a reparentive relationship. *Australian Gestalt Journal, 1,* 38–47.

Erskine, R. G., & Moursund, J. P. (1988/1997). *Integrative psychotherapy in action.* Highland, NJ: Gestalt Journal Press. (Original work published 1988 by Sage, Newbury Park, CA).

Erskine, R. G., & Trautmann, R. L. (1996). Methods of an integrative psychotherapy. *Transactional Analysis Journal, 26,* 316–328. Republished in *Theories and methods of an integrative transactional analysis: A volume of selected articles* (pp. 20–36). San Francisco: TA Press.

Erskine, R. G., & Zalcman, M. J. (1979). The racket system: A model for racket analysis. *Transactional Analysis Journal, 9,* 51–59. Republished in *Theories and methods of an integrative transactional analysis: A volume of selected articles* (pp. 156–165). San Francisco: TA Press.

Evans, N. (1995). *The horse whisperer.* New York: Delacorte Press.

Fairbairn, W. R. D. (1952). *An object-relations theory of the personality*. New York: Basic Books.

Federn, P. (1953/1977). *Ego personality and the psychoses*. London: Maresfield Reprints. (Original work published 1953).

Ferenczi, S. (1988). *The clinical diary of Sandor Ferenczi*. Cambridge, MA: Harvard University Press.

Fraiberg, S. H. (1959). *The magic years: Understanding and handling the problems of early childhood*. New York: Charles Scribner's Sons.

Fraiberg, S. H. (1982). Pathological defenses in infancy. *Psychoanalytic Quarterly, 51*, 612–635.

Fraiberg, S. H. (1987). *Selected writings of Selma Fraiberg*. Columbus, OH: Ohio State University Press.

Freud, A. (1937). *The ego and the mechanisms of defense*. London: The Hogarth Press and the Institute of Psycho-Analysis.

Freud, S. (1938). The interpretation of dreams. In A. A. Brill (Trans. & Ed.), *The basic writings of Sigmund Freud*. New York: Modern Library. (Original work published in 1900).

Fromm, M. G., & Smith, B. L. (1989). *The facilitating environment: Clinical applications of Winnicott's theory*. Madison, CT: International Universities Press.

Goldberg, C. (1991). *Understanding shame*. Northvale, NJ: Jason Aronson.

Goulding, M. M., & Goulding, R. L. (1979). *Changing lives through redecision therapy*. New York: Brunner/Mazel.

Greenberg, J., & Mitchell, S. (1983). *Object relations in psychoanalytic theory*. Cambridge, MA: Harvard University Press.

Greenson, R. (1967). *The techniques and practice of psychoanalysis*. New York: International Universities Press.

Greenspan, S. I., & Pollock, G. H. (Eds.). (1989). *The course of lives: Infancy*. Madison, CT: International Universities Press.

Greenwald, H. (1971). Direct decision therapy. *Voices* (Spring), 38–42.

Greenwald, H. (1978). *Direct decision therapy*. San Diego, CA: EdITS, Publisher.

Guntrip, H. J. S. (1961). The schizoid problem, regression and the struggle to preserve an ego. *British Journal of Medical Psychology, 34*, 223–244.

Guntrip, H. J. S. (1962). In truth the need to regress cannot be taken lightly. In J. Hazell (Ed.), *Personal relations therapy: The collected papers of H.J.S. Guntrip*. Northvale, NJ: Jason Aronson.

Guntrip, H. J. S. (1968). *Schizoid phenomena, object relations and the self*. London: Hogarth.

Guntrip, H. J. S. (1971). *Psychoanalytic theory, therapy and the self*. New York: Basic Books.

Hycner, R., & Jacobs, L. (1995). *The healing relationship in Gestalt therapy*. Highland, NY: Gestalt Journal Press.

Janov, A. (1971). *The anatomy of mental illness: The scientific basis of primal therapy*. New York: G.P. Putnam's Sons.

Jones, J. M. (1995). *Affects as process: An inquiry into the centrality of affect in psychological life*. Hillsdale, NJ: The Analytic Press.

Jordan, J. V. (1989). *Relational development: Therapeutic implications of empathy and shame*. Works in Progress (No. 39). Wellesley, MA: The Stone Center, Wellesley College.

Kagan, J. (1984). *The nature of the child*. New York: Basic Books.

Kaufman, G. (1989). *The psychology of shame*. New York: Springer.

Kepner, J. I. (1987). *Body process: Working with the body in psychotherapy*. San Francisco: Jossey-Bass.

Khan, M. M. (1963). The concept of cumulative trauma. In R. S. Eissler, A. Freud, H. Hartman, & M. Kris (Eds.), *Psychoanalytic study of the child*, XVIII (pp. 286–306). New York: International Universities Press.

Khan, M. M. (1974). *The privacy of the self*. London: The Hogarth Press.

Kohan, G. (Ed). (1986). *The British School of psychoanalysis: The independent tradition.* New Haven, CT: Yale University Press.

Kohler, W. (1938). Physical gestalten. In W. Ellis (Ed.), *A source book of Gestalt psychology* (pp. 17–54). London: Routledge & Kegan Paul.

Kohut, H. (1971). *The analysis of the self.* New York: International Universities Press.

Kohut, H. (1977). *The restoration of the self: A systematic approach to the psychoanalytic treatment of narcissistic personality disorder.* New York: International Universities Press.

Langs, R. (1981). *Classics in psychoanalytic techniques.* New York: Plenum.

Lewin, K. (1938). Will and needs. In W. Ellis (Ed.), *A source book of Gestalt psychology* (pp. 283–299). London: Routledge & Kegan Paul.

Lewis, H. B. (1971). *Shame and guilt in neurosis.* New York: International Universities Press.

Lewis, H. B. (1987). Shame and the narcissistic personality. In D. L. Nathanson (Ed.), *The many faces of shame* (pp. 93–132). New York: Guilford.

Lourie, J. (1966). Cumulative trauma: The nonproblem problem. *Transactional Analysis Journal, 26,* 276–283.

Mahler, M. (1968). *On human symbiosis and the vicissitudes of individuation.* New York: Jason Aronson.

Maslow, A. (1970). *Motivation and personality* (rev. ed.). New York: Harper & Row.

McNeil, J. (1976). The parent interview. *Transactional Analysis Journal, 6,* 61–68.

Meador, B., & Rogers, C. (1984). Person-centered therapy. In R. Corsini (Ed.), *Current psychotherapies* (3rd ed., pp. 142–195). Itasca, IL: F. E. Peacock.

Mellor, K. & Andrewartha, G. (1980). Reparenting the parent in support of redecisions. *Transactional Analysis Journal, 10,* 197–208.

Mendelson, R. M. (1972). *How can talking help?: An introduction to the technique of analytic therapy.* Northvale, NJ: Jason Aronson.

Miller, J. B. (1986). *What do we mean by relationships?* Works in progress (No. 22). Wellesley, MA: The Stone Center, Wellesley College.

Mitchell, S. A. (1993). *Hope and dread in psychoanalysis.* New York: Basic Books.

Morrison, A. P. (1986). Shame, ideal self, and narcissism. In A. P. Morrison (Ed.), *Essential papers on narcissism* (pp. 341–371). New York: New York University Press.

Naranjo, C. (1993). *Gestalt therapy: The attitude and practice of an atheoretical experientialism.* Nevada City, CA: Gateways/IDHHB Publishing.

Nathanson, D. (1992). *Shame and pride: Affect, sex, and the birth of the self.* New York: Norton.

Norcross, J. C., & Goldfried, M. R. (Eds.). (1992). *Handbook of psychotherapy integration.* New York: Basic Books.

Orange, D. M., Atwood, G. E., & Stolorow, R. D. (1997). *Working intersubjectively: Contextualism in psychoanalytic practice.* Hillsdale, NJ: The Analytic Press.

Perls, F. S. (1944/1947). *Ego, hunger and aggression: The beginnings of Gestalt therapy.* New York: Vintage Books. (Original work published as *Ego, hunger and aggression: A revision of Freud's theory and method.* Durban, RSA: Knox Publishing, 1944)

Perls, F. S. (1967). *Gestalt therapy verbatim.* Lafayette, CA: Real People Press.

Perls, F. S. (1973). *The Gestalt approach and eyewitness to therapy.* Palo Alto, CA: Science and Behavior Books.

Perls, F. S., & Baumgardner, P. (1975). *Legacy from Fritz: Gifts from Lake Cowichan.* Palo Alto, CA: Science & Behavior Books.

Perls, F. S., Hefferline, R. F., & Goodman, P. (1951). *Gestalt therapy: Excitement and growth in the human personality.* New York: Julian Press.

Piaget, J. (1952). *The origins of intelligence in children* (M. Cook, Trans.). New York: Basic Books.

Pine, F. (1985). *Developmental theory and clinical process.* New Haven, CT: Yale University Press.

Racker, M. (1968). *Transference and countertransference.* New York: International Universities Press.

Rogers, C. R. (1951). *Client centered therapy.* Boston: Houghton Mifflin.

Rogers, C. R. (1961). *On becoming a person.* New York: Houghton Mifflin.

Safran, J. D., McMain, S., Crocker, P., & Murray, P. (1990). Therapeutic alliance rupture as a therapy event for empirical investigation. *Psychotherapy, 27,* pp. 154–165.

Sandler, J., & Nagera, H. (1963). Aspects of the metapsychology of fantasy. *Psychoanalytic study of the child, 18,* 159–194.

Schiff, J. L. (1975). *Cathexis reader.* New York: Harper and Row.

Smith, E. W. L. (1985). *The body in psychotherapy.* Jefferson, NC: McFarland.

Spitz, R. (1945). Hospitalism, *The Psychoanalytic Study of the Child, 1,* 53–74.

Spitz, R. (1946). Hospitalism. *The Psychoanalytic Study of the Child, 2,* 113–117.

Spotnitz, H. (1969). *Modern psychoanalysis of the schizophrenic patient.* New York: Grune & Stratton.

Steiner, C. (1974). *Scripts people live: Transactional analysis of life scripts.* New York: Grove Press.

Stern, D. N. (1985). *The interpersonal world of the infant: A view from psychoanalysis and developmental psychology.* New York: Basic Books.

Stern, D. N. (1995). *The motherhood constellation: A unified view of parent-infant psychotherapy.* New York: Basic Books.

Stern, S. (1994). Needed relationships and repeated relationships: An integrated relational perspective. *Psychoanalytic Dialogues, 4* (3), 317–345.

Stolorow, R. D.. & Atwood, G. (1989). The unconscious and unconscious fantasy: An intersubjective developmental perspective. *Psychoanalytic Inquiry, 9,* 364–374.

Stolorow, R. D., Brandschaft, B., & Atwood, G. E. (1987). *Psychoanalytic treatment: An intersubjective approach.* Hillsdale, NJ: The Analytic Press.

Sullivan, H. S. (1953). The interpersonal theory of psychiatry (H. S. Perry & M. L. Gawel, Eds.). New York: Norton.

Surrey, J. L. (1985). *The "self-in-relation": A theory of women's development.* Works in progress (No. 13). Wellesley, MA: The Stone Center, Wellesley College.

Tustin, F. (1986). *Autistic barriers in neurotic patients.* London: Karnac Books.

Weiss, E. (1950). *Principles of psychodynamics.* New York: Grune & Stratton.

Wheeler, G. (1991). *Gestalt reconsidered.* New York: Gardner Press.

Winnicott, D. W. (1965). *The maturational processes and the facilitating environment: Studies in the theory of emotional development.* New York: International Universities Press.

Wolf, E. S. (1988). *Treating the self: Elements of clinical self psychology.* New York: Guilford.

Wurmser, L. (1981). *The mask of shame.* Baltimore: John Hopkins University Press.

Yalom, I. (1980). *Existential psychotherapy.* New York: Basic Books.

Yontef, G. M. (1993). *Awareness, dialogue and process.* Highland, NY: Gestalt Journal Press.

Zinker, J. (1977). *Creative process in Gestalt therapy.* New York: Brunner/Mazel.

INDEX

Acceptance, 131–136, 316
Acknowledgment, 86–91, 159, 162,
    164–166, 170, 177–178, 209, 346
"Acting out," 77–79
Adler, G., 78, 89
Affect, 108–115, 141–144, 337, 340–341
    anger, 111–112, 195–197, 245–246
    coping/choices/decisions, 361
    fear, 112–113
    history/expectations, 355
    joy, 114–115
    phenomenology, 349
    sadness, 113–114
    vulnerability, 366–367
Affective attunement, 57–59, 159, 162,
    164, 166, 170, 320, 346
Ainsworth, M. D., 6
Andrewartha, G., 263
Andrews, J., 9
Anger, 111–112, 195–197, 245–246
Arlow, J., 9
"As if," 54–55
Attunement, 16–18, 46–82, 84, 116–120,
    122–123, 155, 159, 162, 164, 166,
    170, 173–174, 211, 346
    affective, 57–59, 159, 162, 164, 166,
        170, 320, 346
    case examples, 48, 50–53, 55–62,
        64–67, 69–72, 76–78, 80
    cognitive, 54–57, 159, 162, 164, 166,
        170, 346
    conveying, 68–75
    developmental, 62–66, 159, 162, 164,
        166, 170, 321, 246
    false, 61–62
    functions, 47–53
    kinds, 53–68

regression, 66–68
rhythmic, 59–61, 159, 162, 164, 166,
    170, 320, 346
tasks, 75–80
Atwood, G. E., 9, 21, 27–28
Awareness
    blocking, 166
    enhancing, 28-29, 161–162, 186–187,
        218
    new, 117
    restricted, 158

Bach, S., 92, 123, 127, 131
Baker, E., 71
Balint, M., 63, 79
Basch, M. F., 7, 30, 58, 123, 124, 127, 131
Baumgardner, P., 9, 117
Behavior, 337, 341–343
Behavioral therapy, 1, 19
Bergman, S. J., 4
Berne, E., 7–10, 31, 40, 62–63, 67, 77
Bettelheim, B., 6, 12, 44, 46, 58
Bias, 26–27
Blehar, M. C., 6
Bollas, C., 25, 28, 31, 67, 85, 99, 119
Bowlby, J., 3, 5–6
Brandschaft, B., 21, 50
Brisser, A. R., 34
Buber, M., 83, 98, 173

Case examples
    attunement, 48, 50–53, 55–62, 64–67,
        69–72, 76–78, 80
    couples therapy, 314–335
    defense maneuvers, 237–261
    inquiry, 22, 27, 30, 32–44
    introjects, 262–313

Case examples, *continued*
  involvement, 87–97, 100–102, 104–107,
    109–120
  regressed client, 205–236
  relational needs, 125–126, 128–131,
    133, 135–136, 138–139, 142–143,
    145–146, 150
  therapeutic relationship, 338–339,
    342, 348–351, 353–367
Cashdan, S., 31
Child abuse, 6
  case example, 176–204
Children, 2–5, 11–12, 157
  molestation, 205–226
Choices, 168–172, 358–365
  affect, 361
  behavior, 361–362
  cognition, 360
  family/social relationships, 359
  fantasy, 362–363
  physiology, 363–364
  therapeutic
Clark, B. D., 123
Client-centered therapy, 1, 19
Cognition, 337, 339–340
  coping/choices/decisions, 360
  history/expectations, 354–355
  phenomenology, 348–349
  vulnerability, 366–367
Cognitive attunement, 54–57, 159, 162,
    164, 166, 170, 346
Commitment, 85–86
Conclusions, 40–41
Confrontation, 77–79, 88–90
Consistency, 105–106, 238
Contact, 2–5
  disruptions, 158–163, 165–168
  internal, 4–5
Contracting, 29–30, 266–267
Coping skills, 12, 358–365
  affect, 361
  behavior, 361–362
  cognition, 360
  family/social relationships, 359
  fantasy, 362–363
  humor, 241
  physiology, 363–364
  surliness, 243, 245–246
  therapeutic relationship, 365
Countertransference, 67, 152–153
Couples therapy, 314–335
Crocker, P., 15

Dashiell, S., 263
Decentering, 69–70, 130
Decisions, 40–41, 168–172, 358–365
  affect, 361
  behavior, 361–362
  cognition, 360
  family/social relationships, 359
  fantasy, 362–363
  physiology, 363–364
  therapeutic relationship, 365
Defensive maneuvers, 30, 70–72, 151–155,
    158–163, 165–168, 228
  case example, 237–261
  pretending, 266–268
  responding, 153–155
Denial, 161
Depersonalization, 7, 161
Desensitization, 161
Developmental appropriateness, 85
Developmental attunement, 62–66, 159,
    162, 164, 166, 170, 321, 246
*Diagnostic and Statistical Manual of Mental
  Disorders*, 12
Dinkmeyer, D. C., 66
Disavowal, 161
Dissociation, 161, 295

Efran, J. S., 41, 54, 73
Emotions, 37–38
Epstein, S., 26, 42
Erikson, E. H., 66
Erskine, R. G., 2, 5–6, 10, 12, 14, 33, 59,
    63, 81, 108, 112, 122–123, 129–130,
    146, 152, 171
Evans, N., 47
Existential therapy, 19
Expanding awareness, 28–29
Expectations, 42–43, 167, 353–358
  affect, 355
  behavior, 355–356
  cognition, 354–355
  family/social relationships, 353–354
  fantasy, 356–357
  physiology, 357–358
  therapeutic relationship, 358
Expressing love, 148–151, 316

Failure to thrive, 3
Fairbairn, W.R.D., 3, 7, 44, 85, 263
False attunement, 61–62
Family relationships, 337, 345
  coping/choices/decisions, 359

history, 353–354/, 353–354
phenomenology, 347–348
vulnerability, 366
Fantasy, 44–45, 244, 321–322, 337,
    343–344
    coping/choices/decisions, 362–363
    history/expectations, 356–357
    phenomenology, 350–351
    vulnerability, 367
Fear, 112–113, 124–127, 179–180, 187,
    195–199
Federn, P., 7, 63, 79, 108
Ferenczi, S., 50, 63, 84
Fixed gestalten, 9–11, 13–14, 157–158
Fraiberg, S. H., 3, 11, 66
Freud, A., 7, 20
Freud, S., 1, 48, 351
Fromm, M. G., 65, 111, 124

Genuine interest, 23–25, 99–101
Gestalt
    fixed, 9–11, 13–14, 157–158
    therapy, 1, 8–9, 147
Goldberg, C., 59, 77, 95
Goldfried, M. R., 2
Gone With the Wind, 162
Goodman, P., 5
Goulding, M. M., 40, 169
Goulding, R. L., 40, 169
Greenberg, J., 2
Greenson, R., 71
Greenspan, S. I., 66
Greenwald, H., 40, 169
Guntrip, H.J.S., 3, 6–7, 20, 49, 79, 108,
    128, 263

Habitual responses, 10
Hefferline, R. F., 5
History, 353–358
    affect, 355
    behavior, 355–356
    cognition, 354–355
    family/social relationships, 353–354
    fantasy, 356–357
    physiology, 357–358
    therapeutic relationship, 358
Hopes, 43–44
Human development, 2–7, 123
    internal contact, 4–5
    relationships, 5–7
Humor, 241
Hycner, R., 17, 81, 368

Identity, 238
Infants, 2–3, 59–60, 177
Inquiry, 16–17, 19–45, 84, 116–120,
    123–124, 159, 162, 164, 166, 170,
    326–327, 330–335, 346
    case examples, 22, 27, 30, 32–44
    characteristics, 22–27
    contact, 27–29
    phases of
        coping/choices/decisions, 361–362
        phenomenology, 350
        vulnerability, 366–367
    menu, 36–45
    techniques, 29–36
Insight, 117–118
Internal contact, 4–5
Intervention, 337
Introjects, 262–313
Involvement, 16–18, 83–120, 159, 162,
    164, 166, 170, 346
    acknowledgment, 86–91
    affect, 108–115
    case examples, 87–97, 100–102,
        104–107, 109–120
    commitment, 85–86
    nature of, 84–107
    normalization, 94–98
    presence, 98–107
    validation, 91–94

Jacobs, L., 17, 81, 368
Janov, A., 58, 60
Jones, J. M., 37, 60, 108
Jordan, 4, 80, 121
Joy, 114–115
Juxtaposition, 151–155
    responding, 153–155

Kagan, J., 66
Kaufman, G., 59
Kepner, J. I., 22, 28, 37, 68, 87, 126
Khan, M.M.R., 5–6, 105, 128
Klein, 44
Kohan, G., 2
Kohler, W., 9
Kohut, H., 50, 91, 104, 124, 127, 131,
    134

Langs, R., 32
Language, 73–75, 219
Lewin, K., 9
Lewis, H. B., 59, 95

Life scripts, 339–340
Lokens, M. D., 41
Lokens, R. J., 41
Lourie, J., 5–6

Making an impact, 141–144, 315
Marasmus, 3
Maslow, A., 122, 124
McMain, S., 15
McNeil, J., 263
Meador, B., 133
Meanings, 41
Mellor, K., 263
Memories, 38–39
    reclaiming, 49–50
Mendelson, R. M., 21, 30
Miller, J. B., 4, 80
Mitchell, S. A., 2, 43
Morrison, A. P., 95
Moursund, J. P., 2, 10, 33, 63, 81, 146
Murray, P., 15
Mutuality, 134–137, 316
Myerson, B. G., 78, 89

Nagera, H., 44
Naranjo, C., 26, 31
Nathanson, D., 38, 59
Needs, 7–9
    relational, 121–155, 159, 162, 164,
        166, 170, 315
Neglect, 6–7
New behaviors, 118–120
Nonverbal communication, 68–69,
        147–148
Norcross, J. C., 2
Normalization, 95–98, 130, 159, 162,
        164, 166, 170, 171–172, 177–178,
        220, 248–249, 346

Object-relations therapy, 1
Open-endedness, 25–26
Openness, 101–103
Orange, D. M., 27–28, 42, 51
Other initiating, 144–148, 316–318

Patience, 105–106, 165
Perls, F. S., 5, 8–10, 33, 49, 74, 99, 117,
        140, 263
Phases of therapy
    choices and decisions, 168–172
    full contact, 172–173

making connections, 165–168
    starting, 164–165
Phenomenology, 160, 162, 164, 166,
        170
    affect, 349
    behavior, 350
    cognition, 348–349
    family/social relationships, 347–348
    fantasy, 350–351
    physiology, 351–355
    therapeutic relationship, 352–353
Physical reactions, 36–37
Physical sensations, 36
Physiology, 337, 344–345, 351–352
    coping/choices/decisions, 363–364
    history/expectations, 357–358
    phenomenology, 351–355
Piaget, J., 66
Pine, F., 72
Pollock, G. H., 66
Predictability, 238
Presence, 98–107, 159, 162, 164, 166,
        170, 346
    consistency, 105–106
    contact, 99
    curiosity, 99–101
    interest, 99–101
    openness, 101–103
    patience, 105–106
    professional intent, 106–107
    vulnerability, 103–105
Presuppositions, 30–32
Professionalism, 86
Projection, 315–316
Psychoanalysis, 1
Psychodynamic therapy, 19

Racker, M., 25
Rape, 205–226
Reclamation, 49–50, 130–131
Regression, 58, 62–68, 79–80, 85, 244,
        315–316, 322–323
    case example, 205–226
    supporting, 79–80
Relational needs, 121–155, 159, 162,
        164, 166, 170, 315, 317–335, 346
    acceptance, 131–134, 316
    case examples, 125–126, 128–131,
        133, 135–136, 138–139, 142–143,
        145–146, 150
    expressing love, 148–151, 316

juxtaposition, 151–155
making an impact, 141–144, 315
mutuality, 134–137, 316
other initiation, 144–148, 316–318
security, 124–127, 316, 318–319,
325
self-definition, 137–140, 316, 318
valuing, 127–131, 316
Resistance. See Defense maneuvers
Resolution, 171
Resonance, 84–85
Respect, 23, 47–49, 70–72
Restricted awareness, 158
Retraumatization, 14–16
Rhythmic attunement, 59–61, 159, 162,
164, 166, 170, 320, 346
false, 61–62
Rogers, C., 1–2, 49, 84, 124, 133, 141

Sadness, 113–114
Safety, 49, 116–117
Safran, J. D., 15, 19, 30, 51, 90
Sandler, J., 44
Scheduling, 73
Schiff, J. L., 162
Script beliefs, 10–11, 81
Security, 124–127, 316, 318–319, 325
Self-definition, 137–140, 316, 318
Sexual molestation, 205–226
Shame, 59, 95, 220–223, 231–233,
318–319
Smith, B. L., 65, 111, 124
Smith, E.W.L., 32, 36, 68, 127
Social relationships, 337, 345
coping/choices/decisions, 359
history, 353–354/, 353–354
phenomenology, 347–348
vulnerability, 366
Spitz, R., 3
Spotnitz, H., 49
Stability, 238–239
Steiner, C., 30, 147
Stern, D. N., 3, 9, 42, 46, 57, 66
Stolorow, R. D., 9, 21, 27–28, 69, 99,
122, 130
Sullivan, H. S., 26, 31, 122
Surliness, 243, 245–246
Surrey, J. L., 4

Techniques
acceptance, 131–136, 316

acknowledgment, 86–91, 159, 162,
164–166, 170, 177–178, 209, 346
attention, 32–34, 68–69
attunement, 16–18, 46–82, 84, 116–120,
122–123, 155, 159, 162, 164, 166, 170,
173–174, 211, 346
confrontation, 77–79, 88–90
contracting, 29–30, 266–267
decentering, 69–70
defensiveness, 70–72
giving information, 75–77
inquiry, 16–17, 19–45, 84, 116–120,
123–124, 159, 162, 164, 166, 170,
326–327, 330–335, 346
language, 73–75
normalization, 94–98, 130, 159, 162,
164, 166, 170, 171–172, 177–178,
220, 248–249, 346
open mindedness, 30–32
respect, 34–36
scheduling, 73
supporting regressive work, 79–80
timing, 72–73
validation, 91–94, 127, 159, 162, 164,
166, 168, 170, 318, 346
Therapeutic misses, 50–53, 142–144
Therapeutic relationship, 156–175,
347–348
case examples, 338–339, 342, 348–351,
353–367
coping/choices/decisions, 365
disruptions, 160–163, 165–167
expectations, 358
facets, 337
function, 12–14
history, 358
phases, 164–173
phenomenology, 352–353
vulnerability, 367–368
Therapist initiating, 144–148
Thoughts, 39–40
Timing, 72–73
Transactional analysis, 1, 147
Transference, 132–134, 148–151
Trauma, 6, 123
cumulative, 6–7, 131, 155, 157–158
retraumatization, 14–16
symptoms, 11–12
Trautmann, R. L., 130
Trust, 21–22
Tustin, F., 6, 12, 46, 58, 94

Validation, 91–94, 127, 159, 162, 164,
166, 168, 170, 318, 346
Valuing, 127–131, 316
Vulnerability, 103–105, 159, 162, 164,
166, 170, 172–173, 346, 365–368
affect, 366–367
behavior, 363–367
cognition, 366–367
family/social relationships, 366
fantasy, 367
therapeutic relationship, 367–368

Wall, S., 6
Waters, E., 6
Weiss, E., 7, 63
Wheeler, G., 2
Winnicott, D. W., 3, 85, 111
Wolf, E. S., 91, 124, 138
Wurmser, L., 77, 95

Yontef, G. M., 11, 17, 21, 98, 121, 368
Zalcman, M. J., 10, 81
Zinker, J., 28

Printed in Great Britain
by Amazon